Teach Yourself
WordPerfect®

Teach Yourself
WordPerfect®

Mary Campbell

Osborne **McGraw-Hill**

Berkeley   New York   St. Louis   San Francisco
Auckland   Bogotá   Hamburg   London   Madrid
Mexico   Milan   Montreal   New Delhi   Panama
Paris   São Paulo   Singapore   Sydney
Tokyo   Toronto

Osborne **McGraw-Hill**
2600 Tenth Street
Berkeley, California 94710
U.S.A.

For information on translations and book distributors outside
of the U.S.A., please write to Osborne **McGraw-Hill** at the
above address.

A complete list of trademarks appears on page 601. Screens
produced with InSet, from InSet Systems, Inc.

Teach Yourself WordPerfect®

1234567890 DOCDOC 89

ISBN 0-07-881481-2

A Gift from the Estate of
Michael Hart
www.gutenberg.org

To my husband, Dave

Acknowledgments

I would like to extend my thanks to all the people who contributed to producing this book:

Gabrielle Lawrence, for all her work on this project. Her ideas helped make this a better book and added variety to chapter examples and exercises.

Cindy Hudson, for her idea to do this series and for all of her behind-the-scenes efforts.

Fran Haselsteiner, for coordinating editorial phases; and all the great staff at Osborne who worked on this book: Ilene Shapera, Margaret Flynn, Laura Sackerman, Richard Hack, Deborra Knotts, and Stefany Otis.

Bob Wanetick, for all his work as both a technical reviewer and a copy editor. Bob's thoroughness and skills ensured that none of the details were overlooked.

Bob Wanetick and Matt Mahjer, for their double and triple checks of the answer keys to be certain that they were letter perfect.

Judy Wohlfrom, for her expert design.

Contents

2   Creating a WordPerfect Document   27

3   Printing a Document   57

Part III Special Features

Introduction

If you have ever tried to learn a new software program on your own, chances are that you were left somewhat frustrated by the experience. Even if you learned to use the program, you probably wondered if you were doing things correctly. Without an expert tutor in the office or the time and money to attend a seminar, you may have felt as if there were no solution. *Teach Yourself WordPerfect* is designed to provide that solution.

The short, easy-to-follow lessons in *Teach Yourself Word-Perfect* present basic WordPerfect skills step by step. Each new skill builds on the skills learned previously. Before long, you will be able to create all types of documents.

The book uses a learning-by-example approach and avoids lengthy discussions of features. The chapters are organized by lessons, each focusing on a learning objective. As you master a learning objective, you will acquire a new WordPerfect skill. Each lesson takes about 15 minutes to complete.

Every chapter (except the first) begins with a Skills Check. The Skills Check exercises test your readiness to begin the chapter. The sequences of keystrokes used in the exercises are given in Appendix C, along with the number of the section where the skills were initially covered. If you experience difficulty with an exercise, you will want to go back to the referenced section and work through the examples to improve your skill level before proceeding with the new material.

Once you have mastered the Skills Check, you are ready to tackle the first learning objective. A brief description of the skill is followed by the steps it involves and one or more practical applications. By following these steps you will be able to create the applications. You will want to enter the examples at your keyboard if at all possible, since reading about the feature does not offer the same reinforcement as trying it out on the computer. The examples are followed by a set of exercises, which test your ability to use the feature covered in the learning objective. Appendix C provides the answers for each exercise.

Each chapter concludes with two additional sets of exercises: the Mastery Skills Check and the Integrated Skills Check. Unlike the section exercises, which focus on one learning objective, the Mastery Skills Check tests your skill with all the chapter's objectives. The Integrated Skills Check brings together your new skills and skills mastered in earlier chapters. Appendix C provides the keystrokes and a reference to the chapter and section where skills needed to complete the exercise are covered in detail.

As you complete a chapter, you will find that you can use the skills immediately to create a wide variety of documents. After completing the last chapter, you will have a set of both beginning- and intermediate-level skills with WordPerfect. You will have gained these skills through hard work and repetition but without the frustration so often associated with learning a new package.

How This Book Is Organized

Teach Yourself WordPerfect is divided into 3 parts and 19 chapters. Parts I and II are designed to be covered in sequential order. Part I covers the basic skills needed to create WordPerfect documents. Part II covers intermediate-level features that enhance the appearance of your documents and add flexibility to your basic skills. Part III focuses on special topics. You may be interested in all of these topics or just a few. The chapters in Part III can be read in any sequence you choose, as you need to learn about a topic, since each special topic is not dependent on other special topics.

Appendixes A and B cover installation and hyphenation; Appendix C provides answers to all exercises.

Conventions Used in This Book

- *User Input*   Text to be typed into the computer is shown in **bold** type. When entering text, type it continuously, without pressing ENTER at the end of each line, and do not insert hyphens. In general, use two spaces after a period. You should press ENTER only at the end of a paragraph or a short line, or as otherwise instructed.

- *Keys*   Keys are shown in SMALLCAPS. Keys to be pressed simultaneously are separated by hyphens. For example: SHIFT-F3. The names of function keys are followed by the key you should press. For example: Cancel (F1).

- *Answer Key*   Appendix C provides answers to the exercises in the form of keystroke sequences. These sequences provide one workable solution; others are possible. The keystroke sequences you use may differ from those in Appendix C depending on the configuration and defaults of your computer system. The system used for developing the answers in this book included an IBM System 2 Model 60 with a VGA monitor and a Hewlett-Packard LaserJet Series II printer.

In the answers for Chapter 1, the entry [SPACEBAR] is used every time you need to press the spacebar. In subsequent chapters, it is only included where the required keystrokes would not be obvious without it.

In the answer key, a set of brackets is used to encase function keys. For example: [SHIFT-F3]. A set of braces {} is used to encase descriptive information and directions. For example: {Move the cursor to the top line}. Section references for the Skills Checks, Mastery Skills Checks, and Integrated Skills Checks are found at the outer edge of the page.

·Part I·

Essential WordPerfect Features

CHAPTER OBJECTIVES

After completing this chapter, you should be able to

1.1 Start a WordPerfect session

1.2 End a WordPerfect session

1.3 Clear the screen

1.4 Locate and use special keyboard keys

1.5 Master the use of the Help and Cancel keys

1.6 Control the entry of uppercase and lowercase

·1·

WordPerfect's Basic Components

There are a few basic skills that you need to master before creating WordPerfect documents. You need to learn how to begin and end a WordPerfect session. You will want to become acquainted with the keyboard. Even if you have used a typewriter, you will need to learn how WordPerfect makes use of many of your computer's special keys.

1.1   START A WORDPERFECT SESSION

Computer programs make it possible for your computer to perform a specific set of tasks. To use any program, you must load the program into the memory of your computer. WordPerfect is a computer program that provides sophisticated word processing capabilities to your computer. You must load WordPerfect to make these word processing features available. Once WordPerfect is loaded in your machine, you can think of everything that you do as part of a WordPerfect session.

The process for loading WordPerfect is different for a hard disk than for a floppy disk. In either case, a copy of the operating system (for example, DOS 4.0) must be in your machine, and WordPerfect must already be installed. You will want to consult Appendix A for instructions if you are uncertain of either condition.

The two sets of instructions are for hard disk and floppy disk users who wish to invoke WordPerfect directly. If your screen displays a menu selection to begin WordPerfect, you can skip the directions that follow.

To start a WordPerfect session on a hard disk system:

a. Activate the subdirectory that contains the WordPerfect files. If you installed WordPerfect according to the directions in Appendix A or the package documentation, you can type **cd \wp50**.

b. Type **wp** to start the WordPerfect program.

c. Press ENTER.

To start a WordPerfect session on a floppy disk system:

a. Type **b:** to make drive B the current directory.

b. Place the disk labeled WordPerfect 1 in drive A.

c. Place a formatted disk for storing your word-processing documents in drive B.

d. Type **a:wp**.

e. Replace the WordPerfect 1 disk with the WordPerfect 2 disk when you see the message prompting you to do so.

f. Press any key to continue.

When WordPerfect is loaded, the program displays a blank *document*, as shown in Figure 1-1. A document is WordPerfect's basic structure for letters, reports, and other text entries. Everything you type is held in the current document, which you can store on disk.

The screen displays a blinking rectangle called the *cursor*. As you type, WordPerfect places each character at the cursor location and moves the cursor one position to the right. You can determine the current location of the cursor from the information in the *status line*. The status line indicates the current document, the current page number, and the cursor's distance from the top and left edges of the paper.

Examples

1. To start WordPerfect on a hard disk system, activate the directory where your WordPerfect files are stored by typing **cd \wp50** and pressing ENTER. Then type **wp** and press ENTER again to start the program. WordPerfect displays a blank screen like the one in Figure 1-1. Note the initial location of the cursor.

2. On a floppy disk system, place the WordPerfect 1 program disk in drive A and the data disk that will contain your text files in drive B. Type **b:** and press ENTER to change the current disk drive to drive B. Next, type **a:wp** and press ENTER. At the prompt, replace the WordPerfect 1 disk with

Doc 1 Pg 1 Ln 1" Pos 1"

FIGURE 1-1.   The initial WordPerfect screen

the WordPerfect 2 disk and press any key to continue. WordPerfect is loaded into memory, and the screen looks like Figure 1-1.

Exercise

1. Begin a WordPerfect session on your computer.

1.2   END A WORDPERFECT SESSION

When you have finished using WordPerfect, you end the WordPerfect session by exiting the program. Exiting Word-Perfect removes the program from the computer's memory, allowing you to use other programs. When you exit, Word-Perfect checks to see if you want to save the current document. If you exit WordPerfect without saving, the text you have in memory will be lost. In Chapter 2, you will learn how to save a document.

To exit WordPerfect:

a. Press the Exit (F7) key.

b. Type an **n** in response to WordPerfect's prompt for saving the file.

c. Type a **y** in response to WordPerfect's prompt for exiting WordPerfect. When you end a WordPerfect session, you are returned to the DOS prompt. On a hard disk, the prompt might appear as C> or C:\WP50>. On a floppy disk system, the prompt will probably appear as B>.

Examples

1. You can exit from WordPerfect at any time. After loading WordPerfect, press the A key seven times. The screen looks like this:

aaaaaaa_

Press the Exit (F7) key to exit. Type an **n** in response to WordPerfect's prompt for saving the document. Type a **y** in response to WordPerfect's prompt for exiting WordPerfect. The DOS prompt appears on your screen.

2. When you load WordPerfect again, the text that was on the screen from an earlier session does not reappear. Type **wp** (for a floppy disk system, **a:wp**) to begin a session. Note that the "a"s do not appear on the screen. Press the Exit (F7) key to exit again. Type an **n** and a **y** to return to DOS.

Exercise

1. Begin a WordPerfect session. End the current WordPerfect session.

1.3   CLEAR THE SCREEN

You can clear the screen without exiting from WordPerfect. This feature allows you to create many WordPerfect documents in a single WordPerfect session. When you want to remove the document on the screen, you clear the screen by telling WordPerfect that you do not want to save the file and you do not want to exit WordPerfect.

To clear the screen:

a. Press the Exit (F7) key.

b. Type an **n** in response to WordPerfect's prompt for saving the file.

c. Type an **n** in response to WordPerfect's prompt for exiting WordPerfect.

These steps provide you with a blank screen identical to the initial screen that appeared when you started your WordPerfect session. In step c, you could press ENTER instead, since WordPerfect offers **No** as the default response to the prompt.

Remember to clear the screen after each exercise and example throughout the book unless the instructions indicate otherwise. This chapter will include reminders, but after that you're on your own.

Example

1. You can remove the text on a screen quickly if you do not need to save it. First, type

this text will be cleared from the screen quickly

Next, press the Exit (F7) key.

Type an **n** in response to WordPerfect's prompt for saving the document.

Type an **n** in response to WordPerfect's prompt for exiting WordPerfect, or press ENTER to accept the default. A blank screen results from your entries.

Exercises

1. Type **accounting**, and then clear the screen.

2. Type **trees**, and then clear the screen.

3. Type **1989 holidays**, and then clear the screen.

4. Type **bills, bills, and more bills.** Clear the screen.

LOCATE AND USE SPECIAL KEYBOARD KEYS

1.4

You must become familiar with some of the special keyboard keys to use WordPerfect effectively. These keys move the cursor around in a document, provide access to WordPerfect features, and help you make changes to text. Figures 1-2 and 1-3 show the location of these keys on two popular keyboards. Table 1-1 lists some of the special keys that you will use when working with WordPerfect documents.

As you move around in a document, WordPerfect indicates the current location in the status line. The **Ln** (line)

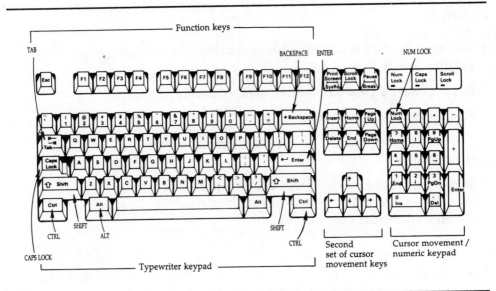

FIGURE 1-2.   The IBM XT and IBM enhanced keyboards

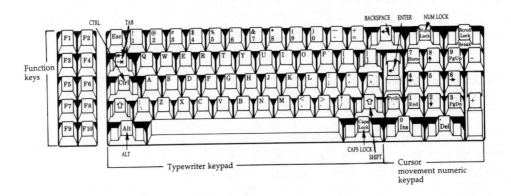

FIGURE 1-3.   The IBM standard keyboard

TABLE 1-1.   WordPerfect's Special Keys

Key Sequence	Action Taken
ENTER	Ends a short line or a paragraph
BACKSPACE	Deletes the character to the left of the cursor
UP ARROW	Moves the cursor up one line
DOWN ARROW	Moves the cursor down one line
LEFT ARROW	Moves the cursor one character to the left
RIGHT ARROW	Moves the cursor one character to the right
PGUP	Moves the cursor to the preceding page
PGDN	Moves the cursor to the next page
END	Moves the cursor to the end of the line
HOME	Moves the cursor in the direction of the arrow key that is pressed next. If you press the HOME key once before pressing an arrow key, the cursor moves to the edge of the screen in the direction of the arrow. Using the HOME and RIGHT ARROW key combination moves the cursor to the end of the line rather than to the edge of the screen if the line is not as wide as the screen. Pressing the HOME key twice before pressing the UP ARROW or DOWN ARROW key moves the cursor to the top or the bottom of the document
TAB	Moves the cursor to the next tab stop. The initial settings for tabs are every 1/2 inch
NUM LOCK	Switches the numeric keypad at the side of the keyboard between numbers and the arrow keys
CTRL-ENTER	Inserts a hard page break
ESC	Repeats a keystroke a specified number of times
CTRL-RIGHT ARROW	Moves the cursor one word to the right
CTRL-LEFT ARROW	Moves the cursor one word to the left
SCREEN UP (GREY −)	Moves the cursor to the top of the screen; if pressed again, moves the cursor to the previous screen
SCREEN DOWN (GREY +)	Moves the cursor to the bottom of the screen; if pressed again, moves the cursor to the next screen
CTRL-HOME	Moves the cursor to a specified character or page
Function keys	The keys on the side or the top of the keyboard, labeled F1 through F10. These keys are used alone or combined with the SHIFT, CTRL, and ALT keys to access. These keys are discussed in the chapters where their features are introduced.

indicator tells you the position of the cursor from the top of a piece of paper. The **Pos** (position) indicator tells you the position of the cursor from the left edge of the paper. Both line and position are measured in inches in WordPerfect's original setup.

As you become proficient with the basic uses of WordPerfect's special keys, you will want to become familiar with the keys listed in Table 1-2.

Examples

1. You can use the ENTER key to create blank lines in the document. Beginning with the initial WordPerfect screen, press ENTER three times. The cursor moves down three lines from its original position. The **Ln** indicator in the status line shows **1.5**". Press the Exit (F7) key and type **n** twice to clear the screen.

2. You can use the DEL and BACKSPACE keys to remove characters from the screen. First, type **abc**. Then press the BACKSPACE key to delete the character to the left of the cursor. Next, press the LEFT ARROW key twice to position the cursor under the letter "a." Press the DEL key to delete the character above the cursor, leaving only the "b." Press the Exit (F7) key and type **n** twice to clear the screen.

3. You can enter the same character repetitively with two shortcut features. You can use the ESC key to repeat a keystroke; for example, you can create a line of hyphens by using ESC to repeat a single hyphen (-). When you press the ESC key, the left side of the status line shows the number of times WordPerfect will repeat the character and looks like this:

Repeat Value = 8

You can control the number of repeats by typing a new number. For example, type **65** to tell WordPerfect how many times it should repeat the keystroke that follows, and then type a hyphen. The result looks like this:

```
----------------------------------------------------------------- _
```

You can also repeat a keystroke by holding down a key. However, it is more difficult to control the exact number of repeats with this approach. First, press ENTER to move to the next line. Create another hyphenated line by holding down the hyphen key. After creating the second line of

hyphens, press ENTER to move to the next line. Press the Exit (F7) key and type **n** twice to clear the screen.

4. You can use the arrow keys to move in any direction on the screen. Type **abc** and press ENTER. Next, type **def** and press ENTER. Type **ghi** and press ENTER to place text on the third line of the document. The screen looks like this:

```
abc
def
ghi
_
```

When you press the UP ARROW key once, the cursor moves to the "g." When you press the RIGHT ARROW key twice, the cursor moves to the "i." Pressing the UP ARROW key two more times moves the cursor to the "c." Pressing the LEFT ARROW key twice moves the cursor to the "a." Press the DOWN ARROW key once to move to the "d." Press the Exit (F7) key and type **n** twice to clear the screen.

5. The numeric keypad keys provide an alternative when you need to enter many numbers. You can use the NUM LOCK key to switch the numeric keypad between number keys and cursor movement keys. When you press the NUM LOCK key to turn it on, the **Pos** indicator in the status line flashes. Type **46.73** on the numeric keypad keys and press ENTER. When you press the NUM LOCK key again, the **Pos** indicator stops flashing. When NUM LOCK is not on, you can use the numeric keypad keys for the functions that are shown below the numbers. For example, if you press 8 on the numeric keypad, the keypad registers an UP ARROW to move the cursor back to the line containing "46.73." Press the Exit (F7) key and type **n** twice to clear the screen.

6. Special keystroke combinations make it easy to move the cursor more than one position at a time through the document. First, type

   a stitch in time saves nine.

   Pressing the LEFT ARROW key while holding down the CTRL key moves the cursor one word to the left. Press CTRL-LEFT ARROW six times to move to the word "a." You can move the cursor one word to the right with the CTRL-RIGHT ARROW combination. Press CTRL-RIGHT ARROW six times to move back to the end of the line. To move to the end of the line more quickly, press the END key. Press the Exit (F7) key and type **n** twice to clear the screen.

7. Three keys, ALT, CTRL, and SHIFT, must be used in combination with other keys; they do not perform any action by themselves. Press the ALT key; nothing happens. Press the SHIFT key and then the ALT key; in both cases, nothing happens. However, when used with other keys, these keys provide features that are not otherwise available. You can press the CTRL key simultaneously with the ENTER key to create a page break. This feature overrides WordPerfect's

automatic page breaks and causes a new page to start at the current location. Press the CTRL-ENTER key combination to generate this display:

```
================================================================================
-
```

WordPerfect displays the current page number after **Pg** in the status line. Press the Exit (F7) key and type **n** twice to clear the screen.

8. You can use the PGUP and PGDN keys to move from page to page in a document. Create the first page in a two-page document by typing **existing clients** and pressing CTRL-ENTER. To complete the second page, type **prospective clients**.

   When you press PGUP, you move from page two to page one. When you press PGDN, you move from page one to page two. WordPerfect displays the first line of the page at the top of the screen. Another way of moving to a different page is using CTRL-HOME. When you hold down CTRL and press HOME, WordPerfect prompts you for the number of the page on which you want the cursor placed. When you type a **1** and press ENTER, WordPerfect moves the cursor to the top of page 1. Press the Exit (F7) key and type **n** twice to clear the screen.

9. You can move from screen to screen in a document with the SCREEN DOWN (GREY +) and SCREEN UP (GREY -) keys. First, type the number **2** 24 times, following each entry with ENTER. Next, type the number **2** 24 times, following each entry with ENTER. If NUM LOCK is on, press the NUM LOCK key to turn it off. When you press the SCREEN UP (GREY -) key, WordPerfect moves the cursor to the top of the current screen. When you press the SCREEN UP (GREY -) key again,

WordPerfect displays the preceding screen, containing the 1s. If you press the SCREEN DOWN (GREY +) key once, WordPerfect moves the cursor to the bottom of the current screen. If you press it again, WordPerfect moves down to the next screen. Use the entries in this example for the one that follows.

10. You can use the HOME key in combination with other keys to move through the entries in the current document. If you press the HOME key and then press the UP ARROW key, the cursor moves to the top line in the screen. If you press the HOME key and the DOWN ARROW key, the cursor moves to the bottom line of the screen. If the text is too short to fill the screen, the cursor moves to the last line of the document. Press the HOME key twice and the UP ARROW key once to move the cursor to the beginning of the document. Press the HOME key twice and the DOWN ARROW key once to move the cursor to the end of the document. Press the Exit (F7) key and type **n** twice to clear the screen.

11. Once you have a line of text, you can move quickly through it by using the HOME key in combination with other keys. First, press ESC, type **20**, and type an equal sign (=). When you press the HOME key and then the LEFT ARROW key, the cursor moves to the first character in the line. When you press the HOME key and then the RIGHT ARROW key, the cursor moves to the end of the line. As you saw in example 7, you can also press END to move the cursor to the end of the line. Press the Exit (F7) key and type **n** twice to clear the screen.

12. The TAB key moves the cursor to the next tab stop to the right. Initially, these tab stops are set for every 1/2 inch. You can use the TAB key to indent the beginning of an entry. Press the TAB key and then type **the meeting is scheduled for the 19th**. Next, press ENTER. Press the TAB key six times. When you do, the **Pos** indicator shows that the cursor is 4 inches from the left edge of the paper. Pressing

the LEFT ARROW key moves the cursor to the preceding tab stop because there is no text between the cursor location and the previous tab stop. Press the Exit (F7) key and type **n** twice to clear the screen.

13. Some of the keys can be confused with one another, since they perform similar functions. For example, the LEFT ARROW key is frequently confused with the BACKSPACE key. The BACKSPACE key removes the character to the left of the cursor and moves the cursor and the character above it to that position. The LEFT ARROW key moves the cursor one character to the left but leaves all characters intact. You can see how this works by pressing ESC, typing **10**, and typing a period. Next, press the LEFT ARROW key three times. This moves you to the eighth period. Next, press the BACKSPACE key three times. This removes three periods. Although the cursor is still below the third period from the end of the line, that period is now the fifth one. Press the Exit (F7) key and type **n** twice to clear the screen.

14. Two other keys that can be confused with each other are the SPACEBAR and the RIGHT ARROW key. The SPACEBAR inserts a space and moves the cursor and any character above it to the right. All characters to the right of the cursor also move to the right. The RIGHT ARROW key moves the cursor one character to the right but leaves all characters intact. To illustrate how these keys work, press ESC, type **10**, and type an **x**. To move to the beginning of the line, press the HOME key and the LEFT ARROW key. Press the RIGHT ARROW key four times. Then press the SPACEBAR four times. The text looks like this:

XXX   XXXXX

The SPACEBAR has inserted four spaces and moved the text four characters to the right. The RIGHT ARROW key moved the cursor four characters to the right but did not insert any spaces or move any characters. Press the Exit (F7) key and type **n** twice to clear the screen.

Exercises

1. Press ENTER six times. Use the arrow keys to move to the top of the document and then to the bottom of the document. Clear the screen.

2. Create ten "a"s using the ESC key. Create another ten "a"s by holding down the A key. Use the LEFT ARROW and RIGHT ARROW keys to move through this line. Move to the end of the line and press ENTER. Clear the screen.

3. Use the TAB key to move the cursor to 3 inches from the left edge of the page. Use the LEFT ARROW key to move back to the left side of the screen. Clear the screen.

4. Press CTRL-ENTER four times. Use the PGUP and PGDN keys to move among the five pages. Use CTRL-HOME to move to specific pages. Clear the screen.

5. Type

   the early bird gets the worm.

   Press ENTER and the UP ARROW key. Use WordPerfect's cursor movement keys to move from word to word and to the beginning and the end of the line. Clear the screen.

6. Create a six-page document with four blank lines on each page. Move a screen at a time to the top and the bottom of the document. Use the HOME key and the arrow keys to

move to the top and the bottom of the document. Check the status line after each move to see where you are. Clear the screen.

7. Use the numeric keypad to enter the following:

123456789

Clear the screen.

8. Type the following:

abc

Use the BACKSPACE key to delete the "c." Use the LEFT ARROW key to position the cursor under the "a" and delete the "a."

MASTER THE USE OF THE HELP AND CANCEL KEYS

1.5

WordPerfect has two function keys that are useful for all tasks. The Help key, F3, provides help on any topic. The Cancel key, cancels a WordPerfect command or recovers deleted text. You can use the Cancel (F1) key to restore any of the last three deletions you have made. If you accidentally press one of the function keys, you will invoke a WordPerfect command. To cancel a WordPerfect command, press the Cancel (F1) key until you are returned to your document.

To use the Help key:

a. Insert the WordPerfect 1 disk in drive B if you are using a floppy disk system.

b. Press the Help (F3) key.

c. Type the first letter of the subject for which you want help, or press the function key for which you want help.

d. Press ENTER or the SPACEBAR to return to your document.

If you press F3 twice, the WordPerfect template displays all the function key assignments.

To use the Cancel key to cancel a command:

a. Press the Cancel (F1) key until your document displays on the screen.

To use the Cancel key to restore text:

a. Press the Cancel (F1) key. WordPerfect displays the most recently deleted text at the cursor location.

b. Type a **2** or a **p** if you want to restore a previous deletion.

c. Type a **1** or an **r** to restore the displayed deletion.

Examples

1. You can use the Help (F3) key to display information about the cursor movement keys. Press the Help (F3) key; then type a **c**, for cursor movement. The screen displays information on features that begin with the letter "c." Type **1** to see the second screen of topics, on which you will find "Cursor Movement." You could also press any of the cursor movement keys to display their functions. Press the SPACEBAR or ENTER to leave Help.

2. You can use the Cancel (F1) key to cancel any command request. You press the Exit (F7) key to request WordPerfect to save a file. If you change your mind, you can cancel this request by pressing the Cancel (F1) key.

3. You can use the Cancel (F1) key to restore deleted characters. First, type

fourscore and seven years ago

With the cursor at the end of this phrase, press the BACKSPACE key until all of the text is removed. Then, press the Cancel (F1) key. WordPerfect displays the deleted text in a different color or highlighted. To restore this text, type a 1 or an **r**. Press the Exit (F7) key and type **n** twice to clear the screen.

4. You can restore the most recent deletion or either of the prior two deletions. Type **first** and press ENTER. Next, type **second** and press ENTER. Type **third** as the last entry, without pressing ENTER. Move to the first line and delete the word "first" with the BACKSPACE key. Next, press the DOWN ARROW key, and delete the word "second" by pressing the DEL key six times. Press the DOWN ARROW key again, and press the DEL key five times to delete the word "third." When you press the Cancel (F1) key, the word "third" is displayed. If you type a **2**, WordPerfect displays the word "second." Typing a **2** again displays the word "first." Typing a **1** restores this selection. Press the Exit (F7) key and type **n** twice to clear the screen.

Exercises

1. Use the Help (F3) key to determine how to move to the next screen down or up.

2. Type this sentence:

he suddenly left.

Delete "suddenly" and use the Cancel (F1) key to place it after the word "left." Clear the screen.

3. Use the Help (F3) key to view the template for the function keys.

4. Use the Help (F3) key to look at the keys used to delete characters.

5. Type the following:

it was a cold, dark, scary evening

Delete the word "dark" and the comma and space that follow it. Using the Cancel (F1) key, place it in front of "cold" as the first adjective in the sentence. Clear the screen.

1.6   CONTROL THE ENTRY OF UPPERCASE AND LOWERCASE

When you are typing text in WordPerfect, you will want to make some of the letters uppercase and some lowercase. Your keyboard has two types of keys to change the case of letters that you type. The SHIFT key changes the case of any letter that you type when you are pressing this key. The SHIFT key also enables you to type special characters that appear on the number keys and on other keys. The CAPS LOCK key allows you to switch between typing uppercase and lowercase letters without having to hold down the SHIFT key.

To type a capitalized letter or a special character with the SHIFT key:

a. Press the SHIFT key and hold it down.

b. Type the letter that you want capitalized, or press the key displaying a special symbol above a number or above another character.

c. Release the SHIFT key.

To type capitalized letters with the CAPS LOCK **key:**

a. Press the CAPS LOCK key.

b. Type the letters that you want capitalized.

c. Press the CAPS LOCK key.

Using the SHIFT key with CAPS LOCK on causes WordPerfect to enter lowercase characters.

Examples

1. You can type a series of capital letters with the SHIFT key. Hold down the SHIFT key and type

MEMORANDUM

Press the Exit (F7) key and type **n** twice to clear the screen.

2. You can capitalize some letters and enter others in lowercase by selectively pressing the SHIFT key. Hold down the SHIFT key and type

ABC C

These letters are entered in uppercase. Release the SHIFT key and type

orporation

These letters appear in lowercase. The screen looks like this:

ABC Corporation_

Press the Exit (F7) key and type **n** twice to clear the screen.

3. You can use the SHIFT key to type special characters. Hold down the SHIFT key and type

   TO:

   Without the SHIFT key, the entry would have produced a semicolon (;). The SHIFT key causes WordPerfect to use the symbol at the top of the key. Press the Exit (F7) key and type **n** twice to clear the screen.

4. You can use the CAPS LOCK key when you want to type many capitalized letters. First, press CAPS LOCK. The **Pos** in the status line changes to **POS**. For some keyboards, a CAPS LOCK indicator lights up. Type

   MEMORANDUM

   Press CAPS LOCK again to return to lowercase letter entries. The **POS** in the status line changes back to **Pos**. Using the CAPS LOCK key is easier than holding down the SHIFT key when you have many capital letters to type. Press the Exit (F7) key and type **n** twice to clear the screen.

5. You can type capital letters and use number keys at the same time. When CAPS LOCK is on, the keyboard still treats the number keys at the top of keyboard as numbers. Press CAPS LOCK and type

   SATURDAY 15TH

   Even though the letter keys behave as if you are pressing the SHIFT key, the number keys do not. To type the symbols above the numbers, you still must press the SHIFT key while you press the number. Press the Exit (F7) key and type **n** twice to clear the screen.

Exercises

1. Use the SHIFT key to type these characters:

JQLYZBEANL

Clear the screen.

2. Use the SHIFT key selectively to type

The ABC Corporation makes Tiger sedans.

Clear the screen.

3. Without using the separate numeric keypad, type

The lending rate is 15%.
(16*2)+7=39
Profit & Loss Statement

Clear the screen.

4. Use the CAPS LOCK and SHIFT keys to type

CAPITALIZATION CAN EMPHASIZE TEXT
WORDPERFECT makes typing FUN.

Clear the screen.

5. Use the CAPS LOCK key to type

THE LOCAL CAR DEALERSHIP IS OFFERING 16% APR.
COMPANY PICNIC 8/19/89

Clear the screen.

EXERCISES

MASTERY
SKILLS CHECK

1. Exit WordPerfect.

2. Load WordPerfect.

3. Type the following lines. If you make a mistake, use the DEL or BACKSPACE key.

August 15th or SEPTEMBER 3RD
3^2 + (8*9)

4. Find help on exiting WordPerfect.

5. Clear the screen.

6. Type the following lines. If you make a mistake, use the DEL or BACKSPACE key.

10:34 AM
ACME CORPORATION

7. Exit WordPerfect.

CHAPTER OBJECTIVES

After completing this chapter, you should be able to

2.1 Use WordPerfect's defaults to enter text

2.2 Save a document

2.3 Retrieve a document

2.4 Add missing characters (Insert mode)

2.5 Replace existing characters (Typeover mode)

2.6 Delete characters, words, and lines

·2·

Creating a WordPerfect Document

WordPerfect records your every keystroke in a document. You can create a document for a memo, a letter, a list of names and addresses, a report, and so on. As you type, your document is stored in the memory of your computer system. WordPerfect handles the placement of the words you type on a page and provides default settings that can be used for all your documents. These settings automatically control many features, such as the amount of white space at the edges of your document. After creating a document, you can save it onto a disk for use at a later time.

The ability to recall documents can significantly increase your productivity. No longer will you need to retype an entire document because of an error. You can recall the document and correct the text in error. If you have a document stored on disk that is similar to one you currently need, you can retrieve the document from disk and revise it as necessary. Again, the time required is only a fraction of the time required to type a new document.

SKILLS CHECK

(Do not clear the screen unless instructed to do so.)

1. Start WordPerfect, and type the following exactly as shown:
   A PENNY SAVED IS A penny earned.

   Clear the screen.

2. Type the following:
   TO: John Smith
   FROM: Mary Brown
   SUBJECT: 1989 Holiday Schedule

3. Use the ESC key to add a line of dashes under the entries from skills check 2.

4. Add three blank lines after the entry from skills check 3. Then type the following:

   The attached holiday schedule should be circulated to all employees as soon as possible. Note that company holidays have increased to 8.

5. Add a hard page break below your entries and type the following on page 2:

   January 1   New Year's Day
   January 12   Founders' Day
   March 30   Easter holiday
   April 10   Spring holiday
   May 30   Memorial Day
   July 4   Independence Day
   November 28   Thanksgiving
   December 25   Christmas

6. Move the cursor to page 1 using the CTRL-HOME option.

7. Move to the end of the document.

8. Move to the beginning of the document.

9. Clear the screen.

10. Review the Help screen for exiting WordPerfect.

11. Exit WordPerfect.

USE WORDPERFECT'S DEFAULTS TO ENTER TEXT

2.1

WordPerfect provides a set of default settings for each new document that you create. Default settings are available to you automatically, without any work on your part. The availability of these settings means that you can begin typing without having to worry about laying out the format for your document. Figure 2-1 shows a printed copy of a WordPerfect page. The white space at the top, bottom, and sides is referred to as the *margins*. WordPerfect allows for a 1-inch margin on all sides of a document. The lines of the document are single-spaced on the page. Later you will learn to change the basic document format, but for now you will need to understand what WordPerfect provides.

When you type on a typewriter, you need to be conscious of the bell that signals the end of a line. With WordPerfect, you can type without regard for the end of the line, since WordPerfect uses a feature called *word wrap*. This feature breaks each line at an appropriate place to maintain the right margin. WordPerfect moves additional text to the next line without requiring you to press ENTER. As you edit the text in a paragraph, WordPerfect automatically adjusts the lines to fit

2 Creating a WordPerfect Document
WordPerfect records your every keystroke in a document. You can
create a document for a memo, a letter, a list of names and
addresses, a report, and so on. As you type, your document is
stored in the memory of your computer system. WordPerfect handles
the placement of the words you type on a page and provides default
settings that can be used for all your documents. These settings
automatically control many features, such as the amount of white
space at the edges of your document. After creating a document you
can save it on a disk for use at a later time.
        The ability to recall documents can significantly increase
your productivity. No longer will you need to retype an entire
document because of an error. You can recall the document and
correct the text in error. If you have a document stored on disk
that is similar to one you currently need, you can retrieve the
document from disk and revise it as necessary. Again, the time
required is only a fraction of the time required to type a new
document.
CHAPTER OBJECTIVES
2.1 Use WordPerfect's defaults to enter text
2.2 Save a document
2.3 Retrieve a document
2.4 Add missing characters (Insert mode)
2.5 Replace existing characters (Typeover mode)
2.6 Delete characters, words, and lines
SKILLS CHECK
(Do not clear the screen exercises unless instructed to do so.)

1. Start WordPerfect, and type the following exactly as shown:

A PENNY SAVED IS A penny earned.

Clear the screen.

2. Type the following:

TO: John Smith
FROM: Mary Brown
SUBJECT: 1989 Holiday Schedule

3. Use the ESC key to add a line of dashes under the entries from
skill check 2.

4. Add three blank lines after the entry from skill check 3. Then
type the following:

        The attached holiday schedule should be circulated to all
employees as soon as possible. Note that company holidays have
increased to 8.

5. Add a hard page break below your entries and type the following
on page 2:

January 1   New Year's Day
January 12   Founder's Day
March 30   Easter holiday
April 10   Spring holiday
May 30   Memorial Day

FIGURE 2-1.   Manuscript from *Teach Yourself WordPerfect*, printed with WordPerfect's defaults

the width of the document. WordPerfect manages the placement of text on the page, creating a professional appearance as in the sample output in Figure 2-1.

You can tell WordPerfect exactly where you want a line to end by pressing ENTER. The next text you type will be placed on a new line. You should use ENTER to end a paragraph or a short line.

NOTE: On account of typesetting considerations, the lengths of lines in the entries you will type will not exactly match the text shown in the book. When entering text, remember to press ENTER only at the end of a paragraph or a short line, or as otherwise instructed.

To enter text using WordPerfect's word wrap feature:

a. Type the text without pressing ENTER at the end of each line.

b. Press ENTER at the end of each paragraph.

To enter text without using the word wrap feature:

a. Type the text that you want on the line.

b. Press ENTER to end the line.

Examples

1. WordPerfect's word wrap feature and default margin settings are automatically applied to the text you type. To see how WordPerfect handles text entries that extend for more than one line, type

ABC's new dryer automatically stops when the clothes are dry. It determines when to stop by checking the humidity inside the dryer. This feature prevents shrinkage that occurs from overdrying clothes.

Since you did not press ENTER, the screen looks like this:

```
ABC's new dryer automatically stops when the clothes are dry.  It
determines when to stop by checking the humidity inside the dryer.
This feature prevents shrinkage that occurs from overdrying
clothes._
```

Depending on the initial settings for your printer, Word-Perfect may wrap your text differently, causing your screen to appear different from the examples. Your screen may also appear different if you type only one space, rather than two, after a period. You will use this entry in the next example, so do not clear the screen.

2. Word wrap and margin settings remain in effect when you edit the text entered in example 1. First, press the UP ARROW key twice, the HOME key once, the LEFT ARROW key once, CTRL-RIGHT ARROW three times, and the LEFT ARROW key once to move the cursor to the space between "dryer" and "auto-matically". Next, type a comma, press SPACEBAR, type **Just-Dri** as the dryer's name, and type another comma. WordPerfect does not realign the entries on the screen until you move the cursor. After you press the RIGHT ARROW key, the screen looks like this:

```
ABC's new dryer, Just Dri, automatically stops when the clothes
are dry.  It determines when to stop by checking the humidity
inside the dryer.  This feature prevents shrinkage that occurs from
overdrying clothes.
```

3. Pressing ENTER forces WordPerfect to begin a new line even if the first line is not full. Use ENTER to type short lines, such as the ones in address labels. First, type

Carol Gallagan

Since this is the only text for this line, press ENTER. Next, type

Medical Associates, Inc.

After you type this, end this line by pressing ENTER. Enter the street address by typing

4511 Valley Street

To end this line, press ENTER. Finally, finish the address information by typing

New Haven, CT 03421

Press ENTER to end the line. The screen looks like this:

```
Carol Gallagan
Medical Associates, Inc,
4511 Valley Street
New Haven, CT 03421
-
```

4. ENTER is also used to end paragraphs. First, press TAB and type

   Enclosed are the insurance forms that Dr. Wilbur must fill out for my insurance claim. I will stop by next Tuesday to pick them up.

   To end the paragraph, press ENTER. For the next paragraph, press TAB and type

   I have enclosed a check to cover my August 20th visit. Please note this payment on the insurance form.

Since you have finished the second paragraph, press ENTER. The screen looks like this:

```
     Enclosed are the insurance forms that Dr. Wilbur must fill out
for my insurance claim. I will stop by next Tuesday to pick them
up.
     I have enclosed a check to cover my August 20th visit. Please
note this payment on the insurance form.
-
```

If you had not used ENTER to separate the paragraphs, WordPerfect would have combined them.

Exercises

1. Type these lines, using the ENTER key to separate them:

   January 21, 1989
   The meeting is next Friday.
   They are planning to have lunch at the Cozy Corner restaurant.
   Johnston Company stock is currently selling at 8 3/8.

2. Type this paragraph using WordPerfect's word wrap feature:

   The Stone Corporation is merging with the Johnston Company. The new company's name will be Johnston Stone Corporation. The Stone Corporation manufactures jewelry. Johnston's main product line, raw stones, ensures the Stone Corporation a constant supply.

3. Type this list, using ENTER at the end of each item in the list. Allow WordPerfect's wordwrap feature to wrap the items that extend for more than one line.

Stones and Their Descriptions
Opal - Comes in various colors and varieties, all of which have an iridescent reflection of light
Garnet - Primarily crimson but also can be brown, green, yellow, or black
Topaz - A yellow, white, green, or blue stone that is transparent or translucent
Sapphire - A blue stone that is almost as hard as a diamond

4. Type the following paragraphs:

One frequent cause of problems is the use of an incorrect word or expression. Incorrect word usage can cause readers to lose part of the meaning in your writing.

"Casual" and "causal" are two words that are sometimes interchanged. "Casual" is synonymous with "relaxed" and "low-key." "Causal" relates to involvement with a cause.

SAVE A DOCUMENT 2.2

As you type a document, it is stored in the memory of your computer system. Although WordPerfect can save documents automatically, it does not normally save them unless you specifically request it to do so. If the power to your system goes off, you will lose your entire document if you have not saved it. If the power is lost after you save a document, you will lose any changes or additions you made since the last time you saved the document. Saving frequently is a way to minimize the risk of losing the text you type.

When you save a WordPerfect file, you must follow the rules of the DOS operating system for naming the file. A filename is a combination of up to eight letters, numbers, and certain symbols. It cannot contain spaces. You can also use an optional one- to three-character filename extension after the filename. If you use a filename extension, you must separate it from the filename with a period (.). Each filename on a disk or in a subdirectory must be unique on that disk or in that subdirectory. To make files easier to find, give each document a name that relates to the document's contents.

To save a document and clear the screen or exit WordPerfect:

a. Press the Exit (F7) key.

b. Type a **y** in response to WordPerfect's prompt for saving the document.

c. Type a filename.

d. Optionally, type a period followed by a filename extension.

e. Press ENTER.

f. Type an **n** or press ENTER to clear the screen or type a **y** to exit WordPerfect.

To save a document without clearing the document from the screen:

a. Press the Save (F10) key.

b. Type a filename.

c. Optionally, type a period followed by a filename extension.

d. Press ENTER.

If you have already named the file, WordPerfect prompts you with the filename when you press the Exit (F7) key and type a **y** or when you press the Save (F10) key. You can press ENTER to accept that filename or type a new one before pressing ENTER. If you accept the current filename, you will need to confirm that you want the current document to replace the old contents of the file by typing a **y**.

Examples

1. You can save a document and clear the screen. First, type the following document:

Current Sales	$456,000
Last Year's Sales	$400,000
Growth in Sales	14%

To save this file, press the Exit (F7) key. When WordPerfect asks you whether or not you want to save the document, type a **y**. Next, WordPerfect prompts you for the filename. Type **sales** and press ENTER. The document is saved on your disk. WordPerfect asks if you want to leave WordPerfect. Type an **n**. The screen is cleared.

2. You can save a document without clearing the screen. First, type

Memo
To: All Employees
From: Human Resources
Re: Christmas Party

Press ENTER and then the TAB key, and type

The company Christmas party will be on December 21 at 6:30 p.m.

Next, press the Save (F10) key. When WordPerfect prompts you for the filename, type **xmas** and press ENTER. Word-Perfect returns to the document instead of clearing the screen. Also, WordPerfect displays the filename in the status line. You will use this file in the next example.

3. There is one added step when you save a file a second time. Add the following text to the document from example 2:

Dinner will be served at 8. Dancing will begin at 9:30.

Next, press the Exit (F7) key and type a y to save the file. WordPerfect displays the filename XMAS, which you used when saving the file the first time. Since this is the correct filename, press ENTER.

WordPerfect prompts you to see if you want to replace the data stored on disk with the data in the current document. Type a y to override the default of **No** that would be selected if you pressed ENTER.

WordPerfect asks if you want to exit WordPerfect. Press ENTER to accept the default and clear the screen.

4. You can create multiple copies of a document on a disk by saving it under different names. This allows you to create a document and modify a copy of it for another purpose. First, type

    Jim Allen
    Allen & Associates, CPA's
    412 Oakland
    Tallahassee, FL 31245

    If you need to send two letters to Jim Allen, you can save the name and address with two different filenames to avoid having to type them twice. Press the Save (F10) key.

    Next, WordPerfect prompts you for the filename. Type **allen1** and press ENTER.

    To save it again, press the Save (F10) key.

    WordPerfect displays the filename ALLEN1 for the document. Since you want to save the document under a different name, type **allen2** and press ENTER. After completing the letter in ALLEN1, you can save that document and begin typing the other letter in ALLEN2.

Exercises

1. Type the following and save it as STITCH:

A stitch in time saves nine.

2. Type the following and save it as NAME:

Jim Allen
1123 Fork Rd.
Baltimore, Maryland 21237

Save this document again as NAME2, and clear the screen.

3. Type the following:

Insanity is hereditary. You can get it from your kids.
Sam Levenson

Save the file as KIDS, and clear the screen.

4. Type the following:

A man who has never gone to school may steal from a freight car; but if he has a university education, he may steal the whole railroad.
Theodore Roosevelt

Save the file as TEDDY. Save it again as SCHOOL, and clear the screen.

RETRIEVE A DOCUMENT _____ 2.3

Documents saved to a disk can be retrieved. If a document is retrieved when the screen is clear, the document in memory will consist of the document from the disk. If there is already text in the current document, the text in the document stored on disk will be added to the text in memory at the position of the cursor.

To retrieve a document:

a. Press the Retrieve (SHIFT-F10) key.

b. Type the filename of the document that you want.

c. Press ENTER.

After WordPerfect retrieves the file, it displays the filename in the status line. If WordPerfect cannot find the document, it displays a message, such as this one it displayed when it could not find BUDG_RPT:

ERROR: File not found -- BUDG RPT

Examples

1. To work with a document you created and saved earlier, you can retrieve it. First, press the TAB key and type the following:

The next meeting of the WordPerfect User Group is April 20th.

Press ENTER to end the paragraph. Press the Exit (F7) key to save the document and clear the screen. Press ENTER, type **user**, and press ENTER twice more. The screen is cleared. At this point, you can type a new document or retrieve any document on disk. Press the Retrieve (SHIFT-F10) key. Word-

Perfect displays this prompt:

`Document to be retrieved:`

Type **user** and press ENTER. The document saved as USER appears on the screen like this:

_   The next meeting of the WordPerfect User Group is April 28th.

The filename appears in the status line. Do not clear the screen.

2. You can retrieve a file with a document already on the screen. Retrieve USER again. There will be two copies of the text on the screen. Clear the screen. Retrieve the ALLEN1 file you saved in section 2.2 by pressing the Retrieve (SHIFT-F10) key, typing **allen1**, and pressing ENTER. Move to the end of the document by pressing HOME, HOME, and the DOWN ARROW key. Next, press ENTER twice to add two blank lines. Retrieve the USER file by pressing the Retrieve (SHIFT-F10) key, typing **user**, and pressing ENTER. The screen looks like this:

Jim Allen
Allen & Associates CPA's
412 Oakland
Tallahassee, FL 31245

_   The next meeting of the WordPerfect User Group is April 28th.

Before you retrieve a file, be sure that the screen is clear, unless you want to combine files.

Exercises

1. Retrieve the file STITCH created in exercise 1 of section 2.2.

2. Retrieve the file NAME created in exercise 2 of section 2.2. Next, retrieve STITCH again without clearing the screen first.

3. Retrieve the file TEDDY created in exercise 4 of section 2.2. Without clearing the screen, retrieve the file a second time. Clear the screen.

4. Type

Favorite Quotes

Press ENTER and retrieve the file KIDS. Retrieve the file TEDDY. Clear the screen.

2.4   ADD MISSING CHARACTERS (INSERT MODE)

WordPerfect allows you to add a missing character, word, or paragraph at any location in a document. After typing a document, you can edit it to add the information omitted initially. Since WordPerfect's default setting is the Insert mode, you only need to check that the setting has not been changed. The Insert mode places any character you type to the left of the cursor. If the insertion causes text to extend beyond the right margin, WordPerfect automatically reformats the text to change the word wrap location when you move the cursor.

To use Insert mode:

a. Check to ensure that the left side of the status line displays the filename or is blank. If the word "Typeover" is displayed, press the INS key to set the keyboard for Insert.

b. Type the text you want to insert.

Examples

1. You can use the insert mode to add a few words to the current document. First, type

   The company is releasing a new product that stops kitchen odors.

   Next, move the cursor to the space between "product" and "that." The screen looks like this:

   The company is releasing a new product_that stops kitchen odors.

   Type **, Odor Gone,**. Now, the screen looks like this:

   The company is releasing a new product, Odor Gone,_that stops kitchen odors.

   When you press any cursor movement key, WordPerfect adjusts the display.

2. You can use the Insert mode to insert new lines. First, type

   Tasks
   Review Salary Proposals
   Review Budget from Department 439

You can use "Tasks" as a title by inserting a blank line between the word "Tasks" and the first task. Move to the "R" in the second line and press ENTER. Now the screen looks like this:

Tasks

Review Salary Proposals
Review Budget from Department 439

Exercises

1. Type this sentence:

Company sales reached 1.2 million dollars.

Insert **ABC** and a space before the word "Company."

2. Type this sentence:

Cost of goods sold was 135 dollars.

Change the cost of goods sold to 135,975.

3. Type these sentences:

The company's sales increased to 1,654,834. Net income after taxes was 60,245.

Insert the following sentence between the two you just typed:

Cost of goods sold was 983,473.

4. Type the following sentence:

She served cake for dessert.

Change the sentence so it reads

She served rich, warm, chocolate cake and creamy, rich, vanilla ice cream for dessert.

5. Type the following:

Biography is a region bounded on the north by history, on the south by fiction, and on the west by tedium.
                    Philip Guedalla

Add **on the east by obituary,** in front of "and."

REPLACE EXISTING CHARACTERS (TYPEOVER MODE)   2.5

Sometimes you need to replace the characters in a document with other characters. Typeover mode allows you to replace the character at the current cursor location with another character. If you press the INS key when WordPerfect is in Insert mode, it will change to Typeover mode. Each character that you type will replace a character on the screen until you press the INS key again to switch back to Insert mode. When WordPerfect is in Typeover mode, the word "Typeover" appears at the left edge of the status line.

When you enter text in Typeover mode, the text is not reformatted, since the number of characters in the document does not change. An exception to this is changing a space to a character, or vice versa, since this could change the length of a word at the end of a line. In Typeover mode, the BACKSPACE key deletes the character to the left of the cursor and moves the cursor to that space, but it does not move the remaining characters on the line.

To enter replacement characters in Typeover mode:

a. Press the INS key to activate Typeover mode. Check for the indicator in the status line.

b. Type the replacement text.

c. Press INS again to turn off Typeover mode.

Examples

1. You can use Typeover mode to replace an entry when the replacement is the same length as the original entry. First, type:

The chairman of the publicity department is Daryl Smith.

If Daryl Smith resigns and Donna Jones takes his place, you can change this sentence by moving the cursor to the "D" in "Daryl" and pressing the INS key. WordPerfect displays **Typeover** at the left edge of the status line. Now, type

Donna Jones

The screen now looks like this:

The chairman of the publicity department is Donna Jones.

You will use this entry for the next example.

2. The typeover mode can also be used when the new entry is almost as long as the existing entry. The DEL key can remove the extra characters. You can replace the words "Donna Jones" with the words "Jim Lee." Move to the "D" in "Donna" and press INS if **Typeover** is not displayed in the status line. Type **Jim Lee.** The screen looks like this:

The chairman of the publicity department is Jim Leeones,

Press the DEL key four times to delete the extra four characters.

3. If the replacement entry is longer than the original entry, Typeover mode will extend the original entry by adding characters before the end of a short line. For example, type

Adele Altourne
114 Marymont Avenue
Sunrise, FL 33252

When Adele moves, you need to change the address. First, move the cursor to the first 1 in 114. Next, press INS to invoke Typeover mode, and type

4756 N.E. 27th Avenue

Since the new street address is longer than the old one, no characters from the old address will need to be deleted. This is a feature that prevents you from typing over more text than you planned. WordPerfect inserts space for the text you type where you pressed ENTER in the original entry.

Finally, you can move to the beginning of the third line and type

Ft. Lauderdale, FL 33115

The screen now looks like this:

```
Adele Altourne
4756 N.E. 27th Avenue
Fort Lauderdale, FL  33115_
```

Exercises

1. Type these sentences:

In the March issue of Growing Businesses, Carol Summers described how she started her metal-etching company as a hobby. Soon her business expanded to creating molds for other manufacturers.

Replace "Carol" with "Ellen".

2. Type this sentence:

The answering machine automatically picks up all calls after 2 rings.

Change the 2 to a 4. Change "picks up all calls" to "answers the phone".

3. Type these sentences:

The company is located at W. 125th and Lorain. The company started in the founder's basement.

Replace the first occurrence of "company" with "J. L. McGregor Corporation".

4. Type the following:

The new prices for copies are
1 to 100   .08 each
101 to 500   .05 each
501 +   .02 each

Change the .08 to .09. Change the .05 to .06 and change the .02 to .03.

5. Type the following:

Your current balance is $789.95.

Change $789.95 to $389.95.

DELETE CHARACTERS, WORDS, AND LINES

2.6

In Chapter 1, you learned how to use the DEL and BACKSPACE keys to remove unneeded characters. WordPerfect provides some speedy deletion options that are useful when you have a number of characters to remove. You can use these options to delete a word or a sentence.

Examples

1. To delete the character at the cursor, use the DEL key. First, type

Joan Kelley is the Assistant Production Manager.

After she is promoted, you need to remove the "Assistant" from her title. First, move the cursor to the "A" in "Assistant."

Next, press the DEL key ten times. You could also hold the DEL key down until the word "Assistant" was deleted. Now, the screen looks like this:

Joan Kelley is the Production Manager.

2. An alternative to the DEL key is the BACKSPACE key. First, type

The company's house boat is under repair.

Since "houseboat" is one word, you need to remove the space between the two words. Move the cursor to the word "boat." Then press the BACKSPACE key to remove the space. Now the screen looks like this:

The company's houseboat is under repair.

3. When you have to delete several words, you can use CTRL-BACKSPACE to remove a word at a time. First, type

John is assuming Katie's position until the end of the year.

If the change becomes permanent, you will want to remove the last six words. Move the cursor to the word "until." Then, hold down CTRL and press BACKSPACE six times.

Release CTRL. Finally, press BACKSPACE once and type a period. Now the screen looks like this:

John is assuming Katie's position._

4. You can also use the CTRL-END key combination to delete several words at one time. Type

Tasks
Review Salary Proposals
Review Budget from Department 439
Prepare Master Budget

When you finish the second task, you can delete the entry. First, move the cursor to the beginning of the word "Review" in the second task.

Next, hold down CTRL and press END. All of the text in that line disappears. Finally, press the DEL key to delete the hard return that marks where you pressed ENTER at the end of the line. The screen now looks like this:

Tasks
Review Salary Proposals
Prepare Master Budget

Exercises

1. Type this sentence:

The ABC Corporation and the XYZ Corporation are merging together to form the Alphabet Corporation next month.

Use the DEL key to remove the word together.

Use the BACKSPACE key to remove the phrase "next month".

2. Type this paragraph:

The ABC Corporation manufactures personalized license plates, mugs, name plates, and glassware. The XYZ

Corporation produces personalized garment tags, shirts, purses, and pillows.

Delete "name plates," and "purses,".

3. Type these lines:

ABC Corp and XYZ slogans:
We'll name anything.
Names are down our lane.
We'll fit any name onto anything.

Delete the second slogan.

4. Type the following:

The major issues to be discussed at the next sales meeting are
    New bonus program
    Smaller sales regions
    Strategies for developing new customers.

Delete the third line.

5. Type the following:

NAME	DEPARTMENT	SALARY
Jan Smith	Biology	25,600
Bill Black	Accounting	29,800
Jeff Jones	Finance	35,400

Delete the word "SALARY" and all the salary figures.

EXERCISES

MASTERY
SKILLS CHECK

(Do not clear the screen between exercises unless instructed to do so.)

1. Type this paragraph:

At a press conference last Tuesday, XY Graphics Inc. demonstrated its new product, See 'N' Draw. This product is intended for both novices and experts.

2. Insert "June 17" and a comma before "XY Graphics" in the first sentence.

3. Delete "Inc." using the DEL key.

4. Type "July" over "June".

5. Insert a hard return between the two sentences.

6. Save as SEENDRAW, clearing the screen as you save.

7. Retrieve the file SEENDRAW.

8. Delete the word "both" in the second sentence.

9. Delete the second sentence.

10. Save as DRAW.

(Do not clear the screen between exercises unless instructed to do so.)

INTEGRATED SKILLS CHECK

1. Type these lines:

   **CHOCOLATE CHIP COOKIES TASTE GOOD.
   However, they are fattening.**

2. Use Help to determine which key saves a file.

3. Save as COOKIE.

4. Clear the screen.

5. Type the following line:

A few of my favorite things:

Press ENTER, add a line of dashes under the entry, and press ENTER again.

6. Retrieve COOKIE.

7. Insert the phrase **"AND BUTTERSCOTCH CHIP"** between "CHIP" and "COOKIES."

8. Delete the last line.

9. Save as LIST.

10. Exit WordPerfect.

CHAPTER OBJECTIVES

After completing this chapter, you should be able to

3.1 Print the current document

3.2 Print a selected page from the current document

3.3 Preview before printing

3.4 Print from a file

·3·

Printing a Document

Normally you will want at least one printed copy of every document you create. Some people prefer to proof first drafts of their documents from printed copies. Also, a printed copy is usually the medium used to share the information in your documents with others.

WordPerfect offers a considerable amount of flexibility in its print features. You can print from memory or from a disk file. Even with the basic options in this chapter, you will find that you can print a document while continuing to make changes to the copy in memory. The disk-file option allows you to process a request for a copy of another document while continuing to work in the current document. You can print an entire document or only some of its pages.

To perform any of these tasks, WordPerfect needs an assigned printer. Appendix A covers how to select a printer if one has not already been selected for your system. Chapter 12 covers additional enhancements possible with WordPerfect's print features.

SKILLS CHECK   (Do not clear the screen unless instructed to do so.)

1. Type the following, including the misspelling:

   Fourscore and seven years ago our fathers brought forth on this continent, a new nation, conceived in liberty, and dedicated to the propsition that all men are created equal.
   Gettysburg Address

2. Delete the first three words, and type **87** in their place.

3. Restore "Fourscore and seven" and delete "87."

4. Change "propsition" to "proposition" by inserting an **o** between the "p" and the "s."

5. Type **Abraham Lincoln** over "Gettysburg Address," using Typeover mode and the DEL key.

6. Save this as LINCOLN.

7. Exit WordPerfect.

8. Load WordPerfect, and retrieve the file LINCOLN.

9. Clear the screen.

3.1   PRINT THE CURRENT DOCUMENT

WordPerfect can print the current document without disrupting your work with the document. You can continue to make changes to the document or save it to disk while WordPerfect is printing. These actions will have no effect on the printed document.

You can use this printed copy to give your eyes a break from the screen as you proof a section of the document, or you might want to give the preliminary version of the document to someone else to review while you continue to make changes.

To print the current document:

a. Press the Print (SHIFT-F7) key.

b. Type an **f** or a **1** to print the entire document.

Examples

1. You can print a document with a single command. First type the following:

Dear Sir:

According to our records, your balance is past due. Please send the balance of your account, $150, within 30 days to prevent any legal action.

Press ENTER twice, press TAB five times, and type **Sincerely,**. Press ENTER four times, press TAB five times, and type **Ellen Fitzpatrick**.

Once you have finished the letter, you can start printing by pressing the Print (SHIFT-F7) key and typing **f**, for full document. WordPerfect will also accept **1** for this entry, since the options in the print menu, shown in Figure 3-1, are activated by either a letter or a number. The menu disappears, and the document is displayed again as printing begins. You can then edit the document without affecting the print output.

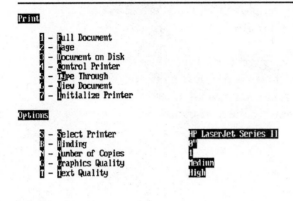

FIGURE 3-1.   Print menu

Save this file as PASTDUE and clear the screen the screen by pressing the Exit (F7) key, pressing ENTER, typing **pastdue**, and pressing ENTER twice more.

2. You can print a multipage document with the same command. First, type

New Hires
Brown, Jim
Scott, Mary

Press CTRL-ENTER to start a new page. Type the following:

Offers Extended
Smith, Jason
Walker, Nancy

Request a printed copy by pressing the Print (SHIFT-F7) key and typing an **f.**

Exercises

1. Retrieve and print the file LINCOLN.

2. Type and print the following letter:

> 12345 Commerce Parkway
> Beachwood, OH 44123
> December 1, 1988

Samantha Koln
Small Business Administration of Cleveland
1235 Public Square
Cleveland, OH 44115

Dear Ms. Koln,

I am starting a business to manufacture mechanical
pencils. Can you provide information on the services that
your organization provides to new companies?

> Sincerely,

> Tom Lu
> President, Various Sundries, Inc.

Save the letter as SBA.

3. Type the following:

There is hardly anything in the world that some man
cannot make a little worse, and sell a little cheaper.

> John Ruskin

Print a copy of the document. Do not clear the screen.

4. Press ENTER twice; then add the following quote:

> It is just as important that business keep out of govern-
> ment as that government keep out of business.
>   Herbert Hoover

Print the document.

3.2   PRINT A SELECTED PAGE FROM THE CURRENT DOCUMENT

If you make a correction to a single page of a document, there is no need to print pages not affected by your change. WordPerfect allows you to print the current page from a document in memory.

To selectively print a page from a document:

a. Move the cursor to the page that you want printed.

b. Press the Print (SHIFT-F7) key.

c. Type a **p** or a **2**.

Examples

1. You can print a single page from a document. First, type the following document as shown, using the ESC key and the equal sign (=) to draw the dividing line:

                              MEMORANDUM

To: Fran Stoll, Director, Human Services
From: John Smith, Division Manager
Re: Job Opening
= =
Fran:

Deborah Winters has accepted a position with another firm. We need someone to fill her vacancy immediately. The following job description can be used for local advertisements.

Next, press CTRL-ENTER to add a hard page break. This places the cursor at the top of the second page of the document. Type the following:

Accountant - Responsibilities include the preparation of budget-analysis and cost-variance data. Must have an MBA or an M.Acct. with 2 years' experience. Salary commensurate with experience.

Move to the first page by pressing PGUP. Then press the Print (SHIFT-F7) key. Enter a **2** or a **p** to print the page.

2. You can print any page in a multipage document. First, type the following:

THINGS TO DO TODAY
Complete filing
Prepare budget report

Press CTRL-ENTER to begin a new page, and type

THINGS TO DO NEXT WEEK
Prepare invoices
Order preprinted forms
Complete Part I of Teach Yourself WordPerfect

Press CTRL-ENTER to end the second page and type

END-OF-MONTH ACTIVITIES
Prepare performance reports
Close books

Press ENTER to end the last line. Next, press the Print (SHIFT-F7) key and type **p** to print the current page (page 3). Word-Perfect prints only page 3. Save this file as TODO.

Exercises

1. Retrieve the file SBA created in exercise 2 of section 3.1. Print the document. Add the following paragraph to the end of the letter:

   I have enclosed a notice of our upcoming open house for your monthly newsletter.

   Move to the end of the document, begin a new page, and type

   Attend the Open House Celebration at Various Sundries on May 15 from 7:30 to 9:30 P.M.

   Print a copy of page 2.

2. Assume that you have three sales personnel reporting to you. Their names are John Smith, Mary Brown, and Nancy Caster. Create a document with a page for each employee. Each page should contain "Significant Accomplishments 1989 -" followed by the name of the employee. The first page would look like this:

   `Significant Accomplishments 1989 - John Smith`

   After creating the three pages, print a copy of page 3. Do not clear the screen.

3. Print a copy of page 2 from the document created in the previous exercise. Print a copy of page 1.

4. Type the following:

Follow pleasure, and then will pleasure flee;
Flee pleasure, and pleasure will follow thee.

John Heywood

Begin a new page; then type

But pleasures are like poppies spread—
you seize the flower, its bloom is shed.

Robert Burns

Print a copy of page 1.

PREVIEW BEFORE PRINTING   3.3

It can be difficult to imagine exactly what your document will look like when it is printed. If your computer has a graphics card WordPerfect provides a way for you to "preview" your print output without taking the time to print the document. The preview that displays on your screen is an exact duplicate of a WordPerfect printed page.

You can choose to display an overview of a page to see the effect of various formatting selections. You can change the display to view two facing pages at once. If you prefer, you can expand the size of the image to either 100% or 200% to read the words in the document.

To view a document before printing:

a. Press the Print (SHIFT-F7) key.

b. Type a **v** or a **6.**

c. To change the size of the image displayed, type **1** for 100%, **2** for 200%, **3** for the default full page, or **4** for facing pages.

d. Press the Exit (F7) key to return to editing the document.

If you choose either of the first two options, you will not be able to see an entire page at once. You can use the arrow keys to move around within a page. You can press PGUP and PGDN to move from page to page in the print image.

Examples

1. When you preview a document, it displays on the screen exactly as it will appear on the printed page. You can see the margins at the edges of the document and look at how the text will appear on the printed page. First type

Ignio Gonzolez
Italia Buena
765 Coltman Avenue
Cleveland, OH 44106

Dear Ignio,

   Thank you for your assistance with the family reunion. Your excellent foods were delightfully prepared, delivery was punctual, and the service was pleasant. We will think of Italia Buena for our next festive occasion.

Press ENTER twice, press TAB five times, and type **Sincerely,**. Press ENTER four times, press TAB five times, and type **Alonzo Benito.**

View the letter to see how it will look when you print it. First, press the Print (SHIFT-F7) key. Next, type a **v.** If you have a graphics card your screen looks like Figure 3-2. While you cannot read the text, you see the general appearance of the letter. Press the Exit (F7) key toend this preview.

FIGURE 3-2. Full-page print preview

You will use this letter for the next example.

2. You can enlarge the preview of the letter shown in exercise 1. Depending on the type of monitor you have, the expanded size of the words may allow you to read them. Press the Print (SHIFT-F7) key and type a **v**. Type a **1** to expand the current document to its full size. Your screen looks like Figure 3-3. Type a **2** to double the size of the display. Use the arrow keys to move around within the display.

Finally, press the Exit (F7) key to return to editing the document. Save the document and clear the screen by pressing the Exit (F7) key, pressing ENTER, typing **ITALIA** as the document name, and pressing ENTER twice.

Exercises

1. Retrieve and view the LINCOLN file created in the skill check in this chapter. Preview the file at the 100% size. Preview the file at the 200% size.

FIGURE 3-3. Print preview at 100%

2. Type the following document and preview it as a full page, at 100%, and at 200%. Use the ESC and equal sign (=) keys to create the dividing line.

To: Sarah Graham, Chief Financial Officer
From: Bob Kelly, Chief Accounting Officer
Re: Financial Statements
= =
Sarah,

Enclosed are the preliminary financial statements. The attached text includes all of the footnotes. If you find any corrections or additions, please contact me immediately.

3. Type the following list of entries:

Meeting on April 20th to discuss new construction.
Make appointment with Harry to discuss new book series.
Meet with marketing to discuss new advertising strategies.

Preview the document. Press CTRL-ENTER at the end of each entry, and preview the document again.

4. Type the following quotations, pressing CTRL-ENTER at the end of each one:

One sees things for the first time only once.

Theodore White

Ignorance is never out of style. It was in fashion yesterday, it is the rage today and will set the pace tomorrow.

Frank Dane

Horatio Alger started by shining shoes and within one year made a million dollars. He must have used very little polish.

Sam Levenson

Nothing is so good as it seems beforehand.

George Eliot

It takes twenty years to become an overnight success.

Eddie Cantor

Preview the document, using the facing-pages view to look at two pages at once. Move to the top of the document and then to the bottom while previewing. Save the document as QUOTES.

PRINT FROM A FILE

3.4

Printing from a file offers convenience since you do not have to interrupt your current activities to print a copy of a document. You can print all the pages of the disk file, or you can specify which pages to print. You have greater flexibility in controlling which pages to print when you print from a file.

To print from a file:

a. Press the Print (SHIFT-F7) key.

b. Type a **3** or a **d**.

c. Type the name of the document that you wish to print from disk.

d. Press ENTER to print the entire document, or type the numbers of the pages that you want printed and then press ENTER.

You can specify one or more pages to print. The page numbers you select are separated by commas. To print a range of pages, you can enter the first page number, a hyphen, and the last page number. You can enter a number preceded by a hyphen to print all pages up to and including that number. Specifying a number followed by a hyphen prints the page specified and all of the pages that follow it. Sample page-number specifications are

1,5-8,12	Prints pages 1, 5, 6, 7, 8, and 12
-5,10-	Prints all pages except 6, 7, 8, and 9
3	Prints page 3

Examples

1. You can print the file ITALIA created in section 3.3. First, press the Print (SHIFT-F7) key. Next, type a **d** for "Document on Disk." When WordPerfect prompts you for the name of the document, type **italia** and press ENTER. WordPerfect displays **Pages** and prompts you with a default of **All**. Press ENTER to have WordPerfect print the entire document.

2. You can print a single page from a document stored on disk. First, create a document that consists of short entries on many pages. Type

This is page 1.

and press CTRL-ENTER to begin a new page. Repeat this process, using consecutive page numbers, until you have entered "This is page 7." End this line with ENTER. Save the document as PAGES by pressing the Exit (F7) key, pressing ENTER, typing **pages**, and pressing ENTER twice. Press the Print (SHIFT-F7) key, and type a **d**. When WordPerfect prompts you for the name of the document on disk, type **pages**, and press ENTER. When WordPerfect prompts you for the page numbers to print, type **4**, and press ENTER. A copy of page 4 is printed.

3. You can print a range of pages from a document stored on disk. First, press the Print (SHIFT-F7) key. Next, type a **d**. When WordPerfect prompts you for the name of the document on disk, type **pages**, and press ENTER. When WordPerfect prompts you for the page numbers to print, type **2-5**, and press ENTER. WordPerfect prints pages 2, 3, 4, and 5.

4. You can exclude a group of pages when printing a document stored on disk. First, press the Print (SHIFT-F7) key. Next, type a **d**. When WordPerfect prompts you for the name of the document, type **pages**. When WordPerfect prompts you for the page numbers to print, type **-3,6-**, and press ENTER. The 3 represents the last page printed before the group of pages excluded, and the 6 represents the first page printed after the excluded pages. WordPerfect prints pages 1, 2, 3, 6, and 7.

Exercises

1. Print the SBA file, created in exercise 2 of section 3.1.

2. Enter the following:

RESIDENTS OPPOSED TO ROAD PAVING
Black
Smith
Campbell
Gilbert
Long
Jackson

Start a new page and enter

RESIDENTS SUPPORTING ROAD PAVING
Wilson
Boswell
Dike

Save the document to disk as ROAD, and clear the screen. Print a copy of the entire document from disk. Print another copy of page 2.

3. Print page 2 of QUOTES, created in exercise 4 of section 3.3.

4. Print pages 2 through 4 of QUOTES.

5. Print pages 1 and 4 of QUOTES.

EXERCISES

MASTERY
SKILLS CHECK   (Do not clear the screen unless instructed to do so.)

1. Type this letter:

To: All Managers
From: Fred Jones, Director of Human Services
Subject: Meetings on the New Benefit Package

The Human Services Department will be conducting a one-hour information meeting on the new benefit package. We have attempted to schedule these meetings at convenient times. Please route the sign-up sheets to your employees and encourage everyone to attend one of these sessions.

Create four new pages in the same document, with one of the following entries at the top of each page:

Benefit Package meeting - April 5 9:30 A.M.
Benefit Package meeting - April 5 2:30 P.M.
Benefit Package meeting - April 6 8:30 A.M.
Benefit Package meeting - April 6 4:00 P.M.

Preview the letter looking first at the full-page view, then at facing pages, and finally at the two enlarged views.

2. Print this letter and the four attachment pages.

3. Print another copy of page 1.

4. Save the file as BENEFITS and clear the screen. Print the four attachment pages from disk.

(Do not clear the screen unless instructed to do so.)

1. Type this as it appears:

INTEGRATED SKILLS CHECK

A meeting is scheduled at 5 PM on January 20 to discuss the company's participation in the CLEVELAND CORPORATE OLYMPICS. The meeting will be held in the fourth-floor conference room.

This year, we need a slogan for the banner and a

T-shirt design. We also need a list of the employees participating in each activity. Please encourage your staff members to participate.

Interested individuals unable to attend the scheduled meeting should contact Steve Spear. His extension is 3963.

2. Delete the second sentence of the third paragraph.

3. Change the date to the 25th.

4. Print the document.

5. Go to the end of the document.

6. Insert a hard page break.

7. Type this as it appears:

Name	Activity
Sue Marianetti	Bike Race
Sharon Campbell	Tug-of-War
John Peterson	Tug-of-War
Tim Smith	5K Race
Ted McGregor	Tug-of-War
Brandon Leidy	Swimming
Marge Thomas	5K Race
Anne Kettlewood	Bike Race

8. Preview the document.

9. Print page 2.

10. Save this document as OLYMPICS and clear the screen.

11. Begin typing the following in a new document:

CORPORATE SLOGAN SUGGESTIONS
Our Team's the Best

Print page 1 of OLYMPICS; then continue typing these slogans:

The Best at All We Do
Scientific Services Employees Have Brains and Brawn
Sticks and Stones Won't Break Our Bones

CHAPTER OBJECTIVES

After completing this chapter, you should be able to

4.1 Underline text as you type

4.2 Boldface text as you type

4.3 Center text as you type

4.4 Reveal the hidden codes for special features

4.5 Search for and delete hidden codes

4.6 Mark and delete block text

4.7 Apply special attributes to blocked text

·4·

Using Features
to Alter the Appearance
of Text

WordPerfect's special features can help you add emphasis to text. Underlining, boldfacing, and centering help to set off text from the rest of your document. WordPerfect changes the appearance of your text on the screen to indicate these special features. WordPerfect also adds special hidden codes to the document for each of these features.

If you do not add these special features to your text as you type it, WordPerfect allows you to add them later. To add the special features to existing text, you must first block the text and then have WordPerfect apply the feature.

SKILLS CHECK   (Do not clear the screen until instructed to do so.)

1. Type the following, including the mistakes:

   The next meting of the WordPerfect User's Group will be January 5. Each attendeee will receive a free on the use of the new graphics features.

2. Correct the document by changing the spelling of the third word to "meeting," removing the last "e" from "attendeee," and inserting the word "handout" after the word "free."

3. Request help for the function key template. Determine the correct key for saving a document.

4. Save the document as MEETING.

5. Clear the screen.

6. Print the document from disk.

4.1   UNDERLINE TEXT AS YOU TYPE

You can use underlining to add emphasis to words in a document. You should use underlining to maintain the correct form for entries such as book titles. You can also use underlining to represent division in a formula or an equation.

To underline characters as you type:

a. Press the Underline (F8) key.

b. Type the characters to be underlined.

c. Press the Underline (F8) key to stop underlining text.

The monitor in your computer system determines the appearance of underlined text on your screen. Some monitors display underlined text with a different background color. Other monitors actually display the underlining beneath the text.

Examples

1. You can underline text at the beginning of a line. First, press the Underline (F8) key, and type

   Project Review

   Next, press the Underline (F8) key again. The screen looks like this:

   <u>Project Review</u>_

2. You can underline several words in the middle of a sentence. First, type the following words, which do not require underlining, and include a space after the last word:

   The project review committee will meet on

   Next, press the Underline (F8) key, and type

   Monday, January 4

   Finally, press the Underline (F8) key to end underlining, and type

   at 3:00 PM.

   The display looks like the following.

The project review committee will meet on ▇Monday, January 4,▇ at
3:00 PM._

Exercises

1. Create the following bibliography entries:

Acerson, Karen L.,WordPerfect: The Complete Reference,
Series 5 Edition, Osborne/McGraw-Hill, 1988.
Alderman, Eric, and Lawrence J. Magid, Advanced Word-
Perfect, Series 5 Edition, Osborne/McGraw-Hill, 1988.
Mincberg, Mella, WordPerfect Made Easy, Series 5
Edition, Osborne/McGraw-Hill, 1988.

2. Type the following document:

We will honor employees with more than twenty-five years
of service at the annual appreciation dinner. The following
employees are honorees at this year's dinner:

EMPLOYEE	YEARS OF SERVICE
J. Smith	25
R. Taylor	35
P. Volker	31

3. Type the following formula:

Cost per square foot = $\dfrac{\text{Total cost}}{\text{Square feet}}$

4. Type the following exactly as shown:

There are many interesting tales in mythology. The
gods, goddesses, and heroes in these stories have un-
usual names and adventures. The names of each of the
gods and other special characters in the following pas-
sage are underlined to highlight them.

Aconteus looked at **Medusa's** head and turned into stone. **Medusa** was a monster whose hair was made of serpents. **Perseus**, the son of **Danae** and **Jupiter**, killed **Medusa**. To make himself invisible to **Medusa**, he wore **Pluto's** helmet and a pair of winged shoes.

BOLDFACE TEXT AS YOU TYPE

4.2

Bold text is text that is darker than the surrounding text. Using the bold feature can add emphasis to text.

To boldface characters as you type:

a. Press the Bold (F6) key.

b. Type the characters you wish to show in boldface.

c. Press the Bold (F6) key to stop boldfacing text.

The monitor on your computer system determines the appearance of bold text on your screen. On some monitors, WordPerfect displays bold text with increased intensity. Other monitors display bold text in a different color.

Examples

1. You can use the Bold feature to highlight a date and time in an entry. First, type the following text, which does not require boldface:

   The next meeting is scheduled for

   Next, add a space after the last word, press the Bold (F6) key, and type

   11 P.M. on Friday, January 14

Finally, end the bold text by pressing the Bold (F6) key, and type a period to end the sentence. When you print the text, it looks like this:

The next meeting is scheduled for 11 P.M. on Friday, January 14.

2. You can invoke the Bold feature once and continue to type boldface text until you turn it off. To enter a list of bullet items in boldface, request Bold before typing the first bullet item, and turn off Bold after typing the last item. First, type the following text, which does not require Bold:

We will discuss the following topics at the next meeting:

Next, press ENTER and press the Bold (F6) key. Then, for each bullet item, press the TAB key, type the text, and press the ENTER key:

* Part-time versus full-time benefits
* Training opportunities
* Stock option plan eligibility

Press the Bold (F6) key to end boldfacing. The text looks like this:

We will discuss the following topics at the next meeting:
   * Part-time versus full-time benefits
   * Training opportunities
   * Stock option plan eligibility

3. You can combine Bold and Underline to add extra emphasis to any text. The appearance of boldface, underlined text will vary on different monitors. To begin an entry that uses both Bold and Underline, press the Bold (F6) key, and then press the Underline (F8) key. Type

ANNUAL REPORT

The text should appear different from both underlined text and bold text. The appearance of the text depends on your computer monitor. Next, press the Underline (F8) and Bold (F6) keys to end both features. The printed text looks like this:

ANNUAL REPORT

Exercises

1. Type the following accounts and their balances. Use Bold for all accounts with negative balances (shown in parentheses).

ACCOUNT	BALANCE
Rent	$5,125
Utilities	**(1,250)**
Phone	**(950)**

2. Type the following sentences. Use Bold for "more than 90 days' past due" and "immediately."

   Your account balance is **more than 90 days' past due. Unless you contact us immediately, we will begin legal action to collect the balance of your account.**

3. Type the following. Use Bold and Underline for the labels at the top of the columns:

DEPT	HEAD COUNT
ACCT	14
FIN	10
MFG	84

4. Type the following, using Bold for the foreign phrases.

Foreign words can add variety to your writing. When you select foreign phrases, you will want to be certain that both you and your readers understand their meaning. **Deo gratias** means thanks to God. **Dei gratia** means by the grace of God. **Deo volente** means by God's will. **Dieu vous garde** means God protect you.

5. Type the following quotations. Use Bold for the author of each quote and Bold and Underline for the title of each book:

Noble by birth, yet nobler by great deeds.
    Henry Wadsworth Longfellow, Tales of a Wayside Inn
Who fears t'offend takes the first step to please.
    Colley Cibber, Love in a Riddle
The art of praising is the beginning of the art of pleasing.
    Voltaire, La Pucelle

4.3   CENTER TEXT AS YOU TYPE

You can use centering to place a report title in the center of a line in your document. You can also center a company name or department name using the same techniques.

To center characters on a line as you type them:

a. Press the Center (SHIFT-F6) key.

b. Type the characters you wish to center on the line.

c. Press ENTER to end centering. WordPerfect displays the text centered on the line.

Examples

(Do not clear the screen between examples unless instructed to do so.)

1. You can center a company name in the middle of a line by pressing the Center (SHIFT-F6) key. Next, type the following company name:

ABC COMPANY

Finally, press ENTER to indicate the end of the entry, producing this result:

ABC COMPANY

–

2. You can center additional lines on a page by invoking the Center feature at the beginning of each line. Press the Center (SHIFT-F6) key, and type

111 North Ave

Press ENTER to end the line, press the Center (SHIFT-F6) key and type

Chicago, IL 30211

After you press ENTER, the screen looks like this:

ABC COMPANY
111 North Ave,
Chicago, IL 38211

–

Clear the screen.

3. You can enter text at the left margin on the same line as centered text. First, type

Roger Smith

Next, press the Center (SHIFT-F6) key, and type

ABC Company

After you press ENTER, the results look like this:

Roger Smith   ABC Company
-

Clear the screen.

4. You can use Center with Underline and Bold. Press the
   Bold (F6) key, press the Underline (F8) key, and then press
   the Center (SHIFT-F6) key. Type

ABC Company

Press the Bold (F6) key, the Underline (F8) key, and ENTER. If
you print the page, the line looks like this:

<u>**ABC Company**</u>

Clear the screen.

Exercises

1. Type your name, street address, and city and state on three
   separate lines, using the Center feature for each line.

2. Using Center and Bold, type **Tinsel Company** on a line.

3. Invoke the Center feature and type the following text,
   watching the screen as you type:

> This text is too long for one line. WordPerfect cannot fit the entire entry on one line. When you print the text, you will notice that WordPerfect centers only the text in the first line.

As you type this text, you cannot see the centering on the screen, because of the length of the lines. Initially, the first characters of the first sentence seem to disappear.

4. Center the following lines as you type them:

> ABC COMPANY
> PERFORMANCE REPORT
> FOR THE QUARTER ENDING JUNE 30, 1989

REVEAL THE HIDDEN CODES FOR SPECIAL FEATURES

4.4

WordPerfect marks special features, such as the end of a line or the end of a page, with hidden codes. The codes provide specific information about each feature used and its exact location within a document. Although some features may be obvious as you look at the screen, others are not apparent unless you reveal the codes within the document. Word-Perfect splits the screen to display the codes, using the top window for the normal display and showing the text and codes in the bottom window. You cannot type a new code over an existing code to make a change. You must delete the existing code or insert a new one after it in the document.

To reveal hidden codes in a document:

a. Press the Reveal Codes (ALT-F3) key.

b. Use the arrow keys to highlight the codes in the document.

c. Press the Reveal Codes (ALT-F3) key to return to the normal display.

If your keyboard has 12 function keys, you can press the F11 key instead of ALT-F3 to reveal codes.

Examples

1. Even without using special attributes (such as bold and underlining), you can find special codes in your documents. Type

   ABC Company

   Next, press ENTER. This adds a hidden code for a hard return. Press the Reveal Codes (ALT-F3) key to produce the split screen display shown in Figure 4-1. The [HRt] code represents a hard return where you pressed ENTER. WordPerfect inserts a soft return code [SRt] when it uses its word wrap feature to begin the next line. A soft page break is generated when WordPerfect fills a page. The code for a soft page break is [SPg]. When you force WordPerfect to end a page by pressing CTRL-ENTER, a hard page break code [HPg] is inserted.

2. You can use Reveal Codes to look at the special attributes in your documents. Press the Bold (F6) key, and type

   BUDGET SUMMARY

   Press the Bold (F6) key to end Bold. Next, press ENTER twice and the Underline (F8) key once. Then type

   ACCOUNTING DEPARTMENT

   Press the Underline (F8) key to end underlining. To look at the codes for these features, press the Reveal Codes (ALT-F3)

ABC Company

Press **Reveal Codes** to restore screen

FIGURE 4-1.   WordPerfect Reveal Codes screen

key. As you examine the Reveal Codes screen, you will
notice that each attribute uses a code at the beginning and
at the end of the affected text.

[BOLD]BUDGET SUMMARY[bold][HRt]
[HRt]
[UND]ACCOUNTING DEPARTMENT[und]

WordPerfect places [BOLD] and [bold] codes around bold
text. It uses [UND] and [und] for underlined text. You can
remove the Reveal Codes display from the screen by
pressing the Reveal Codes (ALT-F3) key again.

3. You can watch WordPerfect add codes to a document as you type by displaying the Reveal Codes screen before making entries. Press the Reveal Codes (ALT-F3) key. Next, press the Center (SHIFT-F6) key. Type the following, and press ENTER:

ABC Company

WordPerfect places Center codes at the beginning and at the end of the centered entry. WordPerfect uses [Cntr] at the beginning and [C/A/Flrt] at the end of the centered text.

Exercises

1. Type the following lines, using the Center feature for each line:

ABC COMPANY
BUDGET REPORT
FISCAL 1990

Use Reveal Codes to find the Center codes at the beginning and end of each entry.

2. Type the following, using Bold where indicated:

New Sunday store hours are Noon to 5 P.M.

Use Reveal Codes to locate the Bold codes.

3. Activate Reveal Codes. Type the following, using Bold and Underline:

Overdue Accounts

Note the addition of the codes to the document.

4. Center the following lines:

I think, therefore I am.
Rene Descartes

Reveal the hidden codes for Center. Save the file as THINK.

SEARCH FOR AND DELETE HIDDEN CODES   4.5

You do not need to delete text to remove special attributes that you used for the text. You can delete the code for an attribute from either the Reveal Codes display or the normal display. To delete a code from the normal display, you can first search for the attribute code you want to delete. Your search will pinpoint the exact location of the specific code. To remove underlining, boldface, or centering, you can remove either of the pair of special codes marking the attribute.

To delete a code in the Reveal Codes display:

a. Press the Reveal Codes (ALT-F3) key.

b. Use the arrow keys to move the cursor to the code you wish to remove.

c. Press the DEL key.

d. Press the Reveal Codes (ALT-F3) key to return to the normal display.

You can also delete a code by moving the cursor to the right of the code and pressing the BACKSPACE key. When you delete codes after pressing the Reveal Codes (F3) key, WordPerfect does not ask for a confirmation. If you try to delete a code when it is hidden, WordPerfect prompts you for a confirmation before deleting the code.

To delete codes in the normal display:

a. Press the HOME key three times and the UP ARROW key once to move to the very top of the document, before any codes.

b. Press the Search (F2) key.

c. Press the function key representing the code, for example, the Bold (F6) key.

d. Press the Search (F2) key again to begin the search.

e. Press the BACKSPACE key to delete the code.

f. Type a **y** to confirm the deletion.

g. Press the Search (F2) key twice to look for the next occurrence of the code. If the search is successful, repeat the procedure from step e.

Examples

1. You can enter text with a special attribute and later remove the attribute. First, press the Bold (F6) key and type

BUDGET REPORT

Next, press the Bold (F6) key to end Bold. To look at the codes, press the Reveal Codes (ALT-F3) key. If you position the cursor in the Reveal Codes screen on either the [BOLD] or [bold] code and press DEL, WordPerfect deletes both codes. The text remains on the screen.

Press the Reveal Codes (ALT-F3) key to return to the normal display.

2. You can assign multiple attributes to text and delete any of them without affecting the remaining codes or the text. Press the Bold (F6) key and then the Underline (F8) key. Next, type

Expenses

Press the Bold (F6) key and then the Underline (F8) key to end both features. After invoking Reveal Codes by pressing the Reveal Codes (ALT-F3) key, use the arrow keys to highlight [und], and press DEL. This action removes the underlining but retains the text and the boldface. Press the Reveal Codes (ALT-F3) to return to the normal display.

3. You can use the BACKSPACE or DEL key to remove either text or codes from the normal display. However, unless you search for a specific code, you may have difficulty determining the correct location of a code in this display. Press the Center (SHIFT-F6) key and type

Lawrence Aluminum

Next, press ENTER twice, and begin Bold by pressing the Bold (F6) key. Type

Salary Expense

After pressing the Bold (F6) key again, move to the top of the document by pressing HOME, HOME, HOME, and UP ARROW. Press the Search (F2) key and then the Bold (F6) key. Press the Search (F2) key again to search for the first Bold code. Press the BACKSPACE key to delete the hidden code, and type a **y** to confirm the deletion. To find the next occurrence of Bold, press the Search (F2) key twice.

Exercises

(Do not clear the screen between exercises unless instructed to do so.)

1. Enter the following text exactly as shown, using Center for the indented lines.

Quality Corporation is pleased to announce the following Christmas bonus structures:
  Less than 2 years of service - 2% bonus
  2 years or more of service - 5% bonus
Checks will be available for distribution on <u>December 23.</u>

Find the codes for Bold, Underline, and Center in the Reveal Codes screen. Delete the Center codes.

2. Deactivate the Reveal Codes display. Move to the beginning of the document, before any codes, and use the Search feature to locate the Bold code. Clear the screen.

3. Retrieve the file THINK, and delete the codes for Center.

4.6   MARK AND DELETE BLOCK TEXT

Normally, the DEL and BACKSPACE keys affect only a single character or code or one pair of codes at a time. Using the Block feature to mark adjacent characters and codes allows you to perform an action on all the marked material at one time.

To mark a block of text:

a. Use the cursor movement keys to position the cursor on the first character or code in the block you wish to define.

b. Press the Block (ALT-F4) key. If you have a keyboard that has 12 function keys, you can use F12 as well as ALT-F4 to block text.

c. Use the arrow keys to move the cursor one position past the last character in the block.

The text within the block appears with black letters against a highlighted background. On color monitors, the blocked text may appear with a background color different from that of normal text. If you wish to remove the highlighting without taking an action, press the Block (ALT-F4) key again or press the Cancel (F1) key.

Examples

1. You can block a word in a document and delete it. First, type the following sentence:

The next loan payment is due January 14.

Use the arrow keys to move to the "p" in "payment." Next, press the Block (ALT-F4) key. WordPerfect changes the background display of the position number on the status line to indicate that Block has been activated. Press CTRL-RIGHT ARROW to place the cursor on the "i" in "is." WordPerfect changes the display of the blocked text. The screen looks like this:

The next loan payment is due January 14,

To delete the blocked text, press the DEL or BACKSPACE key.

2. You can block larger portions of a document with the same method or with some shortcuts. For example, when Block is activated, typing any character causes everything up to the next occurrence of that character to be included within the block. First, type the following:

The first Advanced WordPerfect seminar is scheduled for February 22, 1989. Employees must complete the exercises in Teach Yourself WordPerfect to be eligible for enrollment.

Next, use the arrow keys to move to the "E" at the beginning of the second sentence. Press the Block (ALT-F4) key to activate the Block feature. To block the entire sentence, press the PERIOD (.) key. Press the DEL key to remove the sentence. WordPerfect displays a prompt on the status line. Type a y to confirm that you want to delete the block.

Exercises

1. Type the following. Then block the second sentence.

New members must pay an initiation fee of $300. In addition, new members must volunteer for association programs a minimum of 25 hours during their first year.

2. Type the following:

An excuse uncalled for becomes an obvious accusation.
Law Maxim

Block the word "excuse." Remove the Block feature, and save the file as EXCUSE.

3. Type the following text:

You must submit expense reports by the 15th of the month following travel.

Use the Block feature to block "15th." Turn off the Block feature. Do not clear the screen.

4. Insert the word **previous** before the word "month." Block the new word and delete it.

5. Retrieve the file named THINK. Block and delete "Rene Descartes."

APPLY SPECIAL ATTRIBUTES
TO BLOCKED TEXT

4.7

Using special attributes, such as boldface, underlining, and centering is simplest if you invoke the feature before typing the text. However, if you forget, or if you wish to change the appearance of text that has already been typed, you can still add these attributes. You first block the text that you wish to change and then invoke the attribute.

To apply special attributes to a group of characters:

a. Block the text.

b. Press the function key representing the attribute you wish to use, for example, the Underline (F8) key.

c. If you are adding a code for centering, you must confirm your request by typing a **y** when WordPerfect prompts you for confirmation.

Examples

1. You can underline text without retyping it. First, complete these entries, pressing ENTER at the end of each line:

   A few box office hits are
   Who Framed Roger Rabbit?
   Coming to America
   Bull Durham
   Big

   Press ENTER after typing the last title. Although you did not underline the movie titles when typing them, you can do so now. Move the cursor to the "W" in the first title, and press the Block (ALT-F4) key. Use the DOWN ARROW key to move the cursor to the line below the last title. Next, press the Underline (F8) key. WordPerfect underlines the titles.

2. You can add centering with the same method. First, type:

Productivity Report

Since you can block from either direction, press the Block (ALT-F4) key and move the cursor to the beginning of the entry. Press the Center (SHIFT-F6) key, and type a y to confirm the request. The actions center the entry like this:

Productivity Report

3. You can add more than one attribute to existing text. Type the following:

The last date for renewing your membership at this year's rate is December 31.

You can add both bold and underlining to "last date" and "December 31" by blocking the entries. First, move the cursor to the "l" in "last." Press the Block (ALT-F4) key, and move to the space following the "e" in "date." Press the Underline (F8) key. To add bold, block the data again by pressing the Block (ALT-F4) key. To return quickly to the first character of the block, hold down CTRL and press HOME twice. Press the Bold (F6) key to add the second attribute. You can repeat this procedure for "December 31." The printed sentence will look like this:

The <u>last date</u> for renewing your membership at this year's rate is <u>December 31.</u>

Exercises

1. Type the following:

After completing this book, you can continue to build your skills with WordPerfect 5 Made Easy. Soon you will be your company's WordPerfect expert.

Use the Block feature to underline "WordPerfect 5 Made Easy". Do not clear the screen.

2. Use the Block feature to make "WordPerfect expert" bold.

3. Type the following:

ACCOUNTS RECEIVABLE AGING

Underline and center the text without retyping it.

4. Retrieve the file EXCUSE. Add the following at the end of the document:

A bad excuse is better, they say, than none at all.
Stephen Gosson

Block the word "excuse" in each quotation, and make it boldface.

5. Type the following:

A cruel story runs on wheels, and every hand oils the wheels as they run.
Ouida

Underline and boldface both occurrences of "wheels" after completing the entry.

EXERCISES

(Do not clear the screen between exercises unless instructed to do so.)

MASTERY
SKILLS CHECK

1. Underline the following text as you type it:

   Bylaws of the WordPerfect Users Group

   Clear the screen.

2. Enter the following, using Bold for the company name, location, and date:

   ABC Company will hold its annual picnic at the **Loch Raven Pavilion** on **July 17th.**

3. Use Reveal Codes to look at the hidden codes for Bold. Delete the Bold codes for "Loch Raven Pavilion."

4. Move to the top of the document. With Reveal Codes activated, type the following using Center and Underline:

   COMPANY PICNIC ANNOUNCEMENT

5. Add two blank lines. Deactivate Reveal Codes. Use the Search feature to locate the codes for Underline. Print the document, and clear the screen.

6. Type the following memo as shown:

   ABC COMPANY
   INTERNAL MEMORANDUM

   TO: All staff
   FROM: John Smith
   SUBJECT: Completion of parking lot resurfacing
   DATE: February 15, 1989

   The resurfacing of parking lots A and B is complete. Resurfacing of parking lot C is scheduled to begin Monday, February 20. Your continued cooperation is appreciated.

   Use Reveal Codes to remove the hard return before the last line. Save the memo as PARKING.

7. Add bold to the word "complete" in the first sentence. Use Block to mark the second sentence and delete it. Clear the screen.

8. Type the following:

ACCT NO	BALANCE
1204	$12,350
1567	$17,865
2569	$23,789

Use the Block feature to add boldface and underlining to the headings at the top of the columns.

(Do not clear the screen between exercises unless instructed to do so.)

INTEGRATED
SKILLS CHECK

1. Type the following document as shown:

ABC BOOKS
1115 Warren Avenue
Cleveland, OH 44017

Mr. John Myers
Winsom Corporation
111 North St.
Akron, OH 43124

Dear Mr. Myers:

We are holding a copy of Successful Office Management for you. We will hold this book for you until October 12.

Sincerely,

Ralph Jones
Customer Service

2. Save the document as MYERS, and clear the screen. Print a copy of the letter from disk.

3. Retrieve the file, and make the following changes: Use Typeover mode to change "North" to **South**. Add underlining to "Successful Office Management". Add boldface to the date in the last sentence.

4. Activate the Block feature, and block the letter body. Then cancel the Block request.

5. Save the document to disk, replacing the previous copy. Preview the document on the screen. Print a copy.

CHAPTER OBJECTIVES

After completing this chapter, you should be able to

5.1 Set right and left margins

5.2 Use indentation

5.3 Use the Margin Release feature

5.4 Set tabs

5.5 Use the Flush Right feature

5.6 Change the line spacing

5.7 Alter justification

·5·

Changing the
Appearance of Lines
Within a Document

WordPerfect's line-formatting features allow you to change the appearance of one or more lines of text. You can alter the margin settings to add more or less white space at the edges of the paper. Lines can also be indented from the left and right edges of the paper, allowing you to offset bullet items or other important text. You can change the tab settings to conform with the structure of the entries you wish to make.

WordPerfect lets you change the line spacing to provide extra space between lines when printing a draft of a document. Two additional options affect the right margin of a document: The Flush Right feature allows you to place text such as the date or a letter heading at the right edge of a document. While WordPerfect's default right justification is designed to provide a consistent right margin when a document is printed, you can turn off that feature if you desire.

Each of the line-formatting options affects the document beginning at the line in which it is invoked. If you want a formatting change to affect every line in a document, you must invoke the feature at the top of the document.

SKILLS CHECK

(Do not clear the screen until you are instructed to do so.)

1. Type the bibliography shown below, centering the head and underlining the book titles as you type them.

Bibliography

Mincberg, Mella, <u>WordPerfect 5 Made Easy</u>, Osborne/McGraw-Hill, 492 pages.
Campbell, Mary, <u>1-2-3 Made Easy</u>, Osborne/McGraw-Hill, 400 pages.

2. Insert the year for each book—1988 and 1986, respectively—between the publisher and the page count.

3. Save the document as BIBLIO.

4. Search for the underline codes and delete them.

5. Clear the screen.

6. Print the file BIBLIO.

5.1 SET RIGHT AND LEFT MARGINS

The left and right margins are the blank area at the left and right sides of a printed page. WordPerfect measures the margins as the number of inches between the edge of the paper and the text and ensures that text entered conforms to the margin settings.

Margin settings can be changed throughout a document. WordPerfect uses the default margin settings unless it finds hidden codes representing other margin specifications. WordPerfect initially has 1" left and right margins. When you change a margin setting, WordPerfect automatically rewraps the text for the new margin and continues to use that setting unless it finds another hidden code for a margin change.

To change the left and right margins:

a. Press the Format (SHIFT-F8) key.

b. Select Line by typing a letter l or a number 1.

c. Select Margins by typing an **M** or a **7**.

d. Type the number of inches WordPerfect should leave between the left edge of the paper and the text.

e. Press ENTER.

f. Type the number of inches WordPerfect should leave between the right edge of the paper and the text.

g. Press ENTER.

h. Press the Exit (F7) key to return to the document.

Examples

1. You can decrease the margins to increase the amount of text that fits on each page. For example, you can decrease the margins to .5". First, type

   A presentation on WordPerfect's exciting new graphics features is scheduled for the next meeting of the WordPerfect User Group. This meeting will be held at noon on April 28th.

   Move to the top of the document by pressing HOME, HOME,

and UP ARROW. Next, press the Format (SHIFT-F8) key. Type **l** to select the line-formatting options. Type **m** to select the margin-formatting option. Type **.5** and press ENTER. Then, type **.5** and press ENTER again. This allows an additional inch of text on each line. Press the Exit (F7) key to return to the document. Then press the DOWN ARROW key to make Word-Perfect reformat the paragraph. The reformatted lines are shown below:

A presentation on WordPerfect's exciting new graphics features is scheduled for the next meeting of the WordPerfect User Group. This meeting will be held at noon on April 28th.

Press the Reveal Codes (ALT-F3) key. WordPerfect displays [L/R Mar:0.5",0.5"] as the code for the half-inch-margins setting. Use this entry in the next example.

2. You can increase the margins to decrease the text that fits on each page. If you set the new margins when the cursor is past the hidden code for the current margin setting, you do not have to delete the hidden code. However, if you are changing the margins for the entire document, the best strategy is to eliminate the margin settings that are not needed.

   Codes are still revealed from the last example. Press HOME, HOME, and UP ARROW, and press the BACKSPACE key to remove the [L/R Mar:0.5",0.5"] code for the current margin setting. (You can either remain in the Reveal Codes screen or remove it by pressing the Reveal Codes (ALT-F3) key again.) Press the Format (SHIFT-F8) key and type a **l**. Next, type **m** to select Margins. Type a **2** for the left-margin setting, and press ENTER. Type a **2** for the right-margin setting, and press ENTER again. Finally, press the Exit (F7) key to return to the document. Press the DOWN ARROW key to reformat the para-graph. The text now appears with the wider margins, as shown below:

A presentation on WordPerfect's exciting new
graphics features is scheduled for the next
meeting of the WordPerfect User Group. This
meeting will be held at noon on April 28th.

Exercises

1. Type the following:

**Some are born great, some achieve greatness, others
have greatness thrust upon 'em.**
                    William Shakespeare

Change the left margin to 2″ and the right margin to 1.5″.

2. Type the following:

**What makes us discontented with our condition is the
absurdly exaggerated idea we have of the happiness of
others.**
                    Proverb

Change the left and right margins to 2″. Reveal the hidden
codes to see the code for the new margins. Return to the
normal screen, and change the margins to 1.5″.

3. Type the following:

**The plural of most compound nouns is formed by adding
"s" or "es" to the main word in the grouping. For example:**

   mothers-in-law
   runners-up
   daughters-in-law

Change the left margin to 2.5″ and the right margin to 1.5″.

4. Type the following lines:
ABC COMPANY - MEMO
Date: Friday, Sept 10, 1989

— —

When using the copier by the coffee machine, only use the paper stacked next to the machine. Since the machine is old, if you use different paper (envelopes, letterheads, etc.), the machine jams.

At the beginning of the document, set the left and right margins to 3″. Preview how WordPerfect prints the document. Delete the hidden code for the margin settings.

5.2   USE INDENTATION

WordPerfect allows you to indent a paragraph of text from the left margin. Each time you press the Indent (F4) key, WordPerfect moves one tab stop to the right and establishes a temporary margin at that position. When you press ENTER, the normal margin setting is resumed. This feature allows you to indent bullet items and other special text to set it off from the regular text. The hidden code inserted for Indent is [→ Indent]. If you delete this code, the indentation is removed.

A similar feature allows you to indent the text from both margins at the same time. WordPerfect's Indent Left and Right feature moves the paragraph in from the margins without changing the margins of the remaining text. When you press the Indent Left and Right (SHIFT-F4) key, the margins move in one tab stop from the left edge of the document and an equal amount of space from the right edge. Indentation from both sides may be used to set off a long quote from the body of a letter or report. The hidden code added to a document when this feature is used is [→ Indent ◄].

To indent a paragraph from the left margin:

a. Move the cursor to the beginning of the paragraph that you want to indent.

b. Press the Indent (F4) key one or more times to move to the tab setting to which you want the paragraph indented.

To indent a paragraph from both margins:

a. Move the cursor to the beginning of the paragraph that you want to indent.

b. Press the Indent Left and Right (SHIFT-F4) key one or more times to move to the tab setting to which you want the paragraph indented.

You can perform these steps before or after you type the text.

Examples

1. You can indent paragraphs from the left margin to set them off from other text. First, type

   On January 3, 1959, Alaska became the 49th state. Congress defeated an earlier bill that would have granted it statehood. Alaska was the first state admitted to statehood since 1912.

   Next, press ENTER to end the paragraph. Then, press the Indent (F4) key, and type

   The land was purchased from Russia during Lincoln's administration. The purchase was referred to as Seward's Folly after the secretary of state who supported the purchase.

   The second paragraph is indented. The two paragraphs look like the following.

On January 3, 1959, Alaska became the 49th state. Congress defeated an earlier bill that would have granted it statehood. Alaska was the first state admitted to statehood since 1912.
The land was purchased from Russia during Lincoln's administration. The purchase was referred to as Seward's Folly, after the secretary of state who supported the purchase.

You can display the hidden code for the indent feature by pressing the Reveal Codes (ALT-F3) key. If you delete this code, the indentation is removed.

2. You can indent both sides of a paragraph. This is customary when typing a quotation that uses several lines. To indent both sides of a paragraph, type

Isaac Newton, a mathematician, philosopher and scientist, said:

Next, press the Indent Left and Right (SHIFT-F4) key, and type

I do not know what I may appear to the world, but to myself I seem to have been only like a boy playing on the sea-shore, and diverting myself in now and then finding a smoother pebble, or a prettier shell than ordinary, whilst the great ocean of truth lay undiscovered before me.

After you type the text, the screen looks like this:

Isaac Newton, a mathematician, philosopher and scientist, said:
I do not know what I may appear to the world, but to myself I seem to have been only like a boy playing on the sea-shore, and diverting myself in now and then finding a smoother pebble, or a prettier shell than ordinary, whilst the great ocean of truth lay undiscovered before me.

Exercises

1. Type the following paragraph after pressing the Indent

Left and Right (SHIFT-F4) key four times:

Next Monday, the executive officers are meeting to discuss five-year growth projections for the firm. The agenda for this meeting will include these topics: financial planning and new debt issues, new product lines, the competition, and foreign market opportunities.

2. Type the paragraph used in exercise 1 after pressing the Indent (F4) key once. After pressing ENTER to end the paragraph, type the following:

The meeting is scheduled for 9:00 a.m. in the board room.

Do not clear the screen.

3. Reveal codes, and delete the indent code from the first paragraph.

4. Type the following paragraph, pressing the Indent (F4) key and the Indent Left and Right (SHIFT-F4) key where indicated.

[→Indent←]You can use the two indentation keys in the middle of [→Indent] typing a paragraph. When you press the Indent or the [→Indent←]Indent Left and Right key, WordPerfect indents all new lines that appear until you press ENTER.

USE THE MARGIN RELEASE FEATURE   5.3

WordPerfect's Margin Release feature allows you to type text to the left of the left margin setting. If the text fills more than one line, WordPerfect will wrap subsequent lines to the left margin. You can also use the feature to start the first line of an indented paragraph at the left margin; the other lines will wrap to the designated tab stop. The hidden code for the Margin Release feature is [←Mar Rel].

To use the Margin Release feature:

a. Move to the beginning of the line on which you want to use the Margin Release feature.

b. Press the Margin Release (SHIFT-TAB) key one or more times. WordPerfect moves the cursor one tab stop to the left each time.

c. Type the text.

You can use Margin Release only when there are tab stops to the left of the cursor. If there are no tab stops to the left, or if the "Pos" indicator on the status line shows that the cursor is at 0", the cursor stays in its current location.

Examples

1. You can use the Margin Release feature when you create forms. To create an invoice form, you can use the Margin Release feature to put the labels for the data to the left of the margins. First, press the Margin Release (SHIFT-TAB) key, and type

Invoice:

Press ENTER once, and press the Margin Release (SHIFT-TAB) key twice. Type

Company Name:

Press ENTER and the Margin Release (SHIFT-TAB) key. Type

Address:

The screen looks like this:

```
    Invoice:
Company Name:
    Address:
```

2. You can use the Margin Release feature to remove the indentation from the first line of an indented paragraph. Press the Indent (F4) key for indentation. To move back to the margin for the first line, press the Margin Release (SHIFT-TAB) key. Then type

When you have an indented paragraph, you may want the first line to align with paragraphs that are not indented. Margin Release allows you to do this.

The paragraph looks like this:

```
When you have an indented paragraph, you may want the first line
    to align with paragraphs that are not indented. Margin
    Release allows you to do this.
```

3. When you move the cursor through a line that has a margin release, it may behave unexpectedly. Moving the cursor through lines with Margin Release codes is easier when you reveal the codes. First, press the Margin Release (SHIFT-TAB) key twice. Then type

This line does not start at the left margin.

Press ENTER to move to the next line. Press the UP ARROW key. This moves the cursor to the "d" in "does." Press the RIGHT ARROW key. The cursor moves to the "l" in "line." Press the LEFT ARROW key. The cursor moves back to the "d" in "does." To understand why this occurs, press the Reveal Codes (ALT-F3) key. The [◄Mar Rel] code is highlighted. When you pressed the UP ARROW key, the cursor moved to the first [◄Mar Rel] code. When you pressed the RIGHT ARROW key to move past that code, the cursor moved left five spaces to the first tab stop left of the margin. When you pressed the LEFT ARROW key, the cursor moved one code to the left. Because the code was a [◄MarRel], the cursor moved five spaces to the right, back to the left margin. Press the Reveal Codes (ALT-F3) key to return to the normal screen display.

Exercises

1. Type the following paragraph, first invoking the Margin Release feature until you cannot move the first line any further to the left:

   You can use the Margin Release feature to make an indented paragraph begin at the left margin. You can also use it to fit additional characters on a line.

2. Create an employment application form like the one below. Use the Margin Release feature to align the form labels for the name, address, phone number, and social security number.

```
          Name:
       Address:
  Phone Number:
  Social Sec. #:
```

5.4   SET TABS

Tab stops provide an easy way to align text at locations other than the left margin. The traditional settings for tab stops are every five characters. This allows you to use the first tab stop for paragraph indentation. You can change the tab stops when you have columns of entries that you want to align. You might also change them when you want to place a column of entries near the middle or right edge of the page. Eliminating unnecessary tab stops allows you to press the TAB key once to position the cursor correctly.

When you press the TAB key, the cursor moves to the next tab stop and inserts the hidden code [TAB] in your document. Initially, WordPerfect has tab stops at every half inch. These settings conform to the traditional tab stop placement of every 5 characters if you are using 10-pitch type (10 characters to the inch). You can change the tab stops to any positions you want.

To change tab stops:

a. Press the Format (SHIFT-F8) key.

b. Type an **l** or a **1** to select the line-formatting options.

c. Type a **t** or an **8** to select Tab Set.

d. Using the cursor control keys or the SPACEBAR, move the cursor to where you want a tab stop inserted, and type an **l, r, c,** or **d.**

e. Move the cursor to an existing tab stop that you want to remove, and press the DEL key.

f. Press the Exit (F7) key when you have finished modifying the tab stops.

To move the cursor in steps d and e, you can press the LEFT ARROW or RIGHT ARROW key or the SPACEBAR to move one position at a time. Press HOME and the LEFT ARROW or RIGHT ARROW key to move 3.2″ in either direction, or press HOME twice and the LEFT ARROW or RIGHT ARROW key once to move to the beginning or the end of all tab stops.

The letter you type in step d determines the alignment at the tab stop. "L" left-aligns the text typed at the tab stop. "R" right-aligns the text typed at the tab stop. "C" centers the text typed at the tab stop. "D" right-aligns all characters typed before a decimal point or period.

An alternative to steps d and e is typing the number of the desired tab stop position (for example, **2.5**) and pressing ENTER. This inserts a left-aligned tab stop at the specified location and places the cursor there. You can then change the type of tab stop by typing an **r, c,** or **d** or delete the tab stop by pressing DEL.

When you press the Exit [F7] key after changing tab settings, a hidden code is inserted to indicate the change. The hidden code indicates the locations of the tabs you set but does not identify the type of alignment. It looks like this: [Tab Set:0",0.5",1.5",4"].

To remove all the tab stops:

a. Press the Format (SHIFT-F8) key. Type an l and a t.

b. Press HOME twice and the LEFT ARROW key once. The cursor is at the 0" position.

c. Press the Delete EOL (CTRL-END) key.

Examples

1. When you type lines of numbers, you may want the numbers aligned in a column. You can right-align the numbers by creating a special tab stop. First, press the Format (SHIFT-F8) key. Next, type an l and a t. The bottom of the screen looks like this:

```
L....L....L....L....L....L....L....L....L....L....L....L....L....L....L....L....L...
!    ^    !    ^    !    ^    !    ^    !    ^    !    ^    !    ^    !    ^
1"       2"       3"       4"       5"       6"       7"       8"
Delete EOL (clear tabs); Enter Number (set tab); Del (clear tab);
Left; Center; Right; Decimal; .= Dot Leader
```

The default left-aligned tab stops at .5-inch intervals are indicated by the "L"s on the Tab Set screen. Each caret (^) between the inch indicators marks a half inch. Press the Delete EOL (CTRL-END) key to remove all tab stops to the right of the cursor position. Move the cursor to the 1.5" position, and type an l. Move the cursor to the 6" position, and type an r. The Tab Set screen now looks like this:

```
ııııLıııııııııııııııııııııııııııııııııııııııııııRıııııııııııııııııııııııııııııı
 ¦    ^    ¦    ^    ¦    ^    ¦    ^    ¦    ^  T ^    ¦    ^    ¦    ^
 1"      2"      3"      4"      5"      6"      7"      8"
Delete EOL (clear tabs); Enter Number (set tab); Del (clear tab);
Left; Center; Right; Decimal; .= Dot Leader
```

Press the Exit (F7) key twice to return to the document. To enter each right-aligned number, press the TAB key twice, type the number, and press ENTER.

2. When you type letters, you usually need only two tab stops: one for the beginning of paragraphs and the other for the initial address or the date and the closing. Having extra tab stops can be cumbersome and prevent the address from aligning with the closing. You can remove the extraneous tab stops by pressing the Format (SHIFT-F8) key. Next, type an l and a t, and move the cursor to the right of the 1.5" position. Then, press the Delete EOL (CTRL-END) key to remove the tab stops to the right. To create a tab stop for the initial address and the closing, type a 4 and press ENTER. You could also create this tab stop by moving the cursor to the 4" position and typing an l. Now the screen looks like this:

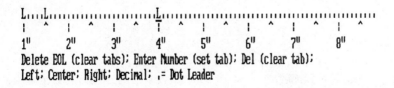

```
Lıı.Lıııııııııııııııııııı.ııııLıııııııııııııııııııııııııııııııııııııııııııııııı
 ¦    ^    ¦    ^    ¦    ^  T ^    ¦    ^    ¦    ^    ¦    ^    ¦    ^
 1"      2"      3"      4"      5"      6"      7"      8"
Delete EOL (clear tabs); Enter Number (set tab); Del (clear tab);
Left; Center; Right; Decimal; .= Dot Leader
```

Press the Exit [F7] key twice to begin typing the letter. Press the TAB key once to start a paragraph and twice to type each line of the first address, the date, or the closing.

3. When you create reports, you often want numbers or text to appear in columns. You can use tab stops to ensure that the information aligns properly. First, press the Format (SHIFT-F8) key. Then, type an l and a t. Once the Tab Set screen appears, press HOME twice and the LEFT ARROW key once to move the cursor to the 0" position. Then, press the Delete EOL (CTRL-END) key to remove the existing tab stops. Next, type 1.5 and press ENTER to create a left-aligned tab stop for text at 1.5". You could also create this tab stop by moving the cursor to the 1.5" position and typing an l. Next, since you will align numbers with decimals in a column to the right, type a 5, press ENTER, and type a d, or move to the 5" position and type a d. This will align text to the left of the decimal points. Press the Exit (F7) key twice to return to the document. Now you can type the following text, pressing the TAB key where indicated:

Expenses [TAB] **Amount**
[TAB]**Insurance** [TAB]5,600
[TAB]**Rent**[TAB]2,135.50
[TAB]**Salaries**[TAB]128,937.13

The screen looks like this:

```
Expenses              Amount
   Insurance            5,600
   Rent                 2,135.50
   Salaries           128,937.13
```

4. You can set the tab stops to any regular interval. First, press the Format (SHIFT-F8) key. Then, type an l and a t. Once the Tab Set screen appears, press HOME twice and the LEFT ARROW key once to move the cursor to the 0" position. Then, press the Delete EOL (CTRL-END) key to remove the existing tab stops. Next, type a 1, a comma, and .6, and press ENTER. WordPerfect sets left-aligned tab stops at every .6" inches, starting at the 1" positon. If you had first typed an r, c, or d

at the 1″ position, the other tab stops also would have been the type that you had indicated.

Exercises

(Do not clear the screen between exercises unless instructed to do so.)

1. Add a tab stop at 3.3″.

2. Remove all tab stops after 6″.

3. Create a right-aligned tab stop at 4″.

4. Create a decimal tab stop at 2.5″.

5. Remove all existing tab stops and set stops at 2″ and 4.5″. Type the following entries, using the TAB key to place the names at the 2″ position and the salaries at the 4.5″ position:

   Jones 17,850
   Culver 23,489
   Walker 32,500

   Clear the screen.

6. Change the tab stops to every .75″ starting at 2″.

7. Return the tab stops to WordPerfect's default of every .5″ starting at 0.

USE THE FLUSH RIGHT FEATURE   5.5

WordPerfect's Flush Right feature allows you to align a line of text at the right margin. It is normally used for short entries, such as a company name, the date, or an address.

To enter text flush right:

a. Move to the line on which you want to place the flush-right text.

b. Press the Flush Right (ALT-F6) key.

c. Type the text you want aligned at the right margin.

d. Press ENTER. The hidden codes WordPerfect inserts for this feature are [FlshRt] and [C/A/Flrt].

Examples

1. You can use the Flush Right feature when you add a date to a document. A special WordPerfect feature can be used to enter the current date. First, press the Flush Right (ALT-F6) key. Next, press the Date (SHIFT-F5) key, and type a **1** or a **t** for Date Text. Press ENTER. The screen looks like this:

November 2, 1989

If the date is not correct, exit WordPerfect, type **date**, press ENTER, type the correct date using the format indicated at the prompt, press ENTER, and reload WordPerfect.

2. The Flush Right feature aligns text only at the right margin. The position of the first character in a flush-right line will depend on the number and size of the characters in the line. Press the Flush Right (ALT-F6) key, type **ABC COMPANY**, and press ENTER. Press the Flush Right (ALT-F6) key again, type **First Quarter Sales**, and press ENTER. The last characters in the lines are aligned at the right margin, but the first characters are not aligned.

3. You can enter text on the same line as right-aligned text by typing the other text before invoking the Flush Right feature. First, type **Date:**, press the Date (SHIFT-F5) key, and type a **1** for Date Text. Then, press the Flush Right (ALT-F6) key, type **ABC Company**, and press ENTER. The text looks like this:

Date: March 30, 1989   ABC Company

Exercises

1. Using the Date feature, enter the current date flush right in the top line of a new document.

2. Enter the following text flush right:

ABC COMPANY

3. Type the following memo, using the Date feature to provide the current date.

MEMO
To: All Employees   Date: August 11, 1989
From: Arnold Smith   Re: Cleaning Computer Screens
– –

Do not use alcohol-based window cleaners to clean your computer screen. Use the special cleaner that is stored with the blank disks.

CHANGE THE LINE SPACING   5.6

Many letters and other types of correspondence use single spacing. Long reports or documents are often double spaced to make them easier to read. You can set the spacing in WordPerfect for an entire document or for a portion of a document. WordPerfect's default is to use single line spacing.

When you change the line spacing, WordPerfect inserts a hidden code that looks like this: [Ln Spacing:3]. The number after the colon indicates the spacing selected.

To set the line spacing:

a. Press the Format (SHIFT-F8) key.

b. Type an **l** or a **1** to select line-formatting options.

c. Type an **s** or a **6** to select Line Spacing.

d. Type the number of spaces you want between lines.

e. Press ENTER.

f. Press the Exit (F7) key.

The line spacing selected with these steps begins at the cursor location. The new spacing is used up to the end of the document unless a new line-spacing code is encountered. The change does not affect the text before the cursor location.

Examples

1. Lengthy documents are often easier to read if they are double spaced. To set double spacing for an entire document, you need to place the hidden line-spacing code at the top of the document. Type the following:

   This text initially displays and prints with single spacing. It is not necessary to retype text to use other spacing. A quick menu selection applies the change beginning at the current location in the document.

Move to the top of the document by pressing HOME, HOME, and UP ARROW. Next, press the Format (SHIFT-F8) key. Then, type an l and an s. Next, type a 2. Finally, press ENTER and the Exit (F7) key. This inserts blank lines between lines of text in the document.

2. A lengthy quote in a document can be single spaced and indented from both sides to set it off from the rest of the text. First, press the Format (SHIFT-F8) key. Next type an l, an s, and a 2. When you press ENTER and the Exit (F7) key to return to the document, WordPerfect inserts a code to change the text to double spaced. Type

Quotes from famous people can be fun to read. The language is often a little different from English as we know it today.

Before typing the quote on the next line, press the Format (SHIFT-F8) key, type an l, an s, and a 1, and press ENTER and the Exit (F7) key to change the line spacing. All of the text after this point will be single spaced. Next, press the Indent Left and Right (SHIFT-F4) key, and type

I do not know what I may appear to the world, but to myself I seem to have been only like a boy playing on the sea-shore, and diverting myself in now and then finding a smoother pebble, or a prettier shell than ordinary, whilst the great ocean of truth lay undiscovered before me.
Isaac Newton

Press the Format (SHIFT-F8) key, type an l, an s, and a 2, and press ENTER and the Exit (F7) key to return the document to double spacing after the quote. Press ENTER, and type

The diverse interests of some famous individuals may seem surprising. The quote from Isaac Newton is very simplistic when contrasted with some of his scientific theorems.

This last paragraph is double spaced.

Exercises

1. Type the following paragraph:

    A sense of humor sharp enough to show a man his own absurdities will keep him from the commission of all sins, or nearly all, except those that are worth committing. (Samuel Butler from Life and Habit)

    Move to the first character in the paragraph. Change the spacing to double spacing. Next try triple spacing. Set the spacing back to single spacing.

2. Type the following paragraphs. Use the default of single spacing for the first paragraph. Change the line spacing to double spacing before typing the second paragraph. Set the line spacing to triple spacing before typing the third paragraph.

    The new Widget maker will expand our current capacity to meet expected demand levels for the next five to ten years. It has a net present value of $25,687.

    The manufacturer gives a 10% trade-in value on its old Widget maker. This is a slightly lower price than expected in the open market. The capital budgeting plan contains the lower trade-in value, but the company will probably sell the used machine in the second-hand market.

    The new Widget maker has many new features. One of these, a free one-year service contract, will save the company $50,000 in the first year.

    Make the first and third paragraphs double spaced and the second paragraph triple spaced.

3. Type the following paragraph. After typing the first sentence, set the line spacing to double spacing.

When you set the line spacing, WordPerfect uses it for all lines after the code in the document. If you change the spacing to double spacing in the middle of a paragraph, the lines above the change are single spaced, and the lines after the change are double spaced.

ALTER JUSTIFICATION

5.7

Initially, WordPerfect is set to right-justify text when you print it. WordPerfect inserts space between the words in each line so that all full lines end at the right margin. Since WordPerfect does not display the text right justified, the printed document will be different from the screen display. If your screen can display graphics, a screen preview of the document will display the text exactly as it will appear when printed. If you want to retain the ragged right edge that appears in the screen display on the printed document, you can turn Justification off.

To change the right justification:

a. Press the Format (SHIFT-F8) key.

b. Type an **l** or a **1** to select line-formatting options.

c. Type a **j** or a **3** for Justification.

d. Type a **y** if you want the text right justified or an **n** if you want a ragged right edge.

e. Press the Exit (F7) key to return to the document.

Example

1. You can change the right justification to change the appearance of printed lines. First, type

The company's financial position is improving. The company retired a million dollars of debt this year and will retire another million next year. The company is retiring the debt by buying stock on the open market and retiring the certificates. Also, the lag between invoice dates and payment dates has decreased by 3 days.

Move the cursor to the beginning of the paragraph. Press the Format (SHIFT-F8) key, type an l, a j, and an n, and press the Exit (F7) key. Now the paragraph will look like this when printed:

```
The company's financial position is improving.  The company
retired a million dollars of debt this year and will retire
another million next year.  The company is retiring the debt by
buying stock on the open market and retiring the certificates.
Also, the lag between invoice dates and payment dates has
decreased by 3 days.
```

Exercises

1. Type the following paragraph. If your screen can display graphics, preview the document. Then turn off Justification, and preview the document again. Turn Justification back on.

   The Accounts Receivable computer system was installed last January. Due to this new system, the average daily accounts receivable amount dropped by $50. Also, the percentage of bad accounts has dropped from 4% to 2%, mostly due to quicker action on overdue accounts.

2. Type the first paragraph below. Turn off Justification, and type the second paragraph. Preview how WordPerfect will print the document.

   When a paragraph is right justified, WordPerfect inserts additional space into lines of the printed copy of the document. This creates even left and right margins. The extra spaces appear only in the printed copy and do not appear on the screen.

When a paragraph is not right justified, WordPerfect does not insert additional space. The right margin has a jagged appearance.

EXERCISES

1. Increase the right and left margins by 1" each, and type the following paragraph:

   Disks store information using magnetized material to hold information. The basic unit of storage is a byte. A byte stores one character of information.

   Save this file as DISK.

2. Type the following paragraph, indenting the left margin of the paragraph by an inch.

   Disk drives read information from a disk. The disk drive spins the disk quickly. A read/write head above the disk reads the information as it spins past the head.

   Save this file as DISKREAD.

3. Remove all tab stops. Set one tab stop at 4", and use the TAB key to create this letter heading:

   Acme Corporation
   496 Prospect Road
   Cleveland, Ohio 44115
   January 3, 1989

4. Retrieve the file DISK, and change the line spacing to double spacing. Save the file.

5. Retrieve DISKREAD, and turn off Justification. Save the file.

MASTERY
SKILLS CHECK

6. Enter the following account numbers flush right, with one account number per line:

ACC-9876
HDG-3218
CRC-9873

7. Duplicate the following, using the Margin Release and Indent features:

Campbell, Mary, <u>Teach Yourself WordPerfect</u>, Osborne/ McGraw-Hill, 1989.

INTEGRATED
SKILLS CHECK

1. Type the following bibliography entries. Increase the left margin by .5″ so that all of the entries will appear indented. Use the Margin Release feature to make the first line of each entry begin five spaces to the left of the indent position.

Crosby, Samuel, "Mergers and Acquisitions," <u>Business Yearly</u>, (OMB Publishing, 1983), June, p. 46-49. Lee, Jane and Lifeson, Tom, "Effectively Combining Companies," <u>Journal of Business Results</u>, (AMBA, 1987), vol 36, Fall, p. 101-9.

2. Use Margin Release and other formatting features to create a heading with the following information on a single line:

Acme Corporation
1560 Main Street
Cleveland, Ohio 44103

Place the company name at the left edge of the page. Center the street address. Right align the city, state, and ZIP code. Underline the line.

3. Type the following letter:

Joan Smith
President, Widgets Inc.
7946 Madison Avenue
New York, New York 10061

Dear Ms. Smith:

Enclosed is the pamphlet you requested, Wrapping Consumer Goods. Our products can shrink-wrap any product. If you send the dimensions of the products that you want to shrink-wrap, one of our representatives will prepare a list of the materials and equipment you will need.

Sincerely,

Larry Kennedy
Plastic Covering Co.

Turn off right justification for the letter. Underline the pamphlet name. Reveal the codes, and delete the Underline code. Print the document.

4. Match the following codes with the features they represent:

1. Soft return	a. [Ln Spacing:3]
2. Underline	b. [◄Mar Rel]
3. Flush Right	c. [►Indent]
4. Margin Release	d. [BOLD][bold]
5. Indent	e. [UND][und]
6. Hard return	f. [Cntr]
7. Hard page return	g. [Flsh Rt]
8. Triple line spacing	h. [►Indent◄]

9. Boldface text   i. [HRt]

10. Justification on   j. [SRt]

11. Set tabs   k. [Just On]

12. Indent Left and   l. [HPg]
    Right

13. Center text on line   m. [Tab Set:0″,0.5″,2.5″]

5. Enter the date flush right. Search for the Flush Right code and delete it.

CHAPTER OBJECTIVES

After completing this chapter, you should be able to

6.1 Center text on a page

6.2 Adjust top and bottom margins

6.3 Add page numbers

6.4 Change the paper size and type

·6·

Changing the Format of a Page

Using a pleasing page format can help you create a document with a professional appearance. Rather than continuing to use the default features, you can enhance the presentation quality of your output with page-format changes.

Such options as centering the text between the top and the bottom of the page allow you to create a short document that still presents a professional image. You can alter the margin settings for the top and bottom of the page, add page numbers, and adjust the page length to make additional appearance enhancements.

SKILLS CHECK

(Do not clear the screen until you have completed the last exercise.)

1. Type the following text, using Bold for "Education:".

   John Doe
   23405 Lander Road
   Cleveland, Ohio 44130
   (216)229-8976

   Education: Cleveland State University, Cleveland, Ohio
   Business Administration, August 1983
   Dean's List 7 Quarters, GPA 3.75

2. Center the name, address, and phone number.

3. Boldface the name.

4. Underline the word "Education."

5. At the beginning of the document, create a tab stop at 2.2", and remove the ones at 1.5" and 2".

6. Indent the three lines containing educational information.

7. Move the first line containing educational information back to the left margin using the Margin Release feature.

8. Print the document.

6.1   CENTER TEXT ON A PAGE

A short memo or letter can present a strong impression if it is centered vertically on the page. Such other text as the title page of a report is also most effectively presented centered between the top and the bottom of the page. This feature is different from the line-centering option covered in Chapter 4. It can be used separately or in combination with line-centering features.

The page-centering command adds the hidden code [Center Pg] to your document at the location of the cursor. To remove the feature, you must delete the code.

To center text on a page:

a. Move the cursor to the top of the page on which you want the text to be centered.

b. Press the Format (SHIFT-F8) key.

c. Type a **p** or a **2** to select page-formatting options.

d. Type a **c** or a **1** to center the text on the page.

e. Press the Exit (F7) key to return to the document.

f. Type the text if it is not already in the document.

g. Press CTRL-ENTER to end the page.

Examples

1. When you create a title page for a report, you often want the title to appear in the middle of the page. Rather than pressing ENTER until the cursor is in the middle of the page, you can have WordPerfect automatically center the text for you. First, press the Format (SHIFT-F8) key, and type a **p** and a **c**. Then, press the Exit (F7) key to return to the document. Press the Center (SHIFT-F6) key and type

   Horton Corporation Financial Statements

   Press ENTER to move to the next line. Press the Center (SHIFT-F6) key, and type

   As of July 30, 1989

FIGURE 6-1.   Print preview of lines centered on a page

When you press the Print (SHIFT-F7) key and type a **v** and a **3** to view the full page, your screen looks like Figure 6-1.

2. You can improve the appearance of short business letters by centering them vertically on the page. To center a short letter, press the Format (SHIFT-F8) key, and type a **p** and a **c**. Press the Exit (F7) key to return to the document, and type

Tracy Smith
2647 Chillecothe Road
Kirkland, Ohio 44296

Dear Tracy,

I have enclosed the information you requested. Please contact me at (212)555-5931 if you have any questions.

Sincerely,

Darren Jeck

When you preview this letter before printing, it looks like Figure 6-2.

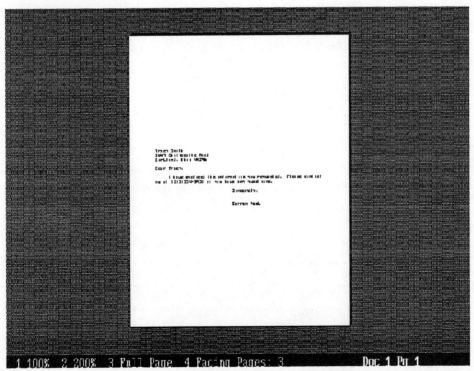

FIGURE 6-2.   Print preview of a short letter centered on a page

Exercises

1. Create a title page with the following three lines centered horizontally and vertically:

Investigation into the Physical Properties of Rust
Dissertation
Angus McPhearson

2. Create a short thank-you letter to **Jules McBride** at **234 Main Street, Lawrence, PA 28634**, thanking him for promptly sending the information you have requested. Center the letter on the page.

3. Create a title page with the following lines centered horizontally and vertically. Preview how WordPerfect will print it.

1989 Financial Statements
Acme Corporation

4. Create the following memo, centering it on the page. Preview how WordPerfect will print it.

MEMO:
To: All Employees
Re: Paychecks

To receive a paycheck September 10th, submit your time card to payroll by September 3rd.

6.2   ADJUST TOP AND BOTTOM MARGINS

The top and bottom margins are the white areas at the top and bottom of a printed page. Increasing the size of these margins lessens the amount of text that can be shown on a page. You may need to increase the top margin when you are printing on letterhead paper to begin printing below the letterhead.

WordPerfect measures each margin as the number of inches from the text to the edge of the paper. WordPerfect initially has 1″ top and bottom margins. WordPerfect uses the default margin settings unless it finds a hidden code representing another margin specification. When you change the margins, WordPerfect inserts a hidden code and adjusts the number of lines that print on each page.

To change the top and bottom margins:

a. Move the cursor to the top of the document or the top of the page on which you wish to change the margins.

b. Press the Format (SHIFT-F8) key.

c. Select Page by typing a **p** or a **2**.

d. Select Margins by typing an **m** or a **5**.

e. Type the number of inches WordPerfect should leave between the top of the paper and the printed text.

f. Press ENTER.

g. Type the number of inches WordPerfect should leave between the bottom of the paper and the printed text.

h. Press ENTER.

i. Press the Exit (F7) key to return to the document.

WordPerfect inserts a hidden code to represent your top and bottom margin settings at the cursor location. For a top margin of 2″ and a bottom margin of 3″, the code looks like this: [T/B Mar:2″,3″]. To see the hidden code, use the Reveal Codes (ALT-F3) key.

Examples

1. You can decrease the margins to increase the amount of text that fits on a page. For example, you can decrease the margins to .5″. First, press the Format (SHIFT-F8) key. Then, type a **p** to select the page-formatting options. Next, type an **m** to select the margin-formatting option. Type **.5** and press ENTER to set the top margin. Type **.5** and press ENTER to set the bottom margin. Finally, press the Exit (F7) key to return to the document. These changes add an inch of space on each page.

2. You can increase the margins to decrease the amount of text that fits on a page. First, press the Format (SHIFT-F8) key and type a **p**. Next, type an **m** to select Margins. Then, type **1.5** to set the top margin, and press ENTER. Next, type **1.5** to set the bottom margin, and press ENTER. Finally, press the Exit (F7) key to return to the document. The document has 1″ less space for text on the page.

Exercises

1. Change the top and bottom margins to 3″ at the beginning of a document. Determine how many times you can press ENTER before WordPerfect inserts a page break.

2. Change the top and bottom margins to 0″. Determine how many times you can press ENTER before WordPerfect inserts a page break.

3. Set the top margin to 9.5″, leaving the bottom margin at 1″. Type the following paragraphs. Preview how WordPerfect will print the document.

    The top margin determines the space WordPerfect skips on a page when printing a document. You must specify this measurement in inches.
    The bottom margin determines the space WordPerfect leaves on a page when printing a document. As Word-Perfect prints a document, it determines how much room is left on the page. When the amount of remaining space

equals the size of the bottom margin, WordPerfect inserts
a soft page break.

ADD PAGE NUMBERS _____ 6.3

WordPerfect does not print page numbers in a document
automatically. This is convenient, since you probably will not
want page numbers on letters, memos, and other similar
documents. However, you can have WordPerfect add page
numbers in a number of locations on a page. If you plan to
combine two or more files into one document, you can specify
the page number for WordPerfect to use at the beginning of
each file to ensure continuous pagination.

To number the pages:

a. Press the Format (SHIFT-F8) key.

b. Type a **p** or a **2** to select the page-formatting options.

c. Type a **p** or a **7** to select the page-numbering options.

d. Select the number that corresponds to the location where
you want WordPerfect to place the page numbers.

e. Type an **n** or a **6** to select a new page number if you want
the page numbers to start with a number other than the
one indicated on the status line. Type the new page
number and press ENTER.

f. Press the Exit (F7) key to return to the document.

Examples

1. You can instruct WordPerfect where to place page numbers
in a printed document. First, press the Format (SHIFT-F8) key,
and type a **p** twice to display the page-numbering format
options, shown in Figure 6-3.

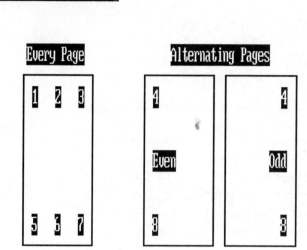

FIGURE 6-3.   Page-numbering options

Each number on the screen represents a specific location for page numbers. Selections 4 and 8 put the page numbers at the left on even-numbered pages and at the right on odd-numbered pages. Type a **7** and press the Exit (F7) key. When you print the document, WordPerfect will place page numbers in the lower right corner on every page.

2. You can change the number WordPerfect uses to start counting page numbers. You can use this feature when you are combining files. For example, if you are creating a page to insert at the end of another document that has 3 pages, you will want to begin the new document with page number 4. First, press the format (SHIFT-F8) key and type a **p**

twice and a **4** once to place the page numbers in the upper left corner on even-numbered pages and in the upper right corner on odd-numbered pages. Next, type an **n** for the New Page Number option, type a **4**, and press ENTER. After you press the Exit (F7) key, you can press the Reveal Codes (ALT-F3) key to see the hidden codes [Pg Numbering: Top Alternating] and [Pg Num:4], which WordPerfect has inserted. Press the Reveal Codes (ALT-F3) key again to remove the codes from view.

Next, type

This is the first page of this document, although we will ask WordPerfect to number it as page 4.

Then, press CTRL-ENTER to create a page break. The status line shows that you are on page 5. Press the Print (SHIFT-F7) key and type an **f** to print the pages.

Exercises

1. Instruct WordPerfect to place page numbers in the center at the bottom of each page. Type **Travel Expenses**, and press CTRL-ENTER. Type **Benefits**, and press CTRL-ENTER. Type **Salary Expense**, and press ENTER. Preview the document to see where the page numbers will appear.

2. Instruct WordPerfect to number the pages at the bottom center. Next, type the numbers **1** to **5**, pressing CTRL-ENTER between numbers to place each one on a separate page. Preview the page. Starting with the last page, renumber each page so that WordPerfect numbers them in reverse order; for example, WordPerfect will print page 1 as page number 5.

6.4   CHANGE THE PAPER SIZE AND TYPE

Most documents are printed on 8 1/2″ X 11″ standard-stock paper. Since this is standard-size paper, WordPerfect's default paper-size setting establishes the page length based on this size as the default. You can print on other sizes of paper, including legal-size sheets and envelopes, by changing the paper-size setting. The paper-size format menu, shown in Figure 6-4, lists the size options.

Instead of printing on standard-stock paper, you might choose to print on bond, letterhead, cardstock, or label sheets. The paper-type format menu, shown in Figure 6-5, lists the

Format: Paper Size

1 – Standard	(8.5″ x 11″)
2 – Standard Landscape	(11″ x 8.5″)
3 – Legal	(8.5″ x 14″)
4 – Legal Landscape	(14″ x 8.5″)
5 – Envelope	(9.5″ x 4″)
6 – Half Sheet	(5.5″ x 8.5″)
7 – US Government	(8″ x 11″)
8 – A4	(210mm x 297mm)
9 – A4 Landscape	(297mm x 210mm)
0 – Other	

Selection: 1

FIGURE 6-4.   Paper-size options

Format: Paper Type

    1 - **S**tandard

    2 - **B**ond

    3 - Letter**H**ead

    4 - **L**abels

    5 - **E**nvelope

    6 - **T**ransparency

    7 - **C**ardstock

    8 - **O**ther

Selection: 1

FIGURE 6-5.   Paper-type options

various types of forms WordPerfect supports. When you change these settings, WordPerfect places the hidden code [Paper Sz/Typ] in your document.

These options help WordPerfect work with printers that have special locations for different forms. When you change the paper-size setting, WordPerfect checks to see if your selection is compatible with the options chosen when you selected your printer. (See Appendix A for information on selecting a printer.) If the selection is acceptable, WordPerfect automatically adjusts the document for the new paper size. If the chosen selection is not available for your printer, Word-Perfect displays an error message and selects the closest match.

To change the page length:

a. Press the Format (SHIFT-F8) key.

b. Type a **p** or a **2** to select the page-formatting options.

c. Type an **s** or an **8** to select the paper-size and -type options.

d. Select the size of the paper you will use.

e. Select the type of paper or other material you will use.

f. Press the Exit (F7) key to return to the document.

Examples

1. You can set the page size and style to print addresses on envelopes. First, press the Format (SHIFT-F8) key and type a **p** and an **s**. Next, type an **e** twice to select Envelopes as both the paper size and type. Finally, press the Exit (F7) key to return to the document. Now you can type addresses on separate pages and have WordPerfect print each address on an envelope. If you press the Reveal Codes (ALT-F3) key, you can see the code [Paper Sz/Typ:9.5" x 4",Envelope] at the top of the document. If your printer cannot handle the size or type you select, WordPerfect displays **(∗requested form is unavailable)** in the page-format menu.

2. When you change the paper size and type, it affects all pages after the code. You can use multiple codes to have pages of a document print on different sizes or types of paper. First, type

Dear Jim,

   Here is the information that you wanted.

To create an envelope for this message, press CTRL-ENTER to start a new page. Press the Format (SHIFT-F8) key, type a **p,** and then type an **e** twice. Press the Exit (F7) key to return to the document. Type

Jim Adler
514 Washington Avenue
Columbus, OH 43213

To see how WordPerfect has changed the paper size, press the Print (SHIFT-F7) key and type a **v**. WordPerfect shows the name and address on an envelope-shaped page. When you press PGUP, WordPerfect shows the letter on a normal page. Press the Exit (F7) key to return to the document.

Exercises

1. Set the paper size and type for legal-size (8 1/2″ X 14″) standard paper (assuming that your printer supports this size paper). Type **Legal-Size Paper**, and create a hard page break. For the second page, return the paper size and type to standard (8 1/2″ X 11″). Type **Standard-Size Paper**. Preview how WordPerfect will print the pages.

2. Type the address from the second example in this section in a document set for a half sheet of standard paper (5.5″ X 8.5″). Preview how WordPerfect will print it.

EXERCISES

(Do not clear the screen until you have completed the last exercise.)

MASTERY
SKILLS CHECK

1. Type the following, centering each line as well as centering the document on the page:

Wilbur Horse Supplies
Financial Statements
For the Year Ending December 31, 1989

Preview the document as WordPerfect will print it.

2. Set the top margin to 3". Preview the document again.

3. Set WordPerfect to print page numbers in the center at the top of each page.

4. Move to the bottom of the document, and enter a hard page break. Set WordPerfect to number the second page of the document as page 10.

5. Change the paper size to half.

INTEGRATED
SKILLS CHECK

(Do not clear the screen until you have completed the last exercise.)

1. Center the following lines as you type them:

Archie's California Grapes
Production Records
For the season ending September 30, 1989

2. Center the three lines vertically on the page.

3. Boldface the first line, and underline the second line.

4. Move to the bottom of the document, and insert a hard page break. Set the page numbers to appear in the upper right corner, starting with 1.

5. Change the spacing to double spacing, and type the following paragraph:

This year's crop is the largest in the last 20 years. It is primarily due to improved fertilization methods and increased rainfall. The plants damaged by last year's drought were replaced.

6. Change the paragraph so that it is not right justified.

7. Print the document.

CHAPTER OBJECTIVES

After completing this chapter, you should be able to

7.1 Search for a word or phrase from the beginning of a document

7.2 Search from the end of a document

7.3 Use the Replace feature

·7·

Search and Replace Options

WordPerfect can assist you in searching through your document to pinpoint the exact location of a word or phrase. This feature provides a significant time savings over visually searching the document and is usually more accurate as well. WordPerfect can search the entire document from the beginning or the end. You can also have it search in either direction from any point in between. In addition to finding an entry, WordPerfect's Replace feature allows you to replace the entry with a new entry. This feature helps you make corrections in several places with ease. Tasks such as correcting the spelling of a name used throughout a document can be handled quickly with this feature.

WordPerfect can find text, numbers, special characters, hidden codes, and any combination of them. Chapter 4 introduced you to searching for hidden codes. You will find that searching for text follows a similar pattern.

SKILLS CHECK

(Do not clear the screen until you have completed the last exercise.)

1. Type the following paragraph:

   Product Announcement

   The XY Graphics Company has announced the release of its new product, See 'N' Draw. This package creates custom pictures by combining existing drawings and advanced graphics features. Since each new feature added to an image is considered a unique layer, you can edit one layer without affecting the others. The print options offer features unavailable in any competing product.

2. Boldface the title.

3. Center the title.

4. Remove the boldfacing in the title by removing the hidden codes.

5. Indent the paragraph on both sides.

6. Double-space the paragraph.

7. Center the text on the page.

8. Print the page.

SEARCH FOR A WORD OR PHRASE FROM THE BEGINNING OF A DOCUMENT

7.1

WordPerfect's Search feature can find a match for a *string*, or series of characters or codes. You can place from 1 to 59 characters (including spaces) in the search string. Since you will be searching forward (from the beginning to the end), it is important to begin with the cursor in front of all the text that you want to include in the search.

If you use one or more capital letters in a search string, WordPerfect conducts a case-sensitive search. If you use only lowercase letters in the search string, WordPerfect ignores case when searching for a match. If WordPerfect finds a match, it positions the cursor immediately past the matching letter, word, or phrase. If WordPerfect cannot find a match, the computer beeps, the message "* Not found *" appears on the screen briefly, and the cursor remains where it was. You can also use this feature to search for hidden codes alone or as part of a string.

To have WordPerfect search for a word or phrase:

a. Press the Search (F2) key.

b. Type the word or phrase that WordPerfect should find.

c. Press the Search (F2) key again.

To search for the same word or phrase a second time, press the Search (F2) key twice. If you have already used the Search command, WordPerfect displays the last string that you searched for. You can edit this text rather than typing the new search text or codes. When WordPerfect prompts you for the search string, press INS, DEL, or the RIGHT ARROW key, and change the text displayed in the prompt.

Examples

1. WordPerfect's Search feature can perform a case-sensitive search. A case-sensitive search matches only words or phrases with the exact capitalization found in the search string. WordPerfect conducts a case-sensitive search anytime you include capital letters in the search string. First, type the following:

   There are many stores that sell computer software. Discount stores, office supply houses, full-service computer stores, and specialized software stores are all options. I prefer to shop at Upgrade Computer.

   Next, move the cursor to the beginning by pressing HOME, HOME, UP ARROW. To find the word "Computer" in "Upgrade Computer," press the Search (F2) key, and type **Computer**. Then, press the Search (F2) key again. WordPerfect moves the cursor to the period following "Computer." WordPerfect skipped the first two occurrences of the word, since they did not begin with a capital "c." Use this paragraph to look at the other Search features in the next two examples.

2. You can conduct a search that ignores the case of entries by entering the search string in lowercase letters. First, move to the top of the document by pressing HOME, HOME, UP ARROW. Next, press the Search (F2) key and type **computer**. When you press the Search (F2) key again, WordPerfect positions the cursor on the space following "computer" in the first sentence.

   If you press the Search (F2) key again, WordPerfect redisplays the search string. You can type a new entry or press the Search (F2) key to use the one displayed. When you reuse the first search string, WordPerfect positions the cursor on the space following "computer" in the second sentence. Pressing the Search (F2) key twice again positions the cursor on the period following "Computer." If you press the Search (F2) key twice again, your computer beeps and displays the message "* Not found *."

3. You can use the Search feature to help locate a word or phrase you wish to delete. To find and delete the phrase "office supply houses" in the paragraph, move to the top of the paragraph by pressing HOME, HOME, UP ARROW. Press the Search (F2) key, and type

office supply houses,

When you press the Search (F2) key again, WordPerfect positions the cursor at the end of this phrase. Press HOME and BACKSPACE three times to eliminate the phrase.

4. You can use the search feature to find a combination of text and hidden codes. This can help you pinpoint a specific location of a word that may occur many times in a document. First, type the following quote from Shakespeare, adding underline to the word "His" in the last line:

His words are bonds, his oaths are oracles;
His love sincere, his thoughts immaculate;
His tears, pure messengers sent from his heart;
His heart as far from fraud as heaven from earth.

Move to the top of the entry by pressing HOME, HOME, UP ARROW. Press the Search (F2) key. Then, press the Underline (F8) key, type **his**, and press the Underline (F8) key again. The search entry looks like this:

-> Srch: [UND]his[und]

The [UND] and [und] symbols are part of the hidden codes for the document. When you press the Search (F2) key again, WordPerfect finds the entry "His" in the last line.

5. You can use the Search feature to look for part of a word. If you know that you are searching for a name that begins with "Smith" but are not certain if it is "Smithson," "Smithsonian," or "Smithfield," you can search for "Smith" to find all words that begin with "Smith." First, type

We have invited the Smithfields and the Harpers for dinner on Friday.

Press HOME, HOME, UP ARROW to move to the beginning of the document. Press the Search (F2) key, type **Smith**, and press the Search (F2) key again. WordPerfect places the cursor on the "f" in "Smithfield." If you want to find "Smith" alone in the middle of a sentence, you can search for it by typing Smith for the search string and pressing the SPACEBAR. To find any occurrences of "Smith" at the end of a sentence, type Smith and a period for the search string.

Exercises

1. Type the following paragraph. Use the Search feature to locate the name "Jill Smith."

   On Saturday, May 16, XY Graphics is holding a press conference for their new product, See 'N' Draw. At this conference, the public relations director, Jill Smith, will reveal the company's marketing strategy for the product.

2. Type the following lines. Move to the beginning of the file, and use the Search feature to locate the "5" used to specify the number of disks.

   Memory Requirements: 512K
   Storage Space Required: 200K
   Number of Disks: 5
   Tutorial: Yes
   Demo: Yes

3. Type the following text. Then find all occurrences of the word "forgive."

   "I can forgive but I cannot forget," is only another way of saying, "I cannot forgive."
                                    Henry Ward Beecher

Forgive! How many will say "Forgive" and find
A sort of absolution in the sound
To hate a little longer.
Alfred, Lord Tennyson

4. Type the following paragraph. Find all occurrences of the three-letter combination "sea." Find all occurrences of the word "sea" without finding words that have that letter combination in it.

Searching for seashells is enjoyable. You do not have to leave the seashore or beach to find them. It is a wonderful way to spend your time by an ocean or a sea in any season.

SEARCH FROM THE END OF A DOCUMENT 7.2

WordPerfect can search backward from any point in a document to the beginning of the document. It is important to begin with the cursor past all the text that you want to include in the search. The cursor stops at the position immediately following the match, if one is found. If WordPerfect cannot find a match it beeps and displays the "* Not found *" message, and the cursor remains where it was.

To search backward for a word or phrase:

a. Press the Reverse Search (SHIFT-F2) key.

b. Type the word or phrase that you want WordPerfect to find.

c. Press the Reverse Search (SHIFT-F2) key or the Search (F2) key. (You get the same result, since WordPerfect sets the direction by the command used in step a.)

To search for the same word or phrase a second time, press the Reverse Search (SHIFT-F2) key twice more. If WordPerfect does not find the word or phrase, it beeps and displays "* Not found *" in the status line. If the text you type in step b is all lowercase, WordPerfect finds both upper- and lowercase letters. If any part of the search string is uppercase, WordPerfect will find only matches with identical capitalization.

Examples

1. You can perform a search through a document you have just completed typing without first moving to the beginning of the document by using the Reverse Search (SHIFT-F2) option. First, type the following paragraph:

   The See 'N' Draw package is easy to install. The installation program creates a subdirectory and copies the files to it. After running the installation program, the See 'N' Draw program is ready to run.

   To find where the text mentions "subdirectories," press the Reverse Search (SHIFT-F2) key, and type

   subdirector

   Because you did not include the suffix, WordPerfect can find either "subdirectory" or "subdirectories." Press the Search (F2) key. WordPerfect moves the cursor to the "y" in "subdirectory" in the second sentence.

2. You can also use Reverse Search to find hidden codes. For example, when you type a paragraph, you might keep WordPerfect from wrapping the lines correctly by pressing ENTER at the end of a line that is not the end of the paragraph. You can locate the [HRt] symbol by pressing ENTER when prompted for the search string. You can locate other attributes, such as centering, boldface, and underlining, just as easily. First, type the following, without pressing ENTER:

A strong feature of See 'N' Draw is the

Continue the entry on the same line by pressing the SPACEBAR and the Bold (F6) key and typing

automatic detection of the hardware components.

Press the Bold (F6) key again, press the SPACEBAR twice, and type the following without pressing ENTER:

When you initially load See 'N' Draw, the program prompts you for information about the equipment you are using. The program determines the proper settings to use for your equipment. You can change these assumptions during installation or later through the menu.

To find the code representing the end of boldfacing, press the Reverse Search (SHIFT-F2) key. Since you want the code that turns Bold off, press the Bold (F6) key twice, and use the LEFT ARROW and BACKSPACE keys to remove the first Bold code. Next, press the Search (F2) key. WordPerfect moves the cursor to the end of the first sentence.

Exercises

1. Type the following sentence:

The entire project was moved to Tobler Hall under the direction of John Tomita.

Use Reverse Search to find all occurrences of the string "to."

2. Type the following sentences:

The meeting is Friday, August 11th. <u>All must attend.</u> Discuss previous commitments with Carol Stevens.

Use Reverse Search to find the ending underline code.

3. Type the following paragraph:

The next forum for the Secretary's Association is in Buffalo. Since it is close to the Canadian border, they are expecting an increased number of foreigners. The cost, including dinner, is forty dollars.

Use Reverse Search to find all occurrences of the string "for." Then use Reverse Search to find all occurrences of the word "for" without finding other words that have that letter combination in them.

7.3   USE THE REPLACE FEATURE

In addition to searching for text, WordPerfect can replace a string of characters with another string of characters. Further, this feature provides *global* replacement, meaning that Word-Perfect searches the entire document and changes each occurrence of the search string to the replacement string. You can choose to confirm every replacement or allow Word-Perfect to make the replacements without waiting for confirmation. To restrict the text to be affected by the replace operation, you can use the Block feature to mark the text to be searched.

The Replace feature provides a convenient method for correcting names entered incorrectly, incorrect product numbers, or any other information you wish to change. You must supply both the original search string and its replacement.

To have WordPerfect find and replace a word or phrase:

a. Press the Replace (ALT-F2) key.

b. Type a **y** or an **n** to indicate whether you want to confirm each replacement.

c. Press the UP ARROW key if you wish WordPerfect to proceed with the replace operation toward the beginning rather than the end of the document.

d. Type the word or phrase that WordPerfect should find.

e. Press the Search (F2) key.

   If the text you type in step d is all lowercase, WordPerfect finds both upper- and lowercase letters. If any part of the search string is uppercase, WordPerfect finds only matches with identical capitalization.

f. Type the replacement text.

   Use the exact capitalization that you wish to appear in the replacement text.

g. Press the Search (F2) key.

   If you perform step c and you have already performed a search or replace during the current WordPerfect session, you need to remove the previous search string. You can do so by using the DEL or DELETE EOL (CTRL-END) key. If you begin typing the new search string *before* pressing the UP ARROW key, however, WordPerfect will delete the first search string automatically.

   When WordPerfect replaces text or codes working toward the beginning of the document, it does not reformat the document. You will need to scroll forward through the document after WordPerfect has finished to make it adjust the text.

   You can press the Cancel (F1) key at any time during the Replace procedure if you make a mistake or change your mind.

Examples

1. You can use the Replace feature to change every occurrence of a word or phrase to another word or phrase. First, type the following text.

See 'N' Draw is a product designed for first-time users and artists who want to push the limits of a graphics package. Compared with competitors' products, See 'N' Draw has the easiest user interface to learn. See 'N' Draw is available at most retail software dealers.

Next, to change the package name to "Scene Draw," press the Replace (ALT-F2) key. WordPerfect displays this prompt in the status line:

w/Confirm? (Y/N) No

Type an **n** so that WordPerfect will not prompt you to confirm every replacement. If you typed a **y**, WordPerfect would prompt you at every occurrence of the search string to see if you want it replaced.

Next, since the cursor is at the end of the text, press the UP ARROW key so that WordPerfect will perform the search and replace toward the beginning of the document. The arrow in the "→Srch" prompt changes to "←." Next, tell WordPerfect what text to find. Remove any previous search string by pressing the DELETE EOL (CTRL-END) key, and type

See 'N'

Next, press the Search (F2) key. WordPerfect prompts you for the text or codes to replace the search text. Type

Scene

Press the Search (F2) key. WordPerfect beeps when it completes the replacements. Press the Scroll Down (GREY +) key to rewrap the paragraph. The paragraph now looks like this:

Scene Draw is a product designed for first-time users and artists who want to push the limits of a graphics package. Compared with competitors' products, Scene Draw has the easiest user interface to learn. Scene Draw is available at most retail software dealers.

2. You can use search and replace to selectively replace text or codes. If you have a document in which you have pressed ENTER at the end of each line, changing the margins might cause the lines to display incorrectly. To correct the problem, you need to remove all the hard returns that do not end a paragraph. This allows WordPerfect to adjust the text correctly within any margin settings you select.

First, type the following lines, pressing ENTER at the end of each sentence:

The product will be released on August 17th.
The initial press conference is on August 11th.
The distributors will have the package on August 14th.
A product review in a monthly newsletter was excellent.
The newsletter is considering another article for a later issue.

Next, press the Replace (ALT-F2) key. WordPerfect prompts you to ask whether you want all replacements confirmed. Type a **y**. Next, press ENTER. WordPerfect deletes the previous search string and displays the [HRt] code. Press the UP ARROW key to have WordPerfect move backward to perform the search. The search prompt looks like this:

<- Srch: [HRt]

Next, press the Search (F2) key. WordPerfect prompts you for the text or codes to replace the search text. Since you want the hard returns replaced with two spaces, press the SPACEBAR twice. Press the Search (F2) key. The cursor stops at the "T" at the beginning of the last line, since that is the first character following the hidden [HRt] code, and Word-Perfect displays this prompt:

Confirm? (Y/N) No

Since you want this replacement made, type a **y**. For each of the successive prompts, type a **y**. WordPerfect beeps when it is finished. WordPerfect will not rewrap the text until you move down through the document. Press the Scroll Down (GREY +) key to reformat the paragraph. The paragraph now looks like this:

The product will be released on August 17th. The initial press conference is on August 11th. The distributors will have the package on August 14th. A product review in a monthly newsletter was excellent. The newsletter is considering another article for a later issue.

3. You can find an exact match for a word by preceding and following the word by a space when typing the search string. If you want WordPerfect to replace the name "Green" with "Lime" and skip "Greene," "Greenfield," "Greenjeans," and "Greenly," you can type a space before and after "Green" when you identify it as the search string.

First, type

He invited John Greenly, Howard Greensen, Mary Green-field, Beth Greene, and Paul Green to his St. Patrick's Day party.

Move to the top of the document by pressing HOME, HOME, UP ARROW. Press the Replace (ALT-F2) key, and press ENTER to reject confirmation. Next, type

Green

placing a space to each side of "Green." Press the Search
(F2) key, and type

Lime

You need to include a space to each side of "Lime" to
maintain the proper spacing in the paragraph. When you
press the Search (F2) key again, WordPerfect performs the
replacement. If "Green" had been the last word of the
sentence, WordPerfect would not have found it, because
the period at the end of the sentence would not have
matched the space in the search string.

4. You can restrict the scope of the replacement by blocking
   the text you wish to be affected. Type

**ABC Company had a very profitable year. Five successful
new products helped to make 1989 the best year ever for
ABC Company. ABC Company performed poorly this
year. A record 90 million dollar loss for ABC Company was
recorded.**

Press ENTER to end the paragraph. Next, move to the
beginning of the third sentence. Block the last two sentences by pressing the Block (ALT-F4) key and the DOWN ARROW
key twice. Next, press the Replace (ALT-F2) key. Press ENTER to
accept the default of no confirmation, and type **ABC**. Press
the Search (F2) key, and type **XYZ**. When you press the
Search (F2) key again, WordPerfect beeps after changing the
text to look like this:

ABC Company had a very profitable year. Five successful new
products helped to make 1989 the best year ever for ABC Company.
XYZ Company performed poorly this year. A record 90 million dollar
loss for XYZ Company was recorded.

Exercises

1. Type the following paragraph:

Sam Cook is the production manager. He has five years' experience in this position. Prior to this position, Sam Cook was a sergeant in the army. Sam Cook succeeded Thomas MacNamara in his current position.

Replace all occurrences of "Sam Cook" with **Daniel Jones.**

2. Type the following text:

WordPerfect's Replace feature allows you to selectively replace one string of characters with another character string. You can have WordPerfect prompt you before completing each replacement, or you can have it make the changes automatically.

Use the Replace feature to change all occurrences of "WordPerfect" to **WordPerfect 5.0.**

3. Type the following paragraph:

The Public Relations Director for your area is XX. XX has been with the company for many years and can answer your questions.

Replace "XX" with **Nancy Clark.** Then replace "Nancy Clark" with **Martin Smith.**

4. Type the following paragraph:

You can use WP's Replace feature to shorten typing in a ms or doc. In a ms or doc, you type the abbreviations in place of the words and have WP replace the abbreviations with the words they represent.

Replace "ms" with **manuscript.** Replace "doc" with **document.** Replace "WP" with **WordPerfect.**

EXERCISES

(Do not clear the screen between exercises unless instructed to do so.)

1. Type the following paragraph:

WordPerfect lets you search for text. You can search either backward or forward. This means that you do not have to move the cursor to a specific location before you can use this feature.

Go to the top of the paragraph, and use the Search feature to locate each occurrence of the word "search."

2. Go back to the top of the paragraph, and use the Search feature to determine the number of times that the paragraph uses the word "you."

3. Go to the bottom of the paragraph, and use the Reverse Search feature to determine the number of times that the paragraph uses the letter combination "for." Clear the screen.

4. Type the following:

Aeneades was a Trojan prince. He was the son of Diomedes and Achilles. Aeneades married Lavinia.

Replace all occurrences of "Aeneades" with **Aeneas**.

(Do not clear the screen until you have completed the last exercise.)

1. Type the following paragraph:

Proposal

The Quick Time division of New Men's Look, Inc., would like to expand their product line to include pocket watches. Adding pocket watches would fit into the division's current production capacity. The plant is operating 30% below capacity. The technology required is already available. This product would also complement the suits produced by another subsidiary, the Taylor division.

Use Search to move the cursor to the hidden code for underlining. Use Reveal Codes to determine the cursor's location in relation to the hidden code.

2. Use Replace to change "Quick Time" to uppercase.

3. Replace "Taylor" with **Tailor**.

4. Center the text on the page.

5. Preview the document as WordPerfect would print it.

CHAPTER OBJECTIVES

After completing this chapter, you should be able to

8.1 Move a sentence, a paragraph, or a page

8.2 Move a block of text

8.3 Delete a block of text

8.4 Copy a block of text

·8·

Restructuring Your Documents with Copy, Move, and Delete

One of WordPerfect's greatest advantages over the use of a typewriter is that it gives you the ability to restructure documents without retyping the text. Moving words, sentences, paragraphs, and pages is easy with WordPerfect's convenient features. Menu options allow you to move a sentence or a paragraph. You can move phrases, multiple sentences, and multiple pages of text by first identifying them with WordPerfect's Block feature. You have mastered the first step in this process already, since you have used Block to underline and boldface text.

The ability to copy a section of text is another useful WordPerfect feature. It allows you to create two similar sections of text by copying the original text and modifying the copy. In addition, a quick method for deleting text is provided, since using the DEL or BACKSPACE key alone is a slow procedure when you have a large amount of text to remove.

SKILLS CHECK

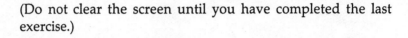

(Do not clear the screen until you have completed the last exercise.)

1. Set all four margins to 2″.

2. Set the page numbers to appear in the upper left-hand corner when you print the document.

3. Remove all of the tab stops, and set new ones at every inch.

4. Type the following letter:

Dale Thompson
Birds of a Feather
2398 Manzanita Park
Stanford, CA 94321

Dear Dale,

According to your advertisement in Feathered Friends, you are interested in purchasing two white cockatoos. I own several and would like to sell them. Please contact me at (813) 212-2634.

Sincerely,

Byron Wilson

Underline "Feathered Friends".

5. Use the Replace feature to change "cockatoos" to **parakeets**.

6. Print the document. Center the document on the page and reprint it.

7. Reset all four margins to 1″ and tab stops to every .5″. Eliminate page numbering.

MOVE A SENTENCE, A PARAGRAPH, OR A PAGE

8.1

Polishing initial drafts of a document can improve the quality and clarity of the writing. Rearranging text is often part of a revision process, since it enables you to place sentences in the most effective order. WordPerfect makes it easy to rearrange text, since you do not have to retype it. WordPerfect provides options for moving a sentence, a paragraph, or a page.

To move text:

a. Move the cursor to the place in the text where you wish to move.

b. Press the Move (CTRL-F4) key.

c. Type an **s** or a **1** to select the current sentence, a **p** or a **2** to select the current paragraph, or an **a** or a **3** to select the current page as the text to move.

d. Type an **m** or a **1** to select moving the text.

e. Move the cursor to where you want the text placed.

f. Press ENTER.

After you perform step d, the text disappears until you press ENTER. In step c, selecting Sentence causes WordPerfect to move everything from the beginning of the sentence up to and including the space following a period, question mark, or exclamation point. Selecting Paragraph causes WordPerfect to move everything from the beginning of the paragraph up to and including the hard return before the next paragraph. Selecting Page causes WordPerfect to move everything from the beginning of the page up to and including the hard or soft page break at the end of the page.

Examples

1. You can move one sentence at a time. First, type

Please return the books immediately! According to our records, Dave, you were the last one borrowing the department's tax reference books.

Since this paragraph makes more sense if you reverse the sentence order, move the cursor to any character in the first sentence. Next, press the Move (CTRL-F4) key. WordPerfect displays this prompt on the status line:

Move: 1 Sentence; 2 Paragraph; 3 Page; 4 Retrieve: 0

Select **s** for Sentence. WordPerfect highlights the sentence and displays these selections:

1 Move; 2 Copy; 3 Delete; 4 Append: 0

Select **m** for Move. The sentence disappears. WordPerfect displays a reminder at the bottom of the screen to press ENTER where you want the text to be placed. Move the cursor to the end of the remaining sentence. If you did not include two spaces at the end of the second sentence when you typed it, press the SPACEBAR twice. Press ENTER. The sentence that was originally first is placed after the other sentence, and the screen looks like this:

According to our records, Dave, you were the last one borrowing the department's tax reference books. Please return the books immediately!

2. Since WordPerfect recognizes a period as the end of a sentence, you can get some unexpected results when trying to move a sentence that contains abbreviations or numbers with decimals. First, type

Dr. and Mrs. Jones bought a St. Bernard puppy.

Press HOME and the UP ARROW to move to the beginning of the sentence. Press the Move (CTRL-F4) key and type an **s**. Instead of highlighting the entire sentence, WordPerfect highlights only "Dr." Because the abbreviations in this sentence require periods, the sentence needs to be moved with the Block Move procedure covered later in this chapter.

3. When you move a paragraph, WordPerfect moves all of the text from the beginning of the paragraph up to and including the hard return before the next paragraph. For example, you can create a list of tasks to perform. Type

To-Do List

 Write instructions for the new subsidiary on the preparation of financial statements to be submitted to the parent corporation. They cannot use electronic transmission for their information until their system is modified to conform to the parent corporation's accounting system.

 Meet with Tom from Purchasing. He wants to streamline the purchasing process for a just-in-time inventory system.

Be sure to press ENTER at the end of the second paragraph. You can move the first item in the list to make it the second item by moving the paragraph. First, move the cursor to the first paragraph. Next, press the Move (CTRL-F4) key. Type a **p** for Paragraph. WordPerfect highlights the entire paragraph. Next, type an **m** for Move. The paragraph disappears. Move the cursor to the blank line below the paragraph still displayed on the screen, and press ENTER. Now, the screen looks like Figure 8-1. If you press HOME,

To-Do List

Meet with Tom from Purchasing. He wants to streamline the
purchasing process for a just-in-time inventory system.
Write instructions for the new subsidiary on the preparation
of financial statements to be submitted to the parent
corporation. They cannot use electronic transmission for their
information until their system is modified to conform to the
parent corporation's accounting system.

FIGURE 8-1.   The effect of moving a paragraph

HOME, and DOWN ARROW, you will notice that the second item
has a blank line below it. WordPerfect moved the blank line
between the two items as part of the paragraph.

4. You can move a page of text to a new location in a
   document. First, type

Preparation and Approval of Building Plans

To start a new page, press CTRL-ENTER. Then, type

Construction of the Building Exterior

Next, press CTRL-ENTER, and type

Interior Finishing Tasks

Next, type

Site Excavation

Press CTRL-ENTER to end page 4. If you review the pages, you
will notice that page 4 ideally should be the second page in
the document. Use the UP ARROW key to position the cursor
on page 4, press the Move (CTRL-F4) key, and type an **a** for
Page. All of the text on the page is highlighted. Next, type
an **m** for Move. Finally, move the cursor to the first
character on page 2, since WordPerfect will insert the text
in front of the cursor position. When you press ENTER,
WordPerfect moves the page, and the screen looks like
Figure 8-2.

Preparation and Approval of Building Plans
===
Site Excavation
===
Construction of the Building Exterior
===
Interior Finishing Tasks
===

FIGURE 8-2. The effect of moving a page

Exercises

1. Type the following paragraph:

A complex sentence consists of an independent clause, which can stand alone, and one or more dependent clauses. A compound sentence is two or more simple sentences joined by a conjunction, such as "and," "or," "but," or "for." A simple sentence expresses a single action or thought.

Change the sentence order so that the first sentence is third and the third sentence is first.

2. Type the following paragraphs:

The sun's temperature is 11,000 degrees Fahrenheit at the surface and 35,000,000 degrees in the center. It releases 1.94 calories per square centimeter per minute.
The diameter of the sun is 865,000 miles. It is small by comparison to other stars. The sun's proximity to the earth makes it appear larger than other stars.

Move the second paragraph to place it before the paragraph that was entered first.

3. Type the following lines, inserting a hard page break after each line. Move the first page to after the third.

A nebula is a mass of gas in space.
A meteoroid is a small object in space.
A constellation is a group of stars.

4. Type the following paragraphs:

Keyboards usually come in two types. A standard keyboard has ten function keys at the side. An enhanced keyboard has twelve function keys across the top.
With WordPerfect, if you have an enhanced keyboard, you can use F11 in place of ALT-F3. You can also use F12 in place of ALT-F4.

Switch the order of the second and third sentences in the first paragraph. Switch the order of the first and second paragraphs.

8.2   MOVE A BLOCK OF TEXT

You must block text when you want to move part of a document that does not fit WordPerfect's definition of a sentence, a paragraph, or a page. This means that when you have periods within a sentence or [HRt] codes to end short lines in a paragraph, you will need to use Block to move the text. If you wish to move a group of words, several sentences, or half of a page, for example, you will need to block the text first. Although moving blocked text requires this additional step, it provides the ultimate flexibility.

To move blocked text:

a. Move the cursor to the first character or code in the text you want to move.

b. Press the Block (ALT-F4) key.

c. Move the cursor to highlight all of the text and the adjacent codes you want to move.

d. Press the Move (CTRL-F4) key.

e. Type a **b** or a **1** to select Block.

f. Type an **m** or a **1** to select Move.

g. Move the cursor to where you want the blocked text placed.

h. Press ENTER.

When you perform step f, the block disappears. When you press ENTER, WordPerfect inserts the block at the cursor's position, moving everything else down. If your computer has 12 function keys, you can use F12 instead of ALT-F4 in step b. You can also define a block by starting at the end and moving the cursor to the beginning of the block.

Examples

1. You can block text to move part of a sentence. Type

In order to complete your request, we need the following information: your address, the date of the purchase, your name, and the salesperson who handled the order.

To move the words "your name" to precede the words "your address," move the cursor to the "y" in "your name" and press the Block (ALT-F4) key. Next, move the cursor to the "a" in "and." The screen looks like this:

```
In order to complete your request, we need the following
information: your address, the date of the purchase, your name, and
the sales person who handled the order.
```

Press the Move (CTRL-F4) key and type a **b** and an **m**. Move the cursor to the "y" in "your address," and press ENTER. Now, the screen looks like this:

In order to complete your request, we need the following information: your name, your address, the date of the purchase, and the sales person who handled the order.

2. You can block text to move it when you have multiple sentences, paragraphs, or pages to move. Type

Last year's sales decreased by 10%. Most of the decrease stemmed from the sale of the Bounce Back Yo-Yo division. Profits increased by 2%.

Be sure to press SPACEBAR twice at the end of the last sentence. You can move the first two sentences to follow the third sentence. First, press PGUP to move the cursor to the "L" in "Last." Next, press the Block (ALT-F4) key and move the cursor to the "P" in "Profits." Press the Move (CTRL-F4) key and type a **b** for Block and an **m** for Move. Next, press END to move the cursor to the second space after the last sentence. Press ENTER, and the text on the screen is reorganized to look like this:

Profits increased by 2%. Last year's sales decreased by 10%. Most of the decrease stemmed from the sale of the Bounce Back Yo-Yo division.

Exercises

1. Type this sentence:

See 'N' Draw, XY Graphics' new product, should capture a large part of the graphics market for first-time users.

Move the product name and the comma and space that follow it after the comma and space that follow "product." The restructured sentence should read

XY Graphics' new product, See N' Draw, should capture a large part of the graphics market for first-time users.

2. Type this sentence:

The new machinery funnels the cake mix into preprinted boxes, weighs a predetermined amount of the cake mix, and seals the bag.

Move "weighs a predetermined amount of the cake mix," to come before "funnels the cake mix into preprinted boxes,". The restructured sentence will read:

The new machinery weighs a predetermined amount of the cake mix, funnels the cake mix into preprinted boxes, and seals the bag.

3. Type these lines:

Review meeting agenda.
Nominate potential candidates for new director position.
Review financial statements.
Review minutes from the last meeting.
Introduce new corporate treasurer to board.

Move the last two lines so that they follow the first line.

4. Type this paragraph:

When you move a block, you should check to include any hidden codes in your text. WordPerfect moves all of the codes within the block. If the text that you move is part of a larger block of text that has special print attributes (for

example, bold or underline), the special print characteristics appear in both the moved text and the original. To view the codes, press the Reveal Codes (ALT-F3) key.

Move the second and third sentences together to the beginning of the paragraph.

8.3   DELETE A BLOCK OF TEXT

When you edit a document, you may want to delete a section of text. Rather than pressing the DEL or BACKSPACE key until the text disappears, you can save time by blocking the text first. You have several options for deleting a block of text. If the block you wish to delete conforms to WordPerfect's definition of a sentence, paragraph, or page, you can use an even faster procedure for deleting it.

To delete a block of text:

a. Move the cursor to the beginning of the text you wish to delete.

b. Press the Block (ALT-F4) key.

c. Move the cursor to highlight all of the text you wish to delete.

d. Press the DEL or BACKSPACE key.

e. Confirm that you wish to delete the text by typing a **y**.

Another method for deleting the text offers the use of menu selections. Steps d and e in the above procedure are replaced by steps d through f below.

d. Press the Move (CTRL-F4) key.

e. Type a **b** or a **1** to select Block.

f. Type a **d** or a **3** to select Delete.

To delete a sentence, paragraph, or page:

a. Press the Move (CTRL-F4) key after positioning the cursor on any character in the text you wish to delete.

b. Type an **s** for Sentence, a **p** for Paragraph, or an **a** for Page as the text to delete.

c. Type a **d** or a **3** to delete the text.

Examples

1. You can block text and then remove it with the DEL key. Type the following sentences, pressing ENTER at the end of each one.

Special rules apply to typing numbers:
Numbers of less than three digits are spelled.
Compound numbers less than 100 are hyphenated.
Numbers that represent measurements are expressed in figures, e.g. 54 miles, 26 feet.

Since the first two rules do not give examples, you can remove the examples from the last entry. Move to the comma after "figures," and press the Block (ALT-F4) key. Move to the end of the sentence by pressing the DOWN ARROW key, and press the LEFT ARROW key once so that the block does not include the period. Press the DEL key, and type a **y**. The blocked text is deleted.

2. You can delete any amount of text by blocking the text you want to delete. First, type

To evaluate investment projects, many companies use the internal rate of return. The internal rate of return is the minimum interest rate that a project must earn to have a net present value of 0.

To remove part of the second sentence, begin by moving the cursor to the period ending the first sentence. Next, press the Block (ALT-F4) key and move the cursor to the space after "is." Press the Move (CTRL-F4) key and type a **b** for Block and a **d** for Delete. Optionally, you could press the DEL or BACKSPACE key and confirm the deletion by typing a **y**. After you type a comma and move the cursor down, the screen looks like this:

To evaluate investment projects, many companies use the internal rate of return, the minimum interest rate that a project must earn to have a net present value of 0.

3. You can use a shortcut if the block of text you wish to delete is a sentence, a paragraph, or a page. Type

   John Adams was the second President of the United States. He served in Europe as the ambassador before his election as the first Vice President. Following Washington's second term, John Adams succeeded Washington as president. He was ambidextrous and could write Greek with one hand while writing Latin with the other.

   After pressing ENTER, press the UP ARROW key to move the cursor to the last sentence. Press the Move (CTRL-F4) key, type an **s** for Sentence and a **d** for Delete.

Exercises

1. Type the following paragraph:

   The Office of Human Resources reports that hiring has increased by 14%. This increase is a result of last year's expansion of the Largo division. The increased hiring, which created 1000 new jobs, should not affect next year's personnel needs.

   Delete the period ending the first sentence and the phrase "This increase is." Add a comma after "14%."

2. Type the following sentence:

As of May 15, the corporation must increase sales by 15,000 units per month, renovate the corporate offices, and divest itself of its Romper division to meet its 1989 objectives.

Delete "renovate the corporate offices" and the comma and space after that phrase.

3. Type the following lines:

Today's Projects
Prepare capital budget request for two computers.
Review receivables older than 90 days.
Prepare next year's forecast.

Block and delete the second and third projects.

4. Type the following paragraph:

Last February, the widget assembler became jammed. While the cause was poor maintenance, the machine's condition requires above-normal maintenance to prevent the problem from recurring. To prevent this problem from recurring, the company should purchase a new machine.

Delete the second sentence.

COPY A BLOCK OF TEXT   8.4

WordPerfect's features for copying text can provide substantial time savings. If you need another copy of existing text, a few menu selections can duplicate the text without any retyping.

Even if you need a modified version of existing text, the Copy feature can provide a better solution than typing. By copying the original text, you can make your modifications more quickly than by typing the entire new section of text.

You can copy a section of text of any size by blocking the text first. If you need to copy a sentence, a paragraph, or a page, you can use an even faster procedure.

To copy blocked text:

a. Move the cursor to the first character in the text you want to copy.

b. Press the Block (ALT-F4) key.

c. Move the cursor to highlight all of the text you want to copy.

d. Press the Move (CTRL-F4) key.

e. Type a **b** or a **1** to select Block.

f. Type a **c** or a **2** to select Copy.

g. Move the cursor to where you want to place the copied text.

h. Press ENTER.

To copy a sentence, a paragraph, or a page:

a. Move the cursor to the section of text you want to copy.

b. Press the Move (CTRL-F4) key.

c. Type an **s** for Sentence, a **p** for Paragraph, or an **a** for Page, depending on the amount of text you wish to copy.

d. Type a **c** or a **2** for Copy.

e. Move the cursor to where you want to place the copied text.

f. Press ENTER.

Examples

1. You can copy a block of any size. First, type the following lines, pressing ENTER at the end of each one.

The policy that applies to borrowing the company's 35mm camera is:
The borrower must return the camera within 24 hours.
The borrower is responsible for film and development.
The borrower is responsible for damage or loss.

To copy the policy, press the Block (ALT-F4) key, and press PGUP to move the cursor to the "T" in the first line. WordPerfect highlights all the text. Next, press the Move (CTRL-F4) key, and type a **b** for Block and a **c** for Copy.

Finally, move the cursor to the bottom of the document by pressing PGDN. Press ENTER to insert a copy of the text. You can modify the copy to produce a policy for borrowing the company's new video camera.

2. You can also copy a sentence, a paragraph, or a page. To copy a paragraph, first type

   The MIS department retains a copy of the manuals for all of the company's software. To borrow a manual, check it out from one of the reference librarians. You may borrow a manual for up to three days.

   After pressing ENTER, move the cursor to any character in the paragraph. Press the Move (CTRL-F4) key, and type a **p** for Paragraph. WordPerfect highlights the entire paragraph. Type a **c** for Copy, and press ENTER to create the second copy of the paragraph.

3. You can use a special procedure when you need multiple copies of text. First, type

   The MIS department retains a copy of the manuals for all of the company's software. To borrow a manual, . You may borrow a manual for up to three days.

The first copy is made with the same procedure you used in example 2. Move the cursor to any character in the paragraph, press the Move (CTRL-F4) key, and type a **p** for Paragraph. WordPerfect highlights the entire paragraph. Type a **c** for Copy, and move the cursor to where you want the new copy to appear. Press ENTER to insert the copy of the paragraph.

To make an additional copy, move the cursor to where you want the next new copy to appear. Press the Move (CTRL-F4) key. Type an **r** for Retrieve and a **b** for Block. WordPerfect inserts a copy of the text that you copied last. You can then edit each paragraph to give different instructions for borrowing a manual.

Exercises

1. Type the following lines, then place a copy of the lines below the original.

Name: Patrick Rabbit
Address: 777 Carrot Lane

Modify the copy to change the second "Patrick" to **Nancy** and the second street number to **515**. Use the Retrieve and Block options to make an additional copy of the original two lines.

2. Type the following paragraph:

First, put the correct pens in the plotter. This is an important step. Next, put the paper or transparency in the plotter.

Copy the second sentence, placing the copy after the third sentence.

3. Type the following lines. Block them, copy them, and make three additional copies.

Current Month: . . . .
Sales: . . . .
Cost of Goods Sold: . . . .

4. Type the following partial paragraph:

Directions to the Cloverleaf Hall: Take the interstate to the Bay Street exit. At the exit, turn right, and take the next left after the light. Stay on this road until you pass the shopping mall on the right. After passing the shopping mall,

Complete the last sentence by blocking and copying "take the next left after the light."

EXERCISES

1. Type the following sentences. Move the first one between the second and third.

The cost of goods sold is $2,363,782. The beginning inventory is $689,578. The ending inventory is $234,245.

MASTERY SKILLS CHECK

2. Type the following sentences:

The new and improved widget maker has several features. One of these features is the internal painter. This feature evenly coats each widget and limits the fumes, which reduces the number of employees needed to operate the machine.

Move the comma and the phrase "which reduces the number of employees needed to operate the machine" to the end of the second sentence. The paragraph should read:

The new and improved widget maker has several features. One of these features is the internal painter, which reduces the number of employees needed to operate the machine. This feature evenly coats each widget and limits the fumes.

3. Type the following paragraph:

Tuesday, the heads of the accounting, production, and MIS departments will review the steps that they can take to reduce the time between the receipt of an order and its completion.

Block and delete the phrase "that they can take." Then delete the entire paragraph.

4. Type the following paragraph:

Today's weather will be lovely. The temperature will rise to 82 and will cool to an evening low of 70. The low humidity will contribute to the day's pleasant weather.

Block the paragraph and make three copies of it.

INTEGRATED SKILLS CHECK

(Do not clear the screen between exercises unless instructed to do so.)

1. Type the following paragraph:

The ABC widget uses point-of-sale displays as its primary marketing strategy. The new point-of-sale displays are designed to fit at the end of an aisle. As an incentive to the retailer, we are selling the widgets in the aisle pre-packs at a slightly lower cost. Each retailer can choose whether to pass the lower cost on to the customer or increase profits.

Insert a hard page break, and move the paragraph to the second page.

2. Indent the paragraph. Clear the screen.

3. Type the following lines:

Marketing Strategy
ABC WIDGETS
Prepared on July 7, 1988

Delete the first two words in the last line. Center this information on the page. Preview how WordPerfect will print the document. Clear the screen.

4. Create a receipt form by typing

   Date:
   Name:
   Amount:
   Explanation:
   Signature:

   Insert a hard page break. Block the lines and the page break, and place a copy below the original.

5. Make three additional copies of the page.

6. Add page numbers in the center at the top of each page, and print the receipt forms.

7. Replace all occurrences of "Explanation" with **For**.

·Part II·

Building on the Basics

CHAPTER OBJECTIVES

After completing this chapter, you should be able to

9.1 Check the spelling of a word

9.2 Check the spelling of an entire document

9.3 Find double words

9.4 Add a word to the supplemental dictionary

9.5 Delete words from the supplemental dictionary

9.6 Replace correctly spelled words that are misused

9.7 Look up a word in the thesaurus

9.8 Replace a word with a word from the thesaurus

·9·

Using the Right Words

When you create a document, you hope that it will convey your message in a clear, concise way. Another objective may be to present a professional image of yourself and your firm.

Part of creating a professional image is creating a document that is flawless in spelling and grammar. Although WordPerfect does not as yet have a grammar-checking feature, it has an excellent spelling checker. WordPerfect's Spell feature allows you to check the spelling of a word, a page, or the entire document. It allows you to create personal dictionaries for specialized terminology. WordPerfect's spelling checker will also find occurrences of double words and provides the added bonus of counting the number of words in a document for you.

In addition to spelling the words correctly, to convey your message effectively, you must use the right words to express the meaning you intend. WordPerfect has a Thesaurus feature to help you find the right words easily.

SKILLS CHECK

(Do not clear the screen until you have completed the last exercise.)

1. Change the left and right margins to 2″.

2. Add page numbers in the upper left corner of the document.

3. Type the following paragraph:

   WordPerfect's Spell feature can find your spelling and typing mistakes. It prompts you with suggested alternatives when it finds a word that is not in one of its dictionaries.

   Find all occurrences of "spell" in the text you just typed.

4. Replace all occurrences of the word "it" with **WordPerfect**.

5. Add the following sentence to the end of the paragraph:

   WordPerfect's Thesaurus feature can help you find a word that has the exact meaning you need.

   Copy the second sentence in the paragraph to the end of the paragraph. Delete "when WordPerfect finds a word that is not in one of its dictionaries," and add **for the word that you look up in its thesaurus**. The completed paragraph should read

   WordPerfect's Spell feature can find your spelling and typing mistakes. WordPerfect prompts you with suggested alternatives when WordPerfect finds a word that is not in one of its dictionaries. WordPerfect's Thesaurus feature can help you find a word that has the exact

meaning you need. WordPerfect prompts you with suggested alternatives for the word that you look up in its thesaurus.

CHECK THE SPELLING OF A WORD — 9.1

If you are uncertain of the correct spelling of a word, you can have WordPerfect check it for you. The ability to check the spelling of a single word is a time-saving feature. Once you have verified it, you can stop questioning the spelling and focus on finishing the document.

To have WordPerfect check the spelling of a word:

a. Move the cursor to the word that you want to check.

b. Press the Spell (CTRL-F2) key.

c. Type a **w** or a **1**.

If you spelled the word correctly, WordPerfect moves the cursor to the next word. If WordPerfect does not find the word in its dictionaries, it displays menu options and, in most cases, similarly spelled or pronounced words, labeled with letters for your selection.

d. Select the correct word or one of the menu options if WordPerfect did not move the cursor to the next word.

e. Press the SPACEBAR, ENTER, ESC, the Cancel (F1) key, or the Exit (F7) key to return to the document.

Examples

1. You can use WordPerfect's Spell feature to check the spelling of a few individual words. To illustrate how the speller works, type the following sentence, including the misspelling of "strategy."

Next Tuesday, the marketing department will present their promotional straegy for the See N' Draw package.

To check the spelling of "promotional" and "straegy," first move the cursor to the word "promotional." Next, press the Spell (CTRL-F2) key. WordPerfect displays this menu:

Check: 1 Word; 2 Page; 3 Document; 4 New Sup. Dictionary; 5 Look Up; 6 Count: 0

Since you want to check a word at a time, type a **w**. WordPerfect checks the spelling of "promotional." Because "promotional" is spelled correctly, WordPerfect moves the cursor to the next word, "straegy." Since you also want to check the spelling of this word, type a **w**. Because it cannot find that word in its dictionary, WordPerfect displays a new menu that looks like this:

Not Found: 1 Skip Once; 2 Skip; 3 Add; 4 Edit; 5 Look Up; 6 Ignore Numbers: 0

It also displays a suggestion for the spelling of the word. Since the suggestion is correct, you can make the replacement by typing an **a**. Since you do not want to check any more words, press the SPACEBAR to leave the Spell feature.

2. When you use the Spell feature on words that are spelled correctly but are not in WordPerfect's dictionary, it still suggests replacements and offers a menu of correction alternatives. You can tell WordPerfect to ignore correctly spelled words it does not recognize. First, type

Adele Stein is representing the European divisions at the stockholders' meeting.

You can check the spelling of this sentence word by word by moving the cursor to the beginning of the sentence, pressing the Spell (CTRL-F2) key, and typing a **w**. WordPerfect highlights "Adele," which it doesn't recognize, and offers suggestions for other spellings. Since you have spelled the name properly, you want WordPerfect to skip this word; type a **2**. By selecting this option, you instruct WordPerfect to ignore "Adele" whenever it finds that word. If you had pressed a **1**, WordPerfect would skip only this occurrence of the word.

3. WordPerfect's Spell feature may offer many alternatives for a word that it does not find in its dictionary. First, type

Lake Erie usualy freezes in November or December.

Next, move the cursor to the word "usualy," press the Spell (CTRL-F2) key, and type a **w**. Since you misspelled this word, the screen looks like Figure 9-1. Each of WordPerfect's

---

Lake Erie usualy freezes in November or December.

===

```
A, usual        B, usually       C, usuary
D, acyl         E, assail        F, azalea
G, easel        H, easily        I, icily
J, ocelli       K, osseously     L, osteal
M, ostial
```

Not Found: 1 Skip Once: 2 Skip: 3 Add: 4 Edit: 5 Look Up: 6 Ignore Numbers: 0

FIGURE 9-1.   Suggested spelling corrections supplied by the spelling checker

suggestions has a different letter next to it. Since the replacement word that you want is "usually," type a **b** to have WordPerfect substitute the correctly spelled word. After checking other words in the sentence, press the Exit (F7) key to exit from the Spell feature.

4. When WordPerfect checks the spelling for you, you may need to modify, rather than replace, a word that it does not recognize. First, type

   For some misspellings, WordPerfect maynot give appropriate suggestions.

   Press ENTER. Then press the UP ARROW key twice to move to the word "For." Press the Spell (CTRL-F2) key. Type a **w** five times. WordPerfect does not recognize "maynot." You can easily fix this typographical mistake by editing it. Type a **4.** Press the RIGHT ARROW key three times and the SPACEBAR once. Then press the Exit (F7) key to end editing. WordPerfect checks the modified text. Since the edited words are correctly spelled, WordPerfect moves to the next word. Continue typing to edit the rest of the sentence. Then press the SPACEBAR to return to the document.

Exercises

1. Type the following words:

   Regrdless
   Disinterested
   Paradox
   Momento
   Subsequentially
   Torturous

   Use the Spell feature to correct the misspelled ones.

2. Type the following sentence as it appears:

WordPerfecty can chek a word at a thime, a blok, or an entear document.

Move to the beginning, and check the sentence's spelling a word at a time.

3. Type the following sentence as it appears:

Arwena McClellan is th product managr.

Move to the beginning, and check the sentence's spelling a word at a time. Assume "Arwena McClellan" is spelled correctly.

4. Type the following:

Ofthe eople, bythe oeople, andfor thepeople.

Move to the beginning, and check the spelling a word at a time. Use the Edit option of the Spell feature to modify the words so that the final result looks like this:

Of the people, by the people, and for the people.

·

CHECK THE SPELLING OF
AN ENTIRE DOCUMENT

9.2

For long documents, pressing keys to check every word whose spelling you are unsure of would be a tedious process. Also, it is likely that you would overlook errors. WordPerfect can check the spelling for the entire document for you with one easy command.

To have WordPerfect check the spelling of a document:

a. Press the Spell (CTRL-F2) key.

b. Type a **d** or a **3.**

WordPerfect reviews the entire document. When it finds a word that is not in its dictionaries, WordPerfect displays its suggestions. After you have instructed WordPerfect how to handle the word it flags as misspelled, it searches for the next misspelled word.

Examples

1. WordPerfect's Spell feature may find a number of words that are not in its dictionary when you check a document. If you elect to make a replacement for any of these words, WordPerfect makes the correction wherever it finds the misspelling throughout the document. First, type

   The factory's new heeting system uses natural gas. Solar panels assist the heeting system by prividing 20% of the power.

   Next, press the Spell (CTRL-F2) key, and type a **d**. The first word WordPerfect flags as misspelled is "heeting." Type an **a** to replace it with WordPerfect's first suggestion, "heating." Since the Spell feature automatically replaces the misspelling wherever it finds the word, WordPerfect corrects "heeting" in the second sentence.

   The next misspelling that WordPerfect brings to your attention is "prividing." Type an **a** to accept WordPerfect's first suggestion, "providing." WordPerfect finishes checking the document and displays a word count. Press the SPACEBAR to exit from the Spell feature.

2. When you check a document's spelling, WordPerfect may question correctly spelled words. Most of the correctly spelled words that WordPerfect will question will be names or technical terms. Type

Jim Wright
2209 Sunrise Boulevard
Ft. Lauderdale, Florida 33304

Dear Mr. Wright,

   We have shipped the supplies that you ordered. You will receive them in a few days. The paper that you ordered is out of stock. We will shipped it once we receive it.

Sincerely,

Adele Stein

To check the spelling of this document, press the Spell (CTRL-F2) key, and type a **d** for Document. Because WordPerfect does not have the word "Adele" in its dictionaries, it prompts you with alternate spellings. Since you spelled the name correctly, type a **2** to skip the word. When WordPerfect finishes checking the document, press the SPACEBAR to leave the Spell features. Notice that WordPerfect does not flag "shipped" as an incorrect word; although it is grammatically incorrect, the spelling is not wrong. The Spell feature is a valuable aid, but it is not a replacement for proofreading your documents.

Exercises

1. Type the following paragraph:

The biologicl lab reports that it has created a new hybrid plant called the Panophile. This plant tolerates extreem differences in humidity and temperature provided that it is adequately watered during its first yeer. Its flowers can be red, yellow, white, or purple.

Use the Spell feature to check the paragraph for spelling errors. Assume "Panophile" is correct.

2. Type the following paragraph:

As part of the city's 100-year celabration, thei are having a fiar, the first since before World War II. The fair will emphsize how the city looked 100 years ago.

Use the Spell feature to correct the misspelled words.

3. Type the following paragraph:

Last Tuesday, Markum Products anounced a dividend of $.30 per share. Thes dividend changes its dividend policy, since the lattest dividend equals the total dividends of the last two years.

Use the Spell feature to make necessary spelling corrections. Assume "Markum" is spelled correctly.

4. Type the following paragraph:

When you use the Spell feature, it finds two types of words. The first type is mispelled words. These words are typographical errors or words that you do not know how to spell. The second type is corectly spelled words that the Spel feature does not recognize. Most of thees words are names or technical terms.

Use the Spell feature to find and correct misspellings.

9.3   FIND DOUBLE WORDS

As you type, you may unintentionally type a word twice. WordPerfect is able to scan your document for occurrences of repeated, or double, words. Checking for double words is an automatic function of WordPerfect's Spell feature.

WordPerfect allows you to approve the occurrence of a double-word pair or delete the second occurrence of the word. It also allows you to edit the document in case one of the words should be changed. As a final option, it allows you to disable further checking for double words in documents in which double words are intended.

To have WordPerfect find double words:

a. Press the Spell (CTRL-F2) key.

b. Type a **d** or a **3**.

When WordPerfect finds a double word, it provides a different set of options than for misspelled words.

Examples

1. Double words are easy to overlook. Type the following paragraph, making sure to include the repeated words "a" and "the":

As part of the city's 100 year celebration, the city is having a a fair, the first since before World War II. The fair will emphasize how the the city looked 100 years ago.

To find the double words, press the Spell (CTRL-F2) key, and type a **d**. WordPerfect highlights the two "a"s before fair. You can select from the following menu options:

Double Word: 1 2 Skip; 3 Delete 2nd; 4 Edit; 5 Disable Double Word Checking

To remove one of the double words, type a **3**. Next, WordPerfect highlights the two "the"s in the second sentence. Since you want to remove one of them, type a **3**.

Finally, since that was the last spelling error or double word occurrence, press the SPACEBAR to return to the document.

2. WordPerfect's Spell feature automatically searches for double words. When your document contains misspelled words and double words, WordPerfect prompts you for the desired actions for misspellings and double words in the order that WordPerfect finds them. Type the following paragraph, making sure to include the misspellings and the repeated words:

The company is redirecting its resources, while remaining in the the personalized items business. This is due to demigraphic changes in its customer base. Its demigraphic base is aging and and has more disposable income.

Press the Spell (CTRL-F2) key, and type a **d**. WordPerfect highlights the two "the"s in the first sentence. Type a **3** to remove the extra word. Next, WordPerfect highlights "demigraphic" as a misspelled word. Type an **a** to substitute WordPerfect's only suggestion. WordPerfect corrects both occurences of the misspelling and highlights the two "and"s in the last sentence. Type a **3** to remove the second "and". When WordPerfect finishes checking the document, press the SPACEBAR to exit from the Spell feature.

Exercises

1. Type the following paragraph:

When ABC Corporation combines its corporate offices into a a central location, they expect to to reduce their staff by 30%. Most of the reduction of personnel costs for the first year will be be consumed by severance pay and other employment termination costs.

Use the Spell feature to remove double words.

2. Type the following paragraph:

The employees that have have been invited to to move to the new new corporate headqurters are in the process of moving. Human Resourses is is providing temporary housing and and moving services. Some of of the staff who are not moving to the new new headquarters have already found new jobs.

Use the Spell feature to remove double words and correct spelling mistakes.

3. Type the following paragraph:

Double words often occur with edited text. When you edit text text, you may add a a word to the end of of a phrase you are are adding, not realizing that it it is already there. Double words often happen with with short words.

Use the Spell feature to remove double words.

4. Type the following lines, pressing ENTER after each line:

WordPerfect does
does not
not check to see if the
the last word of one paragraph is the same word as the
first word word of the next paragraph.

Use the Spell feature to remove double words.

ADD A WORD TO THE SUPPLEMENTAL DICTIONARY 9.4

WordPerfect's main dictionary contains more than 100,000 words. The words in WordPerfect's dictionary have been identified as the words most commonly used in business writing. Despite the extensiveness of this dictionary, it probably will not contain all the properly spelled words that you will use in your documents. Because of this, there may be occasions when properly spelled words are flagged by WordPerfect as potential misspellings. You can circumvent this situation by asking WordPerfect to skip the word.

On a one-time basis, this solution can work. However, if you use a word frequently in your writing, you will soon become frustrated by having to tell WordPerfect to skip the word. WordPerfect offers you a supplemental dictionary to overcome this problem. You can use the supplemental dictionary to expand WordPerfect's word list with your own customized additions. You might want to add proper names (names of persons, company names, geographical names, and so on) or technical terms. Rather than skipping such words every time WordPerfect prompts you for an action, you can add them to your dictionary. WordPerfect maintains a supplemental dictionary file, named WP{WP}EN.SUP., for these entries.

To add a word to the supplemental dictionary:

a. Check the spelling of the word by pressing the Spell (CTRL-F2) key and typing a **1**.

b. Type a **3** when WordPerfect prompts you for action on a properly spelled word.

Examples

1. While WordPerfect's dictionary contains many words, it is missing most technical terms. In given areas of business, you might use some of these terms frequently. If you add these words to the supplemental dictionary the first time you encounter them, WordPerfect will recognize the words when checking subsequent documents. First, type

To assemble the vambrace, align the holes on the largest piece with the holes in the shorter end of the smallest piece. Attach a 2-piece rivet in each hole.

When you press the Spell (CTRL-F2) key and type a **3**, WordPerfect does not find "vambrace" in its dictionary. Since this word, which describes a type of arm protection, is spelled correctly, you can add it to the supplemental dictionary: Type a **3**. As you create other documents that mention "vambrace," WordPerfect will not stop at that word when checking spelling.

2. You will want to add frequently used names to the supplemental dictionary. WordPerfect recognizes many common names such as John, Nancy, Smith, and Jones. Many other, less common names it does not recognize as correctly spelled words. First, type

Jim Johansen
1209 Sunrise Boulevard
Ft. Lauderdale, Florida 33304

Dear Mr. Johansen,

    We have shipped the supplies that you ordered. You will receive them in a few days. The paper that you ordered is out of stock. We will ship it once our inventory is restocked.

                  Sincerely,

                  Adele Stein

When you check the spelling, WordPerfect does not recognize the name "Johansen." If Mr. Johansen is one of your regular customers and you spelled his name correctly, you can add his name to the supplemental dictionary by typing a **3**. When WordPerfect finds "Johansen" in other documents, it will recognize it as a correctly spelled word.

Next, WordPerfect suggests that you have misspelled Adele. Since it is spelled correctly, add it to the dictionary by typing a **3**. WordPerfect finishes checking the document. Press the SPACEBAR to end spell checking.

Exercises

1. Type the following names and addresses:

   Ann Slater
   2573 Curtiswood
   Plantation, Florida 33145

   Timothy McKee
   8964 Lorain Avenue
   Lakewood, Ohio 44106

   Check the spelling. If WordPerfect flags a proper name as misspelled, add it to your supplemental dictionary.

2. Type your full name. Use the Spell feature to determine if each part of it is in WordPerfect's dictionary. If it is not, add it to your supplemental dictionary.

3. Type the following lines, pressing ENTER at the end of each one:

   Abbreviations
   ATMOS - Atmosphere
   IDP - Integrated Data Processing
   OCS - Officer Candidate School
   SWAZ - Swaziland

Check the spelling. If WordPerfect flags a proper name or abbreviation as misspelled, add it to your supplemental dictionary.

4. Type the following paragraph:

Pygmalion was a sculptor who created a beautiful statue called Galatea, which Aphrodite brought to life. George Bernard Shaw wrote a play, called Pygmalion, that relied on this myth for some ideas. The film version of the musical, called My Fair Lady, starred Audrey Hepburn.

Check the spelling. Add any proper names that Word-Perfect suggests to your supplemental dictionary.

DELETE WORDS FROM THE SUPPLEMENTAL DICTIONARY

9.5

As you add more words to your supplemental dictionary, WordPerfect may take longer to check the spelling. If your supplemental dictionary has words that you use infrequently, you should delete them. Since WordPerfect stores all of the words you add in the file WP{WP}EN.SUP, this is the file from which you must remove the words.

To delete words from the dictionary:

a. Clear the screen.

b. Retrieve the file WP{WP}EN.SUP.

c. Move the cursor to a word that you want to remove.

d. Press CTRL-BACKSPACE and then DEL to remove the word and the hard return.

e. Repeat steps c and d for each word that you want to delete.

f. Save the file as WP{WP}EN.SUP, replacing the one on disk.

The instructions presented assume that the supplemental dictionary is in your default directory. If you installed Word-Perfect according to the directions in Appendix A, this will be the correct location. If your dictionary is in another directory, you will need to specify the pathname along with the filename when you retrieve the dictionary in step b.

Examples

1. In example 2 of section 9.4, you added "Adele" to the supplemental dictionary. If you do not expect to use this name often, you can delete it from the dictionary. First, on a clear screen, press the Retrieve (SHIFT-F10) key, type **wp{wp}en.sup**, and press ENTER. The screen looks like Figure 9-2. Next, since "Adele" is the first word, press CTRL-BACKSPACE and then DEL to remove the line from the document. Then, press the Save (F10) key. Since WordPerfect prompts you with the correct filename, press ENTER, and type a **y** to replace the old version of the dictionary with the new version.

2. In the example 1 of section 9.4, you saw that WordPerfect's dictionary does not contain some technical terms. You added "vambrace" to the supplemental dictionary. If you do not expect to use "vambrace" very often, you can delete this word from the dictionary. First, on a clear screen, press the Retrieve (SHIFT-F10) key, type **wp{wp}en.sup**, and press ENTER. Next, press the DOWN ARROW key until the cursor is at the "v" in "vambrace." Press CTRL-BACKSPACE and then DEL to remove the line from the document. Press the Save (F10) key. Since WordPerfect prompts you with the correct filename, press ENTER and type a **y** to replace the old version of the supplemental dictionary with the revised version.

Exercises

1. Remove the words that you added to your supplemental dictionary in the first exercise of section 9.4.

adele
aphrodite
atmos
audrey
curtiswood
galatea
idp
johansen
lakewood
lorain
mckee
ocs
pygmalion
slater
swaz
vambrace

C:\WP50\WP\WP\EN.SUP   Doc 1 Pg 1 Ln 1" Pos 1"

FIGURE 9-2.   WordPerfect supplemental dictionary file

2. Remove the words that you added to your supplemental dictionary in exercise 3 of section 9.4.

3. Remove the words that you added to your supplemental dictionary in exercise 4 of section 9.4.

REPLACE CORRECTLY SPELLED WORDS THAT ARE MISUSED

9.6

WordPerfect's Spell feature checks the spelling in a document; however, it does not check usage. You can have a document with correctly spelled words that are incorrect in usage. Typically, each person makes a mistake or two like this repeatedly. Such habitual mistakes might be caused by a typographical error, for example, typing "form" instead of "from." They might also be caused by the mistaken use of homonyms, as in the use of "their" for "there" or "to" for "too." If you are able to identify any mistakes that you tend to make on a regular basis, you will want to use the Replace feature as part of your document-correction process to check for these potential errors.

Examples

1. One common mistake that you can make is typing "form" when you want "from" and vice versa. First, type

   Enclosed is the order from received form your depart-ment.

   The "form" and "from" are in the wrong places. Since both words are spelled correctly, the Spell feature will not detect the error. To correct this error, press the Replace (ALT-F2) key. Type a **y** since you will need to confirm each replacement. When prompted for the text for which to search, type **from**, and press the UP ARROW, since you are searching from the bottom of the document. Next, press the Search (F2) key. When prompted for the text with which to replace it, type **form**, and press the Search (F2) key again. WordPerfect asks if you want to replace "from" with "form" as the fifth word in the sentence. Type a **y** to confirm the replacement.

   To make the second correction, press HOME, HOME, UP ARROW to move to the top of the document. Press the Replace (ALT-F2) key, and type a **y** to confirm each replacement. When prompted for the text for which to search, type **form**, and press the Search (F2) key. When prompted for the text with which to replace it, type **from**, and press the Search (F2) key.

WordPerfect prompts to see if you want to replace "form" with "from" as the fifth word in the sentence. Since you do not want this replaced, type an **n**. Next, WordPerfect checks to see if you want the second "form" in the sentence replaced. Type a **y** to confirm that you want this replaced.

2. Homonyms present a problem that WordPerfect's Spell feature cannot solve. *Homonyms* are words that sound the same but have different meanings. Examples are "to," "too," and "two." Whenever these words are used in a document, WordPerfect accepts the spelling, although the usage may not be correct. To illustrate the problem, type

Since the dinner had too speakers, the guests were encouraged not two ask to many questions.

This sentence has three occurrences of the homonyms, but none is used correctly: "Too" should have been "two," "two" should have been "to," and "to" which should have been "too." Checking the spelling does not correct these errors. Since "to" is such a common word, searching a document for every occurrence of the word may require a significant investment of time. You probably would not want to do this unless you made this type of mistake on a regular basis; proofreading each document carefully would be a better solution.

Exercises

1. Type the following sentence:

The fair four the bridge to get to the fare is for dollars.

Replace "fair" and "fare" so that each word is in the correct place. Replace "for" and "four" so that each word is in the correct place.

2. Type the following sentence:

Their demonstrating there new product over they're.

Use the Replace feature to place "their," "there," and "they're" in their proper contexts.

9.7   LOOK UP A WORD IN THE THESAURUS

One important aspect of communicating effectively is using words that convey your exact meaning. WordPerfect assists you with finding the right words with its on-line Thesaurus feature.

WordPerfect's thesaurus is similar to *Roget's Thesaurus*, with which you may be familiar. Although its function is the same, WordPerfect's Thesaurus feature is much easier to use. When you ask WordPerfect to find a word in its thesaurus, it provides a listing of synonyms, organized by parts of speech, such as noun, verb, and adjective. Some of the words listed will have synonym lists of their own, which you can review to expand the potential replacement options. The Thesaurus feature provides a handy check for words used infrequently. By looking at the list of synonyms for a word you have used, you can verify its correct usage in your sentence.

To find a word in WordPerfect's thesaurus:

a. Move the cursor to a word that you want to find.

b. Press the Thesaurus (ALT-F1) key.

c. Type the letter of a marked synonym for further synonyms, or select an action from the menu at the bottom of the screen.

d. Press the Cancel (F1) key, the Exit (F7) key, ENTER, or SPACEBAR to return to the document.

If the cursor is not on a word, WordPerfect normally uses the next word in the document. If you are at the end of the document or in a blank one, WordPerfect prompts you for the word you want to look up. If it cannot find a word in its thesaurus, WordPerfect prompts you for another word.

Examples

1. You can use the Thesaurus feature to find a word that you want as you are typing a document. For example, to find words that are similar in meaning to "meet," press the Thesaurus (ALT-F1) key. Since the document is blank, Word-Perfect prompts you for a word to look up. Type **meet**, and press ENTER.

   Now the screen looks like Figure 9-3. As you can see, WordPerfect separates the different parts of speech. Each word with a highlighted dot has its own entry in the thesaurus. Some entries also list antonyms, as shown in this example.

   Once you have looked over the synonyms for the word, press the Cancel (F1) key to return to the document, and type the word that you want to use.

2. You can use a word already in a document to find an entry in the thesaurus. First, type **use**. Although the cursor is to the right of the word, WordPerfect looks for "use" in its thesaurus when you press the Thesaurus (ALT-F1) key. The screen looks like Figure 9-4. Press the Cancel (F1) key to return to the document.

3. You can use synonyms in the thesaurus to find other synonyms. First, type **associate**. Then, press the Thesaurus (ALT-F1) key. The screen looks like Figure 9-5. Several of the words have dots next to them. You can find synonyms for

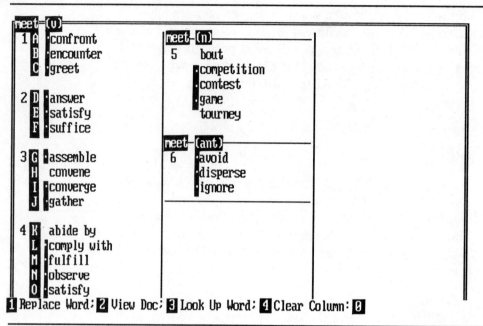

FIGURE 9-3.   Thesaurus entries for "meet"

any of those words by typing the letter to the left of the word.

To find other synonyms for "relate," type an **f.** Now, the screen looks like Figure 9-6. When you look up a synonym's thesaurus entry, WordPerfect puts the word's entry in the next blank column or in the rightmost column if all three are full. Only the current column contains letters next to the synonyms. You can select words to look up only from the current column. To change the current column, use the RIGHT ARROW or the LEFT ARROW key. To remove the current thesaurus entry, type a **4.** As a column is emptied, WordPerfect moves any remaining columns to the left to fill the emptied one. If the thesaurus entry in the rightmost column has more columns to display, it will use the blank column. Press the Cancel (F1) key to return to the document.

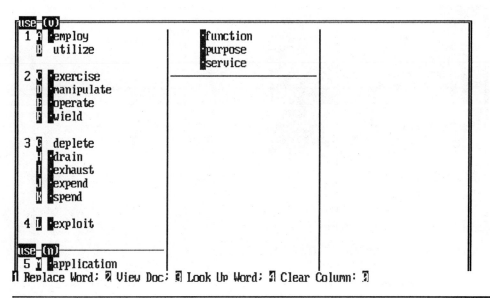

FIGURE 9-4.   Thesaurus entries for "use"

4. You can also look up synonyms for an entry that is not listed in the current thesaurus entry. You can do this when you find synonyms for one word to be unsatisfactory and want to see synonyms for another word. With this approach, you do not have to exit the Thesaurus, move to the other word and activate the feature again. First, type **business**. Then, press the Thesaurus (ALT-F1) key to display the thesaurus entry for "business."

Next, to find the entry for "product," type a **3**, type **product**, and press ENTER. Now the screen shows entries for both "business" and "product." Press the Cancel (F1) key to return to the document.

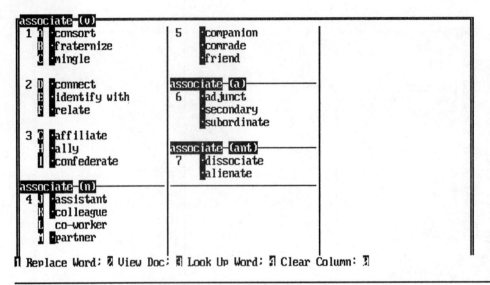

FIGURE 9-5.   Thesaurus entries for "associate"

Exercises

1. Find the thesaurus entry for "table."

2. Find the thesaurus entry for "adjoining."

3. Type **rich,** and find the thesaurus entry for that word. Use that entry to find the thesaurus entry for "prosperous."

4. Activate the Thesaurus feature, and find the entry for "limit." Use this entry to find the entry for "bar." Use this entry to find the entry for "board." Use this entry to find the entry for "cabinet." Use this entry to find the entry for "cupboard." Use this entry to find the entry for "press." Remove the "limit" and "bar" entries from the screen.

associate

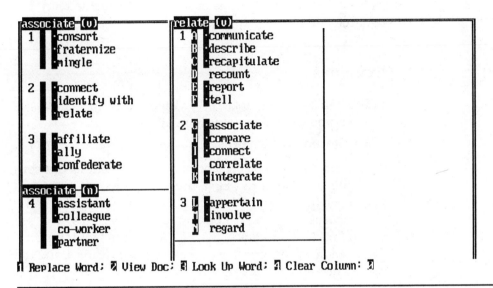

FIGURE 9-6.   Using a thesaurus entry to look up another thesaurus entry

REPLACE A WORD WITH A WORD FROM THE THESAURUS

9.8

You can use any of the thesaurus entries to replace a word in your document. The options available in the thesaurus entries allow you to add variety and color to your writing.

To replace a word with WordPerfect's Thesaurus feature:

a. Move the cursor to the word for which you want to find the thesaurus entry, or type the word.

b. Press the Thesaurus (ALT-F1) key.

c. Type a **1** to select the Replace Word option.

d. Type the letter identifying the word with which you want the original word replaced.

When you replace a word with the Thesaurus feature, WordPerfect inserts the replacement word using the same capitalization as the original word. For example, if the first letter of the original word is capitalized, the first letter of the replacement word is capitalized.

Examples

1. You can use the Replace Word feature of the Thesaurus when you are editing a document. Type

Jim Stevens is the newest associate at Stevens & Stevens.

You can find a replacement word for "associate" by consulting the Thesaurus. First, press CTRL-LEFT ARROW five times to move the cursor to the word "associate." Then, press the Thesaurus (ALT-F1) key. Looking at the selections, you see that "partner" is choice "M." To select this word, type a **1** and an **m**. WordPerfect exits the Thesaurus feature, and the sentence now looks like this:

Jim Stevens is the newest partner at Stevens & Stevens.

2. Although WordPerfect supplies lettered choices for only the active column, you can change the active column. Type

At the end of the day, the store manager totals the daily sales.

To find another word to use in place of "totals," press CTRL-LEFT ARROW four times to move the cursor to the word "totals." Next, press the Thesaurus (ALT-F1) key. The entries for "totals" use three columns, but only the leftmost column offers lettered choices. Looking through the entries, you can see the verb "add" in the second column. Before you can replace "totals" with "add," you must move the letters from the first column to the second column by pressing the RIGHT ARROW key. The screen now looks like

At the end of the day, the store manager `totals` the daily sales.

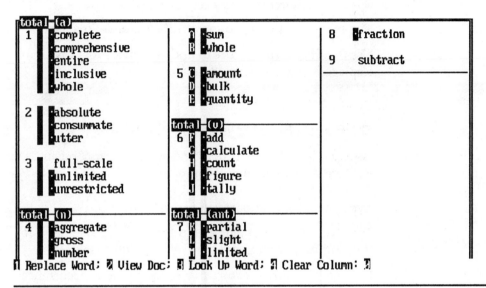

FIGURE 9-7.   Thesaurus entries for "total"

Figure 9-7. To replace "totals" with "add," type a **1** and an
f. Now, the sentence looks like this:

At the end of the day, the store manager add the daily sales.

Type an **s** to change "add" to "adds", and the replacement
is complete.

Exercises

1. Type the following sentence:

The report includes a three-page insert.

Use the Thesaurus feature to find another word for "insert." Replace it.

2. Type the following sentence:

The nylon division reported a 13% increase in sales.

Use the Thesaurus feature to find synonyms for "division." Replace "division" with "branch."

3. Type the following sentence:

The Bargain Business is having a 30% sale.

Use the Thesaurus feature to find synonyms for "business." Replace "business" with "company."

4. Type the following paragraph:

The land holdings include land for raising cattle, land for growing corn, and some land with a high resale value.

Use the Thesaurus feature to replace the four occurrences of "land" with "estate," "ranch," "farm," and "property," respectively. (Naturally, you would also want to add articles to make the sentence read correctly.)

EXERCISES

MASTERY
SKILLS CHECK

1. Type the following words as they appear:

Infomation
Capitalisation
Iregardless
Nevertheless

Use the Spell feature to check the spelling and correct any mistakes.

2. Type the following paragraph, including the errors:

Based on the results of a market study, the XYZ Corporation woll market its its personalized hubcaps nationaly. According to the survey, men are four times more likely to to buy them than women. Also, the product appeals primarily to buyers in the 19- to 34-year-old age group.

Use the Spell feature to correct errors.

3. Type the following letter as it appears:

Ingram Scott
536 S. Green Road
Cleveland Heights, Ohio 44108

Dear Iggy,

Here is the information that you requested. Please return it when you complete your project.

Sincerely,

Tabitha Marletti

Use the Spell feature to check the spelling. Add the proper names that WordPerfect does not recognize.

4. Remove from the supplementary dictionary the names that you added in exercise 3.

5. Type the following paragraph:

Because of the market study, the XYZ Corporation will market it's personalized hubcaps nationally. According to the survey, men are for times moor likely to buy them than women. Also, the product appeals primarily too individuals 19 two 34 years old.

Several words in the paragraph are homonyms. Use the Replace feature to correct the improper usage.

6. Use the Thesaurus feature to find synonyms for "bar," "block," and "light."

7. Type the following sentence:

   Reviewing the data revealed that people thought that the product was overpriced.

   Use the Thesaurus feature to find synonyms for "data." Replace "data" with "statistics."

INTEGRATED
SKILLS CHECK

(Do not clear the screen until you have completed the last exercise.)

1. Set all margins to 3".

2. Type the following paragraph, including the errors:

   The company is reducing its products aimed at the do-it-youself market. It is applying these resources towards manufaturing more higher-proced items. The company expects to increace sales by 15% with this stratagy.

   Use the Spell feature to correct errors.

3. Type the following paragraph, including the errors:

   Howard Moore designed an instant-strip wallpaper removr. The product can be used by inexperienced home owners. It removes wallpaper in half the time required for conventonal methods. The trade name for the product is Wall-Off.

   Check the spelling. Add the proper names to the supplemental dictionary if WordPerfect does not recognize them.

4. Move the paragraph created in exercise 3 to precede the paragraph created in exercise 2.

5. Block and copy the paragraph created in exercise 2. Place two additional copies in the document.

6. Type the following sentence:

   All of the McGregors had light complexions.

   Use the Thesaurus feature to find synonyms for "light."
   Replace "light" with **fair.**

7. Print the document.

8. Save the file as WORDS.

9. Remove from the supplemental dictionary the words that
   you added in exercise 3.

CHAPTER OBJECTIVES

After completing this chapter, you should be able to

10.1 Control widow and orphan lines

10.2 Use headers and footers on pages

10.3 Add footnotes

·10·

Page Breaks, Paragraph Breaks, and Other Options

The appearance of a document can help convey its message to the reader. This chapter covers some features that provide additional options for controlling the appearance of the text on a page. Widow and orphan protection features prevent single lines of a paragraph from appearing at the top or bottom of a page. By controlling the text placement in this way, you can ensure that your documents have greater clarity for the reader, since an entire paragraph can be presented without the need for the reader to turn the page.

In addition, this chapter introduces headers and footers, which allow you to add fixed lines of text at the top and bottom of every page. You can use these features to include, for example, your name or a report name and number on each page of a document. Footnotes provide the opportunity for removing technical data, equations, and bibliographic references from the main text. WordPerfect's features allow you to automatically number footnotes and print them at the end of your document.

SKILLS CHECK

(Do not clear the screen until you have completed the last exercise.)

1. Type the following paragraph, including the errors:

Cash dividents distribute earnings to the shareholders. Cash dividends have several important dates. The declaraction date is the date the board of directors declares the dividend. The date of record is the date that decides which stockholders are paid the dividend. The date of record is the day used to establish stock ownership. The payment date is the date that the company pays its dividents.

Use the Spell feature to check and correct the spelling.

2. Use the Thesaurus feature to replace "decides" with "determines."

3. Move the first sentence to the end of the paragraph.

4. Use the Search feature to find each occurrence of "date."

5. Delete the last sentence.

10.1   CONTROL WIDOW AND ORPHAN LINES

When you work on a document, the first or the last line of a paragraph may appear by itself on a page with the rest of the paragraph on the next or the preceding page. In WordPerfect, the first line of a paragraph placed alone at the bottom of a page is called a *widow*. The last line of a paragraph placed alone at the top of a page is called an *orphan*. Both can cause the reader to lose the line of thought of the paragraph. Widows and orphans also detract from the appearance of a document. WordPerfect lets you prevent widows and orphans from appearing in a document.

To prevent widows and orphans:

a. Move to the beginning of the document.

b. Press the Format (SHIFT-F8) key.

c. Type an l or a **1** to select the line-formatting options.

d. Type a **w** or a **9** to select Widow/Orphan Protection.

e. Type a **y** to activate the feature.

f. Press the Exit (F7) key.

When you enable Widow/Orphan Protection, Word-Perfect adds the hidden code [W/O On] to your document.

Examples

1. WordPerfect's Widow/Orphan Protection feature prevents the last line of a paragraph from appearing as an orphan at the top of a page. To see the effect of orphans while minimizing typing, you can increase the top and bottom margins to limit the amount of text on a page. If you set the top and bottom margins to 5", only six lines will display on each page. First, press the Format (SHIFT-F8) key, and type a **p** and an **m**. Type a **5** and press ENTER for the top margin, and type a **5** and press ENTER for the bottom margin. Press the Exit (F7) key to return to the document.

Next, type

The company picnic is scheduled for July 15 at Waverly Park. A full day of activities is planned for employees and their families. Food, games, clowns, bingo, and prizes are a few of the attractions. This year's food selections include fried chicken, hamburgers, hot dogs, roast beef, cakes, pies, ice cream, and an array of salads. Please stop by the Human Resources office before July 1 to pick up your tickets.

Now, the screen looks like Figure 10-1. The last line of the paragraph is an orphan at the top of a new page.

Move to the top of the document by pressing HOME, HOME, UP ARROW. Press the Format (SHIFT-F8) key, and type an 1 for Line

---

```
The company picnic is scheduled for July 15 at Waverly Park.  A
full day of activities is planned for employees and their families.
Food, games, clowns, bingo, and prizes are a few of the
attractions.  This year's food selections include fried chicken,
hamburgers, hot dogs, roast beef, cakes, pies, ice cream, and an
array of salads.  Please stop by the Human Resources office before
```

```
July 1 to pick up your tickets.
```


                                              Doc 1 Pg 2 Ln 1.83" Pos 1"

FIGURE 10-1.   Orphan line at the top of a page

and a **w** for Widow. Type a **y** to turn on Widow/Orphan Protection. Press the Exit (F7) key to return to the document. Press the DOWN ARROW key to move to the bottom of the paragraph, which now looks like the one in Figure 10-2. The last two lines of the paragraph are both on the second page.

2. Preventing widows also makes documents easier to read. You can obtain protection from widows with the same procedure. First, clear the current document, and set the top and bottom margins to 5″ by pressing the Format (SHIFT-F8) key and typing a **p** and an **m**. Type a 5, press ENTER,

---

```
The company picnic is scheduled for July 15 at Waverly Park.  A
full day of activities is planned for employees and their families.
Food, games, clowns, bingo, and prizes are a few of the
attractions.  This year's food selections include fried chicken,
hamburgers, hot dogs, roast beef, cakes, pies, ice cream, and an
```

```
array of salads.  Please stop by the Human Resources office before
July 1 to pick up your tickets.
```

Doc 1 Pg 2 Ln 5.33″ Pos 1″

FIGURE 10-2. Orphan eliminated with Widow/Orphan Protection

and type a 5 and press ENTER again. Press the Exit (F7) key to return to the document. Type

The company picnic is scheduled for July 15 at Waverly Hills Park. A full day of activities is planned for employees and their families. This year's special activities include softball, bingo, horseshoes, an executive dunktank, carnival rides, and a puppet show.
You can pick up ticket books for your entire family any day before July 15. These books include coupons for the carnival rides and door prize registration forms. Special food stands have been set up for employees. Coupons are not required at these stands.

```
The company picnic is scheduled for July 15 at Waverly Hills Park.
A full day of activities is planned for employees and their
families.  This year's special activities include softball, bingo,
horseshoes, an executive dunktank, carnival rides, and a puppet
show.
You can pick up ticket books for your entire family any day before
```

July 15. These books include coupons for the carnival rides and door prize registration forms. Special food stands have been set up for employees. Coupons are not required at these stands.

Doc 1 Pg 2 Ln 1.5" Pos 1"

FIGURE 10-3.   Widow line at the bottom of a page

The screen looks like Figure 10-3. The first line of the second paragraph displays as a widow at the bottom of page 1.

Move to the top of the document by pressing HOME, HOME, UP ARROW. Invoke Widow and Orphan Protection by pressing the Format (SHIFT-F8) key. Type an l for Line and a w for Widow/Orphan Protection. Type a y to enable the feature, and press the Exit (F7) key to return to the document. When you move the cursor down the screen, the text is rearranged as in Figure 10-4. The widow line now appears on the second page along with the rest of the paragraph.

The company picnic is scheduled for July 15 at Waverly Hills Park. A full day of activities is planned for employees and their families. This year's special activities include softball, bingo, horseshoes, an executive dunktank, carnival rides, and a puppet show.

You can pick up ticket books for your entire family any day before July 15. These books include coupons for the carnival rides and door prize registration forms. Special food stands have been set up for employees. Coupons are not required at these stands.

Doc 1 Pg 2 Ln 1.66" Pos 1"

FIGURE 10-4.   Widow eliminated with Widow/Orphan Protection

Exercises

1. Type the following paragraphs with the top and bottom margins set to 5". Include a blank line between the paragraphs when you type them.

   The company's contingent liabilities are as follows: The company has guaranteed a loan on behalf of a subsidiary that was recently spun off. The loan is for $500,000 and matures on March 30, 1990.

   Estimated loss from a pending lawsuit is $65,000. The suit should be concluded within the next two months.

   Prevent widows and orphans.

2. Type the following paragraph with the top and bottom margins set to 5":

   Cost-flow assumptions affect inventory valuation. If a company uses the LIFO method, it assumes that the last inventory items purchased are the first ones sold. This assumption makes the cost of goods sold closely reflect the current cost of the inventory sold. On the other hand, the ending inventory is valued at prior-period purchase costs. This method is best used when purchase costs are rising and the inventory turnover is low.

   Prevent widows and orphans. Save the document as LIFO.

3. Retrieve LIFO. Remove the top and bottom margin settings. Set the margins to 1" on top and 9" at the bottom. Press the DOWN ARROW key to reformat the paragraph. Save the document and clear the screen.

4. Retrieve LIFO. Leaving the top and bottom margins intact, reset the left and right margins to 3" on each side. Press the DOWN ARROW key to reformat the paragraph. Save the document and clear the screen.

USE HEADERS AND FOOTERS ON PAGES 10.2

Headers are lines of text that appear at the top of every page of printed output. *Footers* are lines of text that appear at the bottom of every printed page. Header and footer lines are handy options. WordPerfect provides two headers and footers so that you can use one header or footer on even-numbered pages and another on odd-numbered pages. The first header or footer you create is referred to as header or footer A. The second is referred to as header or footer B. WordPerfect supports many formatting features (for example, bold and centering) in headers and footers.

Neither headers nor footers display on the screen with the text. To keep a header or a footer from printing, or to make changes to either, you need to issue a command.

To include a header or footer on every page:

a. Move the cursor to the top of the first page on which you want a header or footer.

b. Press the Format (SHIFT-F8) key.

c. Type a **p** or a **2** to select page-formatting options.

d. Type an **h** or a **3** for Headers or an **f** or a **4** for Footers.

e. Type an **a** or a **1** for header or footer A, or type a **b** or a **2** for header or footer B.

f. Type a **p** or a **2** to have the header or footer appear on every page.

g. Type the header or footer text.

h. Press the Exit (F7) key to return to the page-formatting menu.

i. Press the Exit (F7) key to return to the document.

Headers and Footers do not appear on your screen with the document; they appear only when you print or preview the document. WordPerfect puts the header on the first line after the top margin, using additional lines as required for multiline headers. It adds a blank line between the header and the main part of the document. For a footer, WordPerfect stops printing the body of the document before reaching the bottom margin, skips a line, and prints the footer.

To stop printing a header or footer, move to the beginning of the first page that will not have the header or footer. Perform steps b through e, as you did to create the header or footer, type a **d** or a **1**, and press the Exit (F7) key.

You can also remove a header or footer for an entire document by deleting the hidden code for it. The hidden code for a header is [Header X:Y;Z]. "X" represents either A or B, depending on which header the code represents. "Y" represents the number that you selected in step f to indicate where the header will occur. "Z" represents the text in the header. It ends with an ellipsis if the header contains more than 50 characters. Footers use the same hidden code, but with the word "Footer" in place of "Header."

Examples

1. You can use headers to place a repeating line at the top of each page of a document. First, press the Format (SHIFT-F8) key. Type a **p** and an **h**, and type an **a** for header A. Next, type a **p** to have the header appear on every page. Then, type

   1989 Financial Report

   Finally, press the Exit (F7) key twice to return to the document. The header does not appear on the screen. Type the following lines of text in the document:

   Consolidated Changes in Financial Position
   Limestone Corporation
   Sources of Funds:
   Operations:

   When you press the Print (SHIFT-F7) key and type a **v** and a **1**, the screen looks like Figure 10-5. The header that appears on this page will appear on every page in the document.

2. You can use WordPerfect's formatting features in headers and footers. First, press the Format (SHIFT-F8) key. Type a **p**

FIGURE 10-5. View showing header and text

and an **f**, and type an **a** for footer A. Next, type a **p** to have the footer appear on every page. Press the Center (SHIFT-F6) key and the Underline (F8) key, and type

Prepared on 7/1/89

Press the Exit (F7) key twice. Press the Print (SHIFT-F7) key, type a **v** and a **1**, and press the HOME and DOWN ARROW key to move to the bottom of the page. The screen looks like this:

The footer line on this page will appear at the bottom of each page of the document.

3. You can print page numbers as part of a header or footer. Placing the page number in the header or footer gives you additional control over how WordPerfect prints the page numbers, since you can add the word "page" or other constants before or after the page number. First, press the Format (SHIFT-F8) key. Type a **p** and an **h**, and type an **a** for header A. Next, type a **p** to have the header appear on every page. Press the Flush Right (ALT-F6) key, type **Page**, and press the SPACEBAR. To have WordPerfect automatically place page numbers on the line, hold down the CTRL key and type a **b**. The screen looks like this:

Page ^B

Finally, press the Exit (F7) key twice. When you press the Print (SHIFT-F7) key and type a **v**, the screen looks like this:

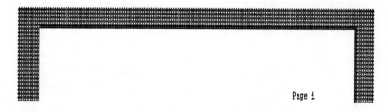

WordPerfect replaces "^B" with the appropriate page numbers when it prints documents.

4. You can define two headers or footers for a document. For example, you may want one header on even pages and another on odd pages. First, press the Format (SHIFT-F8) key. Next, type a **p** and an **h** and type an **A** for header A. Next, type an **o** to have the header appear on odd-numbered pages. Type: **1989 Financial Report**. Next, press the Exit (F7) key once to return to the page-formatting options. Type an **h** and a **b** for header B. Type a **v** to have the header appear on even-numbered pages. Press the Flush Right (ALT-F6) key, type **Ace Corporation**, and press the Exit (F7) key twice. Press the CTRL-ENTER key twice to create additional pages in the document. When you press the Print (SHIFT-F7) key and type a **v** and a **4**, the screen looks like this:

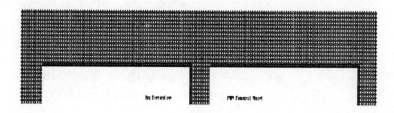

Exercises

1. Create a header that says "Acme Inc. Income Statement". Preview how WordPerfect will print it.

2. Create a footer that displays your name in boldface. Preview how WordPerfect will print it.

3. Create a header consisting of the page number encased between hyphens and centered on the page. Preview how WordPerfect will print it.

4. Create a header that prints the page numbers on odd-numbered pages and your name on even-numbered pages. Preview how WordPerfect will print it.

10.3   ADD FOOTNOTES

Footnotes allow you to store supplemental information in notes at the bottom of each page. Financial reports, legal documents, and academic research papers normally contain footnoted text. The footnote may contain explanatory information or a reference to a source for a specific piece of information in the document.

WordPerfect automatically inserts sequential reference numbers for footnotes. Each footnote number is printed as superscript; that is, it appears slightly smaller and higher than the other text on the line. WordPerfect prints each footnote at the bottom of the page containing the footnote reference. If a footnote is long or near the bottom of a page, WordPerfect allows space for a minimum of three lines of footnote text on the page and continues the footnote at the bottom of the next page. A single footnote can contain as many as 16,000 lines.

To create a footnote:

a. Press the Footnote (CTRL-F7) key.

b. Type an **f** or a **1** for the Footnote options.

c. Type a **c** or a **1** to create a footnote.

d. Type the footnote text.

e. Press the Exit (F7) key.

    A [Footnote[Note Num]] code is inserted in the document at the location of each footnote. You can delete a footnote by removing the hidden code or by deleting the footnote number that displays on the screen.

Examples

1. You can use a footnote to identify the source of a quote. Type

Getting over the hurdle of learning something new can feel uncomfortable and takes both time and practice, so you must be patient with yourself as you learn WordPerfect. Work at your own pace. Tackle a chapter or two a day, whatever is appropriate for you. And make sure that you don't just read the chapters, but that you follow along on the computer, step by step. Pretty soon you'll be using WordPerfect like a pro.

Once you have typed this quote, press the Footnote (CTRL-F7) key. Type an **f** and a **c** to create a footnote. Next, type a space and the following footnote text:

Mella Mincberg, WordPerfect Made Easy**, Osborne/ McGraw-Hill, 1988, pp. xiii-xiv.**

Now, the screen looks like this:

```
    1 Mella Mincberg, WordPerfect Made Easy, Osborne/McGraw-Hill,
1988, pp. xiii-xiv.
```

Finally, press the Exit (F7) key. If you are using a color monitor, the footnote number may appear in a different color to indicate that it is superscript.

2. WordPerfect's Footnote feature keeps track of the footnote numbers as you add or delete footnotes. To illustrate this, you need at least two footnotes. First, increase the bottom margin so that you will be able to see the text and the footnotes together in a print preview. Press the Format (SHIFT-F8) key, type a **p** and an **m**, and press ENTER. Then type an **8**, press ENTER, and press the Exit (F7) key. Next, type

The company's EPS is 3.48. The dividend date is August 15.

Move the cursor to the end of the first sentence. Press the Footnote (CTRL-F7) key and type an **f** and a **c**. Press the SPACEBAR, and type the footnote text:

$1,169,280 1988 income / 336,000 shares

Press the Exit (F7) key to return to the document. For the second footnote, move to the end of the second sentence, press the Footnote (CTRL-F7) key, and type an **f** and a **c**. Press the SPACEBAR, and type

The date of record is August 1.

Press the Exit (F7) key to return to the document. When you press the Print (SHIFT-F7) key and type a **v** and a **1**, the text and the footnotes look like this:

The company's EPS is 3.48.[1] The dividend date is August 15.[2]

_____

[1] $1,169,280 1988 income / 336,000 shares

[2] The date of record is August 1.

Do not clear the screen. Use these entries in the next example.

3. You can delete a footnote without invoking the menu. When you move or delete a footnote, WordPerfect auto-

matically adjusts the footnote numbering. To remove a footnote, move the cursor to the footnote number that you want to eliminate, and press DEL. Using the footnotes from example 2, move to the first footnote, and press DEL. When WordPerfect prompts you for confirmation that it should delete the footnote, type a **y**. Press END to make WordPerfect reformat the other footnote number. Now, the screen looks like this:

The company's EPS is 3.48. The dividend date is August 15.1

Do not clear the screen. Use these entries in the next example.

4. You can edit footnote text. Press the Footnote (CTRL-F7) key, and type an **f** for Footnote, an **e** for Edit, and a **1** for the number of the footnote that you want to edit. Next, move the cursor to the "A" in "August 1," press CTRL-END, and type **July 31** and a period. The screen looks like this:

1The date of record is July 31.

Press the Exit (F7) key to return to the document.

Exercises

(Do not clear the screen between exercises unless instructed to do so.)

1. Type the following:

   WordPerfect Made Easy is written for beginning and intermediate users.

   Add a footnote using the following information.

Mella Mincberg, <u>WordPerfect Made Easy</u>, Osborne/McGraw-Hill, 1988, pp. xiii-xiv.

Clear the screen.

2. Type the first line from each of the following pairs of lines, and use the second line in each pair as a footnote:

Once upon a time,. . .
Grimm Brothers Fairy Tales

Mary had a little lamb
Mother Goose

The Goose That Laid a Golden Egg
Aesop's Fables

3. Block the first line and its footnote number, and move the line to the end of the document.

4. Edit the footnote for the Grimm Brothers to read "Grimm's Fairy Tales."

EXERCISES

MASTERY
SKILLS CHECK

(Do not clear the screen until you have completed the last exercise.)

1. Set the bottom margin to 9". Type the following:

Preparing a Trial Balance

When you prepare a trial balance, you must make several adjusting entries to properly reflect your income and expenses. You must include prepaid expenses as an asset rather than as an expense. You must include unearned revenue, such as unredeemed gift certificates, as a liability. You must include accrued expenses as expenses.

Invoke the Widow/Orphan Protection feature.

2. Insert a page break between the title and the paragraph. Add the following footnote at the end of the paragraph:

   For example, if half of the period between pay days has elapsed, you must include half of the expected salaries and wages.

3. Add the following footnote onto the end of the second sentence:

   For example, if you pay an insurance premium for two years at the beginning of this year, half of what you paid is classified as an expense for this year, and half is a prepaid expense and classified as an asset.

4. Edit the footnote that you created in exercise 3 so that it says

   For example, if you pay a $600 premium insurance for two years at the beginning of this year, $300 is classified as an expense for last year, and $300 is a prepaid expense and classified as an asset.

5. Create a header for every page that consists of the title that you typed in exercise 1. Remove the title from the body of the text.

6. Create a footer with your name in it to appear on odd pages.

   Preview the document. Page through it.

(Do not clear the screen until you have completed the last exercise.)

INTEGRATED
SKILLS CHECK

1. Type the following addresses.

Johann Sebastian
390 Market Street
Newport, Rhode Island 01307
Karl Davis
7439 Coral Drive
Stanford, CA 94237
Angus Fuller
764 Ovine Trail
Kansas City, Missouri 12305

Insert a hard page break after each address.

2. Go to the bottom of the first page and type the following letter:

According to our records, we have not received your subscription renewal for our newsletter. To continue to receive this publication, send the enclosed order blank and a check for $35.00.

         Sincerely,

         Elsie Brown
         Secretary, United Dairy Farmers

Use the Thesaurus feature to review synonyms for "continue" and "receive."

3. Use the Spell feature to check the spelling of the letter.

4. Insert the following footnote after the word "publication":

United Dairy Farmers, <u>Dairy Moo-ving</u>

5. Edit the footnote you just typed to include the publisher, Angus Magazines.

6. Block and copy the letter to follow the other addresses on the other pages.

7. Add a right-justified header that contains your name.

CHAPTER OBJECTIVES

After completing this chapter, you should be able to

·11·

Managing Files

You have already learned that saving files to disk protects your investment in a document. Once a document is stored on a disk, you can retrieve it again even if the system goes down and you lose the copy of the document in memory. There are other file options that increase your control over the documents you store on disk. Understanding these options gives you the power to manage your resources effectively.

In this chapter, you will learn how to create backup copies. You will learn how to create and manage subdirectories for organizing the many documents you create. You will learn how to rename files on the disk and to delete those you no longer need. You will learn how to search for a file based on text stored within the file. You will see how displaying the contents of the file without retrieving it provides a quick way to verify a file selection. You will learn how to create a document summary to provide an overview of a document.

With so many file options to cover, you will find that this chapter is a little longer than some of the others. Your investment of time will prove worthwhile, however, since you will learn a whole tool kit of skills that can be applied to every WordPerfect document you create.

SKILLS CHECK

(Do not clear the screen until you have completed the last exercise.)

1. Type the following lines exactly as shown:

    Companies often issue these types of equity:
    Common stock - This stock closely reflects the value of the company. Stockholders receive a return in value by an increase in price and dividends. Common stockholders have voting control of the company.
    Preferred stock - This stock must pay a required dividend before the common stockholders receive dividends. Preferred stockholders frequently do not have voting rights.
    Convertible bonds - These are bonds that the bond holders may redeem for other stock.

    Move the paragraph about bonds betweeen the two stock paragraphs.

2. Use WordPerfect's Spell feature to check for spelling errors.

3. Use the Thesaurus feature to replace "redeem" with **exchange**.

4. Set the top and bottom margins to 5".

5. Prevent widow and orphan lines.

6. Add the following footnote at the end of the convertible bonds paragraph:

Usually in exchange for common stock

7. Save the document as STOCKS, and clear the screen.

CREATE BACKUP COPIES   11.1

A *backup copy* is a second or third copy of a document that you can retrieve if something happens to the original document. Whenever you have a document that would take a significant amount of time to recreate, you should consider creating a backup copy. It is best to create a backup copy of your document on another disk in the event the disk containing the original is damaged. On a hard disk system, this may mean copying the document during a full disk backup or making a copy on a floppy disk: On a floppy disk system, creating a backup means saving a copy of the document to a second floppy disk.

To create a backup copy of a document:

a. Press the List Files (F5) key.

b. Type the pathname for the directory of the document you wish to back up if it is different from the one displayed.

c. Press ENTER.

d. Move the highlight to the file that you want to back up.

e. Type a **c** or an **8.**

f. Type the drive, directory, and filename under which you want to store the backup of the file.

g. Press ENTER.

h. Press the Exit (F7) key to return to the document.

You can also create backups by retrieving a file and saving it under a different name or in a different directory.

Examples

1. Whether you use a hard disk or a floppy disk system, you can back up a file to a disk and place the backup where it is safe from harm. First, type

   The company is expanding its product line to include more products for the older generation.

   Next, save it as OLDER by pressing the Exit (F7) key, pressing ENTER, typing **older,** and pressing ENTER twice.

   To back up the file, place a disk in drive A, and press the List Files (F5) key. The bottom of the screen looks like this:

   `Dir C:\WP50\*.*`   (Type = to change default Dir)

   Since this is the directory that you want, press ENTER. The screen now looks like Figure 11-1.

   Next, move the highlight to the file named OLDER. Type a c. WordPerfect displays this prompt on the status line:

   `Copy this file to:`

   Type **a:older** for the drive and filename of the backup file, and press ENTER. You can use the same filename because you are copying the file to another disk. If you were storing the backup file in the same directory on the hard disk, you would have to use a different name.

   Finally, press the Exit (F7) key to return to the document.

2. You can also create a backup copy on the same disk by using a different filename. You may create this type of backup when you want to make changes to a document yet retain a copy of the original. First, type

The company is instituting a pension plan for all salaried employees. This pension plan will be operated by a trust fund created for this purpose. The pension plan is a defined-contribution plan. The company's contribution is a percentage of each employee's yearly salary. The contract came into effect April 30, 1989.

Next, save it as PENSION by pressing the Save (F10) key and typing **pension**. Press the List Files (F5) key. Since you want to back up a file from the directory that WordPerfect displays in the prompt, press ENTER.

Next, move the highlight to the PENSION filename. Type a **c**, type **pensions**, and press ENTER. Press the Exit (F7) key to return to the document.

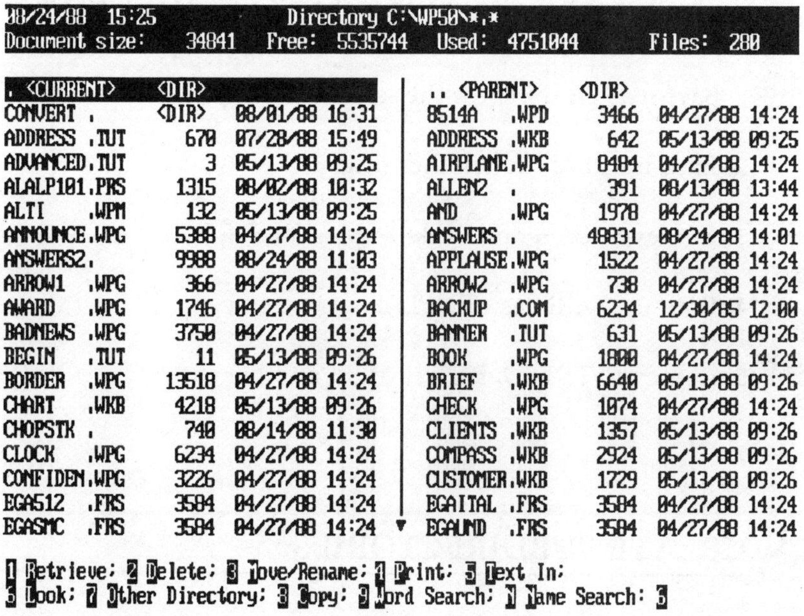

```
08/24/88  15:25            Directory C:\WP50\*.*
Document size:     34041   Free:  5535744   Used:  4751044      Files:  280

.  <CURRENT>    <DIR>                      ..  <PARENT>    <DIR>
CONVERT  .     <DIR>    08/01/88 16:31     8514A    .WPD     3466   04/27/88 14:24
ADDRESS  .TUT     670   07/28/88 15:49     ADDRESS  .WKB      642   05/13/88 09:25
ADVANCED .TUT       3   05/13/88 09:25     AIRPLANE .WPG     8404   04/27/88 14:24
ALALP101 .PRS    1315   08/02/88 10:32     ALLEN2   .         391   08/13/88 13:44
ALTI     .WPM     132   05/13/88 09:25     AND      .WPG     1970   04/27/88 14:24
ANNOUNCE .WPG    5388   04/27/88 14:24     ANSWERS  .       48831   08/24/88 14:01
ANSWERS2 .       9988   08/24/88 11:03     APPLAUSE .WPG     1522   04/27/88 14:24
ARROW1   .WPG     366   04/27/88 14:24     ARROW2   .WPG      738   04/27/88 14:24
AWARD    .WPG    1746   04/27/88 14:24     BACKUP   .COM     6234   12/30/85 12:00
BADNEWS  .WPG    3750   04/27/88 14:24     BANNER   .TUT      631   05/13/88 09:26
BEGIN    .TUT      11   05/13/88 09:26     BOOK     .WPG     1800   04/27/88 14:24
BORDER   .WPG   13518   04/27/88 14:24     BRIEF    .WKB     6640   05/13/88 09:26
CHART    .WKB    4218   05/13/88 09:26     CHECK    .WPG     1074   04/27/88 14:24
CHOPSTK  .        740   08/14/88 11:30     CLIENTS  .WKB     1357   05/13/88 09:26
CLOCK    .WPG    6234   04/27/88 14:24     COMPASS  .WKB     2924   05/13/88 09:26
CONFIDEN .WPG    3226   04/27/88 14:24     CUSTOMER .WKB     1729   05/13/88 09:26
EGA512   .FRS    3504   04/27/88 14:24     EGAITAL  .FRS     3504   04/27/88 14:24
EGASMC   .FRS    3504   04/27/88 14:24  ▼  EGAUND   .FRS     3504   04/27/88 14:24

1 Retrieve; 2 Delete; 3 Move/Rename; 4 Print; 5 Text In;
6 Look; 7 Other Directory; 8 Copy; 9 Word Search; N Name Search: 6
```

FIGURE 11-1.   List Files screen

3. You can also back up a file by saving it with two different names. You can use this method when you want to back up the file that you are currently using. First, type

The company is paying accrued pension costs over a fifteen-year period and will amortize the costs over a twenty-year period.

Save the file by pressing the Save (F10) key, typing **accrue**, and pressing ENTER. To create a backup copy, press the Save (F10) key, type **accrue2**, and press ENTER.

Exercises

1. Type the following paragraph:

The pension plan is expected to earn 6% per year. New employees become vested in the plan after five years with the company.

Save it as PLAN. Clear the screen. Back up the file as EARN.

2. Back up PLAN to another disk.

3. Retrieve PLAN and back it up as VESTED.

4. Back up EARN as PENPLAN.

5. Retrieve VESTED. Back it up to another disk.

11.2   CREATE SUBDIRECTORIES

Subdirectories are logical divisions of a disk that you can create and use to organize data. If you placed all of your documents on a hard disk without any organization, after a

while you would have difficulty finding particular documents, since you would need to read through a list of all the
files on the disk. To make it easier, you can place related
documents or specific types of documents in subdirectories.

You can create just a few subdirectories or many, depending on how many ways you categorize the documents that
you create. If you installed WordPerfect as instructed in
Appendix A or your WordPerfect manual, you already have
your first subdirectory, named WP50. You can create additional subdirectories on this same level, or you can create
subdirectories beneath it.

To create a subdirectory:

a. Press the List Files (F5) key.

b. Type an equal sign (=).

c. Type the name for the new directory.

d. Press ENTER.

e. Type a **y** to create the subdirectory.

Another method for creating a subdirectory is

a. Press the List Files (F5) key.

b. Press ENTER.

c. Type an **o** or a **7** to change directories.

d. Type the name for the new directory.

e. Press ENTER.

f. Type a **y** to create the directory.

g. Press the Exit (F7) key to return to the document.

Subdirectories are directories within an existing directory.
The first-level directory is the root directory. To indicate the
root directory on drive C, you would type **c:**. You use a

pathname to tell the computer where to find the files in a subdirectory. A full pathname includes the drive, a colon, a backslash, and any subdirectory levels. To indicate a subdirectory named LEGAL in the root directory on drive C, you would type **c:\legal**. If LEGAL were a subdirectory under the WP50 subdirectory, you would type **c:\wp50\legal**.

Examples

1. You can create a subdirectory on the same level as Word-
   Perfect. You might do this to put all your budget files into
   one subdirectory to use with different software packages.

   First, press the List Files (F5) key.

   Next, type =**c:\budget** and press ENTER. The screen now
   displays this prompt:

   `Create c:\budget? (Y/N) No`

   Type a **y** to create the subdirectory. The structure of the
   disk now looks like Figure 11-2.

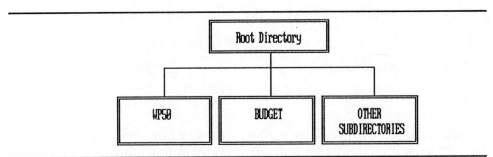

FIGURE 11-2.   Creating a subdirectory at the same level as WP50

2. You can create a subdirectory below the WordPerfect
subdirectory. For example, you can create a subdirectory
for all of the form letters that you use in WordPerfect. First,
press the List Files (F5) key. Type **c:\wp50** and press ENTER.
Next, press ENTER and type an **o**. Type **formlett** for the
subdirectory name, and press ENTER. Since you did not
specify a different pathname, WordPerfect places the new
subdirectory under the current one. Type a **y** when Word-
Perfect prompts you to confirm that you want to create the
subdirectory. The screen now looks like this:

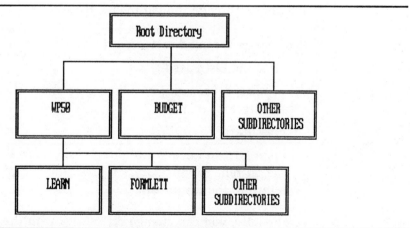

FIGURE 11-3.   Creating a subdirectory under WP50

The structure of the disk now looks like Figure 11-3. Press the Exit (F7) key to return to the document.

Exercises

1. Create a subdirectory called FINANCE on the same level as the WordPerfect subdirectory.

2. Create a subdirectory called LETTERS beneath the Word-Perfect subdirectory.

3. Create a subdirectory of FINANCE called FINC1989.

4. Create a subdirectory of FINANCE called FINC1990.

11.3   CHANGE SUBDIRECTORIES

It is not necessary to work in one subdirectory for an entire WordPerfect session. You can access files without changing subdirectories by typing the full pathname for each file. If you plan to work within a different subdirectory for a while, however, it is easier to make that subdirectory active. You can then save and retrieve files in the subdirectory without having to provide the pathname every time.

To change the subdirectory:

a. Press the List Files (F5) key.

b. Type an equal sign (=) followed by the pathname for the subdirectory that you want to use.

c. Press ENTER.

d. Press ENTER to have WordPerfect display the list of files for the current subdirectory, or press the Cancel (F1) key to return to the document.

Optionally, you can change directories with these steps:

a. Press the List Files (F5) key.

b. Press the ENTER key.

c. Type an **o** or a **7** to use another subdirectory.

d. Type the pathname of the subdirectory that you want to use.

e. Press ENTER to have WordPerfect display the list of files for the current subdirectory.

f. Press the Exit (F7) key to return to the current document.

You can also change subdirectories by moving the highlight on the List Files screen to the subdirectory that you want and pressing ENTER twice. This method is more practical when the subdirectory that you want is contained within the current subdirectory.

Examples

1. You can change directories from the List Files menu. You can use the BUDGET subdirectory that you created in example 1 of section 11.2. First, press the List Files (F5) key. Next, type **c:**, press ENTER, and type an **o**. Next, type **budget**, and press ENTER twice. Press the Exit (F7) key to return to the document. When you subsequently save or retrieve a file, WordPerfect will use the BUDGET subdirectory unless you provide a different pathname.

2. You can change directories immediately after pressing the List Files (F5) key. This approach is actually the simplest method to use to make the change. To change to the FORMLETT subdirectory that you created in example 2 in section 11.2, first press the List Files (F5) key, and type an equal sign (=). Then type **\wp50\formlett**, and press ENTER twice. WordPerfect displays the contents of this subdirectory. Press the Exit (F7) key to return to the document. When you later save or retrieve a file, WordPerfect will use this subdirectory unless you provide a different pathname.

Exercises

1. Change to the FINANCE subdirectory, which you created in exercise 1 in section 11.2.

2. Change to the LETTERS subdirectory, which you created in exercise 2 in section 11.2.

3. Change to the FINC1989 subdirectory, which you created in exercise 3 in section 11.2.

4. Change to the FINC1990 subdirectory, which you created in exercise 4 in section 11.2.

5. Change to the WP50 subdirectory.

11.4   DELETE FILES

Even when you create a document for one-time use, you normally want to save it in case you need another copy of the document. Periodically, you should review the contents of your disk to ensure that it is not cluttered with files that you no longer need. Unneeded files waste disk space and slow access time. WordPerfect provides an easy-to-use option that removes files that are no longer needed.

To delete a file from disk:

a. Press the List Files (F5) key.

b. Type the pathname if you wish to change subdirectories.

c. Press ENTER.

d. Move the highlight to the file that you want to delete.

e. Type a **d** or a **2**.

f. Type a **y** to confirm that you want to delete the file.

g. Press the Exit (F7) key.

Examples

1. You can delete a backup file that you no longer need. To delete the backup file that you made in example 2 of section 11.1, first press the List Files (F5) key.

Next, press ENTER, since WordPerfect displays the subdirectory that you want to use. Move the highlight to the file PENSIONS. When you type a **d**, WordPerfect displays this prompt:

`Delete C:\WP50\PENSIONS? (Y/N) No`

Type a **y** to confirm that you want to delete this file. Press the Exit (F7) key.

2. You can delete a subdirectory with the Delete option in the List Files menu. For example, you can delete the FORM-LETT subdirectory created in example 2 in section 11.2. First, press the List Files (F5) key, and press ENTER, since WordPerfect displays the subdirectory that you want to use. Move the highlight to the FORMLETT subdirectory that you want to delete. When you type a **d**, WordPerfect displays this prompt:

`Delete C:\WP50\FORMLETT? (Y/N) No`

Type a **y** to confirm that you want to delete this subdirectory, and press the Exit (F7) key. A subdirectory must be empty before you can delete it. If the FORMLETT subdirectory had contained any files, you would have had to delete all the files in it before you could delete the subdirectory.

Exercises

1. Delete the file PLAN, which you created in exercise 2 of section 11.1, from the disk in drive A.

2. Delete the subdirectory LETTERS, which you created in exercise 2 in section 11.2.

3. Delete the subdirectory FINC1989, which you created in exercise 3 in section 11.2.

4. Delete the subdirectory FINC1990, which you created in exercise 4 in section 11.2.

11.5 RENAME FILES

You should always give files names that are meaningful. Using standards that apply to all filenames provides a consistent way to name files. You can rename files on disk that do not conform to the rules that you establish. This renaming process does not require you to recreate the file; the only thing you change is the filename. When you choose the new filename, you need to use a name that is unique for the current disk or subdirectory.

To rename a file:

a. Press the List Files (F5) key.

b. Type the pathname if you wish to change subdirectories.

c. Press ENTER.

d. Move the highlight to the file that you want to rename.

e. Type an **m** or a **3**.

f. Type a new name for the file.

g. Press ENTER.

h. Press the Exit (F7) key.

You can edit the filename in step f instead of retyping it. Press the RIGHT ARROW or END key to begin the editing process.

Examples

1. You can rename the OLDER file, which you created in example 1 in section 11.1. First, press the List Files (F5) key. Press ENTER to accept the default directory, move the highlight to the file named OLDER, and type an **m**. Type the new filename, **pension1**, and press ENTER. Press the Exit (F7) key.

2. You can edit a filename to rename a file. You can rename the ACCRUE file, which you created in example 3 in section 11.1. First, press the List Files (F5) key. Next, press ENTER to accept the current directory. Move the highlight to the file ACCRUE, and type an **m**. Press the END key to move the cursor to the end of the filename, type a period, and type **pen**. The prompt on the status line looks like this:

```
New name: C:\WP50\ACCRUE.pen
```

Press ENTER to accept the new name, and then press the Exit (F7) key.

Exercises

1. Rename the file PLAN, which you created in exercise 1 in Section 11.1, to PENSION3.

2. Rename the file EARN, which you created in exercise 1 in Section 11.1, to EARNED.

3. Retrieve the file EARNED. Save it as ERN_INC, and clear the screen. Rename ERN_INC to EARN_INC.

11.6   CREATE DOCUMENT SUMMARIES

Document summaries allow you to store descriptive information about every document file you create. In a document summary, you can provide a Descriptive Filename containing as many as 40 characters to supplement the information conveyed by the filename. You can also enter up to 40 characters each for the subject, the author, and the typist. WordPerfect displays the first 400 characters of the document in the Comments section, or you can enter your own comments. Later, you can use this information to provide an overview of the file's contents and use the overview to make decisions concerning the disposition of the file.

To create a document summary:

a. Press the Format (SHIFT-F8) key.

b. Type a **d** or a **3** to select Document.

c. Type an **s** or a **5** to select the Summary option.

d. Select the desired menu option, type the entry, and press ENTER. When you enter comments, you must use the Exit (F7) key rather than ENTER to complete the entry.

e. Press the Exit (F7) key to return to the document.

In step d, you can type a **d** or a **1** to add a descriptive filename. You can type an **s** or a **2** to describe the subject or enter an account name. Type an **a** or a **3** for Author and a **t** or a **4** for Typist. Type a **c** or a **5** to enter the Comments section.

While completing a document summary requires many steps, WordPerfect uses several defaults to reduce the amount of typing required. WordPerfect uses the Author and Typist entries from the last document summary if you created one in the current WordPerfect session. WordPerfect uses the beginning text of the document if you do not provide a comment in the summary. If you have not already saved your file when you create the document summary, WordPerfect offers some of the nonspace characters of the descriptive filename in the prompt that appears when you save it.

Examples

1. You can create a document summary before creating the document. With a clear screen, press the Format (SHIFT-F8) key. Type a **d** and an **s**. The screen looks like Figure 11-4.

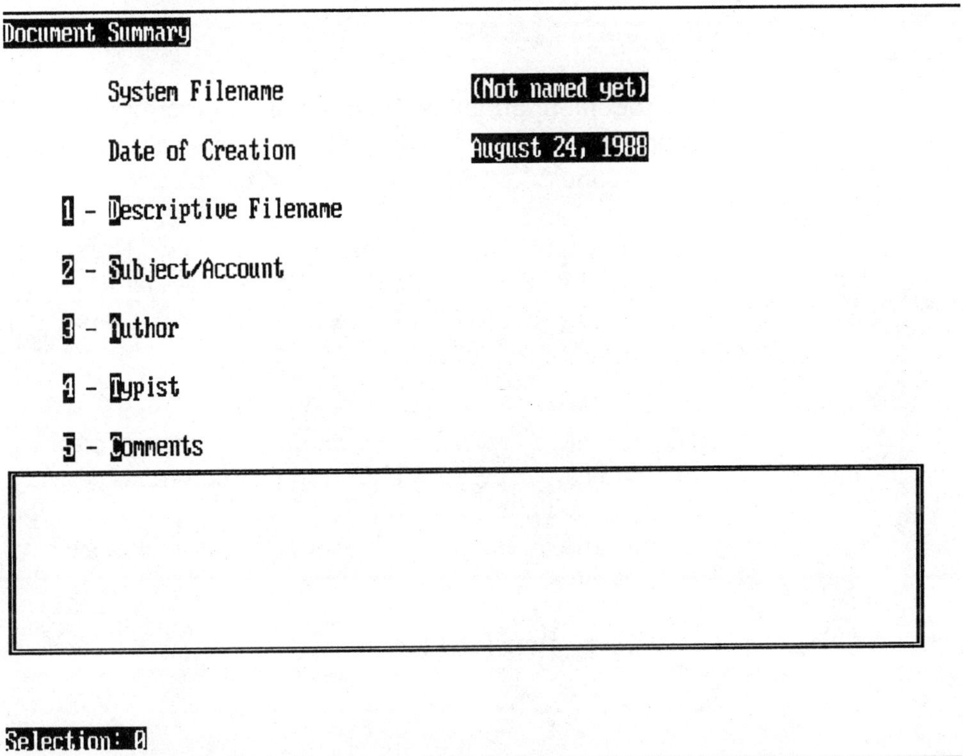

```
Document Summary

        System Filename          (Not named yet)

        Date of Creation         August 24, 1988

    1 - Descriptive Filename

    2 - Subject/Account

    3 - Author

    4 - Typist

    5 - Comments
    ┌──────────────────────────────────────────────────┐
    │                                                    │
    │                                                    │
    │                                                    │
    │                                                    │
    └──────────────────────────────────────────────────┘

Selection: 0
```

FIGURE 11-4.   Blank document summary screen

Type a **d** to select Descriptive Filename, and type

Pension Plan

Press ENTER, type an **s** to select Subject/Account, and type

Acme Corporation

Press ENTER, type an **a** to select Author, and type

Allen Jones

Press ENTER, type a **t** to select Typist, and type

Jim Smith

Press ENTER, type a **c** to select Comments, and type

This document contains the original contract on pages 1 through 17. Pages 18 and 19 contain the addendum passed June 30, 1989.

Press the Exit (F7) key to complete the comment. The screen now looks like Figure 11-5. Press the Exit (F7) key to return to the document. Save this file by pressing the Save (F10) key, typing **penscont**, and pressing ENTER.

2. Once you have created one document summary, creating others is easy, especially if the other documents already contain text. First, press the Retrieve (SHIFT-F10) key, type **pension**, and press ENTER. Press the Format (SHIFT-F8) key. Type a **d**, an **s**, and a **d**. Next, type

Acme Corp - Pension Plan

Press ENTER, type an **s**, and type

Public Announcement 7/1/89

```
Document Summary

        System Filename            PENSIONP.LA

        Date of Creation           August 24, 1988

  1 - Descriptive Filename         Pension Plan

  2 - Subject/Account              Acme Corporation

  3 - Author                       Allen Jones

  4 - Typist                       Jim Smith

  5 - Comments
```

This document contains the original contract on pages 1 through 17. Pages 18 and 19 contain the addendum passed June 30, 1989.

```
Selection: 0
```

FIGURE 11-5.   Completed document summary

Press ENTER to complete the Subject/Account entry. WordPerfect automatically supplies the Author and Typist information that you provided in the first example. WordPerfect also automatically uses the text from the beginning of the document in the Comments section. Press the Exit (F7) key, to return to the document. Press the Save (F10) key, press ENTER, and type a y to save this new version.

Exercises

1. Create a document summary with this information:

Descriptive Title: **Blank Quit Claim Sales Contract**

Subject/Account: **Undeveloped Real Estate**
Author: **Jonas Smith**
Typist: **Karen Polk**
Comments: **This blank contract covers most undeveloped land sales in the state of Florida. This contract has four Xs where you must fill in information. Paragraphs contained in braces are optional. Remove them if they are unnecessary for a particular contract.**

Save the document as CONTRACT.

2. Type the following new document:

**The August 17th meeting discussed the following issues:
Installation of new parking lot lights
Hiring of security personnel to patrol the parking lots after dark
Completion of new research and development building
Improved insurance benefits**

Create a document summary with the following descriptive title:

August 17th meeting notes

Note the entries for Comments, Author, and Typist. Save the document as ISSUES.

3. Enter the following paragraph:

WordPerfect's Graphics features are among the most advanced in the industry. Investing some time in mastering these features could offer a significant payoff for our company. Outside service costs for creating newsletters and brochures can be reduced significantly.

Create a document summary with this information:

Descriptive Filename:
Cut costs with WordPerfect's Graphics
Comments: **Reduce newsletter and brochure development costs with Graphics features. We can recover the cost of the upgrade to 5.0 with the first job.**

Note that the author and typist entries from the previous document summary appear automatically.

Save the document as SAVING.

4. Retrieve the ISSUES file. In the document summary, change the name of the typist to **Martha King.**

SEARCH FOR A WORD WITHIN DOCUMENTS ON DISK

11.7

WordPerfect provides a document-search feature that can examine the contents of files on disk. WordPerfect marks the files that contain the word or phrase that you enter for a search string. You can have WordPerfect check the document summaries, the first page of each document, or the entire text of the documents. Once WordPerfect has marked the files containing your entry, you can use the Look feature to examine them more closely, or you can use other options in the List Files menu.

To search for a word or a phrase in documents:

a. Press the List Files (F5) key.

b. Type the pathname containing the files you wish to check if it is different from the one displayed.

c. Press ENTER.

d. Type a **w** or a **9** to select Word Search.

e. Type a **d** or a **1** to search document summaries, an **f** or a **2** to search the first pages, or an **e** or a **3** to search entire documents.

f. Type the text for which WordPerfect should search.

g. Press ENTER.

WordPerfect searches through the files and marks the ones that contain the specified word or phrase. You can then highlight a marked file and type an **r** or a **1** to retrieve it, or press the Exit (F7) key to return to your current document.

Examples

1. You can search through files in the current directory to find all of the document summaries that contain the word "contract." First, press the List Files (F5) key.

   Next, press ENTER since WordPerfect prompts you for the current directory.

   Then, type a **w**, a **d**, and **contract**, and press ENTER. After completing its search of the document summaries, Word-Perfect displays asterisks to the right of some of the filenames. Some of the marked files should include PEN-SION, CONTRACT, and PENSCONT, each of which contains the word "contract" in its document summary.

   Finally, press the Exit (F7) key to return to the current document.

2. You can search for a phrase on the first page of each file in the current directory. You can find all of the documents that contain the phrase "pension plan" on the first page. First, press the List Files (F5) key.

Next, press ENTER, since WordPerfect prompts you for the current directory.

Then, type a **w** and an **f**. When WordPerfect prompts you for a search string, type a double quote ("), the phrase **pension plan**, and another double quote. Enclosing the phrase in quote marks tells WordPerfect to treat the words in the phrase as a single unit. Press ENTER. After completing its search, WordPerfect displays asterisks to the right of some of the filenames.

Finally, press the Exit (F7) key to return to the document.

3. You can search through all the text in documents in the current directory for a specific word, for example, the name "Jones." First, press the List Files (F5) key, and press ENTER, since WordPerfect prompts you for the current directory. Next, type a **w**, an **e**, and **Jones**. When you press ENTER, WordPerfect searches the documents and displays asterisks to the right of some of the file entries. Each of these files contains the name "Jones" somewhere in the document. Finally, press the Exit (F7) key to return to the current document.

4. You can search for more than one word or phrase at a time when you have WordPerfect search your disk files. You can have WordPerfect mark all documents that contain both entries, or you can elect to mark any file that contains either of the entries.

   The ability to satisfy multiple conditions uses what Word-Perfect refers to as *logical operators*. The semicolon (;) and the comma (,) are the two special operators that Word-Perfect uses to join multiple conditions. If you join two words with a semicolon, WordPerfect will search for files that contain both words, since WordPerfect uses the semi-colon to imply a logical "and" between the two words.

If you join two words with a comma, WordPerfect will search for files containing *either* word, since a comma implies a logical "or."

You can find all documents that contain the word "pension" or "Mary." First, press the List Files (F5) key, and press ENTER, since WordPerfect prompts you for the current directory. Then, type a **w** and an **e**. When WordPerfect prompts you for the search string, type **pension, Mary**, and press ENTER. After selecting the files, WordPerfect displays asterisks to the right of some of the filenames. Each marked file contains the word "pension" or the name "Mary," or both, somewhere in the document. Finally, press the Exit (F7) key to return to the current document.

Exercises

1. Find all documents that contain the word "August" in the document summary.

2. Find all documents that contain the phrase "Acme Corporation" in the first page.

3. Find all documents that contain the word "plan" in the entire document.

4. Find all documents that contain your first name. Find all documents that contain your last name. Find all documents that contain both your first name and your last name. Find all documents that contain either your first name or your last name.

5. Find all documents that contain the words "company" and "product" in the document summary.

6. Find all documents that contain either the word "pension" or the word "contract."

LOOK AT FILES ON DISK   11.8

Sometimes when you are looking for a particular file, you might narrow the choice down to a few files but still be uncertain of the one that you want. A quick way to find the correct file is to use WordPerfect's Look feature. With this feature, you can see a document's contents on the screen without having to retrieve the file. Once you have identified the correct file, you can print it, rename it, delete it, copy it, or retrieve it for editing.

To use the Look feature:

a. Press the List Files (F5) key.

b. Type the pathname if you want to look at files in a different directory.

c. Press ENTER.

d. Move the highlight to the file that you want to view.

e. Type an 1 or a 6, or press ENTER to accept WordPerfect's default.

f. Read the document summary, or use the cursor-control keys to view the document.

g. Press the Exit (F7) key to return to the List Files menu.

h. Press the Exit (F7) key to return to the current document.

Examples

1. You can use the Look feature to display a document without retrieving it. First, press the List Files (F5) key and press ENTER, since WordPerfect prompts you with the correct directory. Highlight the filename PENSION3, and press ENTER. WordPerfect displays the document. You can use the UP ARROW, DOWN ARROW, PGUP, PGDN, SCREEN UP, and SCREEN DOWN keys

to view the document. WordPerfect does not let you change the document. When you finish viewing the document, press the Exit (F7) key twice to return to the document in memory.

2. You can use the Look feature to review document summaries when you display documents. First, press the List Files (F5) key, and press ENTER. Highlight the filename PENSION, and press ENTER. WordPerfect displays the document summary. If you press a cursor-control key, the text of the document appears. The document summary will not reappear; you need to repeat the Look procedure to see it again.

When you finish viewing the document, press the Exit (F7) key twice to return to the current document.

Exercises

1. Use the Look feature to view the EARNED file, which you used in exercise 2 in section 11.5.

2. Use the Look feature to view the CONTRACT file, which you created in exercise 1 in section 11.6.

3. Use the Look feature to view the ISSUES file, which you created in exercise 2 in section 11.6.

4. Use the Look feature to view the PENPLAN file, which you created in exercise 4 in section 11.1.

5. Use the Look feature to view the STOCKS file, which you created in the Skills Check in this chapter.

EXERCISES

(Do not clear the screen between exercises unless instructed to do so.)

1. Create a subdirectory named BUDGET90.

2. Type the following lines:

   Acme Corporation - 1990 Budget

Estimated Sales	**$1,000,000**
Fixed Costs	**$ 400,000**
Variable Costs	**$ 400,000**
Gross Profit	**$ 200,000**

   Save the document as BUDGET. Clear the screen. Copy the BUDGET file to the BUDGET90 subdirectory under the WordPerfect subdirectory.

3. Make the BUDGET90 subdirectory the current subdirectory.

4. Back up the BUDGET file in the BUDGET90 subdirectory to a file named BDGT1990.

5. Delete the BUDGET file in the BUDGET90 subdirectory.

6. Change the BDGT1990 filename to BDGT90.

7. Retrieve BDGT90, and create a document summary with the following information:

   Descriptive Title: **Budget 1990**
   Subject/Account: **Acme Corporation**
   Author: **Jane Smith**
   Typist: **John Dow**
   Comments: **Michael McCormick must have this report by September 30, 1989.**

8. Save the file.

9. Search through document summaries for the word "budget."

10. Clear the screen. View the BDGT90 file.

11. Make the WP50 subdirectory the current subdirectory.

INTEGRATED
SKILLS CHECK

(Do not clear the screen between exercises unless instructed to do so.)

1. Type the following paragraphs:

Discussions about preferred stock use the following descriptive terms:

Participation - This feature determines if the preferred stock can receive an additional dividend after the common stock receives a dividend at the same rate of the preferred stock dividend. The additional dividend is determined by whether the stock is fully or partially participating stock.

Callable - This feature allows the corporation to buy back the preferred stock at a specific price. This feature often places a ceiling on the preferred stock's price.

Cumulative - This feature determines whether dividends that were not declared in prior years must be paid before current dividends are paid.

Conversion - This feature allows the stockholder to convert the preferred stock into common stock. If preferred stock has this feature, the stock often fluctuates with the common stock, although not to the same extent.

Use WordPerfect's speller to determine if you have introduced any spelling errors.

2. Save the document as PREFER.

3. Back up the file as PREFERRD.

4. Create a subdirectory named STOCK.

5. Clear the screen.

6. Back up the PREFERRD file to the STOCK subdirectory.

7. Make the STOCK subdirectory current, and retrieve the PREFERRD file.

8. Rearrange the paragraphs so that the four features are in alphabetical order.

9. Change the top and bottom margins to 5″.

10. Prevent widow and orphan lines.

11. Save the file.

12. Delete the PREFER file from the original subdirectory.

13. Use the Search feature to locate the first occurrence of "dividend."

14. Use the Thesaurus to find synonyms for "fluctuates" and "extent."

CHAPTER OBJECTIVES

After completing this chapter, you should be able to

12.1 Print multiple copies

12.2 Display the print queue

12.3 Cancel a print request

12.4 Rush a print request

12.5 Affect the print quality

12.6 Change print fonts

12.7 Change the size of printed characters

·12·

Changing Print Options

WordPerfect's print features offer more than just printing a copy of your document. You can request printed copies of many documents at a time. WordPerfect keeps track of print priorities and sends jobs to the printer in the proper order.

WordPerfect maintains a print queue to manage print requests that have not yet been fulfilled. You can display the jobs in this queue and cancel a job or specify a rush print job.

Another print option allows you to print multiple copies of a document with one print request. You can select from draft-quality to high-quality print output if your printer supports multiple quality options.

WordPerfect provides options for changing the font, size, and color of your printed text. (Naturally, to use these features, your printer must support these options.) Word-Perfect's font support allows you to use different character sets. It also supports changes that affect the size of the characters. If your printer has proportional fonts, which use a different amount of space for different characters, Word Perfect supports these as well.

SKILLS CHECK

(Do not clear the screen until you have completed the last exercise.)

1. Type the following paragraph as shown, including the misspellings and repeated words:

   In Chapter 3, you learned the basic skills for printiing your your document. This chapter covers other printer feetures that allow you to customize your document's appearence.

   Use the Spell feature to correct spelling errors and eliminate double words.

2. Use the Thesaurus feature to find synonyms for "customize." Replace "customize" with "tailor."

3. Add a header that will print **WordPerfect Print Features**. Add a centered footer that will print **Page** followed by the page number. Preview how WordPerfect will print this document.

4. Create a document summary with the following:

   Descriptive Title: **Describing WordPerfect's Print features**
   Subject/Account: **Teach Yourself WordPerfect**
   Author: [your name]
   Typist: [your name]

5. Save the document as ADVPRINT. Make a copy of this file as PRINTADV. Rename ADVPRINT to PRNTFEAT. Delete PRINTADV.

PRINT MULTIPLE COPIES

12.1

If you need a second copy of a document, you can have WordPerfect create it during your original print request. For a short document, this is usually a quicker solution than a trip to the copy machine.

You can request multiple copies through the Print menu. The number of copies you select remains in effect for the current WordPerfect session.

To print multiple copies:

a. Press the Print (SHIFT-F7) key.

b. Type an **n** to select the Number of Copies option.

c. Type the number of copies you want.

d. Press ENTER.

e. Type an **f**, a **p**, or a **d** to start printing.

Examples

1. You can use this option when you need multiple copies. First, type

The print options allow you to customize your printer output.

Next, press the Print (SHIFT-F7) key, type an **n** and a **2**, and press ENTER. To start printing, type an **f**. WordPerfect returns to the document and prints two copies. Press the Exit (F7) key, press ENTER, type **printopt**, press ENTER, and type an **n** to save the file and clear the screen.

2. WordPerfect continues to use the multiple-copy setting for the current WordPerfect session. First, type

WordPerfect retains some settings for all documents used in the current session. Other settings are saved with a document and do not apply to other documents.

Next, press the Print (SHIFT-F7) key. The setting that you selected in the first example is still in effect. To print two copies of this new document, type an **f**. WordPerfect prints two copies of the document. Press the Exit (F7) key, press ENTER, type **wpset**, press ENTER, and type an **n** to save the file and clear the screen.

Exercises

1. Type the following paragraph:

   You should delete files when you no longer need them. Deleting files frees up needed space on your hard disk or floppy disks.

   Print three copies of the document. Save it as FILEDEL.

2. Type the following paragraph:

   When you save a file, you should use a name that describes the document's purpose. If you do not select meaningful names, you will have difficulty remembering what each document contains. You can rename a file if you wish to change its name.

   Print two copies of the document. Save it as RENAME.

3. Print three copies of the file PRINTOPT.

4. Print two copies of WPSET.

5. Print two copies of FILEDEL. Print one copy of WPSET.

DISPLAY THE PRINT QUEUE

12.2

WordPerfect permits you to display the *print queue*. This queue shows the status of the current print job as well as other jobs waiting to print. From the display of print jobs, you can make an assessment of how long it will take to complete the print jobs that you have requested.

To display the print queue:

a. Press the Print (SHIFT-F7) key.

b. Type a **c** or a **4** to select the Control Printer option.

c. Press the Exit (F7) key to return to the current document.

Each job that is displayed has a number. WordPerfect starts counting print requests with 1 at the beginning of the session and assigns each subsequent print request the next number. As you will learn in later sections, viewing the print queue allows you to use other WordPerfect Print options.

Examples

1. When you tell WordPerfect to print a document, it creates a print job for the task. When you display the print queue, you can look at the status of every print request that has not yet been fulfilled. First, press the Print (SHIFT-F7) key. Then, type a **d** to print a document on disk, type **printopt**, and press ENTER twice. You will need to make several additional print requests quickly to create a backlog. Type a **d**, type **printopt**, and press ENTER twice. Repeat this request one more time. If you proceed quickly to the print queue display, at least one of the print requests should still be in the queue. Type a **c** to select Control Printer from the Print menu. The screen looks like Figure 12-1 if there is one copy left to print. Print jobs usually disappear from the queue

---

```
Print: Control Printer

Current Job

Job Number: 1                          Page Number: 1
Status:      Printing                  Current Copy: 1 of 1
Message:     None
Paper:       Standard 8.5" x 11"
Location:    Continuous feed
Action:      None


Job List

Job  Document              Destination        Print Options
 1   C:\WP50\PRINTOPT      LPT 1



Additional Jobs Not Shown: 0



1 Cancel Job(s); 2 Rush Job; 3 Display Jobs; 4 Go (start printer); 5 Stop: 0
```

FIGURE 12-1.   Control Printer screen

quickly, depending on the speed of your computer and printer and the sizes of your print requests.

2. The queue display shows the printer backlog. You can use this display to help you estimate the time it will take to print the jobs in the queue. Even though WordPerfect does not estimate the time requirements for you, if you are familiar with the documents in the queue you will have a good idea of their length and the required time for printing. Temporarily stopping the print process allows you to look at print requests in the job queue. First, take the printer off line (a button on your printer allows you to do this). This stops the printing process until you turn the printer to on line. Press the Print (SHIFT-F7) key. Then, type a

d to print a document, type **printopt**, and press ENTER twice. Then, type a **d** to print a document, type **wpset**, and press ENTER twice.

Next, type a **c** to select Control Printer from the Print menu. The queue displays both print jobs. Because the printer is off line, the Status message indicates that the printer is not accepting the information that WordPerfect is sending. Turn the printer to on line to make it accept and print the information the computer sends it. As WordPerfect finishes the first job, it removes the job from the queue and changes the information in the top half of the screen to display the print information for the second document. Press the Exit (F7 key to return to the document.

3. The queue display shows some of the print options that you selected, such as the number of copies, rush requests, and print quality. First, press the Print (SHIFT-F7) key. Next, type an **n** and a **4**, and press ENTER. Type a **d** to print a document, type **wpset**, and press ENTER twice. Type a **c** to select Control Printer from the Print menu. WordPerfect displays the request for four copies in the Print Options column.

Exercises

1. Print three copies of the file RENAME, which you created in exercise 2 in section 12.1. Display the print queue while the job is still printing.

2. Print three copies of the file RENAME. Print two copies of FILEDEL, which you created in exercise 1 in section 12.1. Print one copy of the file WPSET. Display the print queue and watch how it changes as WordPerfect prints each job.

12.3 CANCEL A PRINT REQUEST

If you change your mind about printing a document, you can cancel your print request. If the job has already started printing, your printer will continue to print for a page or two: WordPerfect stops transmitting data to the printer when you cancel a job, but it does not clear the printer's memory. The printer continues to print until all the data in its memory has been printed.

To cancel a print request:

a. Press the Print (SHIFT-F7) key.

b. Type a **c** or a **4** to select the Control Printer option.

c. Type a **c** or a **1** to select the Cancel Job(s) option.

d. Type the number of the print job that you want to cancel, or type an asterisk (*) to cancel all jobs.

e. Type a **y** to confirm your selection if you typed an asterisk in step d.

f. Press the Exit (F7) key to return to the current document.

WordPerfect may display a warning message to initialize the printer if you type an asterisk in step d. To initialize the printer, type an **i** while on the initial print menu screen.

Examples

1. You can cancel a print request that is currently printing. First, type

   WordPerfect lets you perform several DOS commands with the List Files (F5) key.

   Then, press CTRL-ENTER to insert a hard page break. On the second page, type

   Using the List Files (F5) key, you can select commands that are equivalent to DOS's COPY, ERASE, RENAME, CD, and TYPE commands.

To print three copies of this document, press the Print (SHIFT-F7) key, type an **n** and a **3**, press ENTER and type an **f**. To cancel this print request, press the Print (SHIFT-F7) key, type a **c** twice to select Control Printer and Cancel Job(s). Type the number of the current print job, and press ENTER. Your printer may continue to print the information the computer has already sent. To return to the document, press the Exit (F7) key. Press the Exit (F7) key, press ENTER, type **listfile**, press ENTER, and type an **n** to save the document and clear the screen.

2. You can also cancel all print requests when you have many print jobs. First, you must enter several print requests. Press the Print (SHIFT-F7) key. Type a **d** to print a document, type **printopt**, press ENTER twice. To print another document, type a **d**, type **wpset**, and press ENTER twice. Then type a **d** again, type **listfile**, and press ENTER twice.

To cancel the print requests, type a **c** twice to select Control Printer and Cancel Job(s). Type an asterisk to cancel all print jobs and a **y** to confirm your choice. If you get a warning message to initialize the printer, press ENTER to return to the initial print menu, and type an **i**. To return to the document, press the Exit (F7) key.

Exercises

1. Start printing five copies of the RENAME file, which you created in exercise 2 in Section 12.1. Cancel the print job.

2. Start printing three copies of RENAME, FILEDEL, and WPSET, which you created in section 12.1. Cancel all print jobs.

3. Turn the printer off to temporarily disable WordPerfect from printing. Request one print of FILEDEL. Cancel the print job.

4. With the printer turned off, request printouts of WPSET, FILEDEL, and RENAME. Cancel the WPSET and RENAME print requests. Turn the printer on.

12.4   RUSH A PRINT REQUEST

With the ability to create many print requests at one time, a backlog of print requests can accumulate. WordPerfect provides a way to expedite a print request so that the entire backlog does not have to finish printing before an important job is printed. After requesting a job in the normal fashion, you use an option on the Print menu to specify that the job is a "rush" job. When the current job finishes printing, the rush job is printed before any other jobs in the print queue.

To rush a print request:

a. Press the Print (SHIFT-F7) key.

b. Type a **c** or a **4** to select Control Printer.

c. Type an **r** or a **2** to select the Rush Job option.

d. Type the number of the print job that you want to rush.

e. Type a **y** if you want to interrupt the current print job or an **n** if you do not want to interrupt it.

f. Press the Exit (F7) key to return to the document.

If you interrupt the current print job, WordPerfect finishes the page it is printing, prints the rush job and then continues printing the interrupted job. If you do not interrupt the current print job, WordPerfect finishes printing it before printing the rush job ahead of other print jobs in the queue.

Examples

1. You can use the Rush Job option to change the order of the print jobs. Press the Print (SHIFT-F7) key. Type an **n** and a **2**, and press ENTER. Type a **d** to print a document, type **printopt**, and press ENTER twice. Type a **d**, type **wpset**, and press ENTER twice. Type a **d**, type **listfile**, and press ENTER twice. Press the Exit (F7) key to return to the document.

To rush the LISTFILE print job, press the Print (SHIFT-F7) key, and type a **c** and an **r**. Then, type the number of the LISTFILE print job. When WordPerfect asks you whether to interrupt the current job, type a **y**. Finally, press the Exit (F7) key to return to the document.

2. When you rush a print request, you can direct WordPerfect not to print the rush job until it finishes the current job. Press CTRL-ENTER six times to create a multiple-page document. Then, press the Print (SHIFT-F7) key, type an **n** and a **1** for copy, and type an **f**. Once the document starts printing, turn the printer off to temporarily halt the printing process. To print a file from disk, press the Print (SHIFT-F7) key, type a **d**, type **listfile**, and press ENTER twice.

To rush the LISTFILE print request, type a **c** and an **r**. Then, type the number of the LISTFILE print job. When Word-Perfect asks whether you want to interrupt the current job, type an **n**. WordPerfect will not print LISTFILE immediately, even though it is a rush request. WordPerfect must finish printing the seven blank pages of the current document. Turn the printer back on.

Exercises

1. Create a print request for RENAME. Create a print request for FILEDEL. Create a print request for PRINTOPT. Rush the PRINTOPT request, interrupting the current print job.

2. Turn the printer off, and request printouts of WPSET, FILEDEL, and RENAME. Rush the RENAME print request. Turn the printer on.

12.5 AFFECT THE PRINT QUALITY

Many printers support more than one quality of print output. Some printers have a draft mode that prints quickly but is not so high in quality as other modes. WordPerfect supports draft-, medium-, and high-quality print output. It provides separate print-quality selections for text and graphics. These settings also provide a "do not print" option, allowing you to print text and graphics in separate print jobs.

To set the print quality:

a. Press the Print (SHIFT-F7) key.

b. Type a **t** to set the text quality or a **g** to set the graphics quality.

c. Type an **n** or a **1** for Do Not Print, a **d** or a **2** for Draft, an **m** or a **3** for Medium, or an **h** or a **4** for High.

d. Type an **f** or a **p** to start printing.

With some printers, the higher the quality, the longer it takes the printer to print. The Do Not Print option in step c can be used for printing text and graphics on a printer that can print one or the other but not both. The options available for graphics are identical to the options for text. They are not discussed here, since they use skills that you will develop in Chapter 17. Text and graphics quality are saved with the files.

Examples

1. You can set the text quality to draft when you need a quick printed copy. Retrieve PRINTOPT by pressing the Retrieve (SHIFT-F10) key, typing **printopt**, and pressing ENTER. Press the Print (SHIFT-F7) key and type a **t** and a **d**. To see how draft-quality print appears, type an **f**. Use this document in the next example.

2. You use high text quality when you are printing your document for presentation to others. Press the Print (SHIFT-F7) key, and type a **t** and an **h**. To see how high-quality text appears, type an **f**.

Exercises

(Do not clear the screen until you have completed the last exercise.)

1. Retrieve WPSET. Set the text quality to medium. Print the document.

2. Set the text quality to high. Print the document.

3. Set the text quality to draft. Print the document.

CHANGE PRINT FONTS

12.6

Most printers support multiple fonts. These fonts allow you to use character sets that are created in different styles. Some fonts are proportional; that is, different characters take up different amounts of space on a line. The font options that WordPerfect presents depend on the printer that you are using.

You can change fonts within a document, a paragraph or a line. WordPerfect adjusts the text on the screen and how it is word wrapped to reflect new font. For example, changing the font does not change the margins. When you change fonts, you can still use other WordPerfect features, such as boldfacing, underlining, and centering. Figure 12-2 is a preview at 100% showing how WordPerfect will print different fonts.

To change the base font:

a. Press the Font (CTRL-F8) key.

b. Type an **f** or a **4** to choose the Base Font option.

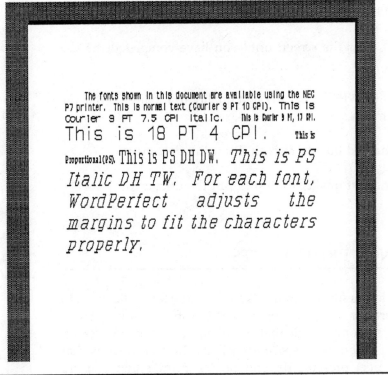

FIGURE 12-2.   Sample fonts

c. Move the highlight to the font that you want, using the cursor-movement keys.

d. Press ENTER.

The fonts available in step c depend upon your printer. When you change the font, WordPerfect inserts the code [Font: font name]. The font name is the font description that you selected in step c.

Examples

1. You can change the default base font for a Hewlett-Packard LaserJet Series II printer to one with smaller characters than the current font has. If you are using this printer, your choices will be the same as those in this example. First, press the Format (SHIFT-F8) key, and type an **l** and an **m**. Type a **1**, press ENTER, type a **4**, and press ENTER. Press the Exit (F7) key. This increases the right margin so that you can see all the text when you preview the document at 200%. Next, type

Larger characters have smaller pitch numbers.

Press the Font (CTRL-F8) key, and type an **f**. WordPerfect displays the available base fonts, like these:

```
* Courier 10 pitch (PC-8)
  Courier 10 pitch (Roman-8)
  Courier Bold 10 pitch (PC-8)
  Courier Bold 10 pitch (Roman-8)
  Line Printer 16.66 pitch (PC-8)
  Line Printer 16.66 pitch (Roman-8)
  Solid Line Draw 10 pitch
```

If you have soft fonts or font cartridges for your printer, additional fonts may be available. With other printers, the selections may be quite different. Press the DOWN ARROW key to move the highlight to the Line Printer 16.66 pitch (PC-8) font, and press ENTER to select this font. Next, type

Smaller characters have larger pitch numbers. Word-Perfect automatically adjusts for the different sizes of characters.

To see how the different fonts appear at 200%, press the Print (SHIFT-F7) key and type a **v** and a **2**. The screen looks like this:

Larger characters have smaller pitch numbers.   Smaller characters have larger pitch numbers. WordPerfect automatically adjusts for the different sizes of characters.

2. If your font options include an italics font, you can change the base font to italics. In this example, options for an NEC P7 dot matrix printer are used to select a font providing large italic characters. The font selections that are available to you depend upon your printer. First, type

Smaller characters have smaller point sizes. WordPerfect abbreviates points as PT.

Press the Font (CTRL-F8) key and type an **f**. WordPerfect displays the available base fonts, like the ones for the NEC P7 printer shown in Figure 12-3. Press the DOWN ARROW key to move the highlight to the Courier 18 PT 7.5 CPI Italic font. Next, type

Larger characters have larger point numbers.

Since the characters are larger, WordPerfect fits fewer characters per line. The italicized characters probably do not appear as italic on your screen. To see how the different fonts will appear in print, press the Print (SHIFT-F7) key, and type a **v** and a **1**. The screen looks like this:

Smaller characters have smaller point sizes. WordPerfect abbreviates points as PT. *larger characters have larger point numbers.*

Exercises

1. Type the first sentence of the following paragraph. Change the font to a larger-character base font and type the second sentence. Preview how WordPerfect will print the document.

When you change the font, all characters after the font change are affected. Characters before the font change use the initial setting of your printer.

Base Font

```
Courier  9 PT  5 CPI
Courier  9 PT  5 CPI Italic
Courier  9 PT  6 CPI
Courier  9 PT  6 CPI Italic
Courier  9 PT  7.5 CPI
Courier  9 PT  7.5 CPI Italic
* Courier  9 PT  10 CPI
Courier  9 PT 10 CPI Italic
Courier  9 PT 12 CPI
Courier  9 PT 12 CPI Italic
Courier  9 PT 15 CPI
Courier  9 PT 15 CPI Italic
Courier  9 PT 17 CPI
Courier  9 PT 17 CPI Italic
Courier  9 PT 20 CPI
Courier  9 PT 20 CPI Italic
Courier 18 PT  4 CPI
Courier 18 PT  4 CPI Italic
Courier 18 PT  5 CPI
Courier 18 PT  5 CPI Italic
Courier 18 PT  6 CPI
```

1 Select; N Name search: 1

FIGURE 12-3.   Sample fonts available for NEC P7 printer

2. Type the first sentence of the following paragraph. If your printer can print proportional spacing (abbreviated PS), change the base font to a proportionally spaced font. If it cannot, change the font to a smaller-character base font. Type the last two sentences of the paragraph. Preview how WordPerfect will print the document.

Fonts can also be proportionally spaced. In proportionally spaced fonts, each character uses a different amount of space. For example, an I takes less space than an m.

12.7 CHANGE THE SIZE OF PRINTED CHARACTERS

When you select the base font, you are actually changing the default size that the rest of your document will use. Word-Perfect has a separate option that changes the size of text without changing the base font. This feature lets you use large characters in a document that has a smaller base font. You can use this feature to create superscript and subscript features. The actual appearance of these characters will depend upon the capabilities of your printer.

To change the size of characters before you type them:

a. Move the cursor to where you want characters to appear in a different size.

b. Press the Font (CTRL-F8) key.

c. Type an **s** or a **1** to choose the Size option.

d. Type the letter or number for the character size that you want.

e. Type the text that you want to appear in that size.

f. To return the character size to normal, press Font (CTRL-F8) and type an **n**, or press the RIGHT ARROW key once.

You may notice a change in the color or intensity of the position indicator on the status line when you use different fonts. With a color monitor, text in a different size may appear in a different color.

To change the size of characters that you have already typed:

a. Block the text that you want in a different size.

b. Press the Font (CTRL-F8) key.

c. Type an **s** or a **1** to choose the Size option.

d. Type the letter or number for the character size that you want.

In step d of both methods, WordPerfect provides you with size options. You can type a **p** or a **1** for Superscript, a **b** or a **2** for Subscript, an **f** or a **3** for Fine, an **s** or a **4** for Small, an **l** or a **5** for Large, a **v** or a **6** for Very Large, or an **e** or a **7** for Extra Large, assuming your printer supports these options.

When you change the size of characters, WordPerfect inserts codes where the special-size text starts and ends. For Superscript, WordPerfect inserts the codes [SUPRSCPT] and [suprscpt]. For Subscript, WordPerfect inserts the codes [SUBSCPT] and [subscpt]. For Fine, WordPerfect inserts the codes [FINE] and [fine]. For Small, WordPerfect inserts the codes [SMALL] and [small]. For Large, WordPerfect inserts the codes [LARGE] and [large]. For Very Large, WordPerfect inserts the codes [VRY LARGE] and [vry large]. For Extra Large, WordPerfect inserts the codes [EXT LARGE] and [ext large]. Step f in the first method for changing text size ends the size change by moving the cursor past the end code for the size.

Examples

1. You can change the size of text that you entered to make it a large heading. First, type

ATTENTION:
The auditors will arrive on Monday. Please provide any
assistance and/or answers they require.

Press ENTER and press the UP ARROW key three times. Then,
press the Block (ALT-F4) key, and press END. Next, press the
Font (CTRL-F8) key, and type an **s** and an **e** to have the
blocked text print as extra-large letters. Finally, press the
Print (SHIFT-F7) key, and type a **v**. The screen looks like this:

```
ATTENTION:
The auditors will arrive on Monday.  Please provide any assistance
and/or answers they require.
```

2. You can use superscripts and subscripts to type formulas.
   First, type an **x**. Press the Font (CTRL-F8) key, and type an **s**
   and a **b** for Subscript text. Then, type a **1**, and press the RIGHT
   ARROW key. Press the Font (CTRL-F8) key, and type an **s** and a
   p for Superscript text. Then, type a **2** and press the RIGHT
   ARROW key and the SPACEBAR.

   Type a plus sign (+), press the SPACEBAR, and type an **x**. Press
   the Font (CTRL-F8) key and type an **s** and a **b** for Subscript
   text. Then, type a **2**, and press the RIGHT ARROW key. Press the
   Font (CTRL-F8) key and type an **s** and a **p** for Superscript text.
   Then, type a **2**, and press the RIGHT ARROW key and the
   SPACEBAR.

   Type an equal sign (=), press the SPACEBAR, and type an **x**.
   Press the Font (CTRL-F8) key, and type an **s** and a **b** for
   Subscript text. Then, type a **3**, and press the RIGHT ARROW key.
   Press the Font (CTRL-F8) key, and type an **s** and a **p** for
   Superscript text. Then, type a **2**, and press the RIGHT ARROW
   key.

   This completes the Pythagorean theorem, which states that
   the square of the longest side of a right triangle is equal to
   the sum of the squares of the other two sides. Press the
   Print (SHIFT-F7) key and type a **v**. The screen looks like this:

$$x_1{}^2 + x_2{}^2 = x_3{}^2$$

Exercises

1. Type the following paragraph:

   Always make sure to read the fine print. It may contain information not found in other parts of the document.

   Block the first sentence and change it to fine print. Preview how WordPerfect will print the document.

2. Type the following lines, including the subscript and superscript information as shown. Press ENTER twice at the end of each line.

   H_2O
   $E = mc^2$
   Subscripted text appears below the normal text.
   Superscripted text appears above the normal text.

   Preview how WordPerfect will print this document.

3. Type the following lines, setting the size of the characters in each line to the size described in the sentence:

   Your printer prints Extra Large text like this.
   Your printer prints Very Large text like this.
   Your printer prints Large text like this.
   Your printer prints Small text like this.
   Your printer prints Fine text like this.

   Preview how WordPerfect will print this document.

EXERCISES

(Do not clear the screen until you have completed the last exercise.)

MASTERY
SKILLS CHECK

1. Type the following paragraph.

WordPerfect uses several abbreviations for font selection. CPI represents the number of characters per inch. The larger the number, the smaller the characters. Points, or PT, represent the height of the character. The larger the number, the larger the characters. Pitch is the number of characters that can be printed per horizontal inch. The larger the number, the smaller the characters.

Move to the top of the document, and change the base font so that the characters will print as italics. (If an italicized font of the same size is unavailable, select any other font.)

2. Change the words "CPI," "PT," and "Pitch" to appear in large print.

3. Print four copies of the document, using draft print quality.

4. Cancel the print request.

5. Print two copies of the document, using high print quality. Print four copies using draft print quality. Rush the draft print job.

INTEGRATED SKILLS CHECK

(Do not clear the screen until you have completed the last exercise.)

1. Type the following paragraph:

When you change the size of the characters, you change the number of characters that WordPerfect fits on each line. WordPerfect automatically adjusts word wrapping for fine, extra-large and small fonts. WordPerfect also automatically adjusts word wrapping for proportionally spaced, larger, and smaller base fonts.

Check the document for spelling errors.

2. Save the document as WORDWRAP. Create a backup called FONTADJ. Delete the WORDWRAP file.

3. Change the size of the words "fine," "extra large," and "small" so that the words will print in the sizes they describe. Include the punctuation for the words when you change the sizes. View how WordPerfect will print the document.

4. Move to the top of the document, and set the base font to a larger font. Move to the last sentence, and set the base font to a smaller font. View how WordPerfect will print the document.

5. Add the following footnote at the end of the first sentence:

   Changing the font does not change WordPerfect's other default settings, such as margins and page size.

6. Print four copies of the document, using high print quality. Print three copies. Set the text quality to draft, and print two copies. Rush the draft print request.

7. Look at the file FONTADJ on disk.

CHAPTER OBJECTIVES

After completing this chapter, you should be able to

13.1 Open and exit from a second document

13.2 Change the size of a document window

13.3 Use two documents at one time

13.4 Copy and move text between documents

·13·

Working with Two Documents

WordPerfect permits you to have two documents in memory at one time. With this feature, you can refer to one document while working on another. You can copy or move information in one document to the other document. You can split the screen to allow part of both documents to be visible on the screen.

WordPerfect maintains the two documents separately; changes to one document do not affect the other. You can switch between documents to edit either one, and you can save the documents in separate files.

SKILLS CHECK

(Do not clear the screen between exercises unless instructed to do so.)

1. Type the following paragraph:

   In March, the company exchanged 30,000 shares of newly issued common stock for $500,000 principal value of its 6% bonds. It recognized a $145,000 extraordinary gain.

   Add the following footnote at the end of the first sentence:

   These bonds were originally issued to upgrade production facilities.

2. Create a footer containing your name.

3. Create a header that will print the word **Page** followed by a space and the page number.

4. Set the text quality to draft.

5. Set the font to print the document in italics. Save the file as XTRAGAIN, and clear the screen.

6. Create a subdirectory called NOTES below the WP50 subdirectory.

7. Back up the file XTRAGAIN to the subdirectory NOTES using the same filename.

8. Print the file XTRAGAIN that is in the subdirectory NOTES.

9. Delete the file XTRAGAIN that is in the subdirectory NOTES.

10. Delete the subdirectory NOTES.

OPEN AND EXIT FROM A SECOND DOCUMENT

13.1

You have been working with only one document at a time in all the WordPerfect tasks you have accomplished thus far. To work in a second document, you need to switch to the second document screen. Once you are in the second document screen, you can begin typing a new document, move or copy text from the first document, or retrieve a document from disk to work with in this screen. The contents of this second document do not affect document 1.

Since WordPerfect stores each document separately in memory, you must exit from each document separately. It does not matter in which order you exit from the documents; for example, you can exit from document 2 and continue to work in document 1. When you exit from the remaining document, you can also exit from WordPerfect.

To open a second document:

a. Press the Switch (SHIFT-F3) key.

To exit from a second document:

a. Press the Exit (F7) key.

b. Press ENTER, type a filename and press ENTER if you want to save the second document; otherwise, type an **n**.

c. Type a **y** to leave the second document.

Examples

1. You can type a document in document 2 while you have a document in document 1. First, type

Rod Taylor
Trenton Inc.
4056 Carnegie Avenue
Cleveland, Ohio 44113

Dear Sir,
Enclosed is an invoice for $278.25. Payment is due by
August 30. This is for the final balance on your account.

Sincerely,

Maud Stevens

After you have typed this letter, you can save it to a file.
Press the Save (F10) key, type **finalbal**, and press ENTER. To
create a second document, press the Switch (SHIFT-F3) key.
The current document disappears from the screen, and the
status line looks like this:

Doc 2 Pg 1 Ln 1" Pos 1"

Doc 2 indicates that you are in WordPerfect's second
document screen. For this document, type

**The next meeting of the board of directors is December
14.**

The first document is still intact, since anything you type in
one document does not affect the other.

You can clear this document from memory and remain on
this screen by pressing the Exit (F7) key and typing **n** when
WordPerfect asks you whether to save the document and **n**
again when WordPerfect asks you whether to exit document 2.

2. You can retrieve a document from disk for document 2. You can retrieve the file that you saved in example 1. First, press the Retrieve (SHIFT-F10) key, type **finalbal**, and press ENTER. The screen displays the letter that you created and saved in document 1. Move to the end of the document, and type

100 Financial Statements	$525.00
6% State tax	$ 31.50
Total	$556.50
Paid to date	$278.25
Total due	$278.25

50% by August 1
Balance upon delivery (August 30)

The original copy in document 1 is still intact. You can see this by pressing the Exit (F7) key. When WordPerfect asks whether you want to save the file, type a **y**, type **final**, and press ENTER. When WordPerfect asks whether you want to exit from document 2, type a **y**. The screen displays the original letter that you typed in example 1.

3. You must exit from each document separately. You can create two documents and exit from both of them. First, type

The corporation owns 83,500 shares of Treasury stock.

To switch to document 2, press the Switch (SHIFT-F3) key. In document 2, type

25,000 shares of the company's Treasury stock is reserved for stock option plans.

To exit from both documents, first press the Exit (F7) key, and type an **n** and a **y**. WordPerfect returns you to document 1. Then, press the Exit (F7) key, and type an **n** twice to clear the first document and remain in Word Perfect.

Exercises

1. Type the following paragraph:

   Production used 1200 ball bearings to replace the machinery's worn ones.

   Switch to document 2. Retrieve FINAL, and insert a page break between the letter and the text you typed in example 2. Save and exit from document 2. Save document 1 as SKATES.

2. Type the following paragraph:

   The company is using a new printer for the current year's financial statements. This allows the company to include pictures of its executive officers and its main office building.

   Save this document as STMT1. Switch to document 2, and retrieve STMT1. Add the following sentence:

   Management felt that the change was necessary, since the company wants to improve its corporate image.

   Save this document as STMT2. Exit from both documents.

3. In document 1, retrieve STMT2. Switch to document 2, and retrieve STMT1. Exit from both documents.

CHANGE THE SIZE OF A DOCUMENT WINDOW

13.2

WordPerfect normally displays 24 lines in a screen. You can reduce the number of lines displayed in document 1 to allow part of document 2 to be displayed on the screen at the same time. The part of the screen used for each separate document is called a *window*. This window feature allows you to review the contents of a document in one window while you work on a document in the other window.

To set the number of lines WordPerfect uses for a window:

a. Press the Screen (CTRL-F3) key.

b. Type a **w** or a **1**.

c. Type a number from 1 to 24 for the number of lines the current window should use.

d. Press ENTER.

WordPerfect uses the number that you provide in step c for the number of lines in the current window and subtracts that number from 22 to determine the number of lines to be displayed in the other window. Each window uses an additional line for the status line. The two windows are separated on the screen by a ruler line, which indicates margin and tab settings for the current window. If you press the Reveal Codes (ALT-F3) key, WordPerfect splits the screen to show the codes hidden in the current window and hides the other window.

Examples

1. You can set the number of lines in a window to allow you to see two documents at once. First, retrieve FINAL by pressing the Retrieve (SHIFT-F10) key, typing **final**, and pressing ENTER.

Next, press the Screen (CTRL-F3) key, and type a **w**. Word Perfect displays this prompt:

`Number of lines in this window: 24`

Type **11**, and press ENTER. The screen now looks like Figure 13-1. Each window has its own filename and status line.

The screen uses 11 lines for document 1 and 11 lines for document 2. The triangles in the ruler line, which represent tab stops, point up, indicating that the cursor is in document 1.

```
Rod Taylor
Trenton Inc.
4056 Carnegie Avenue
Cleveland, Ohio 44113

Dear Sir,
     Enclosed is an invoice for $278.25.  This is due by August
30th.  This is for the final balance on your account.

               Sincerely,
```

```
C:\WP50\FINAL                            Doc 1 Pg 1 Ln 1" Pos 1"
{   ▲   ▲    ▲     ▲    ▲     ▲    ▲    ▲   ▲    ▲    }   ▲    ▲
```

```
                              Doc 2 Pg 1 Ln 1" Pos 1"
```

FIGURE 13-1. Two document windows on the screen

2. You can reset the full screen size for a document by changing the number of lines back to 24. First, press the Screen (CTRL-F3) key, and type a **w**. Next, type **24**, and press ENTER. Although document 2 disappears from the screen, it remains in the computer's memory.

3. You can also set the window size while using the second window. First, press the Switch (SHIFT-F3) key to switch to document 2. Press the Screen (CTRL-F3) key, and type a **w**.

Next, type **15**, and press ENTER. Document 2 now has 15 lines, and document 1 has 7. Document 2 always appears below document 1 on a split screen. When you press the Exit (F7) key and type an **n** and a **y**, you return to the first document, although the window for document 2 remains on the screen. You can remove it by resetting the window for document 1 to 24 lines.

You will find more details on switching in the next section.

Exercises

1. Set the document 1 window to 10 lines. Reset it to 24.

2. Set the document 1 window to 8 lines. Reset it to 18 lines.

3. Set the document 2 window to 14 lines.

4. Set document 2 to 8 lines.

USE TWO DOCUMENTS AT ONE TIME   13.3

You can use the same technique that allowed you to open the second document window to switch back and forth between the two windows. You can use this feature to allow you to read along in one document as you type a response in the second document. You can also use this technique to edit text in either document. Each time you press the Switch (SHIFT-F3) key, WordPerfect activates the other window.

To switch between documents:

a. Press the Switch (SHIFT-F3) key.

Examples

1. You can switch between two documents when you are creating a document that makes use of information contained in another document. You can use the information contained in the file FINAL to write a reminder notice. First, press the Retrieve (SHIFT-F10) key, type **final**, and press ENTER.

   Next, switch to document 2 by pressing the Switch (SHIFT-F3) key. In document 2, type

   Dear Sirs,

   Your account balance of

   To determine the balance due, press the Switch (SHIFT-F3) key. You can see from the schedule at the bottom of the document that the client owes $278.25.

   Return to document 2 by pressing the Switch (SHIFT-F3) key, and type

   $278.25 is overdue. Please remit a check for this amount. As per our agreement, we should have received payment on

   To determine the date the balance was due, press the Switch (SHIFT-F3) key. You can see from the schedule at the bottom of the document that the balance should have been paid by August 30. Return to document 2 by pressing the Switch (SHIFT-F3) key, and type

August 30.

Sincerely,

Maud Stevens

2. You can switch between documents to create two closely
related documents. For example, when you type a summary letter for a contract, you may need to switch between
the contract and the letter to check that both documents
use the same facts. First, type

Know all men by these presents, that I, Tom Jones, the
undersigned, in consideration of the sum of $40,000, in
hand paid, do hereby grant, bargain, sell and convey to
Ron Delaney, of Broward County, Florida, the following
described real estate situated in the county of Orange,
State of Florida, to wit: 1/2 acre lot at the corner of Rio
Pinar Drive and Gator Alley, to have and to hold to his
heirs and assigns forever.

Then, create the summary letter to send with the contract.
Press the Switch (SHIFT-F3) key, and type

Tom Jones
513 Allworthy Lane
Oxford, CT 09134

Dear Mr. Jones,

Enclosed is the contract to sell your land at the corner of
Rio Pinar Drive and Gator Alley to

To check the buyer's name and the price, press the Switch
(SHIFT-F3) key. The contract states that the buyer is Ron
Delaney and the price is $40,000. To return to the letter,
press the Switch (SHIFT-F3) key. Type

Ron Delaney for $40,000. Sign the contract, notarize it, and return it to our office as soon as possible.

Sincerely,

Jane Perez, Attorney

By creating both documents at once, you can ensure that they both use the same information.

Exercises

1. Type the following paragraph. When you get to the four "X"s, switch to document 2, retrieve FINAL, and find the sales tax. Switch to document 1, and type the sales tax in place of the four "X"s.

   The discrepancy between the amount due and what the client believes is the proper amount is the sales tax of XXXX. The client was not aware that sales tax would be added for printing services.

2. Type the following sentence:

   The president, Amanda Williams, started with the company as chief production officer fifteen years ago.

   Switch to document 2, and type

   Ms. Williams' experience includes chief production officer, divisional vice president, production vice president, and president.

Switch to document 1, and type

After four years as production officer, she was promoted to divisional vice president of the appliance division.

Save document 1 as PRESIDNT and 2 as PRESRESU.ME.

COPY AND MOVE TEXT BETWEEN DOCUMENTS

13.4

You can use the techniques for copying and moving text in one document to perform the same tasks in two documents. This feature allows you to recall a file from disk and use it as the basis for another document. When you move data between documents, the data from the current document is removed and placed in the other document. When you copy text, it is left in its original location, and a copy of it is placed in the other document. Either document 1 or document 2 can contain the data to be moved or copied.

To copy or move text between documents:

a. Move the cursor to a character in the sentence, paragraph, or page that you want to copy or move.

b. Press the Move (CTRL-F4) key.

c. Type an **s** or a **1** to copy or move a sentence, a **p** or a **2** to copy or move a paragraph, or an **a** or a **3** to move a page.

d. Type an **m** or a **1** to move the highlighted text or a **c** or a **2** to copy the highlighted text.

e. Press the Switch (SHIFT-F3) key to switch to the other document.

f. Move the cursor to where you want the text to be placed.

g. Press ENTER.

To copy or move blocked text between documents:

a. Move the cursor to the beginning of the text that you want to move or copy.

b. Press the Block (ALT-F4) key.

c. Move the cursor to the end of the text that you want to move or copy.

d. Press the Move (CTRL-F4) key.

e. Type a **b** or a **1** to select Block.

f. Type an **m** or a **1** to move the blocked text or a **c** or a **2** to copy the blocked text.

g. Press the Switch (SHIFT-F3) key to switch to the other document.

h. Place the cursor where you want the blocked text to be copied or moved.

i. Press ENTER.

Examples

1. You can move text from one document to another. First, press the Retrieve (SHIFT-F10) key, type **final**, and press ENTER. Next, switch to document 2 by pressing the Switch (SHIFT-F3) key. Press the Retrieve (SHIFT-F10) key, type **stmt1**, and press ENTER.

To move the paragraph in document 2 to document 1, press the Move (CTRL-F4) key, and type a **p** and an **m**. The paragraph is removed from the current document.

Next, press the Switch (SHIFT-F3) key to return to document 1. Place the cursor below the numbers at the bottom of the document, and press ENTER. WordPerfect inserts a copy of the paragraph from the other document into the current document.

2. You can copy a block of text from one document to another. First, set the number of lines in the document 1 window to 11 by pressing the Screen (CTRL-F3) key, typing a **w** and **11**, and pressing ENTER. Then, press the Retrieve (SHIFT-F10) key, type **finalbal**, and press ENTER.

To copy the inside address to another document, begin by pressing the Block (ALT-F4) key. Move the cursor to the blank line before the salutation. Then, press the Move (CTRL-F4) key, and type a **b** and a **c**. The highlighting disappears, and the block remains in the current document.

Next, switch to document 2 by pressing the Switch (SHIFT-F3) key. Press ENTER to place a copy of the block from document 1 in document 2. Now you can type the remainder of the second document. Even though you have completed the

Copy procedure, the message **Move cursor; press Enter to retrieve** will remain in the first document's status line until you switch back to that window.

Exercises

1. Type the following paragraphs:

Peter Sullivan is production vice president. He has held this position for the past three years.

Paula Atchinson is the financial vice president. She has held this position for the past two years.

Move the first paragraph to document 2.

2. Type the following name and address:

Terry Kesley
Kesley Associates
496 Berry Avenue
Newport, Rhode Island 03563

Copy them to document 2.

EXERCISES

MASTERY
SKILLS CHECK

(Do not clear the screen until you have completed the last exercise.)

1. Type the following paragraphs:

The company has made the following accounting changes:
   Inventory valuation now uses the FIFO method instead of the LIFO method. The change to this year's income is $40,000, last year's income is $48,000. The total effect on income from prior years is $88,000.

Contracts are now accounted for using the percentage-of-completion method rather than the completed-contract method. This increased last year's net income by $40,000 and this year's by $60,000.

Switch to document 2.

2. Set the window for document 2 to 12 lines.

3. Switch to document 1. Set the window for document 1 to 8 lines.

4. Copy the first accounting-change paragraph to document 2.

5. Move the second accounting-change paragraph to the beginning of document 2.

(Do not clear the screen until you have completed the last exercise.)

INTEGRATED SKILLS CHECK

1. Type the following paragraphs:

The company leases most of its office space and mainframe computer equipment. It owns all of its production facilities.

Total rental expense is $1,709,000 for the current year, $998,000 for 1988, and $923,000 for 1987.

Save as LEASES. Back up the file as LEASES.BAK.

2. Switch to document 2. Retrieve LEASES.BAK.

3. Add the following paragraph at the bottom of the document:

   The company's minimum lease obligations are $503,000 for 1990, $432,000 for 1991, $401,000 for 1992, $352,000 for 1993, $318,000 for 1994, and $1,293,000 for later years.

   Copy the last paragraph to the bottom of document 1.

4. Save document 1 as LEASES.NEW, and switch to document 2.

5. Create a document summary with the following information:
   Descriptive Filename: **Notes for financial statements**
   Subject: **For 1989 financial statements**
   Author: [your name]
   Typist: [your name]

6. Delete the file LEASES.BAK.

7. Add the following header:

   Financial Statement Notes

8. Create a footer that will print your name.

9. Turn your printer's power switch to the off position. (If you attempted this exercise with your printer on, it is likely that

the print job would finish before you could activate the Control Printer screen.) Start a print job to create two copies of the current document. Cancel the print job. Turn your printer on.

·Part III·

Special Features

CHAPTER OBJECTIVES

After completing this chapter, you should be able to

14.1 Create a secondary file

14.2 Create a primary file

14.3 Produce the Merge document

14.4 Print the Merge document

·14·

Merging Variable Information into a Standard Letter

Sometimes you need to create many documents that are almost identical. The only difference in the documents may be individualized information, such as a customer name and address or an account balance. Such documents are referred to as form letters since each of them follows an identical format. WordPerfect supports the creation of form letters with its Merge features. The Merge features allow you to integrate variable information with a document that is fixed in content and format. This capability allows you to create letters, invoices, and other documents that are similar without having to type each document from scratch.

You can create a base document with special markers entered where variable information is to be inserted. You can create a second document containing the variable information, such as names, addresses, and account balances. At your command, WordPerfect merges the variable information into the base document to create individualized documents.

To merge files in WordPerfect, you must have primary and secondary document files. The *primary file* contains the form letter or other nonchanging text. It also directs Word-Perfect to the specific locations at which information should be inserted. The *secondary file* contains the variable information that WordPerfect places into the primary document. When the merge operation is complete, you will have individualized documents for the information in the secondary file. These documents will all be stored in one file in memory.

SKILLS CHECK

(Do not clear the screen between exercises unless instructed to do so.)

1. Delete the default tab stops and set tabs stops at 1.5″ and 4″. Type the following letter:

Highland Graphics, Inc.
24257 N.W. 5th Street
Sunrise, FL 33146
305-331-2473

Mark Scheimer
Chairman, Education and Development
Association of Computer Graphic Artists
1347 S.W. 14 Ave.
Davie, FL 33136

Dear Mr. Scheimer,
    Since my company is having a display at your upcoming forum, I need the dimensions for the display space. I also

need the number of electrical outlets available for use in my display and the distance from the display to these outlets.

Sincerely,

Ann Slater
President, Highland Graphics, Inc.

Use WordPerfect's Spell feature to check the spelling.

2. Block the name and address information for Mark Scheimer.

3. Place a copy of the block in a second document.

4. Return to the first document. Change the window size to 12 lines.

5. Save the document as REQUEST.

6. Print two copies of the letter.

7. Request two printed copies two more times. Then cancel all print jobs.

8. Add the following paragraph to the letter:

   I have enclosed a list of the sales representatives who will be attending the forum.

Add a hard page break at the end of the letter. Type the following list of names on the new page:

Jim Styverson
Karen Acermann
Julie Greenlowe
Paul Hatterfield

Check the spelling for this page. Add the proper names that are not recognized by the spelling checker to your supplemental dictionary.

9. Add the following header to the second page:

Forum Attendees

10. Make a backup of the REQUEST file LETTER.BK.

11. Switch to the second document screen. Add the following header:

Booth Assignments

Copy the list of names from the first document to the end of the second.

12. Set the tab stops in the second document to have only one tab stop, at 4″. Use this tab stop to enter the following times in a column next to the names:

8:00 - 10:00
10:00 - 1:00
1:00 - 3:00
3:00 - 5:30

13. Set the number of print copies to 1. Request a copy of the original letter in the REQUEST file twice. Request a print of the page containing booth assignments, and have WordPerfect make it a rush job.

14. Save the document as TIMES. Rename the file as BOOTH.

15. Search your default directory for files that contain the name "Karen."

16. Clear both files from memory. Look at the BOOTH file.

17. Retrieve BOOTH, and create a document summary that contains entries for descriptive filename, author, and typist.

18. If you have a hard disk, change to and look at the root directory. Look at the files on the disk in the other drive if you have a floppy disk system.

19. If you have a hard disk, create a new subdirectory called TRDESHOW at the same level as the WordPerfect subdirectory. If you have a floppy disk, create a TRDESHOW subdirectory in the root directory of the floppy disk. In either system, remove the new subdirectory. Return the current subdirectory to WP50 if you are using a hard disk.

20. Add a footer to BOOTH that shows the date at the left and the page number at the right, preceded by the word "Page." Save the file and clear the screen. Change the window size back to 24 lines.

21. Remove the names you added to the supplemental dictionary in exercise 8.

CREATE A SECONDARY FILE 14.1

Secondary files contain the information that you want Word-Perfect to substitute in place of markers in a primary file. Each unit of information that WordPerfect substitutes is called a *field*. WordPerfect has no limit on the amount of text that a field can contain; different fields may contain one word, one line, or multiple lines, or be blank.

WordPerfect refers to each field by a number; for example, the second field is field 2. The set of fields that WordPerfect uses for each part of a Merge document is called a *record*. WordPerfect has no limit on the number of records that your secondary file can contain.

To create a secondary file:

a. Type the information for the first field.

b. Press the Merge R (F9) key.

c. Type the information for the additional fields of a record, pressing the Merge R (F9) key each time you finish a field.

d. Press the Merge Codes (SHIFT-F9) key.

e. Type an **e**.

f. Repeat steps a through e for each record.

g. Save the file.

As you perform these steps, WordPerfect adds characters to the file. These special characters do not appear in the Merge document; WordPerfect uses them to mark the ends of fields and records. When you press the Merge R (F9) key, WordPerfect puts a ^R symbol at the end of the line and moves the cursor to the next line. (The "R" in "Merge R" stands for "return.") When you press the Merge Codes (SHIFT-F9) key and type an **e**, WordPerfect inserts a ^E symbol and a page break and moves the cursor to the next line. You *cannot* achieve the same result by typing the caret symbol (^) followed by the letter.

Examples

1. You can create a record containing different fields of data in a secondary file. The record can contain fields for a person's name, the person's title, the person's company, the first line of the person's address, the second line of the address, the person's phone number, and a salutation to use in a form letter to the person. First, type **Mary Ann**

Kelley. Next, press the Merge R (F9) key. The screen looks
like this:

Mary Ann Kelley^R
-

Next, fill in the field for the title by typing **President**. Press
the Merge R (F9) key. Fill in the field for the company by
typing **Kelley Graphics**. Press the Merge R (F9) key. The
screen now looks like this:

Mary Ann Kelley^R
President^R
Kelley Graphics^R
-

You can complete the address fields by typing **6035 N.E.
25th Avenue**, pressing the Merge R (F9) key, typing **Lighthouse Point, FL 33041**, and pressing the Merge R (F9) key
again. Next, type **305-275-6582** and press the Merge R (F9)
key to add the phone-number field to the record. You can
add the name to be used in a salutation by typing **Mary
Ann** and pressing the Merge R (F9) key to mark the end of
that field.

Finally, press the Merge Codes (SHIFT-F9) key, and type an **e**.
The record now looks like this:

Mary Ann Kelley^R
President^R
Kelley Graphics^R
6035 N.E. 25th Avenue^R
Lighthouse Point, FL 33041^R
305-275-6582^R
Mary Ann^R
^E
==
-

Press the Exit (F7) key and type **n** twice to clear the screen.

2. You can put multiple lines in a field. The same record that you typed can be entered with two lines in the address field instead of one. First, type **Mary Ann Kelley**, and press the Merge R (F9) key. Next, type **President**, and press the Merge R (F9) key. Then, type **Kelley Graphics**, and press the Merge R (F9) key.

You can use two lines for the address. Type **6035 N.E. 25th Avenue**, press ENTER, type **Lighthouse Point, FL 33041**, and press the Merge R (F9) key. The two lines look like this:

```
6035 N.E. 25th Avenue
Lighthouse Point, FL  33041^R
```

To include the telephone number, type **305-275-6582**, and press the Merge R (F9) key. The last field in this record is the name to be used in the salutation. Type **Mary Ann**, and press the Merge R (F9) key.

Finally, press the Merge Codes (SHIFT-F9) key and type an **e**. The record now looks like this:

```
Mary Ann Kelley^R
President^R
Kelley Graphics^R
6035 N.E. 25th Avenue
Lighthouse Point, FL  33041^R
305-275-6582^R
Mary Ann^R
^E
================================================================================
-
```

Keep this record on the screen to use in the next example.

3. You can create records that do not include information in all fields. However, you must tell WordPerfect which fields are empty so that it will continue to use the proper fields after it reaches a field you are skipping. Create a record without a title or company. First, type **Scott McGregor**, and press the Merge R (F9) key. Next, since he does not have a title, press the Merge R (F9) key again. The record looks like this:

Scott McGregor^R
^R
-

The second ^R tells WordPerfect that the information to the left of it is for the second field. Since there is nothing to the left of it, WordPerfect will recognize that the second field is blank. Since Scott McGregor does not have a company name, press the Merge R (F9) key again.

Fill in the address field by typing **503 S.W. 6th Avenue**, pressing ENTER, typing **Pompano, FL 33167**, and pressing the Merge R (F9) key.

To complete the phone number field, type **305-465-6734**, and press the Merge R (F9) key.

To include the first name for a salutation, type **Scott**, and press the Merge R (F9) key.

Finally, since the salutation field is the last one, press the Merge Codes (SHIFT-F9) key and type an **e**. The completed record for Scott McGregor looks like this:

Scott McGregor^R
^R
^R
503 S.W. 6th Avenue
Pompano, FL 33167^R
305-465-6734^R
Scott^R
^E
===

The document now contains two records that are ready to be combined with a primary file, which you will create in the next section. Save this document as NAMES by pressing the Exit (F7) key, typing **y** and **names**, and pressing ENTER. Type an **n** to stay in WordPerfect.

Exercises

1. Create a secondary file that contains the following four records :

B. J. Smith	231-46-4232
Carroll Lawrence	564-90-5327
Sara Graham	976-95-3194
Ellen Pelton	687-64-6546

2. Retrieve the NAMES file created in example 3. Using the same format, add the following record to the secondary file:

   Paul Stevens
   Vice President
   Stevens & Stevens
   635 Dover Street
   Daytona Beach, FL 34240
   305-287-3863
   Paul

3. Add another record to the NAMES secondary file, using your own information. Save the revised file.

14.2   CREATE A PRIMARY FILE

A primary file contains the text that is to appear in each form letter or other Merge document. It also contains Merge codes that instruct WordPerfect where it should place the different fields when it merges with the secondary file. You do not have to use all of the available fields in the primary file; you can use any of the fields you want, in any order you choose. You can also use a field more than once in the primary file.

You might find it worthwhile to print a copy of a secondary file format to help you correctly identify the field numbers when you create a primary file.

To create a primary file:

a. Type the text as you want it to appear in each Merge document. Where the final documents will display individualized information, leave the primary file blank.

b. Place the cursor where you want WordPerfect to substitute one of the fields from the secondary file.

c. Press the Merge Codes (SHIFT-F9) key.

d. Type an **f** for Field.

e. Type the number of the field containing the information that you want inserted at that spot.

f. Press ENTER.

g. Repeat steps b through f for each field in the secondary file that you want placed in the primary file when WordPerfect merges the files.

h. Save the file.

When you press ENTER during this procedure, WordPerfect inserts a ^F followed by the field number that you specified and a caret (^).

Examples

1. You can create a primary file that generates address labels. Since the address labels will include only text that is in the secondary file, the primary file will consist of only field references. First, press the Merge Codes (SHIFT-F9) key to display the options shown here:

^C; ^D; ^E; ^F; ^G; ^N; ^O; ^P; ^Q; ^S; ^T; ^U; ^V;

Next, type an **f**. When WordPerfect prompts you for a field number, type a **1**, for the field containing the person's name in each record, and press ENTER. Press ENTER to move to the next line. The screen now looks like this:

^F1^

Add the Merge code for the field containing the person's title by pressing the Merge Codes (SHIFT-F9) key, typing an **f** and a **2**, and pressing ENTER. Press ENTER to move to the next line.

Add the Merge code for the field containing the company name by pressing the Merge Codes (SHIFT-F9) key, typing an **f** and a **3**, and pressing ENTER. Press ENTER to move to the next line.

Add the Merge code for the field containing the company address by pressing the Merge Codes (SHIFT-F9) key, typing an **f** and a **4**, and pressing the Exit (F7) key. You use the Exit (F7) key rather than ENTER to avoid adding hard returns to the Merge document. Even though the address uses two lines in the secondary file, the primary file requires only one, since WordPerfect will use the hard return in that field when it merges the files. The primary file looks like this:

^F1^
^F2^
^F3^
^F4^

Finally, save this document as LABELS by pressing the Exit (F7) key, pressing ENTER, typing **labels**, pressing ENTER, and typing a **y**.

2. You can create a form letter that confirms reservations. The first part of a letter is the inside address. This address is the information contained in the secondary file that you created earlier. First, press the Merge Codes (SHIFT-F9) key, type an **f** and a **1**, for the field containing the person's name. Press ENTER. The screen looks like this:

^F1^
-

Next, press ENTER to move to the next line. Add the field name for the title by pressing the Merge Codes (SHIFT-F9) key, typing an **f** and a **2**, and pressing ENTER. Press ENTER to move to the next line.

Add the Merge code for field containing the company name by pressing the Merge Codes (SHIFT-F9) key, typing an **f** and a **3**, and pressing ENTER. Press ENTER to move to the next line.

Add the Merge code for the field containing the company address by pressing the Merge Codes (SHIFT-F9) key, typing an **f** and a **4**, and pressing ENTER. Since WordPerfect will use the hard return in field 4 in the secondary file when it merges the files, you need to use only one line for this field in the primary file. Press ENTER twice to place a blank line between the inside address and the salutation.

To create the salutation, type **Dear**, press the SPACEBAR, press the Merge Codes (SHIFT-F9) key, type an **f** and a **6**, and press ENTER. Type a comma to end the salutation, and press ENTER twice. At this point, the screen looks like this:

```
^F1^
^F2^
^F3^
^F4^

Dear ^F6^,
-
```

Type the body and closing of the letter as follows, using the 3.5" tab stop for the closing:

Enclosed are the registration materials for the upcoming forum, Taking Computer Graphics One Step Further. Please return the completed forms no later than the end of the month to insure that you are registered in time.

Sincerely,

Mark Scheimer
Chairman, Education and Development
Association of Computer Graphic Artists

Enc:(3)

This primary file does not use field 5, which contains phone numbers. Save the file as REGIS.

3. You can modify Merge codes in a primary file so that WordPerfect will not include blank secondary file fields. Press the Merge Codes (SHIFT-F9) key, type an **f** and a **1**, for the field containing the name, and press ENTER. Press ENTER to move to the next line.

Next, press the Merge Codes (SHIFT-F9) key, type an **f** and a **2**, type a question mark (?), and press ENTER. The ? after the field number tells WordPerfect to use this field in a Merge only if the field contains information. If the field is blank, WordPerfect will not include it when it merges the record. Press ENTER to move to the next line. The screen looks like this:

```
^F1^
^F2?^
-
```

To include the third field, company name, press the Merge Codes (SHIFT-F9) key, type an **f** and a **3**, type a **?**, and press ENTER. Press ENTER again to move to the next line.

For the address, press the Merge Codes (SHIFT-F9) key, type an **f** and a **4**, and press ENTER. The address uses two lines, but the primary file requires only one, since WordPerfect will incorporate the hard return in the secondary file when it merges the two. Press ENTER twice to place a blank line between the address and the salutation.

To create the salutation, type **Dear**, press the SPACEBAR, press the Merge Codes (SHIFT-F9) key, type an **f** and a **6**, and press ENTER. Type a comma, and press ENTER twice. The screen now looks like the following.

```
^F1^
^F2?^
^F3?^
^F4^
```

Dear ^F6^,

Type the body and closing of the letter as follows, using the 3.5″ tab stop for the closing:

    Enclosed are the registration materials for the upcoming forum, Taking Computer Graphics One Step Further. Please return the completed forms no later than the end of the month to insure that you are registered in time.

        Sincerely,

        Mark Scheimer
        Chairman, Education and Development
        Association of Computer Graphic Artists
Enc:(3)

If you had not used question marks, WordPerfect would have printed blank lines for Scott McGregor's title and company when it merged this primary file with the secondary file containing his record.

Save this file by pressing the Exit (F7) key, pressing ENTER, typing **register**, and pressing ENTER. Type an **n** to stay in WordPerfect.

Exercises

1. Create a primary file for the following form letter, replacing the information in parentheses with Merge codes for fields.

Assume that the secondary file is in the format of the examples in section 14.1.

The Association of Computer Graphic Artists wishes to thank (person's name) from (person's company) for his or her assistance with the Taking Computer Graphics One Step Further forum.

Save this file as THANKS.

2. Create a primary file for the following form letter, substituting the information in parentheses with Merge codes for fields. Assume that the secondary file is in the format of example 2 in section 14.1. Use the 3.5" tab stop for the closing.

(full name)
(title)
(company)
(address)
Dear (first name),

To stimulate attendance at your display during the upcoming forum, we are providing cards for you to distribute. These cards are professionally printed on high-quality paper. The format of these cards is as follows:
(company name)
(address)
(phone number)
Contact: (person's name)
        (title)
If you prefer a different format, call us at (501) 365-2352 by next Monday.

Sincerely,

Mark Scheimer
Chairman, Education and Development
Association of Computer Graphic Artists

Save the file as CARDS.

14.3   PRODUCE THE MERGE DOCUMENT

Once you have created the primary and secondary files, you are ready to produce the Merge document. When you merge the two files, you create another document that contains a copy of the primary file for each record in the secondary file. The new copies have the information from each field substituted for the Merge code for the field number in the primary file. WordPerfect automatically inserts a page break after merging each secondary file record.

Since WordPerfect creates Merge documents in the computer's memory, you may be limited in the number of records you can have in a secondary file. If a Merge exceeds the computer's memory, break up the secondary file into smaller files, and merge the primary file with each smaller secondary file in turn.

WordPerfect has many other Merge features that are beyond the scope of this book. These features are covered in the WordPerfect manual and in *WordPerfect: The Complete Reference* (by Karen L. Acerson; Osborne/McGraw-Hill, 1988).

To create a Merge document:

a. Be sure the current document screen is empty.

b. Press the Merge/Sort (CTRL-F9) key.

c. Type an **m** or a **1** for Merge.

d. Type the name of the primary file, and press ENTER.

e. Type the name of the secondary file, and press ENTER.

WordPerfect merges the files you specified. It automatically adjusts line spacing and word wrap to accommodate the substitution of the secondary file information for the Merge codes for field numbers.

Example

1. You can combine the primary file created in the examples in section 14.2 with the secondary file created in the examples in section 14.1. Press the Merge/Sort (CTRL-F9) key to display this menu:

1 Merge; 2 Sort; 3 Sort Order: 0

Type an **m** to select Merge. Type **register** for the primary file, and press ENTER. Type **names** for the secondary file, and press ENTER. Figure 14-1 shows one of the letters that result from WordPerfect's replacing the Merge codes for field numbers in the primary file with the contents of the fields in the second record. The letter containing your name should appear on your screen. Press the PGUP key to view the other letters.

Save the merge document by pressing the Exit (F7) key, pressing ENTER, typing **rgstr**, and pressing ENTER. Type an **n** to remain in WordPerfect.

Exercises

1. Merge the THANKS primary file that you created in exercise 1 in section 14.2 with the NAMES secondary file. Save the Merge document as THANKS.OUT.

2. Merge the CARDS primary file that you created in exercise 2 in section 14.2 with the NAMES secondary file. Save the Merge document as CARDS.OUT.

PRINT THE MERGE DOCUMENT   14.4

Once you have produced the Merge document, you can print it. You can print a Merge document from disk if you've saved

```
==============================================================================
Scott McGregor
583 S.W. 6th Avenue
Pompano, FL  33167

Dear Scott,

     Enclosed are the registration materials for the upcoming
forum, Taking Computer Graphics One Step Further.  Please return
the completed forms no later than the end of the month to insure
that you are registered in time.

                    Sincerely,


                    Mark Scheiner
                    Chairman, Education and Development
                    Association Of Computer Graphic Artists

Enc:(3)




                                    Doc 1 Pg 2 Ln 4.16" Pos 1"
```

FIGURE 14-1.   WordPerfect screen showing a Merge document

it or print it directly from memory. You can use the same print features that work with printing regular documents.

To print a Merge document:

a. Press the Print (SHIFT-F7) key.

b. Type an **f** or a **1** to print the full document. WordPerfect prints the Merge document.

To print a Merge document from disk:

a. Press the Print (SHIFT-F7) key.

```
Paul Stevens
Vice President
Stevens & Stevens
635 Dover Street
Daytona Beach,  FL 34240

Dear Paul,

     Enclosed are the registration materials for the upcoming
forum, Taking Computer Graphics One Step Further.  Please return
the completed forms no later than the end of the month to insure
that you are registered in time.

                    Sincerely,


                    Mark Scheimer
                    Chairman, Education and Development
                    Association Of Computer Graphic Artists

Enc:(3)
```

FIGURE 14-2.   Printed copy of a letter created with the Merge feature

b. Type a **d** or a **3**.

c. Type the name of the Merge document that you saved, and press ENTER.

d. Type the numbers of the pages that you want printed and press ENTER, or press ENTER to print the entire document.

Example

1. You can print the Merge document that you created in the example in section 14.3. Press the Print (SHIFT-F7) key, type a **d** and **rgstr**, and press ENTER twice. Figure 14-2 shows a printed page from the Merge document created with the REGISTER primary file and the NAMES secondary file.

Exercises

1. Print the Merge document THANKS.OUT, which you created in exercise 1 in section 14.3.

2. Print the Merge document CARDS.OUT, which you created in exercise 2 in section 14.3.

EXERCISES

1. Create a secondary file that contains records with the following information. Each line represents a separate field.

Karen Simon
34220 Euclid Avenue
Cleveland, OH 44134

Jim Darcy
12353 Carnegie Avenue
Lakewood, OH 44116

Save the file as NAMES2.

2. Create a primary file that creates address labels when merged with the secondary file NAMES2. Save the primary file as LBLS. Merge the primary and secondary files, and print the Merge document.

3. Retrieve the NAMES2 secondary file. Add a field for the first name to be used as a salutation in form letters. Save the revised file as NAMES2.

4. Create a primary file containing a letter to be used with NAMES2. Use the following as the letter body:

According to our records, we cannot finish processing the application until you send two ID-sized photos. Please send these photos so that your application to the Radio Controlled Planes Club may be processed.

Sincerely,

Tim Powers
Membership Director

Save the file as PHOTOS. Merge this file with the NAMES2 secondary file, and print the Merge document.

5. Retrieve the PHOTOS primary file, and modify it so that the person's first name and a comma appear after "According to our records." Save the revised file. Merge the file with the NAMES2 secondary file, and print the Merge document.

(Do not clear the screen between exercises unless instructed to do so.)

INTEGRATED
SKILLS CHECK

1. Create a secondary file that contains records with the following information:

**Thomas Douglas
Dept. Manager, Accounting
X3963
Tanya Smith
Dept. Manager, Data Processing
X3959**

Save the file as NAMES.TWO. Clear the screen.

2. Create a primary file that contains the following memo. Replace the parenthetical information with a Merge code or fill in the information, as appropriate. Use the format of the secondary file created in exercise 1 for field numbers.

**Memo
To: (name)
           (title)
           (phone number)
Date: (today's date)
From: (your name)
Re: Smoking Areas
    In compliance with local ordinances, the company
must limit smoking to a designated area. The designated**

smoking area is the cafeteria's west end. Please inform the staff of your department. This is effective immediately.

3. Center the word "Memo."

4. Place a hyphenated line between "Memo" and "To."

5. Save the file as SMOKERS, and clear the screen.

6. Merge the SMOKERS primary file with the NAMES.TWO secondary file.

7. Print two copies of the Merge document.

8. Clear the screen. Retrieve the secondary file into document 1 and the primary file into document 2. Change the size of the document 2 window to 12 lines.

CHAPTER OBJECTIVES

After completing this chapter, you should be able to

15.1 Obtain a total for a column of numbers

15.2 Use multilevel totals

·15·

Adding a Column of Numbers

WordPerfect is not designed to do heavy-duty calculating like a spreadsheet program. It does, however, have basic math capabilities that can perform simple calculations. In this chapter, you will add a column of numbers to produce a subtotal. You will also add subtotals to produce a total and combine totals into a grand total.

You will want to master the basic math features presented in this chapter to guarantee that expense reports, invoices, and other such documents are accurate.

SKILLS CHECK

1. Clear the default tab stops. Create tab settings at 1.5″, 2″, and 4″. Reset the tab stops to the default setting.

2. Type the following paragraph, using Bold and Underline where indicated:

   We have written several times to inquire about the status of order number 98754. Please check the status of the back-order items. If you are unable to fill the remainder of the order within <u>10 days</u>, please notify us so that we can contact other suppliers.

3. Type the following, using the ESC key to draw the line:

   ```
   150
    50
   100
   ───
   300
   ```

4. Type the following, using bold where indicated:

   You can use an 's to create the plural of letters, numbers, symbols, and words. For example, you could write that there are four s's and four i's in Mississippi.

   Print two copies of the paragraph.

5. Type the following:

   Errors, like straws, upon the surface flow;
   He who would search for pearls, must dive below.

   John Dryden

   Use the Block feature to make two more copies of the quotation and author name.

6. Reset the number of copies to one.

OBTAIN A TOTAL FOR A COLUMN OF NUMBERS

15.1

Many of the documents that you create may contain columns of figures. Rather than use a calculator to obtain the correct total at the bottom of a column, you can use WordPerfect's Math features.

WordPerfect's Math features require a bit of advanced planning and a little extra care on your part. You must follow a set procedure, placing the math entries in columns set with tab stops. The Math features use a special symbol to tell WordPerfect that you wish to add the numbers in a column.

Once you have learned the process, abiding by the rules is not difficult. Your reward is column totals that are always accurate, whether you are preparing commission reports, purchase orders, or the company bowling team's scores.

To calculate a total for a column of numbers:

a. Place the cursor where you wish to use the Math features.

b. Set tab stops for the columns you plan to use.

c. Press the Math/Columns (ALT-F7) key.

d. Type an **m** or a **1** to turn Math on.

e. Type the column entries for the labels and numbers.

f. Type a plus sign (**+**) where you want the total calculated.

g. Press the Math/Columns (ALT-F7) key.

h. Type an **a** or a **2** for Calculate.

i. Press the Math/Columns (ALT-F7) key.

j. Type an **m** or a **1** to turn Math off.

The hidden codes [Math On] and [Math Off] mark the beginning and ending locations for Math. These steps produce what WordPerfect refers to as a subtotal for the column. WordPerfect uses the special code [+] to mark where it will compute the subtotal. In many documents, the subtotal will be all you need.

Examples

1. You can use WordPerfect's Math features to add amounts in an invoice. First, type the top of the invoice: Press the Center (SHIFT-F6) key, and type

ABC COMPANY

Press ENTER. Next, press the Center (SHIFT-F6) key, and type

Invoice Number 889-3452

Press ENTER. Then, press the Center (SHIFT-F6) key, and type

As of August 5, 1989

Press ENTER twice. The screen looks like this:

```
                    ABC COMPANY
              Invoice Number 889-3452
                 As of August 5, 1989
```

You are now ready to set the tabs for the math columns. Since you can store the text descriptions at the left margin, you need only one tab stop for the numeric column. Press the Format (SHIFT-F8) key, and type an l and a t. Clear all the tabs by pressing the DEL EOL (CTRL-END) key. Type **4.5**, and press ENTER. Type a **d** to change the tab set to a decimal tab, which aligns numbers on their decimal points. Press the Exit (F7) key twice.

Press the Math/Columns (ALT-F7) key, and type an **m** to turn on the Math feature. WordPerfect displays **Math** at the left edge of the status line. WordPerfect can perform calculations only in an area of the document where the Math feature is on.

Type **Desk**, press the TAB key, and type **249.95**. WordPerfect places the decimal point at the tab stop. Press ENTER, type **Chair (side)**, press the TAB key, and type **98.75**. Press ENTER, type **Chair (desk)**, press the TAB key, and type **185.00**. For the last item, press ENTER, type **Lamp**, press TAB, type **59.95**, and press ENTER.

You can use a plus sign (+) to make WordPerfect add the numbers in the column. First, press the TAB key to position the cursor in the numeric column. Next, type a **+**. Nothing seems to happen, as the plus symbol only marks the place where you want the calculation; it does not perform the calculation. The screen looks like Figure 15-1. To perform the calculation, you must return to the Math menu. Press the Math/Columns (ALT-F7) key. A revised list of menu options now appears. Type an **a** to calculate the subtotal. The result on the screen should match Figure 15-2. When you print this document, the + symbol will not appear on the printed copy.

```
                      ABC COMPANY
                Invoice Number 889-3452
                As of August 5, 1989


Desk                     249.95
Chair (side)              98.75
Chair (desk)             185.00
Lamp                      59.95
                           +
```

FIGURE 15-1.   Plus sign used for subtotal

```
                    ABC COMPANY
              Invoice Number 889-3452
              As of August 5, 1989

Desk                  249.95
Chair (side)           98.75
Chair (desk)          185.00
Lamp                   59.95
                      593.65+
```

FIGURE 15-2.   Subtotal calculated

You can now turn off the Math feature. Press the Math/Co-lumns (ALT-F7) key, and type an **m**. The Math features are inactive at the current cursor position. A + symbol typed outside of the document area where Math is on will not be effective in totaling a column of numbers.

Use these entries in the next example.

2. You can revise mathematical calculations that have already been defined. Move the cursor to the "8" in "185.00." Notice that the **Math** indicator reappears on the status line. Press the INS key to invoke Typeover mode, type a **7**, and press INS again to turn Typeover mode off. The new number appears in the column, but the subtotal is unchanged. You must invoke the Math menu again to recalculate the subtotal. Press the Math/Columns (ALT-F7) key, and type an **a**. The new subtotal appears at the bottom of the column.

Use these entries in the next example.

3. You can insert a new item in a column and include its value in the subtotal. First, move the cursor to the "L" in "Lamp." Press the ENTER key to add a new line, and use the UP ARROW key to move the cursor to it. Type **Credenza**, and press the TAB key. Type **205.75**. Again, the subtotal needs to be recalculated. Press the Math/Columns (ALT-F7) key, and type

an **a**. The new subtotal, 789.40, appears at the bottom of the column.

Save the file by pressing the Exit (F7) key, pressing ENTER, typing **invoice**, and pressing ENTER. Press ENTER again to remain in WordPerfect.

Exercises

(Do not clear the screen until you have completed the last exercise.)

1. Set a decimal tab stop at 3″, and create math columns for the following entries:

Salaries	50,000
Benefits	8,500
Travel	18,000
Rent	120,000

Since the numbers do not have a decimal point, Word Perfect right-aligns them at the tab stop when you press ENTER. Calculate a subtotal at the bottom of the column. Turn off the Math feature.

2. Change the "Benefits" amount to **8,900**. Recalculate the subtotal.

USE MULTILEVEL TOTALS
15.2

WordPerfect supports multiple levels of totals. You can calculate subtotals for columns of entries, add subtotals, and even create a grand total. Each level requires a different symbol to indicate which entries you want WordPerfect to add together.

You can place all of your totals in the same column, or you can use the columns to the right of your entries to show different levels of totals. If you elect to use extra columns, you must use another Math feature to define the columns before making your entries.

To create multiple levels of totals:

a. Place the cursor where you wish to use the Math feature.

b. Set tab stops for the columns you plan to use.

c. Press the Math/Columns (ALT-F7) key.

d. Type an **e** or a **2** for Math Def (definition).

e. Change the settings as appropriate for each column you will use, and press the Exit (F7) key.

f. Type an **m** or a **1** to turn Math on.

g. Type the column entries for the labels and numbers.

h. Press the TAB key to move the cursor to the appropriate column, and type a **+** to calculate a subtotal, an equal sign (=) to calculate a total from subtotals, or an asterisk (*) to calculate a grand total.

i. Press the Math/Columns (ALT-F7) key.

j. Type an **a** or a **2**.

k. Press the Math/Columns (ALT-F7) key.

l. Type an **m** or a **1** to turn Math off.

The special code [Math Def] marks the Math definition in the Reveal Codes screen; [=] marks where WordPerfect will compute the total; and [*] marks where WordPerfect will compute the grand total.

Examples

1. You can add subtotals together. You can place this total in the same column as the subtotals or in a separate column to the right. If you wish to use a separate column, you must be sure the column is defined appropriately.

You can use this feature to find the total of the salaries paid to sales representatives on the East Coast. In addition to defining the columns for the numeric entries and totals, you can define other text columns to allow for the indentation of various levels of entries.

The first step is to define the tab settings for all of the columns. Press the Format (SHIFT-F8) key, and type an l and a t. Press the DEL EOL (CTRL-END) key to clear the tab settings. Create left-aligned tab stops at 1.2″, 1.4″, and 1.6″. Create decimal tab stops at 4.5″, 5.5″, and 6.5″. The tab settings look like this:

```
,,L,L,L,,,,,,,,,,,,,,,,,,,,,,,,,,,D,,,,,,,,D,,,,,,,,D,,,,,,,,,,,,,,,,,,,,,
¦    ^   ¦    ^   ¦    ^   ¦    ^   ¦    ^   ¦    ^   ¦    ^   ¦    ^
1"      2"      3"      4"      5"      6"      7"      8"
Delete EOL (clear tabs); Enter Number (set tab); Del (clear tab);
Left; Center; Right; Decimal; ,= Dot Leader
```

Press the Exit (F7) key twice to return to the document. Next, press the Math/Columns (ALT-F7) key, and type an e to define the Math columns. The Math Definition screen looks like Figure 15-3. The letters at the top represent consecutive columns in the document, not including the column at the left margin. You need to define only the columns you plan to use. Type of column is defined in the next line. As the information near the bottom of the screen explains, 1 indicates Text columns, 2 is used for Numeric columns, and 3 is used for columns containing calculated totals. If the setting for a column is incorrect, you will need to change the number under the column letter.

The next row in the Math Definition screen defines the appearance of negative numbers. For each column, you can choose a minus sign or parentheses. The entries in the next row indicate the number of digits to be placed after the decimal point in each calculation in each column.

Math Definition	Use arrow keys to position cursor
Columns	A B C D E F G H I J K L M N O P Q R S T U V W X
Type	2 2 2 2 2 2 2 2 2 2 2 2 2 2 2 2 2 2 2 2 2 2 2 2
Negative Numbers	((
Number of Digits to the Right (0–4)	2 2 2 2 2 2 2 2 2 2 2 2 2 2 2 2 2 2 2 2 2 2 2 2

```
Calculation    1
   Formulas    2
               3
               4

Type of Column:
     0 = Calculation    1 = Text    2 = Numeric    3 = Total

Negative Numbers
     ( = Parentheses (50.00)        - = Minus Sign  -50.00
```

Press Exit when done

FIGURE 15-3.   Math Definition screen

For the current example, the first three columns will be Text columns; type a **1** three times to make these changes. The next column will be a Numeric column. Type a **2** for this setting, or press the RIGHT ARROW key if the column is already set to 2. Type **3** twice to set the next two columns to be Total columns.

Press the DOWN ARROW key twice, press the LEFT ARROW key three times, and type **0** three times to eliminate decimal places in calculations in the Numeric and Total columns (D, E, and F). Figure 15-4 shows the completed entries. Press the Exit (F7) key to accept the Math column definitions. Type an **m** to turn on the Math feature.

Next, type **Salary Report**, and press ENTER twice. Press the TAB key, type **East Coast**, and press ENTER twice. Press the TAB key twice, type **New York**, and press ENTER. Press the TAB key three times, and type **Bob Jones**. Press the TAB key again,

Math Definition   Use arrow keys to position cursor

Columns   A B C D E F G H I J K L M N O P Q R S T U V W X

Type   1 1 1 2 3 3 2 2 2 2 2 2 2 2 2 2 2 2 2 2 2 2 2 2

Negative Numbers   (

Number of Digits to   2 2 2 0 0 0 <u>2</u> 2 2 2 2 2 2 2 2 2 2 2 2 2 2 2 2 2
  the Right (0-4)

Calculation   1
  Formulas   2
             3
             4

Type of Column:
    0 = Calculation   1 = Text   2 = Numeric   3 = Total

Negative Numbers
    (= Parentheses (50.00)   - = Minus Sign -50.00

Press Exit when done

FIGURE 15-4. Defining math columns for text, subtotal, total, and grand total

type **25,600**, and press ENTER. Press the TAB key three times, type **Jane Doe**, press the TAB key again, type **26,850**, and press ENTER.

Since these are the only two employees listed in the New York area, you can compute a subtotal for the salaries for New York. Press the TAB key four times, and type a +. WordPerfect displays the + but does not perform the calculation automatically.

Press the ENTER key twice, press the TAB key twice, type **Washington**, and press ENTER. Press the TAB key three times, type **Nancy Smith**, press the TAB key again, type **32,500**, and press ENTER. Press the TAB key three times, type **Mary Marvin**, press the TAB key again, and type **24,350**.

To include the subtotal for Washington, press ENTER, press the TAB key four times, and type a +.

Salary Report

  East Coast

    New York
      Bob Jones   25,600
      Jane Doe   26,850
                  52,450+

    Washington
      Nancy Smith   32,500
      Mary Marvin   24,350
                  56,850+
                        109,300=

FIGURE 15-5.   Using the equal sign to calculate a total

To make WordPerfect add the subtotals, press the ENTER key, press the TAB key five times, and type an =. This symbol represents the total level. Press the Math (ALT-F7) key, and type an **a** to have WordPerfect calculate the total. The results look like Figure 15-5.

Use these entries in the next example.

2. You can add a grand-total level to a WordPerfect report. You can add data for the West Coast to the entries in example 1 and use the grand-total level to produce a total of the salaries in all locations.

First, press the ENTER key twice to begin entering the additional data. Next, press the TAB key, type **West Coast**, and press ENTER twice. Press the TAB key twice, type **California**, and press ENTER. Press the TAB key three times, and type **Cindy Harper**. Press the TAB key again, type **42,870**, and press ENTER. Press the TAB key three times, type **Jeff Parker**, press the TAB key again, type **39,700**, and press ENTER.

Since these are the only two employees in the California area, you can have WordPerfect calculate a subtotal for the salaries. Press the TAB key four times, type a **+**, and press the ENTER key twice.

Press the TAB key twice, type **Nevada**, and press ENTER. Press the TAB key three times, type **Joan Carson**, press the TAB key again, type **18,750**, and press ENTER. Press the TAB key three times, type **Frances Drake**, press the TAB key again, type **16,500**, and press ENTER.

To tell WordPerfect where to place the subtotal for Nevada, press the TAB key four times, and type a +.

To make WordPerfect calculate a total for the two subtotals, press ENTER, press the TAB key five times, and type an =. Then, press the Math (ALT-F7) key, and type an **a**. Word Perfect calculates the subtotals for California and Nevada and a total for the West Coast.

You can have WordPerfect calculate a grand total for the East and West Coasts. Press ENTER once, and press the TAB key six times. Type an * to mark the location of the grand total. Press the Math (ALT-F7) key and type an **a** to make WordPerfect calculate the result. Press the Math (ALT-F7) key and type an **m** to turn off the Math features. Since WordPerfect shifted the screen display when it calculated, move the cursor toward the top of the report to see all the entries. Figure 15-6 displays the results. You can make changes to the numbers that are in the Math area, but you will need to recalculate to revise the totals.

Exercises

1. Set a left-justified tab at 1.5″ and decimal tabs at 3.7″ and 4.7″. Use the Math features to re-create the following information, with decimal places set to 0:

   Machine repairs

   Model 5210
       Factory 1   10
       Factory 2   5
   Total Repairs 5210   +

```
New York
   Bob Jones          25,600
   Jane Doe           26,850
                      52,450+

Washington
   Nancy Smith        32,500
   Mary Marvin        24,350
                      56,850+
                               109,300=

West Coast

California
   Cindy Harper       42,870
   Jeff Parker        39,700
                      82,570+

Nevada
   Joan Carson        18,750
   Frances Drake      16,500
                      35,250+
                               117,820=
                                       227,120*
Math                           Doc 1 Pg 1 Ln 1.66" Pos 2.2"
```

FIGURE 15-6.   Using the asterisk to calculate a grand total

Model 6511
   Factory 1   48
   Factory 2   9
Total Repairs 6511   +

TOTAL ALL MODELS   =

Calculate the subtotals and the total.

2. Set left-justified tabs at 1.3″ and 1.5″ and decimal tabs at 4.5″, 5.5″, and 6.5″. Recreate the following information with the Math features:

EMPLOYEE BENEFIT PARTICIPATION
   Employees in Savings Plan
      Thrift   500

```
S&L                     250
Bonds                   250
Total in Savings              +
Employees in Stock Option Plan
   Plan A               100
   Plan B               100
Total in Stocks               +
Total Employees in Investment Plans   =
Employees in Medical Plan
   White Cross          500
   Cheap Docs           500
Total Medical                 +
Employees in Life Insurance Plan
   Quick Save           100
   High Risk            100
Total Life                    +
Total Employees in Insurance Plans   =
```

TOTAL NUMBERS IN BENEFIT PLANS *

Have WordPerfect calculate the totals.

EXERCISES

1. Set the tabs and Math features, type the following information, and calculate the subtotal:

HEAD COUNT BY LOCATION

```
Chicago             120
Dallas               38
Denver              105
New York            302

TOTAL                      +
```

Do not clear the screen.

2. Edit "TOTAL" to read "U.S. TOTAL." Add the following information to the list, and calculate the subtotal.

MASTERY
SKILLS CHECK

Paris	82
London	106
Lisbon	34
Frankfort	192
FOREIGN TOTAL	+

3. Set a left-justified tab at 1.5″ and decimal tabs at 3.5″ and 4.5″. Use the Math features to recreate the following information, and calculate the subtotals and total, with decimal places set to 0:

Product 1 Sales
Jim	12,500
Fred	38,900
Harry	23,500
Total Product 1	+

Product 2 Sales
Jim	23,450
Fred	56,750
Harry	78,900
Total Product 2	+

Total Products 1 & 2 =

4. Set tabs and the Math features, recreate the following information, and calculate the totals:

Office Supplies
	10.00
	15.50
	25.60
Total Supplies	+
Office Furniture	
	345.00
	545.00
Total Furniture	+
Total Office Products	=

Coffee Supplies	25.00	
	15.80	
Total Coffee		+
Paper Products		
	115.00	
Total Paper		+
Total Miscellaneous		=
TOTAL PURCHASES		*

(Do not clear the screen until you have completed the last exercise.)

INTEGRATED
SKILLS CHECK

1. Type the following:

   Expenses for 1989 have risen dramatically. Please review the following figures with your managers.

   Add a header with ABC Company at the left and the date at the right. Add a footer with the page number in the middle preceded by the word "Page."

2. Type the following information below the paragraph, using the Math features. Use 3″ and 4.5″ left-justified tabs for the column headers and 3.5″ and 5″ decimal tabs for the numbers.

	Last Year	This Year
Travel	52,900	86,900
Consultants	104,585	190,800
Entertainment	3,900	9,800
Supplies	1,200	15,900
Phone	25,000	49,000
TOTALS	+	+

Calculate the totals for the two columns.

3. Turn off Math, reset the tabs, and type the following:

   A meeting has been scheduled for June 20 to discuss emergency measures to cut costs. Please come prepared to offer your suggestions for both proven and innovative cost-cutting measures.

4. Print two copies of the document.

CHAPTER OBJECTIVES

After completing this chapter, you should be able to

16.1 Draw a line

16.2 Create a box with lines

16.3 Erase a line

16.4 Move the cursor without drawing

16.5 Use a special character for the line

16.6 Add text to a box

·16·

Drawing Lines and Boxes

WordPerfect's Line Draw feature allows you to add borders, lines, boxes, and graphs to your documents. You can use lines to create your own custom forms or to add a dividing line beneath a letterhead. Organizational charts and flow diagrams are easy to create with the Line Draw feature.

You can use the Line Draw feature in a blank document, or you can type text and add lines around it. WordPerfect's ESC key allows you to control the length of a line. Special characters can be used to add variety to your drawings or to create graphs with multiple data series; you can use a different character line for each data series. You can erase existing lines or move the cursor without extending the current line.

With these features, you have a full set of options for jazzing up your documents with the addition of lines and boxes. If you are using proportionally spaced text on your printer, however, line draw will not produce satisfactory results.

When you draw lines and boxes, WordPerfect uses special codes to describe the symbols. When you reveal codes, these hidden codes appear different from the other codes you have used, but they operate like other keyboard characters.

SKILLS CHECK

(Do not clear the screen until you have completed the last exercise.)

1. Create a subdirectory called ACCOUNT on the same level as WP50.

2. Create a subdirectory of WP50 called LETTERS.

3. Create a line of 55 asterisks with the ESC key.

4. On the line below the asterisks, type the following text centered, boldfaced, and underlined:

   1989 Statement of Changes in Financial Position

5. Preview the printed document.

6. Block the line of asterisks, and reposition it below the centered text.

16.1 DRAW A LINE

You can draw single or double lines with a simple Word-Perfect menu option. The Line Draw feature provides you the means to develop your own set of forms, to which you can add text. Depending on which direction you move the cursor, you can create lines vertically and horizontally.

To draw a line:

a. Place the cursor where you want the line to start.

b. Press the Screen (CTRL-F3) key.

c. Type an 1 or a **2** to select Line Draw.

d. Type a **1** to draw a single line or a **2** to draw a double line.

e. Move the cursor to where you want the line to end.

f. Press the Exit (F7) key.

An alternative method is

a. Place the cursor where you want the line to start.

b. Press the Screen (CTRL-F3) key.

c. Type an 1 or a **2** to select Line Draw.

d. Type a **1** to draw a single line or a **2** to draw a double line.

e. Press ESC.

f. Type the number of spaces or lines through which you want the drawn line to extend.

g. Press the UP ARROW, DOWN ARROW, LEFT ARROW, or RIGHT ARROW key to provide the direction in which the line should be drawn.

h. Press the Exit (F7) key.

As you move the cursor, WordPerfect draws the line. The arrows that appear on the screen will not be printed. As you draw the line, WordPerfect inserts spaces and hard returns where appropriate to make the line fit the document format.

Examples

1. You can use vertical lines to set off lines of text. First, type

When you use the drill, remember to:

Next, press ENTER to move to the next line. Press the Screen (CTRL-F3) key. Then, type an **1** and a **2**. Press the DOWN ARROW key 3 times. This creates a double line with an arrow at the top and bottom.

Next, press the Exit (F7) key. The screen looks like this:

```
When you use the drill, remember to:
↑
‖
‖
↓
```

You can type the set off text. Press the UP ARROW key twice and the RIGHT ARROW key once to place the cursor next to the first double-line character. Press the SPACEBAR, and type

Wear safety goggles and gloves.

Since WordPerfect inserted a hard return for each line in which the double line was drawn, you do not need to press ENTER. Instead, press the DOWN ARROW key. Press the SPACEBAR, and type

Unplug the drill before changing bits.

The screen now looks like this:

```
When you use the drill, remember to:
↑
‖ Wear safety goggles and gloves.
‖ Unplug the drill before changing bits.
↓
```

When you preview the document at 100% by pressing the Print (SHIFT-F7) key and typing a **v** and a **1**, the screen looks like this:

```
When you use the drill, remember to:

Wear safety goggles and gloves.
Unplug the drill before changing bits.
```

The actual characters that WordPerfect uses for the lines depend upon your printer.

2. You can use horizontal lines to set off text. First, type

When you use the drill, remember to:

Press ENTER to move to the next line. Press the Screen (CTRL-F3) key, and type an l and a 1. Press ESC, type a 5, and press the RIGHT ARROW key to draw a line 4 characters long with arrows at both ends. Exit from the Line Draw by pressing the Exit (F7) key. The screen looks like this:

```
When you use the drill, remember to:
←——→
```

You can type the first line of text next to this line. Press the RIGHT ARROW key, and type

Wear safety goggles and gloves.

Then, press ENTER to move to the next line.

To draw the next line, press the Screen (CTRL-F3) key, and type an l. Since WordPerfect retains the last selection from this menu, you do not have to select the type of line you want to draw. Press ESC, type a 5, and press the RIGHT ARROW key. To finish the line drawing, press the Exit (F7) key. Press the RIGHT ARROW key, and type

Unplug the drill before changing bits.

The screen appears as follows.

When you use the drill, remember to:
←———→Wear safety goggles and gloves.
←———→Unplug the drill before changing bits.

Exercises

1. Type the first paragraph below. Draw a horizontal double line 40 characters long, and type the second paragraph.

> The new accounting system assigns each account a number. The numbers prevent confusion among accounts with similar names but different purposes.
> This change will improve internal control. It should prevent debits and credits to the miscellaneous account that belong in another account.

2. Draw a single line that extends 3 rows down. Then draw a double line 6 characters across. Draw another double line that extends 5 rows down. Preview how WordPerfect will print the lines at 100% and 200%.

16.2   CREATE A BOX WITH LINES

You can create a box with a series of four connecting lines. The secret to creating boxes with same-length lines on opposite sides is to use the ESC key to draw the lines that make up the sides of the box. WordPerfect automatically adds corners to your boxes as you change directions. Text to the right of the cursor is pushed ahead to make room for the box. WordPerfect inserts spaces and hard returns to fill blank areas.

To draw a box:

a. Place the cursor where you want the box's upper left-hand corner to appear.

b. Press the Screen (CTRL-F3) key.

c. Type an **1** or a **2** to select Line Draw.

d. Type a **1** to draw a single line or a **2** to draw a double line.

e. Press ESC, type the number of rows through which the box will extend, and press the DOWN ARROW key.

f. Press ESC, type the number of spaces across which the box will extend, and press the RIGHT ARROW key.

g. Press ESC, type the number you typed in step e, and press the UP ARROW key.

h. Press ESC, type the number you typed in step f, and press the LEFT ARROW key.

i. Press the Exit (F7) key.

Examples

1. You can use boxes to show where information should be provided in a form. First, type

   Total amount remitted:

   Next, press the Screen (CTRL-F3) key, and type an **1** and a **1**. Then, press ESC, type a **3**, and press the DOWN ARROW key. Create the bottom line of the box by pressing ESC, typing **10**, and pressing the RIGHT ARROW key.

   To create the right side of the box, press ESC, type a **3**, and press the UP ARROW key.

   Complete the box by pressing ESC, typing **10**, and pressing the LEFT ARROW key. Press the Exit (F7) key. The screen looks like this:

   Total amount remitted:

2. You can combine lines and boxes to create a blank organizational chart. First, type

Organization Chart

Press ENTER to move to the next line, and press TAB four times.

To begin drawing the first box, press the Screen (CTRL-F3) key, type an 1 and a 2, and press the DOWN ARROW key 3 times. To draw the bottom of the box, press the ESC key, type **15**, and press the RIGHT ARROW key. For the right side of the box, press the UP ARROW key 3 times. To complete the box, press the ESC key, type **15**, press the LEFT ARROW key, and press the Exit (F7) key.

To create a second box, you can block and copy the first one. First, press the DOWN ARROW 3 times, END once, and ENTER twice to move below the box. Next, press the UP ARROW key 5 times and CTRL-RIGHT ARROW to move to the upper left-hand corner of the box. Press the Block (ALT-F4) key, the DOWN ARROW key 3 times, and END once. Then, press the Move (CTRL-F4) key and type an **r**.

As the highlight shows, blocking a rectangle affects only the area between the cursor's first and last position. When you move, copy, or delete a rectangle, WordPerfect ignores the text or other material that is on the same line as any line of the block but not within the rectangle. Type a **c** for Copy. Press the DOWN ARROW key twice and ENTER once to place the copy of the box below and to the left of the original.

To draw the third box, press END once and TAB 5 times to move to the box's location. Press the Move (CTRL-F4) key and type an **r** twice for Retrieve and Rectangle. The screen looks like Figure 16-1.

To draw the connecting lines, press ESC, type a **7**, and press the RIGHT ARROW key to move to the middle of the box that you just drew. Next, press the Screen (CTRL-F3) key, and type an 1 and a **1**. Press the UP ARROW key once to draw a line leading up from the box on the right. Press ESC, type **39**, and

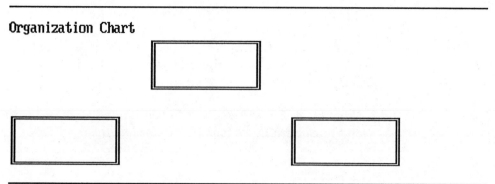

FIGURE 16-1.   Boxes for an organizational chart

press the LEFT ARROW key to draw a line to the box on the left. Press the DOWN ARROW key to connect the line to the box and the Exit (F7) key to complete the line drawing.

Next, press the UP ARROW key, press ESC, type **20**, and press the RIGHT ARROW key to move to the middle of the line that you created. Then, press the Screen (CTRL-F3) key, type an **1**, press the UP ARROW key to connect all three boxes, and press the Exit (F7) key. The organizational chart looks like Figure 16-2.

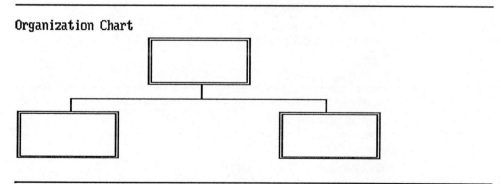

FIGURE 16-2.   Lines connecting the organizational chart boxes

Exercises

1. Create a form that asks for a person's first name and last name. For each place the form prompts for information, create a box to contain the information.

2. Using boxes 5 rows deep and 14 columns wide, draw boxes and lines for a flow chart that looks like this:

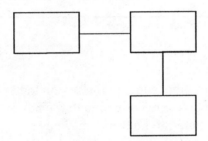

16.3   ERASE A LINE

WordPerfect's erase option in the Line Draw menu lets you correct mistakes without starting over. As you move the cursor over a line, WordPerfect erases that part of the line. You can use this option to shorten or remove a line. WordPerfect adjusts spaces and hard returns to maintain the remaining portions of the line.

To erase a line:

a. Move the cursor to the end or beginning of the part of the line you want to erase.

b. Press the Screen (CTRL-F3) key.

c. Type an 1 for Line Draw.

d. Type a **5**.

e. Move the cursor along the part of the line you want to erase.

f. Press the Exit (F7) key.

Since WordPerfect erases every character over which you move the cursor when you erase lines, do not move the cursor over part of a line that you want to keep. If you want to move to another line to erase, press the Exit (F7) key first so that you can move the cursor without changing the drawing. You can also erase lines and boxes by pressing DEL or typing spaces in Typeover mode.

Examples

1. You can use the erase option when you have drawn a line incorrectly. First, press the Screen (CTRL-F3) key, type an l and a 1, press ESC, type 20, press the RIGHT ARROW key, and press the Exit (F7) key.

   To erase part of the end of the line, press the Screen (CTRL-F3) key, type an l and a 5, press the LEFT ARROW key twice, and press the Exit (F7) key. You have shortened the line by two characters.

2. You can erase part of a line from the middle. First, press the Screen (CTRL-F3) key, type an l and a 1, press ESC, type 12, press the RIGHT ARROW key, and press the Exit (F7) key.

   Next, press the LEFT ARROW key 6 times to move the cursor to the middle of the line. Then, press the Screen (CTRL-F3) key, type an l and a 5, press the RIGHT ARROW key 3 times, and press the Exit (F7) key. The line now looks like this:

←——→ ←→

3. You can use the Line Draw feature to create boxes representing an office layout and erase part of a box to represent
   a door between rooms. First, label the drawing by typing

Office Layout

Next, press ENTER to move to the next line, press the Screen
(CTRL-F3) key, and type an l and a **1**. To draw the first room,
press ESC, type a **4**, press the DOWN ARROW key, press ESC, type
20, press the RIGHT ARROW key, press ESC, type a **4**, press the UP
ARROW key, press ESC, type **20**, press the LEFT ARROW key, and
press the Exit (F7) key.

For the second room, press ESC, type a **4**, and press the DOWN
ARROW key. Then, press the Screen (CTRL-F3) key, type an l and
a **1**, press ESC, type an **8**, press the DOWN ARROW key, press ESC,
type **10**, press the RIGHT ARROW key, press ESC, type an **8**, and
press the UP ARROW key.

For the third room, press ESC, type an **8**, press the DOWN ARROW
key, press ESC, type **10**, press the RIGHT ARROW key, press ESC,
type **8**, press the UP ARROW key, and press the Exit (F7) key.
The screen looks like Figure 16-3.

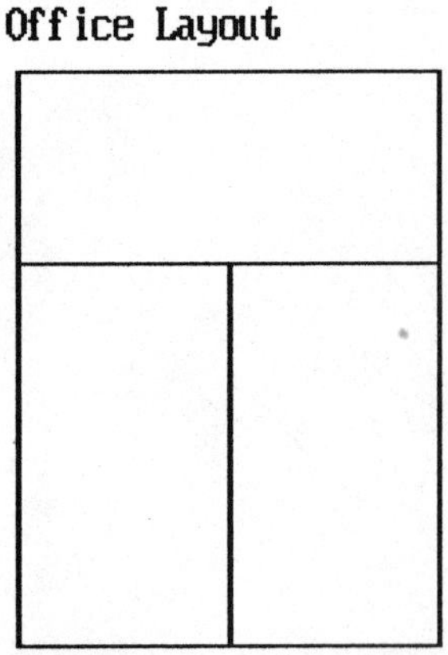

Office Layout

FIGURE 16-3. Office layout with three rooms

To move to the entrance, press the UP ARROW key 4 times, press ESC, type **11**, and press the LEFT ARROW key. To mark the door, press the Screen (CTRL-F3) key and type an l and a **5**, and press the RIGHT ARROW key twice.

To move to the next door without drawing or erasing, press the Exit (F7) key, press the DOWN ARROW key 4 times, and press the LEFT ARROW key 7 times. To indicate the door, press the Screen (CTRL-F3) key, type an l, and press the RIGHT ARROW key twice.

To erase the lines for the last door, type a **1** so that WordPerfect draws a line where you move the cursor. Next, press ESC, type a **9**, and press the RIGHT ARROW key. Then, type a **5** to erase the line, and press the RIGHT ARROW key twice. Press the Exit (F7) key. The screen looks like Figure 16-4.

Exercises

1. Draw a double line 6 characters across. Erase the line.

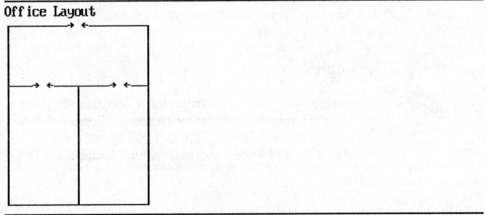

FIGURE 16-4.   Using the erase option to show doors in the office layout

2. Create a single-line box that is 5 characters across and 4 rows deep. Erase the middle character in the top and the bottom of the box to split the box in half.

16.4   MOVE THE CURSOR WITHOUT DRAWING

Entering multiple unconnected lines on the screen requires a method for moving the cursor without extending the lines. WordPerfect's Line Draw feature provides a menu option to support cursor movement without line creation.

To move the cursor without drawing (or erasing):

a. Press the Screen (CTRL-F3) key.

b. Type an **1** or a **2** for Line Draw.

c. Draw the first line.

d. Type a **6**.

e. Place the cursor where you want to draw another line.

f. Type a **1** or **2** to draw another line.

WordPerfect adds the necessary spaces and hard returns to allow you to move in a straight direction.

Examples

1. You can move the cursor around in a document to shorten the steps you must perform when you draw multiple lines. First, type the following lines, pressing ENTER once after "Name" and "Phone" and twice after "Address":

Name:
Address:

Phone:

To draw a line after each entry, press the UP ARROW key and END to move to the end of the "Phone" line. Next, press the Screen (CTRL-F3) key, and type an l and a **1**. Press ESC, type **30**, and press the RIGHT ARROW key. Instead of pressing the Exit (F7) key to move to the second "Address" line, type a **6**, and press the UP ARROW key. WordPerfect automatically inserts spaces at the beginning of the second "Address" line so that you can move up in a straight line.

To draw the line for the second line of the address, type a **1**, press ESC, type **30**, and press the LEFT ARROW key.

Move to the first "Address" line by typing a **6** and pressing the UP ARROW key. To draw the line for the first line of the address, type a **1**, press ESC, type **30**, and press the RIGHT ARROW key.

Move to the "Name" line by typing a **6** and pressing the UP ARROW key. To draw the line for the name, type a **1**, press ESC, type **30**, and press the RIGHT ARROW key. Press the Exit (F7) key. The result looks like this:

```
   Name:←————————————————————→
Address:←————————————————————→
        ←————————————————————→
  Phone:←————————————————————→
```

2. You can draw a competition list using WordPerfect. For this type of list, some of the lines connect and others do not. To draw the lines for the first set of competitors, press the Screen (CTRL-F3) key, type an l and a **1**, press ESC, type **20**, press the RIGHT ARROW key, press the DOWN ARROW key twice, press ESC, type **20**, and press the LEFT ARROW key. The screen looks like this:

```
←————————————┐
             │
             │
←————————————┘
```

To draw the lines for other competitors, type a **6**, press the DOWN ARROW key twice, type a **1** to resume line drawing, press ESC, type **20**, press the RIGHT ARROW key, press the DOWN ARROW key twice, press ESC, type **20**, and press the LEFT ARROW key.

Next, draw lines for the finals. First, type a **6**, press the UP ARROW key, press ESC, type **20**, and press the RIGHT ARROW key to move the cursor to the vertical line. Then, type a **1** to resume line drawing, press ESC, type **20**, and press the RIGHT ARROW key. Next, press ESC, type a **4**, and press the UP ARROW key. Press ESC again, type **20**, and press the LEFT ARROW key.

To draw a line for the winner, first type a **6**, press the DOWN ARROW key twice, and press the RIGHT ARROW key until the cursor is at the vertical line. Then, type a **1** to resume line drawing, press ESC, type **20**, and press the RIGHT ARROW key. Press the Exit (F7) key. The drawing looks like Figure 16-5.

Exercises

1. Create a double-line box that is 4 rows deep and 15 characters across. Move 5 spaces beyond the right edge of the box, and create a box that is 2 rows deep and 12 characters across.

2. Make three "I"s using the Line Draw feature. The "I"s should be 10 rows high and 10 characters wide and be 10 characters apart from each other.

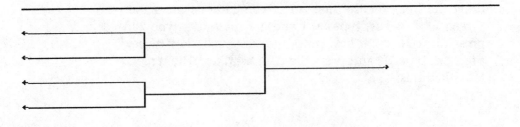

FIGURE 16-5.   A competition list

USE A SPECIAL CHARACTER FOR THE LINE

16.5

You can draw lines with any character you choose. Word-Perfect's default Line Draw menu offers the asterisk (*) as an option for drawing lines when you choose characters other than a single or double line. You can change the setting for this character and draw lines with any character of your choice.

To use the special character to draw a line:

a. Place the cursor where you want the line to start.

b. Press the Screen (CTRL-F3) key.

c. Type an 1 or a **2** to select Line Draw.

d. Type a **3** to draw with the displayed special character.

e. Move the cursor to where you want the line to end, or press ESC, type the number of times you want the special character, and press an arrow key to indicate in which direction to draw the line.

f. Repeat step e for every line you want.

g. Press the Exit (F7) key.

To change the special character:

a. Place the cursor where you want to start drawing with the special character.

b. Press the Screen (CTRL-F3) key.

c. Type an 1 or a **2** to select Line Draw.

d. Type a **c** or a **4** to change the special character.

e. Type the number representing the special character you want or an **o** or a **9** if the one you want is not displayed.

f. Type the character that you want if you typed **9** in step e.

g. Draw your lines with the special character.

Examples

1. You can create a box of asterisks. First, press the Screen (CTRL-F3) key, and type an **l** and a **3**. Next, press the DOWN ARROW key 3 times, the RIGHT ARROW key 4 times, the UP ARROW key 3 times, and the LEFT ARROW key 3 times. Finally, press the Exit (F7) key. The box looks like this:

```
*****
*   *
*   *
*****
```

2. You can change the special character to a shaded pattern. First, press the Screen (CTRL-F3) key and type an **l** and a **4**. Then, type a **1** to select the character indicated by that number.

3. You can use the special character you have just selected to create a gray box. First, press the Screen (CTRL-F3) key, and type an **l** and a **3**.

Next, press the DOWN ARROW key twice, the RIGHT ARROW key 7 times, the UP ARROW key twice, and the LEFT ARROW key 6 times. Finally, press the Exit (F7) key. The box looks like this:

Exercises

1. Set the special character to the number sign (#). Create a box 10 lines deep and 20 characters wide.

2. Set the special character to the solid rectangle (■). Draw a line 30 characters long.

ADD TEXT TO A BOX   16.6

If you create organizational charts or flow diagrams, you will need to place text inside your boxes. You can create the text first and draw boxes around the text, or you can draw the box first and add the text. To add text to an existing box, you need to use the INS key to set WordPerfect to Typeover mode. If you used Insert mode, you would distort the box when you added the text.

To insert text in a box:

a. Press the INS key.

b. Place the cursor inside the box in which you want to include text.

c. Type the text.

d. Press the INS key.

Examples

1. You can put text in boxes to set off the text. First, start Line Draw by pressing the Screen (CTRL-F3) key and typing an **1** and a **2**. Next, press ESC, type a **5**, press the DOWN ARROW key, press ESC, type **35**, press the RIGHT ARROW key, press ESC, type **5**, press the UP ARROW key, press ESC, type **35**, and press the LEFT ARROW key. Then, press the Exit (F7) key.

Next, press the INS key, press the DOWN ARROW key, press the RIGHT ARROW key twice, and type

Bill must be paid by August 20th

For the next line of text, press the DOWN ARROW key, CTRL-LEFT ARROW key combination, and the RIGHT ARROW key twice, and type

To prevent a late payment penalty

The final block looks like this:

```
┌─────────────────────────────┐
│ Bill must be paid by August 20th │
│ To prevent a late payment penalty │
└─────────────────────────────┘
```

2. You can use the text and line drawings to create an organizational chart. First, create a box at the top for the president. Press the Screen (CTRL-F3) key and type an l and a 2. Then, press ESC, type a 3, press the DOWN ARROW key, press ESC, type 25, press the RIGHT ARROW key, press ESC, type a 3, press the UP ARROW key, press ESC, type 25, and press the LEFT ARROW key.

To create a box for the first person who reports to the president, type a 6, and press DOWN ARROW key 6 times. Then, type a 2, press ESC, type a 3, and press the DOWN ARROW key. Press ESC again, type 20, and press the RIGHT ARROW key, press ESC, type a 3, and press the UP ARROW key. To complete the box, press ESC, type 20, and press the LEFT ARROW key.

To create a box for the second person who reports to the president, you can copy the box for the first one. First, press the Exit (F7) key to end Line Draw. Next, press the Block (ALT-F4) key, the DOWN ARROW key 3 times, and END. Then, press the Move (CTRL-F4) key and type an r and a c. Next, press the UP ARROW key 3 times, and press END and ENTER to place the copy of the box next to the original.

To create a box for the third person who reports to the president, press the Move (CTRL-F4) key and type an r twice.

You can center the president's box with WordPerfect's Center features. Press HOME twice, and the UP ARROW key once.

Then, press the Block (ALT-F4) key and the DOWN ARROW key 4 times to highlight the entire box. Press the Center (SHIFT-F6) key, and type a **y**. The screen looks like Figure 16-6.

Once you have created the boxes, you can draw lines between them. First, press the UP ARROW key and the CTRL-RIGHT ARROW key combination. Press ESC, type **13**, and press the RIGHT ARROW key to move to the middle of the bottom line of the top box. Then, press the Screen (CTRL-F3) key, and type an **l** and a **1**. To draw the first line, press the DOWN ARROW key 3 times. To draw the second line, type a **6**, and press the UP ARROW key twice. Then, press ESC, type **22**, and press the LEFT ARROW key. Press the DOWN ARROW key twice. Next, type a **1**, press the UP ARROW twice, press ESC, type **44**, and press the RIGHT ARROW key. Then, press the DOWN ARROW key twice. Since this completes the line drawings, press the Exit (F7) key. The screen looks like Figure 16-7.

Now you can add text to the boxes. First, press the INS key to switch to Typeover mode, and move to the top box by pressing the UP ARROW key 5 times, the CTRL-LEFT ARROW key combination twice, and the RIGHT ARROW key 7 times. Then, type **Paula Stevens**, press the CTRL-LEFT ARROW key combination twice and the DOWN ARROW key once, and type **President**.

Next, press the DOWN ARROW key 5 times, the CTRL-LEFT ARROW key combination twice, and the RIGHT ARROW key 5 times to move to the first box in the second row. Type **Tom Packard**,

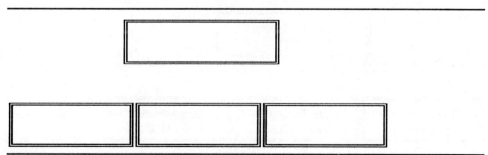

FIGURE 16-6. Organizational chart shell

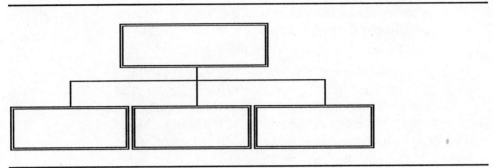

FIGURE 16-7. Organizational chart with connecting lines

press the CTRL-LEFT ARROW key combination twice, press the DOWN ARROW key, and type **Marketing**.

Next, press the CTRL-RIGHT ARROW key combination, the UP ARROW key, and the RIGHT ARROW key 6 times to move to the next box. Type **Sue Kegley,** press the CTRL-LEFT ARROW key combination twice, press the DOWN ARROW key, and type **Controller**.

Next, press the CTRL-RIGHT ARROW key combination, the UP ARROW key, and the RIGHT ARROW key 5 times to move to the last box. Type **George Adams**, press the CTRL-LEFT ARROW key combination twice, press the DOWN ARROW key, and type **Production**. The final organizational chart looks like Figure 16-8.

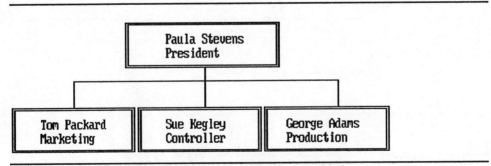

FIGURE 16-8. Completed organizational chart with text added

3. You can add the boxes after you type the text. You can use this feature to create, for example, a diagram of subdirectories, such as a diagram of a root directory containing the WP50 subdirectory and an ACCOUNT subdirectory. The WP50 subdirectory has its own subdirectory, called LETTERS. First, press ENTER three times to create space to draw the boxes later. Then, press TAB 4 times, and type **Root Directory**. Next, press ENTER 4 times, press TAB, type **WP50**, press TAB 8 times, and type **ACCOUNT**. Then press ENTER 3 times, press TAB, type **LETTERS**, and press ENTER.

To draw a box for the root directory, press ESC, type a **9**, press the UP ARROW key, and press TAB 3 times. Then, press the Screen (CTRL-F3) key, and type an **1** and a **2**, press the DOWN ARROW key twice, press ESC, type **23**, and press the RIGHT ARROW key. To complete the box, press the UP ARROW key twice, press ESC, type **23**, and press the LEFT ARROW key. The "y" in "directory" may temporarily disappear, but it will reappear as you work on the document.

To draw the box for the WP50 subdirectory, type a **6**, and press the DOWN ARROW key 4 times. Type a **2**, press ESC, type **15**, press the LEFT ARROW key, press the DOWN ARROW key twice, press ESC, type **15**, and press the RIGHT ARROW key. To complete the box, press the UP ARROW key twice, press ESC, type **15**, and press the LEFT ARROW key.

To draw the box for the ACCOUNT subdirectory, type a **6**, press ESC, type **26**, and press the RIGHT ARROW key. Then, type a **2**, press the DOWN ARROW key twice, press ESC, type **15**, press the RIGHT ARROW key, press the UP ARROW key twice, press ESC, type **15**, and press the LEFT ARROW key.

To draw the box for the LETTERS subdirectory, type a **6**, press the DOWN ARROW key 3 times, press ESC, type **50**, press the LEFT ARROW key, and type a **2**. Then, press the DOWN ARROW key twice, press ESC, type **15**, press the RIGHT ARROW key, press the UP ARROW key twice, press ESC, type **15**, and press the LEFT ARROW

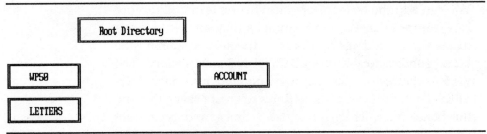

FIGURE 16-9. Boxes added around text

key. Some letters may temporarily disappear, but they will reappear when you move the cursor. The screen looks like Figure 16-9.

Once you have drawn the boxes, you can draw lines to connect them. First, type a **6**, press ESC, type an **8**, press the RIGHT ARROW key, type a **1** and press the UP ARROW key. Next, type a **6**, press the UP ARROW key twice, type a **1**, press the UP ARROW key, press ESC, type **40**, press the RIGHT ARROW key, and press the DOWN ARROW key to connect the WP50 and AC-COUNT subdirectories. To connect the root directory to the subdirectories, press the UP ARROW key, press ESC, type **20**, press the LEFT ARROW key, and press the UP ARROW key. Since this completes the diagram, press the Exit (F7) key. The screen looks like Figure 16-10.

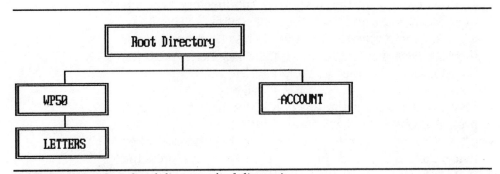

FIGURE 16-10. Completed diagram of subdirectories

4. You can combine text, lines, and boxes to create a graph like the one shown in Figure 16-11. First, insert blank lines at the top of the screen by pressing ENTER 3 times and press the SPACEBAR 8 times to leave blank space at the left. Next, press the Screen (CTRL-F3) key, and type a **2** for Line Draw. Select a single line by typing a **1**, and press ESC, type **18**, and press the DOWN ARROW key. Press ESC, type **55**, and press the RIGHT ARROW key to complete the axes for the graph.

Type a **6**, and press ESC, type **55**, and press LEFT ARROW to move to the intersection of the axes, and press the RIGHT ARROW key 3 times. Type a **1**, and begin drawing the first bar by pressing the UP ARROW 6 times. Then, press the RIGHT ARROW key 6 times and press the DOWN ARROW key 6 times to rejoin the horizontal axis.

To draw the second bar, press the RIGHT ARROW key 5 times, the UP ARROW key 8 times, the RIGHT ARROW key 6 times, and the DOWN ARROW key 8 times. To draw the third bar, press the

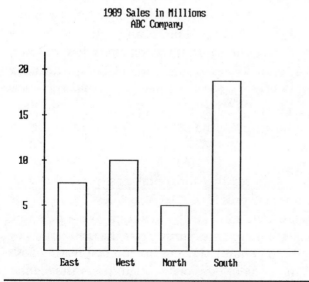

FIGURE 16-11.   A bar chart

RIGHT ARROW key 5 times, the UP ARROW key 4 times, the RIGHT ARROW key 6 times, and the DOWN ARROW key 4 times. To draw the fourth bar, press the RIGHT ARROW key 5 times, press ESC, type **15**, press the UP ARROW key, press the RIGHT ARROW key 6 times, press ESC, type **15**, and press the DOWN ARROW key.

Next, draw the tick marks on the vertical axis. Press ESC, type **42**, and press LEFT ARROW. Type a **6**, press the LEFT ARROW key, press the UP ARROW key 4 times, type a **1**, and press the RIGHT ARROW key twice to draw the first tick mark. To create the next tick mark, type a **6**, press the UP ARROW key 4 times, type a **1**, and press the LEFT ARROW key twice. For the next tick mark, type a **6**, press the UP ARROW key 4 times, type a **1**, and press the RIGHT ARROW key twice. To create the last tick mark, type a **6**, press the UP ARROW key 4 times, type a **1**, and press the LEFT ARROW key twice. Press the Exit (F7) key to end Line Draw. Each tick mark on the screen looks like a short arrow with an arrowhead at both ends.

To label the tick marks, you must be in Typeover mode. Press the INS key if **Typeover** is not displayed in the status line, press the LEFT ARROW key 4 times, and type a **20**. For the next tick mark down, press the DOWN ARROW key 4 times, press the LEFT ARROW key twice, and type **15**. For the next tick mark, press the DOWN ARROW key 4 times, press the LEFT ARROW key twice, and type **10**. For the last tick mark, press the DOWN ARROW key 4 times, press the LEFT ARROW key once, and then type a **5**.

To add the labels for the horizontal axis, press the DOWN ARROW key 5 times, press the RIGHT ARROW key 7 times, type **East**, press the RIGHT ARROW key 8 times, type **West**, press the RIGHT ARROW key 6 times type **North**, press the RIGHT ARROW key 6 times, and type **South**. Move to the top by pressing HOME twice and the UP ARROW key once. Then, press the Center (SHIFT-F6) key, type **1989 Sales in Millions**, and press ENTER.

Press the Center (SHIFT-F6) key again, type **ABC Company**, and press ENTER. When the graph is completed, your screen looks like Figure 16-12.

Although the arrowheads do not appear on the printed graph, their positions are marked by a slight deviation in the straightness of the line on most printers.

You can erase the deviations by replacing the arrows with spaces. First, press the INS key to switch to the Typeover mode if **Typeover** is not displayed in the status line. For each of the arrows you want to remove, move the cursor to an arrow and press the SPACEBAR. When you have removed all the arrows, press the INS key to return to the Insert mode.

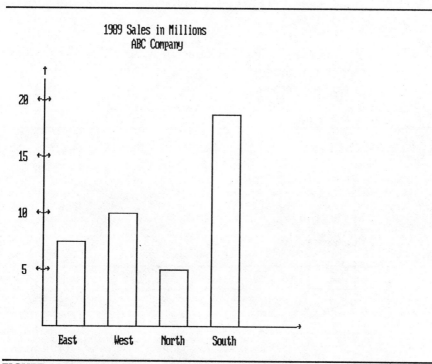

FIGURE 16-12.   A bar chart with lines

Exercises

1. Create a subdirectory diagram with three subdirectories under the root directory. Name them BUDGET, PROD-UCT, and REPORTS.

2. Create a single-line box that is 50 characters across and 4 rows deep. Type the following text inside the box:

   All of the paintings displayed in this
   restaurant are for sale on a consignment
   basis. For more details, see the manager.

EXERCISES

MASTERY
SKILLS CHECK

(Do not clear the screen between exercises unless instructed to do so.)

1. Create a single line 40 characters across. Move 20 spaces to the left in the line, and erase the 3 characters to the right. Clear the screen.

2. Create this flow chart:

Clear the screen.

3. Change the special character to colons.

4. Create the following line diagram. Insert a blank line above the diagram, and press ENTER twice before typing each line of text.

```
Construction Schedule          Dates

Start renovation◄─────────────────────────────┐
Start interior remodeling◄──────────────────┐  │
Start repaving parking lot◄──────────────┐  │  │
End repaving parking lot◄────────────────┘  │  │
End interior remodeling◄────────────────────┘  │
End renovation◄─────────────────────────────────┘
```

5. Delete the portion of the lines under the "Dates" heading. Then, insert the following dates:

Start renovation	5/1
Start interior remodeling	6/15
Start repaving parking lot	7/1
End repaving parking lot	7/31
End interior remodeling	8/30
End renovation	9/30

6. Draw a box of colon characters around the diagram.

1. Create a form for the entry of the following information. After each item, draw a box large enough to contain the information.

Last name:
First name:
Department:
Years with the company:

INTEGRATED
SKILLS CHECK

2. Type the following lines of text:

Acme's Main Product Line
Solder
Silver necklaces
Silver flatware

Add lines that connect the items to the heading "Acme's Main Product Line."

3. Remove the ACCOUNT subdirectory that you created in the Skills Check.

4. Remove the LETTERS subdirectory that you created in the Skills Check.

5. Return the special character for line drawing to asterisks. Create a box 10 lines by 50 characters, and put the following text inside it:

Clark Corporation is Moving
On Friday the 23rd, Clark Corporation is
closing its Lakewood offices. Its new
headquarters are in Barlow, Florida. It is
moving there to move closer to its prospering
land-development subsidiary.

6. Center the box and the text inside.

CHAPTER OBJECTIVES

After completing this chapter, you should be able to

17.1 Create a graphics box

17.2 Place text in a box

17.3 Place a figure in a box

17.4 Add a caption

17.5 Position and size a box

17.6 Edit and delete graphics boxes

17.7 Print documents containing graphics

·17·

WordPerfect's
New Graphics
Features

WordPerfect 5.0 provides exciting new features that allow you to combine text and graphics in a single document. You can use these features to create newsletters, letterheads, customized forms, and other special documents that convey your message with both text and graphics.

You can incorporate graphic images created with computer-aided design (CAD) systems as line drawings and use pictures created with draw packages. If you would prefer not to create the images, third-party developers sell diskettes containing a variety of graphic images. WordPerfect provides a number of sample graphics files that you can use to try out the techniques presented in this chapter.

WordPerfect also enables you to add graphics boxes to a document and display text within the box. Objectives, quotations, sidebars, and other textual materials can be set off from the main text using this method.

The full set of graphics features offered by this package will require some time to explore. In this chapter, you will be introduced to the basic options to get you started using these exciting new features. Even these basic options will require a little more time to master than some of the other topics in this book. You will find the time investment worthwhile if you want to create professional-looking documents that include text and graphics.

SKILLS CHECK

(Do not clear the screen until you have completed the last exercise.)

1. Type the following paragraph:

   The objective of this chapter is to learn how to incorporate graphics boxes into your document. You will learn how to create these boxes and use options to fill the boxes with images or text. WordPerfect also allows you to create captions for the boxes to provide labels and titles. These boxes can be moved and deleted.

   Underline **objective of this chapter**. Save the document as GRAPHBOX.

2. Switch to the second document. Retrieve GRAPHBOX, and add the following paragraph:

   Once your document is complete, you can print it. Many printers can print text and graphics simultaneously.

3. Create a header that says **WordPerfect's Graphics Features**.

4. Boldface the words "captions," "labels," and "titles."

5. Preview document 2. Preview document 1.

CREATE A GRAPHICS BOX 17.1

Before you can add a graphics image to a document, you must create a box. Once the box is created, you can access disk files to obtain the text or graphics data to be shown in the box. Graphics boxes are like footnotes in that WordPerfect numbers them in their order of appearance and renumbers them as necessary when boxes are added, deleted, or moved. Graphics boxes can be placed anywhere in a document, including in headers and footers. Once you create a graphics box, you can view how WordPerfect will print it by previewing the page if your monitor and printer support graphics.

To add a graphics box:

a. Press the Graphics (ALT-F9) key.

b. Type the option number or letter for the type of box that you want.

c. Type a **c** or a **1** to create the box.

d. Define or change features of the box, as necessary.

e. Press the Exit (F7) key or ENTER to return to the document.

WordPerfect has four box types: Figure, Table, Text Box, and User-Defined Box. (The last graphics option, Line, is not used for graphics boxes.) The box type that you select does not affect what can be stored in the box. The differences among the box types are the separate numbering sequences that each type uses and the default settings for each type; these are described in Table 17-1. When you create a graphics box, WordPerfect draws a box on the screen indicating where it will place the graphics box. WordPerfect's default settings keep the document text from overlaying the contents of the

TABLE 17-1. Default Settings for Graphics Boxes

Graphics Box Type	Figure	Table	Text Box	User-Defined Box
Initial caption	Figure #	Table #	#	#
Caption position	Below box, outside border	Above box, outside border	Below box, outside border	Below box, outside border
Numbering	Arabic (1, 2)	Roman (I, II)	Arabic (1, 2)	Arabic (1, 2)
Initial size	3.25″ × 3.25″	3.25″ × 3.37″	3.25″ × 0.6″	3.25″ × 3.25″
Border	Single line on all sides	Thick lines on top and bottom	Thick lines on top and bottom	No border
Alignment	Right	Right	Right	Right

box. If WordPerfect cannot fit the entire graphics box on the current page, it moves the box to the next page.

Once you have created a graphics box, you can preview it. To preview it, press the Print (SHIFT-F7) key, and type a **v**. This displays your text and graphics as they will print. If the graphics do not display, you most likely have a monitor that cannot display graphics or you have a nongraphics printer. You will have a blank preview screen if you have a user-defined graphics box with nothing in it.

Examples

1. You can insert a graphics box and add additional information later. First, press the Graphics (ALT-F9) key. Type an **f** for figure and a **c** to create a figure. Press the Exit (F7) key to accept the default settings for this type of box and return to the document. The screen does not show the bottom of the graphics box until you move the cursor down to that area

FIG 1

Doc 1 Pg 1 Ln 4.83" Pos 1"

FIGURE 17-1.   Sample graphics box

of the document. To see how WordPerfect marks the document area for the graphics box, press ENTER several times to move the cursor toward the bottom of the screen. The screen looks like Figure 17-1.

2. When you create a graphics box, WordPerfect wraps text around it unless you specify otherwise. To illustrate this feature, press the Graphics (ALT-F9) key, and type a **t** for table and a **c** for create. Press ENTER to accept the default

settings for the table and return to the document. Word-Perfect has not drawn the box yet. To see how WordPerfect wraps words around a graphics box, type

WordPerfect allows you to add graphics boxes anywhere in your document. The options let you put graphic images or text into the boxes. You can also move or copy a box or change a box's size.

As you type the text, WordPerfect wraps the words and draws the sides of the graphics box. The screen looks like this:

3. When you preview your document, WordPerfect displays the graphics box. To preview a text box, press the Graphics (ALT-F9) key. Type a **b** for text box and a **c**, and press the Exit (F7) key. Next, press ENTER until WordPerfect draws the entire box. To see how WordPerfect will print this box, press the Print (SHIFT-F7) key and type a **v** and a **1**. The text box looks like this:

4. You can create multiple graphics boxes on the same page. As you add additional ones, WordPerfect makes them smaller whenever necessary to accommodate their correct

placement. To create two adjacent text boxes, press the Graphics (ALT-F9) key, type a **b** and a **c**, and press the Exit (F7) key. Next, press the Graphics (ALT-F9) key, type a **b** and a **c**, and press the Exit (F7) key. Because the default position setting for the first box is at the right margin, WordPerfect places the second box to the left of the first. To see how WordPerfect will print these boxes, press the Print (SHIFT-F7) key and type a **v**. The preview of the text boxes look like this:

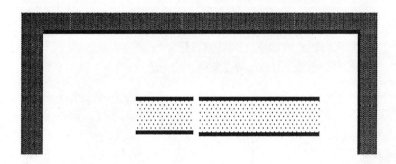

5. You can place graphics boxes below one another in a document. If the boxes are not side by side, WordPerfect does not make the new boxes smaller. To create a figure above a table, press the Graphics (ALT-F9) key. Type an **f** and a **c**, and press the Exit (F7) key. Next, press ENTER 21 times. Then, press the Graphics (ALT-F9) key, type a **t** and a **c**, and press ENTER. To see how WordPerfect will print the figures, press the Print (SHIFT-F7) key, and type a **v** and a **3**. The figures look like Figure 17-2.

Exercises

1. Create a user-defined box. Press ENTER until the cursor reaches the line below the bottom of the box.

2. Create a figure. Type the following text, allowing Word Perfect to draw the box and wrap the text as you type it.

When you create a graphics box, WordPerfect wraps the document text around it. If WordPerfect has not already drawn the box, it draws the box as you type the text. Even as you edit the text that you put next to the box, Word-Perfect adjusts the text so that it is still properly wrapped.

3. Create a table. Preview how WordPerfect will print it.

4. Create a text box. Press ENTER until the cursor reaches the line below the bottom of the box. Create a figure. Preview how WordPerfect will print it.

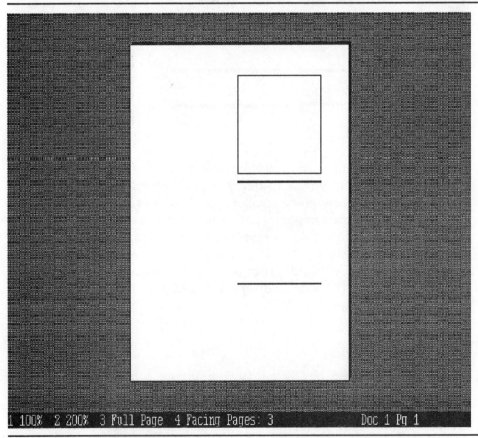

1 100% 2 200% 3 Full Page 4 Facing Pages: 3   Doc 1 Pg 1

FIGURE 17-2. Two graphics boxes

5. Create a table. Create a figure box next to it. Press ENTER until the cursor reaches the line below the bottom of both graphics boxes. Preview how WordPerfect will print them.

PLACE TEXT IN A BOX   17.2

You can display the contents of another document file within a graphics box in the current document. You can also type the text for a graphics box when you define the settings for the box. This can be an effective way to highlight project objectives or to set off quotations or any other important text in the document.

When you use another document as the text for a graphics box, WordPerfect copies the text from the document on disk into the box in the current document. Since the box reflects the disk document's contents at the moment you copy it, it is not updated to include any changes you subsequently make in the original document. Likewise, any changes you make to the duplicate copy in the current document do not affect the original file. When you use a document file in a graphics box, the size of the graphics box changes to accommodate the size of the document.

You can edit or create the text for a graphics box in a screen accessible through the graphics box menu selections. You can preview the contents of a text box using the Print Preview Menu Option.

To use text from a document stored on disk in a graphics box:

a. Press the Graphics (ALT-F9) key.

b. Type the appropriate number or letter for the box type that you want to create.

c. Type a **c** or a **1** to create the graphics box.

d. Type an **f** or a **1** to retrieve a file into the graphics box.

e. Type the name of the file containing the text that you want to appear in the graphics box.

f. Press ENTER.

g. Press the Exit (F7) key to return to the document.

To enter text in a graphics box or edit a graphics box containing a file:

a. Press the Graphics (ALT-F9) key.

b. Type the appropriate number or letter for the box type that you want to create or edit.

c. Type a **c** or a **1** to create a box or an **e** or a **2** to edit an existing box.

d. If you typed an **e** or a **2** in the previous step, type the number of the box you want to edit, and press ENTER.

e. Type an **e** or an **S** to edit the graphics box.

f. Type the text that you want to appear in the graphics box, or edit the existing text.

g. Press the Exit (F7) key twice to return to the document.

When you place text in a graphics box, WordPerfect sets the size of the graphics box to the size needed for the text. When you edit the text in a graphics box, you can use all of WordPerfect's formatting features, such as Bold and Underline. If you are using another document in the graphics box, the text contains all of the codes from the document on disk; if this text contains margin codes, you should remove them.

Examples

1. You can use text in boxes to have the text treated as a unit. First, press the Graphics (ALT-F9) key and type an **f**, a **c**, and an **e** to enter text for the graphics box. WordPerfect places the cursor near the middle of the screen, since the graphics box is set to appear on the right side of the screen. Type

Graphics boxes allow you to treat text as a unit. With text in a box, you can move the box around without affecting the text in it.

Do not press ENTER at the end of the paragraph. Press the Exit (F7) key. WordPerfect changes the size of the graphics box to 3.25" × .69", assuming your printer is set to print six lines to the inch. Press the Exit (F7) key to return to the document, and type

Text in a document containing graphics boxes is automatically moved to accommodate the graphics boxes. As the information in the boxes changes, WordPerfect adjusts the wrapping for the remaining text. Graphics boxes allow some text to be unaffected by the other text.

The screen looks like this:

```
Text in a document containing        ┌FIG 1─────────────────────┐
graphics boxes is automatically      │                          │
moved to accommodate the             │                          │
graphics boxes. As the               │                          │
information in the boxes             │                          │
changes, WordPerfect adjusts the     └──────────────────────────┘
wrapping for the remaining text.  Graphics boxes allow some text
to be unaffected by the other text.

-
```

Press the Print (SHIFT-F7) key, and type a **v** and a **1**. The preview of the printed document appears as follows.

```
Text in a document containing │Graphics boxes allow you to treat│
graphics boxes is automatically │text as a unit.  With text in a│
moved   to   accommodate   the │box, you can move the box around│
graphics  boxes.      As   the │without affecting the text in it.│
information    in    the   boxes
changes, WordPerfect adjusts the
wrapping for the remaining text.  Graphics boxes allow some text
to be unaffected by the other text.
```

2. You can display text from another document in a text box. First, type

   On August 17, 1989, the board of directors approved the company's long-term goals as presented by the Development Committee. The approved goals include:
   Increase the return on investment from 8 to 10 percent.
   Renovate the Hamburg facilities and develop a community-responsible attitude in that area.
   Focus research and development on the electrochemical market.

   Press the Exit (F7) key, type a **y**, type **goals**, press ENTER, and type an **n** to clear the screen. Press the Graphics (ALT-F9) key, type a **t**, a **c**, and an **f**, type **goals**, and press ENTER. WordPerfect retrieves that file and places the filename and the word "Text" enclosed in parentheses next to the Filename option. Press the Exit (F7) key to return to the document. Use this document in the next example.

3. You can edit the text in a graphics box without changing the original document that you used. You may want to take this approach to use WordPerfect's formatting features on text for a table. First, press the Graphics (ALT-F9) key, type a **t**, an **e**, and a **1** or an **i**, press ENTER, and type an **e**. Change the table's appearance by deleting the first paragraph. Then, press the Bold (F6) key, type **The long-term goals approved by the board of directors are:**, press the Bold (F6) key again, and press ENTER. Then, press the Exit (F7) key twice. To view the table, press the Print (SHIFT-F7) key and type a **v** and a **1**. The preview of the table looks like this:

```
The long-term goals approved
by the board of directors are:
Increase   the   return   on
investment  from  8  to  10
percent.
Renovate the Hamburg facilities
and   develop   a   community
responsible attitude in that
area.
Focus research and development
on the electrochemical market.
```

Exercises

1. Create a table with the following text, typing the text directly into the graphics box:

Project	Date
Systems analysis	5/1
Order equipment	6/15
Design software	7/1
Test software	7/31
Implement software	8/30
Evaluation	9/30

   Preview how WordPerfect will print it.

2. Type the following paragraph:

   Besides creating graphics boxes containing text, you can also create graphics boxes with images. The next section will show you how to create a graphics box with an image. You do not need to create the image first, since Word-Perfect provides several ready-made images.

   Save the document as PICTURE, and clear the screen. Create a text box that uses the text from the PICTURE file. Preview how WordPerfect will print it.

3. Create a table with the following text, typing the text directly into the graphics box.

Steps for Creating a Figure with Text in It:
1. Press the Graphics (ALT-F9) key.
2. Type an f for figure.
3. Type a c to create a figure.
4. Type an e to edit the figure's contents.
5. Type the text to appear in the figure.
6. Press the Exit (F7) key to end the edit.
7. Press the Exit (F7) key to return to the document.

Preview how WordPerfect will print the table.

17.3   PLACE A FIGURE IN A BOX

WordPerfect can incorporate graphic images within a graphics box. The WordPerfect program includes 30 graphic images. You can add your own if you have graphic images in one of several formats that WordPerfect can use. Placing a figure in a box is very much like placing text in a box. You can view the graphic images using WordPerfect's print preview if your computer has a graphics card. If your computer does not have a graphics card, you can still create graphic images, although you will not be able to see them until you print them.

To place a graphic image in a graphics box:

a. Press the Graphics (ALT-F9) key.

b. Type the appropriate number or letter for the box type that you want to create or edit.

c. Type a c or a 1 to create a graphics box or an e or a 2 to edit an existing graphics box.

d. If you typed an e or a 2 in the previous step, type the number of the box you want to edit, and press ENTER.

e. Type an f or a 1 to specify the file containing the graphic image.

f. Type the name of the file containing the image that you want to appear in the graphics box, and press ENTER.

g. Press the Exit (F7) key to return to the document.

When you place an image in a graphics box, WordPerfect sets the size of the box to fit the image. WordPerfect uses the same height-to-width ratio that was in effect when the image was created.

Examples

1. You can use WordPerfect's ready-made images, such as the computer image named PC.WPG, to enhance your documents. First, press the Graphics (ALT-F9) key. Type a **u** for User-defined box, a **c**, and an **f**. If your WordPerfect graphic images are in the WP50 subdirectory, type **pc.wpg** and press ENTER. If your graphic images are in a subdirectory of the WordPerfect subdirectory, type the subdirectory name, a backslash, and the figure name (for example, **graphics\pc.wpg**), and press ENTER. If your graphics images are not in the WordPerfect subdirectory, type a backslash and the appropriate subdirectory name in the examples and exercises before typing the graphics image filename. WordPerfect finds the file and loads the image into memory. WordPerfect adjusts the graphics box size to a default setting for the image. Press the Exit (F7) key to return to the document. To view the image, press the Print (SHIFT-F7) key, and type a **v** and a **3**. The image looks like this:

2. You can use WordPerfect images in headers. Press the Format (SHIFT-F8) key, and type a **p**, an **h**, an **a**, and a **p** to create a header for every page. Press the Graphics (ALT-F9) key. Type an **f**, a **c**, an **f**, and **airplane.wpg**, and press ENTER. WordPerfect finds the file and loads the image into the header. WordPerfect adjusts the graphics box size to a default setting for the image. Press the Exit (F7) key three times to return to the document. To view the header, press the Print (SHIFT-F7) key, and type a **v** and a **1**. The screen looks like this:

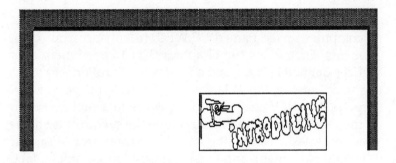

3. WordPerfect can use graphic images from other packages, allowing you to incorporate graphs and drawings that you have already made into your WordPerfect documents. This example requires a .PIC file from Lotus 1-2-3 and is included because many users wish to access this type of data. While you may not have this particular graph or the spreadsheet with which it was created, these steps demonstrate the process. If you do not have a Lotus 1-2-3 file, you can use other graphic image files that various software packages create. You can skip this example if you do not plan to work with graphs.

To use a Lotus 1-2-3 graph in a WordPerfect document, press the Graphics (ALT-F9) key and type an **f**, a **c**, and an **f**. To use a Lotus 1-2-3 .PIC file named GRAPH, which is stored in the default directory for 1-2-3, type **c:\123\graph.pic** as the pathname and filename of the file,

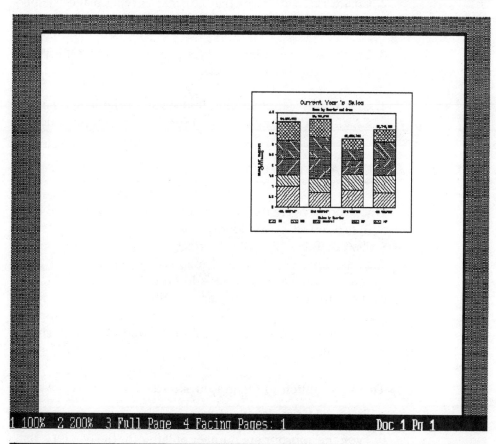

FIGURE 17-3.   Graphics box with Lotus 1-2-3 .PIC file

press ENTER, and press the Exit (F7) key to return to the document. To view this graph, press the Print (SHIFT-F7) key, and type a **v** and a **1**. The screen looks like Figure 17-3.

Exercises

1. Create a table that displays the image MAPSYMBL.WPG. Preview how WordPerfect will print it.

2. Create a text box that displays the image named ARROW1.WPG. Preview how WordPerfect will print it.

3. Create a figure that displays the image BORDER.WPG. Preview how WordPerfect will print it.

4. Create a user-defined box that displays the image named GAVEL.WPG. Preview how WordPerfect will print it.

17.4   ADD A CAPTION

Once you have created a graphics box, you may want to label it. WordPerfect refers to the box label as a *caption*. As described in Table 17-1, WordPerfect provides default captions, such as "Figure" or "Table" followed by the figure or table number. You can provide additional information in the caption; for example, you can use the caption to provide a title for the graphics box. When you have multiple graphics boxes, the numbers and labels in the captions distinguish the various box entries.

To add a caption to the graphics box:

a. Press the Graphics (ALT-F9) key.

b. Type the appropriate number or letter for the box type that you want to create or edit.

c. Type a **c** or a **1** to create a graphics box or an **e** or a **2** to edit an existing graphics box.

d. If you typed an **e** or a **2** in the previous step, type the number of the box you want to edit, and press ENTER.

e. Type a **c** or a **2** to select the Caption option.

f. Type the text that you want to appear in the caption.

g. Press the Exit (F7) key to return to the Graphics menu.

h. Press the Exit (F7) key to return to the document.

When you add a caption, you can use all of WordPerfect's features, such as Underline and Bold. You can change or remove the initial caption that WordPerfect provides by editing that text. To move the default caption from the beginning to another location within the caption area, delete the caption with the BACKSPACE key and reinsert it by pressing the Graphics (ALT-F9) key. WordPerfect wraps the text in the caption to fit the width of the graphics box. While you can place graphics boxes in headers, footers, footnotes, and endnotes, you cannot use captions in these locations.

Examples

1. You can use captions to identify graphic images referenced in your text. With captions, a reader browsing through your document can quickly identify the information that each graphics box presents. First, press the Graphics (ALT-F9) key. Type an **f**, a **c**, an **f**, and **usamap.wpg**. Press ENTER, and type a **c** for Caption. Press the SPACEBAR, type **Acme's Customer Base**, and press the Exit (F7) key. Press the Exit (F7) key again to return to the document. To view this image, press the Print (SHIFT-F7) key, and type a **v** and a **1**. The figure looks like this:

Figure 1 Acme's Customer Base

2. You can also use captions to create titles for tables. First, press the Graphics (ALT-F9) key, and type a **t**, a **c**, and an **e**.

Then, type

Duct Tape
Electrical Tape
Strapping Tape
Epoxy

Press the Exit (F7) key. Type a **c** for Caption. Press the SPACEBAR, press the Bold (F6) key, type **Acme's Product Line**, press the Bold (F6) key, and press the Exit (F7) key twice. To view this image, press the Print (SHIFT-F7) key, and type a **v** and a **1**. The screen looks like this:

Table I Acme's Product Line

_____

Duct Tape
Electrical Tape
Strapping Tape
Epoxy

_____

Exercises

1. Create a blank text box with the caption **To be filled in later**. Preview how WordPerfect will print it.

2. Create a table containing the text **insert Ms. Mitchell's picture here** and a caption that says **Susan Mitchell, President**. Preview how WordPerfect will print it.

3. Create a figure with the image named PHONE.WPG and the caption **When It Rings, We Answer**. Preview how WordPerfect will print it.

4. Create a figure with the image named NO1.WPG and the caption **First in the Business**. Preview how WordPerfect will print it.

POSITION AND SIZE A BOX   17.5

You can control the size and placement of a graphics box on
the page. The placement options allow you to specify vertical
and horizontal positions. The options for both position settings are dependent on the type of box selected. WordPerfect
lets you define a box as a paragraph box, a page box, or a
character box. WordPerfect treats each type of box differently
in relation to the text around it. In this chapter, our focus is on
the default setting, the paragraph type. Paragraph boxes
remain with the text that is wrapped around them. For
paragraph boxes, the vertical setting is the number of inches
that the graphics box is placed from the top of the paragraph.
The horizontal settings are left, right, center, and both left
and right.

   You can accept WordPerfect's calculations for a box size or
change the size of a box by altering its height or its width. You
can also choose to alter both the height and the width with
one menu selection. If you set only one dimension of the box,
WordPerfect calculates the other dimension automatically.

To set the horizontal and vertical positions of a graphics box:

a. Press the Graphics (ALT-F9) key.

b. Type the appropriate number or letter for the box type that
   you want to create or edit.

c. Type a **c** or a **1** to create a graphics box or an **e** or a **2** to edit
   an existing graphics box.

d. If you typed an **e** or a **2** in the previous step, type the
   number of the box you want to edit, and press ENTER.

e. Type a **v** or a **4** to specify the box's vertical position.

f. Type the number of inches between the top of the paragraph and the box, and press ENTER.

g. Type an **h** or a **5** to specify the box's horizontal position.

h. Type an **l** or a **1** to have the box align with the paragraph's left margin, an **r** or a **2** to have the box align with the paragraph's right margin, a **c** or a **3** to have the box centered between the paragraph margins, or a **b** or a **4** to have the box stretch between the left and right margins.

i. Press the Exit (F7) key to return to the document.

   The vertical setting is ignored if it prevents the image from fitting on the page.

To set the graphics box's size:

a. Press the Graphics (ALT-F9) key.

b. Type the appropriate number or letter for the box type that you want to create or edit.

c. Type a **c** or a **1** to create a graphics box or an **e** or a **2** to edit an existing graphics box.

d. If you typed an **e** or a **2** in the previous step, type the number of the box you want to edit, and press ENTER.

e. Type an **s** or a **6** to specify the box's size.

f. Type a **w** or a **1** to specify the box's width, letting WordPerfect determine the height; an **h** or a **2** to specify the box's height, letting WordPerfect determine the width; or a **b** or a **3** to set both the width and the height.

g. Type the number of inches for the box's width if you typed a **w**, a **1**, a **b**, or a **3** in step f, and press ENTER.

h. Type the number of inches for the box's width if you typed an **h**, a **2**, a **b**, or a **3** in step f, and press ENTER.

i. Press the Exit (F7) key to return to the document.

   When you set the size of a graphics box that contains a graphic image, WordPerfect changes the size of the image to fill as much of the box as possible. Once the image is as large as possible, remaining space is left blank. When you set the size of a graphics box that contains text, WordPerfect fits as much of the text as possible into the box. If WordPerfect cannot display all of the text in the box, it displays as much as possible and keeps the rest in memory. If the box has more room than the text requires, WordPerfect leaves the remaining space blank.

Examples

1. You can set the vertical position when you want one or more lines of a paragraph that is wrapped around a graphics box to appear unwrapped above the box. First, type

   Fourscore and seven years ago, our fathers brought forth upon this continent, a new nation, conceived in liberty, and dedicated to the proposition that all men are created equal.

   Next, move the cursor to the "F" in "Fourscore," and press the Graphics (ALT-F9) key. Type an **f**, a **c**, an **f**, and **flag.wpg**, and press ENTER. WordPerfect finds the file and loads the image. Then, type a **v** and **.2**, and press ENTER. Press the Exit (F7) key to return to the document. WordPerfect adjusts the graphics box to fit below the first line of text in the paragraph. To view this image, press the Print (SHIFT-F7) key and type a **v** and a **1**. The screen looks like Figure 17-4. Press the Exit (F7) key. Use this text and the graphics box in the next example.

2. You can set the horizontal position when you want to change how the box aligns with the left or right margin. First, press the Graphics (ALT-F9) key. Type an **f**, an **e**, and **1** for the figure number that you want to edit, and press ENTER. Type an **h** for Horizontal. To stretch the graphics box from the right margin to the left margin, type a **b**, and press the Exit (F7) key to return to the document. Move the cursor to

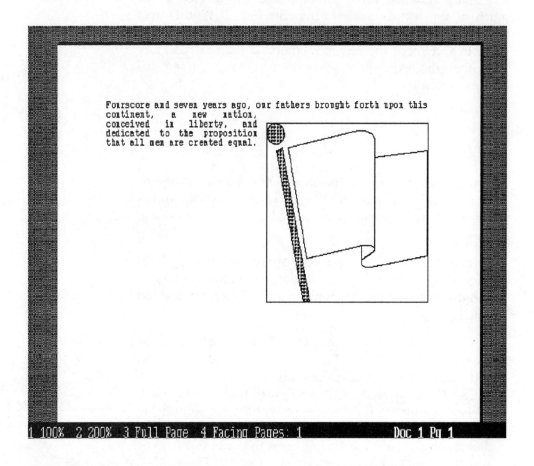

FIGURE 17-4.   Graphics box with a vertical-position setting

the last line of the paragraph. The screen looks like this:

```
Fourscore and seven years ago, our fathers brought forth upon this
┌FIG 1─────────────────────────────────────────────────────────────┐
continent, a new nation, conceived in liberty, and dedicated to the
proposition that all men are created equal.
```

WordPerfect adjusts the graphics box to fit between the first line of the paragraph and the remaining lines. Although the graphics box occupies the entire width of the screen, WordPerfect shows only the first line of the graphics box. When the cursor is on the first line of the paragraph, the **LN** indicator in the status line says **1″**. When the cursor is on the second line of the paragraph, the **LN** indicator in the status line says **4.83″**. To view the image, press the Print (SHIFT-F7) key, and type a **v** and a **3**. The screen looks like Figure 17-5.

3. For most graphics boxes, you can use the height and width settings that WordPerfect creates. However, you can change the height and width settings for a box whenever you wish. First, press the Graphics (ALT-F9) key. Type an **f**, a **c**, an **f**, and **mapsymbl.wpg**, and press ENTER. WordPerfect retrieves the file and sets the graphics box to a predetermined size. To change the size, type an **s**, and a **b** to set both height and width. For the width, type **3**, and press ENTER. For the height, type **1.5**, and press ENTER. To return to the document, press the Exit (F7) key. To view the image, press the Print (SHIFT-F7) key and type a **v** and a **3**. The screen looks like this:

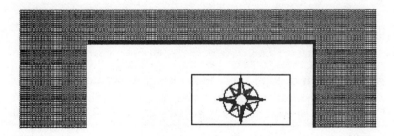

When you change the size, WordPerfect expands or contracts the image to display it as large as possible without changing the height-to-width ratio. The extra space in the box remains empty.

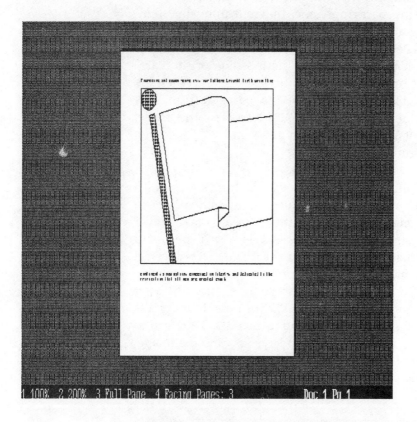

FIGURE 17-5.   Graphics box with horizontal setting at both left and right margins

4. When you change the width of a graphics box containing text, WordPerfect rewraps the text to fit. First, press the Graphics (ALT-F9) key, and type an **f**, a **c**, and an **e**. Then, type

Fourscore and seven years ago, our fathers brought forth upon this continent, a new nation, conceived in liberty, and dedicated to the proposition that all men are created equal.

Then, press the Exit (F7) key. Notice that WordPerfect changed the size of the graphics box to 3.25" by 1.02". Press the Exit (F7) key to return to the document. To view the figure, press the Print (SHIFT-F7) key, and type a **v** and a **1**. The screen looks like this:

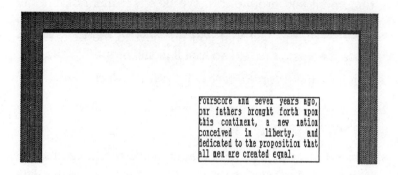

Press the Exit (F7) key to return to the document. To change the size of the box, press the Graphics (ALT-F9) key. Type an **f**, an **e**, a **1**, an **s**, and a **w**. Type 5, and press ENTER for the new width. WordPerfect automatically adjusts the height of the box to accommodate the text. Finally, press the Exit (F7) key to return to the document. To view the figure, press the Print (SHIFT-F7) key, and type a **v**. The screen looks like this:

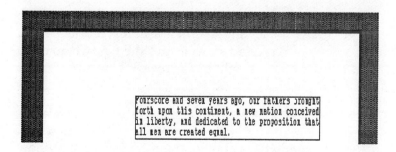

Exercises

1. Create a blank text box, setting the vertical position to .4".
   Now return to the document, and type the following
   paragraph:

   When you create a graphics box, WordPerfect wraps the
   document text around it. If WordPerfect has not already
   drawn the box, it draws the box as you type the text. Even
   as you edit the text that you put next to the box, Word-
   Perfect adjusts the text so that it is still properly wrapped.

   Preview how WordPerfect will print the document.

2. Create an empty figure at the left margin. Preview how
   WordPerfect will print it.

3. Create a user-defined box that contains the image named
   CHECK.WPG. Set the height to 5", and let WordPerfect
   determine the appropriate width. Preview how Word-
   Perfect will print it.

4. Create a table that contains the following paragraph:

   As you change the width of a graphics box that contains
   text, WordPerfect rewraps the text inside it to fit the new
   width. When you set the height of a graphics box that
   contains text, WordPerfect fits as much of the text as
   possible into the box. If it cannot display all of the text, the
   remaining text does not appear, although WordPerfect
   remembers it.

   Preview how WordPerfect will print the box. Change the
   width to 2.5", allowing WordPerfect to set the height.
   Preview how WordPerfect will print the box. Change the
   width to 3" and the height to 2". Preview how WordPerfect
   will print the box.

5. Create a figure that contains the image APPLAUSE.WPG.
   Set the height to 4", allowing WordPerfect to set the width.
   Set the horizontal position to center the box. Preview how
   WordPerfect will print the box.

EDIT AND DELETE GRAPHICS BOXES   17.6

When you edit a graphics box, you can change any of the settings established when the box was initially created. Supplying the same or a new filename updates or changes the contents of a box.

Although you can remove the contents of a box through the edit option, to eliminate a box, you must delete the hidden code for the box. You can accomplish this most easily in the Reveal Codes screen. You can also delete and restore the hidden code to move a box from one location to another.

To edit a graphics box:

a. Press the Graphics (ALT-F9) key.

b. Type the appropriate number or letter for the box type that you want to edit.

c. Type an **e** or a **2**.

d. Type the number of the box you want to edit, and press ENTER.

e. Change any options you want changed.

f. Press the Exit (F7) key to return to the document.

Supplying a new filename replaces the old text or image with the contents of the new file.

To delete a graphics box:

a. Press the Reveal Codes (ALT-F3) key.

b. Move the cursor to the code representing the graphics box.

c. Press the DEL key.

d. Press the Reveal Codes (ALT-F3) key.

When you delete a graphics box, WordPerfect renumbers all of the remaining figures, tables, text boxes, or user-defined boxes.

The hidden code for a figure is [Figure:#; FILENAME;Caption]. The hidden code for a table is [Table:#;FILENAME;Caption]. The hidden code for a text box is [Text Box:#;FILENAME;Caption]. The hidden code for a user-defined box is [Usr Box:#;FILENAME;Caption]. The number sign (#) represents the figure number. "FILENAME" represents the document name or image name that the graphics box contains. "Caption" represents the first 49 characters of the caption that you have provided, which includes [Box Num] for the default caption. The filename and caption are not displayed in the hidden code if the graphics box does not use them.

To move a graphics box:

a. Press the Reveal Codes (ALT-F3) key.

b. Move the cursor to the code representing the graphics box.

c. Press the DEL key.

d. Place the cursor where you want the graphics box to be moved.

e. Press the Cancel (F1) key.

f. Type an **r** or a **1** to restore the graphics box.

g. Press the Reveal Codes (ALT-F3) key.

You can also use the BACKSPACE key instead of DEL if the cursor is to the right of the hidden code for the graphics box.

Examples

1. WordPerfect places a copy of a document or image from disk into the current document when you specify a filename for a graphics box. The copy of the image or text in the graphics box will not include any changes made to the original document at a later time. By resupplying the

filename, you can update the graphics box contents. First, type the following, pressing ENTER after the colon and after "meeting" in the second line:

At the next board of directors meeting, they will discuss:
The upcoming stockholders' meeting
The company's reaction to the negative press involving the Indiana plant closing

Press the Exit (F7) key, type a **y**, type **bodmeet**, press ENTER, and type an **n** to save the document and clear the screen. Next, press the Graphics (ALT-F9) key, type an **f**, a **c**, an **f**, and **bodmeet**, and press ENTER. Press the Exit (F7) key to return to the document. When you preview the document at 100 percent by pressing the Print (SHIFT-F7) key and typing a **v** and a **1**, the screen looks like this:

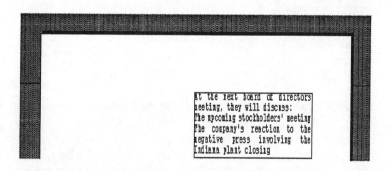

Next, press the Exit (F7) key to return to the document. To show how WordPerfect does not update graphics boxes that use other documents, press the Switch (SHIFT-F3) key, press the Retrieve (SHIFT-F10) key, type **bodmeet**, and press ENTER. Press PGDN to move to the bottom of the document, press ENTER, and type

Suggestions for new board members to replace Ima L. Shark and Jim Pollack

Press the Exit (F7) key, press ENTER twice, and type a **y** twice. When you return to the first document and press the Print (SHIFT-F7) key and type a **v**, the screen does not show the new text that you entered in the BODMEET file. Press the Exit (F7) key to return to the document. To update the figure, press the Graphics (ALT-F9) key, and type an **f**, an **e**, and a **1** for the figure number. Then, press ENTER and type an **f**. Since WordPerfect prompts you with the correct filename, press ENTER. When WordPerfect prompts you for a confirmation, type a **y**. Now the figure uses the updated copy of the BODMEET file. Press the Exit (F7) key to return to the document. Press the Print (SHIFT-F7) key, and type a **v**. The figure looks like this:

```
At the next board of directors
meeting, they will discuss:
The upcoming stockholders' meeting
The company's reaction to the
negative press involving the
Indiana plant closing
Suggestions for new board members
to replace Ima L. Shark and Jim
Pollack
```

2. You can remove the filename from a graphics box setting. First, press the Graphics (ALT-F9) key, type an **f**, a **c**, an **f**, and **bodmeet**, press ENTER, and press the Exit (F7) key. To remove the filename setting, press the Graphics (ALT-F9) key, and type an **f**, an **e**, and a **1** for the number of the graphics box you have created. Press ENTER and type an **f** for Filename. When WordPerfect prompts you with the current filename, press the DELETE EOL (CTRL-END) key, and press ENTER. When WordPerfect prompts you for a confirmation to clear the contents, type a **y**, and press the Exit (F7) key to return to the document. To see the empty figure, press the Print (SHIFT-F7) key and type a **v**. Press the Exit (F7) key to return to the document.

3. You can remove a graphics box from a document. Press the

Graphics (ALT-F9) key, type an **f**, a **c**, an **f**, and **bodmeet**, and press ENTER. Press the Exit (F7) key to return to the document. To remove this figure, press the Reveal Codes (ALT-F3) key, and press BACKSPACE. Press the Reveal Codes (ALT-F3) key to return to the normal screen.

4. You can move a graphics box by using its hidden code. Press the Graphics (ALT-F9) key, type an **f**, a **c**, an **f**, and **bodmeet**, and press ENTER. Press the Exit (F7) key to return to the document, and press ENTER until the cursor is at the bottom of the figure. Press the Graphics (ALT-F9) key, type a **b** and a **c**, and press the Exit (F7) key. Press the ENTER key five times to create extra room below the text box. To move the figure below the text box, press the Reveal Codes (ALT-F3) key, and press HOME, HOME, the UP ARROW key, and the LEFT ARROW key to move the cursor to the right of the hidden code for Figure 1. Then, press the BACKSPACE key to delete the code.

To insert the figure at its new location, press HOME, HOME, and the DOWN ARROW key. Then, press the Cancel (F1) key. Word-Perfect displays the code for the figure. Type an **r** or a **1** to restore the figure. Press the Reveal Codes (ALT-F3) key to return the screen to normal. To see the figure after it is moved, press the Print (SHIFT-F7) key, and type a **v**. Press the Exit (F7) key to return to the document.

Exercises

1. Create a table that uses the image named ARROW1.WPG. Preview how WordPerfect will print it. Change the image to CHECK.WPG. Preview how WordPerfect will print it.

2. Create a text box that uses the image CONFIDEN.WPG. Preview how WordPerfect will print it. Remove the file-name setting. Preview how WordPerfect will print it.

3. Create a table with nothing in it. Delete the table.

4. Create a figure that uses the image named NEWSPAPR.WPG. Press ENTER until the cursor is below the bottom of the figure. Create a figure that uses the image named PRESENT.WPG. Press ENTER until the cursor is below the bottom of the figure. Move the figure with the NEWSPAPR.WPG image to below the figure with the PRESENT.WPG image. Move to the beginning of the document, and delete the hard returns until the figure containing the image in PRESENT.WPG is at the first line. Preview how WordPerfect will print it.

17.7   PRINT DOCUMENTS CONTAINING GRAPHICS

Many printers can print your graphics boxes as they print your document. A few printers can print graphics and text but not both at one time. If you try to print a document containing text and graphics and one or the other does not print correctly, your printer will not support the combined printing of text and graphics.

Depending on your printer, you may be able to set the quality of the printing. As you improve the quality of text or graphics, especially the latter, you increase the time your printer takes to print the document.

To print a document with text and graphics on a printer that can print both at one time:

a. Press the Print (SHIFT-F7) key.

b. Type a **g** to set the graphics quality.

c. Type a **d** or a **2** for Draft, an **m** or a **3** for Medium, or an **h** or a **4** for High.

d. Type a **t** to set the text quality.

e. Type a **d** or a **2** for Draft, an **m** or a **3** for Medium, or an **h** or a **4** for High.

f. Type an **f** or a **p** to start printing the document.

To print a document with text and graphics on a printer that cannot print both at one time:

a. Press the Print (SHIFT-F7) key.

b. Type a **g** to set the graphics quality.

c. Type an **n** or a **1** for Do Not Print.

d. Type a **t** to set the text quality.

e. Type a **d** or a **2** for Draft, an **m** or a **3** for Medium, or an **h** or a **4** for High.

f. Type an **f** or a **p** to print the text of the document.

g. When the text is printed, insert the printed pages into the printer so that it will start printing at the beginning of the first page.

h. Press the Print (SHIFT-F7) key.

i. Type a **t** to set the text quality.

j. Type an **n** or a **1** for Do Not Print.

k. Type a **g** to set the graphics quality.

l. Type a **d** or a **2** for Draft, an **m** or a **3** for Medium, or an **h** or a **4** for High.

m. Type an **f** or a **p** to print the graphics in the document.

Examples

1. Printing documents with text and graphics is a simple process with many printers. To create a document with text and graphics, press the Graphics (ALT-F9) key, type an **f**, a **c**, an **f**, and **arrow2.wpg**, and press ENTER. Align this image with the left margin by typing an **h** and an **l**. Press the Exit (F7) key to return to the document, and type

At next Tuesday's meeting, several important points will be discussed. It is imperative that you be there.

To print this document, press the Print (SHIFT-F7) key, and type a **g**, an **h**, a **t**, and an **h** to set both the graphics and text quality to high. Then, type an **f**. The printed document looks like this:

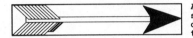

```
At   next   Tuesday's   meeting,
several important points will be
discussed.    It  is  imperative
that you be there.
```

2. If your printer can print text and graphics simultaneously, ignore this example. If you have a printer that cannot print graphics and text at the same time, you must use a different set of steps. First, press the Graphics (ALT-F9) key, type an **f**, a **c**, an **f**, and **arrow2.wpg**, and press ENTER. Align this image with the left margin by typing an **h** and an **l**. Press the Exit (F7) key to return to the document and type

At next Tuesday's meeting, several important points will be discussed. It is imperative that you be there.

To print this document, press the Print (SHIFT-F7) key. Type a **g** and an **n** to suppress the printing of the graphics, and type a **t** and an **h** to set the text quality to high. Type an **f** to start printing the document.

To print the graphics, reinsert the paper into the paper tray, if your printer uses one, or move the paper back in the traction feeders so that WordPerfect will start printing the graphics at the beginning of the document. Press the Print (SHIFT-F7) key, and type a **t** and an **n** to keep WordPerfect from printing the text. Then, type a **g** and an **h** to set the graphics quality to high, and type an **f** to start printing. WordPerfect will skip over where it printed the text and print the graphics in their appropriate places. The results will look like the illustration from the previous example.

Since this can be a cumbersome process, you may want to perform these steps for one page at a time if only a few pages in your document have graphics.

Exercises

1. Create a table with the image named AND.WPG. Print the document using draft quality for the graphics.

2. Create a text box with the image named KEY.WPG. Return to the document, and type the following paragraph:

   To check out a key for the observatory, you must register your name with the department secretary, Karen Martin. Then you must sign up for a night on the calendar outside Martin's office. On the day that you have signed up, you must pick up the key by 5:00 p.m.

   Print the document with graphics set to medium and text set to high.

3. Create a user-defined box with the image QUILL.WPG. Now return to the document, and type the following paragraph:

   Calligraphy is the art of writing beautifully. While some calligraphers use quill pens, you can learn calligraphy using special pens that are available in most art stores. To learn calligraphy, you need a pen, ink, paper, and patience.

   Print the document with the graphics quality set to high.

4. Create a figure with the image named PENCIL.WPG. Without moving the cursor, create a figure with the image named BOOK.WPG. Return to the document, and type the following paragraph.

Each department has a designated person for acquiring office supplies. This person is in charge of ordering and handling the department's transfer of funds for this purpose. Once a year, someone from the internal control department will inspect these records.

Now print the document with the graphics quality set to medium.

EXERCISES

MASTERY
SKILLS CHECK

(Do not clear the screen between exercises unless instructed to do so. Preview the document after completing each exercise.)

1. Create a blank figure.

2. Create another blank figure that has a left horizontal position.

3. Edit figure 1 to use the image in QUILL.WPG.

4. Edit figure 2 to contain the following text:

   A few thoughts to ponder:
   A bird is known by its note, and a man by his talk.
   —Proverb
   The secret of success is constancy to purpose.
   —Benjamin Disraeli
   Thrift is too late at the bottom of the purse. —Seneca

5. Change the image used in figure 1 to the image named THINKER.WPG.

6. Add a caption for figure 1 that says **Rodin's The Thinker**.

7. Change figure 1's height to 2".

8. Change figure 2's width to 4″.

9. Insert blank lines between the sayings in figure 2.

10. Print the document with text quality set to medium and graphics quality set to high. Clear the screen.

11. Create a left-aligned table with the image named ARROW1.WPG and with a caption that says **Read This! It Is Important!**.

(Do not clear the screen between exercises. Preview the document after each exercise.)

INTEGRATED
SKILLS CHECK

1. Type the following paragraph:

   The images that you use for a graphics box can come from a variety of sources. WordPerfect provides 30 images, all with the .WPG extension. You can also use pictures generated by other software. For example, you can use .PIC files that you generate with Lotus 1-2-3. You can learn more about graphics boxes from WordPerfect 5 Made Easy, by Mella Mincberg.

   Save the document as IMAGES. Clear the screen, and create a text box that uses the text in IMAGES. Press ENTER until the cursor is on the line below the bottom of the text box.

2. Create a table that displays the image CLOCK.WPG. Create a caption that says **A stitch in time saves nine.**

3. Set the table height and width to 4″.

4. Switch to the second document. Retrieve IMAGES. Delete the fourth sentence. Save the document.

5. Switch back to the first document. Update the text box to use the new version of IMAGES.

6. Edit the text box to underline "WordPerfect 5 Made Easy."

7. Set graphics and text quality to draft. Print the document.

8. Delete the table.

9. At the bottom of the document, create a figure that uses the image named ANNOUNCE.WPG. Press ENTER until the cursor is on the line below the bottom of the figure.

10. Move the text box to below the figure. Move to the beginning of the document, and remove the blank lines before the figure.

11. Create a header that contains a user-defined box that displays the image named AIRPLANE.WPG. Set the horizontal position to stretch the box from the left to the right margin.

12. Set the graphics quality to high, and print the document.

CHAPTER OBJECTIVES

After completing this chapter, you should be able to

18.1 Create an outline

18.2 Change the outline

18.3 Change the numbering style

·18·
Creating An Outline

You can create outlines with WordPerfect. Your outline entries can be complete sentences or just topic words or phrases. You can use these outlines as the basis for a more detailed document with additional, descriptive text. You can also use them without change to show meeting agendas, project tasks, personnel assignments, and other materials.

If you use WordPerfect's Outline feature as you create your outline, WordPerfect numbers the outline levels automatically. As you add, delete, and move entries in the outline, WordPerfect handles renumbering for you.

WordPerfect supports up to eight levels of outlining, marking each with a different numbering style. Arabic numbers, uppercase letters, lowercase letters, and Roman numerals are combined with periods and parentheses to make each level unique. You can use the default settings for each level, use other predefined style options, or define your own.

SKILLS CHECK

1. Type the following text, indenting it from the left margin:

   WordPerfect has many features that are missing from other word processing packages. Once you master the basics, you will feel comfortable exploring some of the advanced features that WordPerfect offers.

2. Retype the paragraph in exercise 1, indenting it from both margins.

3. Change the tab setting to one tab stop at 4", and type the following:

Joe Jones	Accounting
Paul Balber	Finance
Norlin Rugers	Management
Mary Rogers	Accounting

4. Change the left and right margin settings to 2", and type the following:

   WordPerfect's Outline feature makes outline entry and update an easy process. Although each outline entry requires several steps, once the outline is entered, Word-Perfect updates level assignments.

   Print two copies of the document.

18.1   CREATE AN OUTLINE

An outline can help you organize and focus your thoughts when you have to write a lengthy document. An outline can also serve as a useful end product when you need to share a set of summary data with others.

WordPerfect makes it easy to create outlines. When you turn on the Outline feature, WordPerfect treats each new paragraph as another entry at the highest level in your outline. You press the TAB key to change the level. Word-Perfect takes care of maintaining perfect order for each level in your outline.

To create an outline in WordPerfect:

a. Position the cursor where you want to begin the outline.

b. Press the Date/Outline (SHIFT-F5) key.

c. Type an **o** or a **4** to turn on the Outline feature.

d. Press ENTER to insert a first-level entry, or press ENTER once and press the TAB key one or more times to create a lower-level entry.

e. Press the SPACEBAR or the Indent (F4) key, and type the text for the outline entry.

f. Repeat steps d and e as necessary to complete the outline.

g. Press the Date/Outline (SHIFT-F5) key.

h. Type an **o** or a **4** to turn off the Outline feature.

The default numbering that WordPerfect uses for levels in outlines is I., A., 1., a., (1), (a), i), a). If you want to indent the text of an outline entry, press the SPACEBAR before pressing the TAB key in step d. The Outline feature works as a toggle switch; that is, you select it once to start it, and you select it again to turn it off. Invoking the Outline feature does not generate a hidden code in the document, although pressing ENTER to create a new entry does. The hidden code generated each time you create an outline entry is [Par Num:Auto].

Examples

1. You can use WordPerfect's Outline feature to create a topic outline. You might use such an outline to record the various points that you want to discuss at an upcoming management meeting. First, type the following title for the outline:

August 20 Meeting Agenda

Press ENTER to position the cursor at the beginning of the outline. Press the Date/Outline (SHIFT-F5) key, and type an **o** to turn on the Outline feature. Press ENTER to have Word-Perfect generate the number I. for the first entry. Press the SPACEBAR, and then press the TAB key to move to the next tab stop without altering the outline number. Type

Sales bonus program

Press ENTER and then press the SPACEBAR and the TAB key. Next, type

Insurance coverage options

Press ENTER. Press the SPACEBAR and type

Construction proposals

Pressing the TAB key is not necessary: since the number for this entry requires four characters, the SPACEBAR is sufficient to position the cursor.

Press ENTER, the SPACEBAR, and the TAB key to generate the number IV. Type

Meeting with security personnel

For the last entry, press ENTER, the SPACEBAR, and the TAB key, and type

Position announcements before publication

The completed outline should look like this:

August 20 Meeting Agenda

I.   Sales bonus program
II. Insurance coverage options
III. Construction proposals
IV. Meeting with security personnel
V.   Position announcements before publication

Turn off the Outline feature by pressing the Date/Outline (SHIFT-F5) key and typing an **o**.

Save the document by pressing the Exit (F7) key, pressing ENTER, typing **agenda**, and pressing ENTER again. Press ENTER to clear the screen and remain in WordPerfect.

2. You can use WordPerfect's Outline feature to create a sentence outline. The Indent (F4) key can be used with the Outline feature to maintain indentation of the text at each level. You can outline project tasks in the order in which they will be completed. First, turn on the Outline feature by pressing the Date/Outline (SHIFT-F5) key and typing an **o**. Press ENTER to generate the first outline number, and press the Indent (F4) key. Type

Meet with architect to discuss building plans and zoning requirements.

Press ENTER to create the next number, press the Indent (F4) key, and type

Complete excavation and other site preparation tasks. Complete roadbed preparation.

Press ENTER to create the next number, press the Indent (F4) key, and type

Review architect's drawings, make suggested changes, and discuss construction schedule.

For the last outline entry, press ENTER to create the number, press the Indent (F4) key and type

Begin construction on main building, drive pilings for pier, and begin paving parking lots.

The outline looks like this:

```
I.   Meet with architect to discuss building plans and zoning
     requirements.
II.  Complete excavation and other site preparation tasks.
     Complete roadbed preparation.
III. Review architect's drawings, make suggested changes, and
     discuss construction schedule.
IV.  Begin construction on main building, drive pilings for pier,
     and begin paving parking lots.
```

Turn the Outline feature off by pressing the Date/Outline (SHIFT-F5) key. Press the Exit (F7) key, press ENTER, type **constrt** as the filename for the document, and press ENTER twice to clear the screen without leaving WordPerfect.

3. You can use multiple levels in an outline. The TAB key will indicate to WordPerfect which level you want to use for each entry. You can create an outline structure that shows the winners in a sales contest by region, branch, and employee. The first level of the outline will be the region,

the second level the branch, and the third level will be the employee name. First, type the following title for the outline:

Better Boat Brigade Contest

Press ENTER, and turn on the Outline feature by pressing the Date/Outline (SHIFT-F5) key and typing an **o**. Press ENTER and the Indent (F4) key, and type

Eastern Region

Press ENTER, and press the TAB key to create a number one level down. Press the Indent (F4) key, and type

Boston Branch

Press ENTER and press the TAB key twice to generate a number one more level down. Press the Indent (F4) key, and type

John Jones

Press ENTER, press the TAB key twice, press the Indent (F4) key, and type

Mary Smith

To begin another branch entry, press ENTER and the TAB key once. Press the Indent (F4) key, and type

New York Branch

Press ENTER. To add the names for New York, press the TAB key twice, press the Indent (F4) key, and type

Nancy Carter

Press ENTER once, the TAB key twice, and the Indent (F4) key once, and type

Jeff Greenhoff

The screen looks like this:

Better Boat Brigade Contest

```
I,   Eastern Region
     A,   Boston Branch
          1,   John Jones
          2,   Mary Smith
     B,   New York Branch
          1,   Nancy Carter
          2,   Jeff Greenhoff
```

Complete the entries for the western region with the same approach. Press ENTER twice. WordPerfect generates the number II. when you press ENTER the first time and moves it down a line when you press ENTER again. Press the Indent (F4) key, and type

Western Region

Press ENTER, press the TAB key, press the Indent (F4) key, and type

Las Vegas Branch

Press ENTER, press the TAB key twice, press the Indent (F4) key, and type

Jill Cravens

Press ENTER. For the last entry, press TAB twice, press the Indent (F4) key, and type

George Moore

The screen looks like this:

Better Boat Brigade Contest

```
I.   Eastern Region
     A.  Boston Branch
         1.  John Jones
         2.  Mary Smith
     B.  New York Branch
         1.  Nancy Carter
         2.  Jeff Greenhoff

II.  Western Region
     A.  Las Vegas Branch
         1.  Jill Cravens
         2.  George Moore
```

Press the Date/Outline (SHIFT-F5) key and type an **o** to turn off the Outline feature. Save the file and clear the screen by pressing the Exit (F7) key, pressing ENTER, typing **prizes**, and pressing ENTER twice.

Exercises

1. Create the following outline:

HIGH SCHOOL SPORTS
I.   BASEBALL
II. FOOTBALL
III. SWIMMING
IV. HOCKEY

Save the file as SPORTS.

2. Create the following outline:

BREEDS OF DOGS
I.   Hounds
     A. Greyhound
     B. Whippet

II. Sporting Dogs
   A. Labrador Retriever
   B. Irish Setter
III. Terriers
   A. Airedale
   B. Welsh Terrier
IV. Working Dogs
   A. Collie
   B. Siberian Husky

Save the file as DOGS.

18.2   CHANGE THE OUTLINE

WordPerfect not only creates the level numbering for an outline, it also maintains it as you change the outline. When you add additional items at any level, WordPerfect assigns the appropriate numbers to those items and renumbers entries affected by the addition. Likewise, if you remove an entry, WordPerfect adjusts the numbering of the remaining entries in that level. Moving entries by indenting them farther or moving them to new locations also causes WordPerfect to adjust the number assignments.

Examples

1. You can delete entries in an outline and have WordPerfect maintain the correct numbers for the outline entries. Retrieve the file named AGENDA by pressing the Retrieve (SHIFT-F10) key, typing **agenda**, and pressing ENTER. The outline created in example 1 of section 18.1 should display on your screen. You can delete the fourth item in the outline by

moving to the "I" in "IV.," pressing the DELETE EOL (CTRL-END) key, and pressing the DEL key. Then, press the RIGHT ARROW key. The revised outline will look like this:

August 20 Meeting Agenda

I.   Sales bonus program
II. Insurance coverage options
III. Construction proposals
IV. Position announcements before publication

Save this revised outline by pressing the Exit (F7) key once, pressing ENTER twice, and typing a **y**. Type an **n** to clear the screen and remain in WordPerfect.

2. You can add levels to an existing outline by typing new entries or splitting existing entries. Retrieve the file CON-STRT created in example 2 of section 18.1 by pressing the Retrieve (SHIFT-F10) key, typing **constrt**, and pressing ENTER.

Turn on the Outline feature by pressing the Date/Outline (SHIFT-F5) key and typing an **o**. Move to the last outline entry, placing the cursor on the comma that follows "building." Press the DEL key 3 times to eliminate the comma, the space, and the "d." Type a period, press ENTER, press the Indent (F4) key, and type a **D**.

Move to the comma following "pier," press the DEL key seven times, type a period, and press ENTER. Press the Indent (F4) key, and type a **B**. WordPerfect automatically assigns the two new outline entries the appropriate level numbers, creating a revised outline that looks like the following.

```
I,   Meet with architect to discuss building plans and zoning
     requirements,
II,  Complete excavation and other site preparation tasks,
     Complete roadbed preparation,
III, Review architect's drawings, make suggested changes, and
     discuss construction schedule,
IV,  Begin construction on main building,
V,   Drive pilings for pier,
VI,  Begin paving parking lots,
```

Use this outline in the next example.

3. WordPerfect adjusts the level numbers when you relocate outline entries. You must be sure to move the required hidden codes along with your entries when you relocate them. The revised outline from example 2 indicates that excavation will start before the architect's plans are approved. To delay this step until after approval, you can rearrange the outline.

Move to the second outline entry. Press the Move (CTRL-F4) key. Type a **p** for Paragraph and an **m** for Move. Press the DOWN ARROW twice to move to the beginning of the next outline entry, and press ENTER. After you restore the entry, the level numbers initially will not appear correctly. Move down the screen by pressing the DOWN ARROW key and the level numbers will be adjusted as shown here:

```
I,   Meet with architect to discuss building plans and zoning
     requirements,
II,  Review architect's drawings, make suggested changes, and
     discuss construction schedule,
III, Complete excavation and other site preparation tasks,
     Complete roadbed preparation,
IV,  Begin construction on main building,
V,   Drive pilings for pier,
VI,  Begin paving parking lots,
```

Save this revised file as CONSTRT by pressing the Save (F10) key, pressing ENTER, and typing a **y**.

4. Changing the indentation of an outline entry changes the lettering assigned to the entry. Retrieve the file AGENDA by pressing the Retrieve (SHIFT-F10) key, typing **agenda**, and pressing ENTER. Turn the Outline feature on by pressing the Date/Outline (SHIFT-F5) key and typing an **o**. Move to the end of the first outline entry. Press ENTER, press the SPACEBAR, press the TAB key, type **Branch managers**, and press ENTER. Press the SPACEBAR, press the TAB key, and type **Sales personnel**. Numbers II and III have been assigned to these two entries. The entry for number III appears to be aligned incorrectly; this will be remedied when its number is adjusted. To change the level of the "Branch managers" entry, move to the beginning of the line, and press the TAB key. Press the RIGHT ARROW key, and notice how the number changes. Move to the beginning of the next line, and press the TAB key. Press the DOWN ARROW key to scroll down the screen. Word-Perfect adjusts all of the levels properly, as shown here:

```
August 28 Meeting Agenda

I,   Sales bonus program
     A,   Branch managers
     B,   Sales personnel
II,  Insurance coverage options
III, Construction proposals
IV,  Position announcements before publication
```

You can move an entry back to a higher level by deleting the [TAB] code before the [Par Num:Auto] code.

Save this file as CONSTRT by pressing the Save (F10) key, pressing ENTER, and typing a **y**.

Exercises

1. Retrieve the SPORTS file, created in exercise 1 in section 18.1. Turn on the Outline feature, and add entries for **BASKETBALL** and **TRACK**. Add another level under each sport, and list the names of the team captains. You can use your imagination for these names.

2. Retrieve the DOGS file, created in exercise 2 in section 18.1. Move the entries for "Sporting Dogs" to the end of the outline.

18.3 CHANGE THE NUMBERING STYLE

The default outline numbering style will be adequate for many tasks. If you must conform to a set of established standards, however, you can modify the structure that Word-Perfect uses.

You can select from a number of other predefined styles or create your own. Some of the other predefined options will be explored in this section. You will use the legal and bullet styles for marking the levels in an outline.

To change the outline numbering style:

a. Position the cursor at the location where you want to begin using the new style.

b. Press the Date/Outline (SHIFT-F5) key.

c. Type a **d** or a **6** to define a numbering style.

d. Type the letter or number of the numbering style you want.

e. Press the Exit (F7) key to leave the definition menu.

In step d, you can type an **o** or a **3** for the outline style, an **l** or a **4** for the legal style, or a **b** or a **5** for the bullet style. The hidden code [Par Num Def] marks the location of the new numbering definition in the document. WordPerfect uses the

```
Paragraph Number Definition

    1 - Starting Paragraph Number          1
        (in legal style)

                                       Levels
                       1     2     3     4     5     6     7     8
    2 - Paragraph      1,    a,    i,    (1)   (a)   (i)   1)    a)
    3 - Outline        I,    A,    1,    a,    (1)   (a)   i)    a)
    4 - Legal (1,1,1)  1     ,1    ,1    ,1    ,1    ,1    ,1    ,1
    5 - Bullets        •     o     -     ▪     *     +     ·     x
    6 - User-defined

    Current Definition  I,    A,    1,    a,    (1)   (a)   i)    a)

        Number Style                 Punctuation
        1 - Digits                   #    - No punctuation
        A - Upper case letters       #,   - Trailing period
        a - Lower case letters       #)   - Trailing parenthesis
        I - Upper case roman         (#)  - Enclosing parentheses
        i - Lower case roman         #    - All levels separated by period
        Other character - Bullet          (e,g,  2,1,3,4)


Selection: 0
```

FIGURE 18-1.   Selecting a numbering style

new paragraph-numbering definition for outline entries after the hidden code.

Examples

1. The bullet style offers an attractive solution for an outline of ideas or other entries that do not require numbers or letters. To create an outline in this style, press the Date/Outline (SHIFT-F5) key, and type a **6** for Define. WordPerfect displays the Paragraph Number Definition screen shown in Figure 18-1.

   Select the bullet style by typing a **b**. Press the Exit (F7) key, and turn on the Outline feature by typing an **o**. Press the ENTER key to create the first bullet marker. Then, press the SPACEBAR, press the TAB key, type **Complete filing**, and press ENTER. Press the SPACEBAR and then the TAB key. Type **Create form letter**. Your two entries should be marked with bullet indicators like this:

```
•    Complete filing
•    Create form letter
```

Turn off Outline feature by pressing the Date/Outline (SHIFT-F5) key and typing an **o**.

2. The legal style allows you to create outline entries with each item number displaying all of the levels. For example, if your entry is the third item under the first section, it will be labeled "1.3." The second item one level below this entry would be labeled "1.3.2." To use the legal style, position the cursor where you want to create the outline, press the Date/Outline (SHIFT-F5) key, and type a **d**. Type an **l** for Legal, and press the Exit (F7) key. Turn on the Outline feature by typing an **o**.

Press ENTER to generate a first-level number. Press the Indent (F4) key, and type **Easements to Title**. Press ENTER and the TAB key to generate a second-level number. Press the Indent (F4) key, and type **Water Rights**. Press ENTER, press the TAB key, press the Indent (F4) key, and type **Building Rights**. Press ENTER, and press the TAB key twice to generate a number at the third level. Press the Indent (F4) key, type **Special deed rights**, and press ENTER. Press the TAB key twice, press the Indent (F4) key, and type **Lateral support**. Press ENTER, press the TAB key, and press the Indent (F4) key. Type **Right of Way**, and press ENTER. Press the TAB key, press the Indent (F4) key, and type **Way of Necessity**. The completed outline looks like this:

```
1   Easements to Title
    1.1  Water Rights
    1.2  Building Rights
        1.2.1     Special deed rights
        1.2.2     Lateral support
    1.3  Right of Way
    1.4  Way of Necessity
```

Turn off the Outline feature by pressing the Date/Outline (SHIFT-F5) key and typing an **o**.

Exercises

1. Change the outline style to Legal, and create the following outline:

1. Estate Planning
   1.1. Trust
   1.2. Will

2. Change to the bullet outline style, and create the following entries with the level-four bullet indicators:

The following employees are being honored for 25 years of service:
   ■ **Jane Parker**
   ■ **Bill Black**

EXERCISES

(Do not clear the screen between exercises unless instructed to do so.)

MASTERY
SKILLS CHECK

1. Create the following outline with WordPerfect's automatic level-numbering feature.

PORTFOLIO HOLDINGS
I. Zero coupon bonds
II. Treasury bills
III. Blue chip stocks
IV. Mutual fund shares

2. Revise the outline so that "Treasury bills" is the last entry.

3. Add the following entry to the outline with the Outline feature:

V. Stock options

Save the file as INVEST, and clear the screen.

4. Create the following outline:

I. New Construction
   A. Mayfield Village
   B. Highland Heights
      1. 1114 Miner Road
      2. 4811 Highland Ave.
II. Remodeling Projects
   A. Gates Mills
      1. 112 Sherman Road
      2. 230 Saddleback Lane
   B. Chagrin Falls

5. Add a new entry for a remodeling project in Solon. Add another entry for a new construction project at 5311 Wilson Mills Road in Highland Heights. Save the file as JOBS.

INTEGRATED
SKILLS CHECK

1. Create the following memo, using the Outline feature for the bullet entries:

From: John Smith
To: George Carson
Subject: Expense Reports

A recent audit of expense reports indicated that several of your employees have exceeded the per diem allowed for travel expense on several occasions. A list of the employees violating this policy is enclosed.

- Jim Miller
- Mary Parker
- Paul Drake

Insert a hard page break above the outline entries, and print a copy of the document.

2. Change Outline options, and create the following outline:

1 WordPerfect's Math Features
   1.1 Add numbers
      1.1.1 Produce a subtotal for a column of numbers
      1.1.2 Add subtotals to create totals
      1.1.3 Add totals to produce a grand total
   1.2 Perform formula calculations across columns

Save the outline as MATH.

3. Create the following outline, using Underline for the titles as shown:

I. WordPerfect Books
   A. WordPerfect Made Easy
   B. WordPerfect: The Complete Reference
II. 1-2-3 Books
   A. 1-2-3 Made Easy
   B. 1-2-3: The Complete Reference

Add Teach Yourself WordPerfect as item C in the first section. Print two copies of the outline.

4. Create the following outline:

I. Vacation days
II. Sick leave
III. Holidays
   A. Christmas
   B. Thanksgiving
   C. Memorial Day
   D. Halloween
   E. Independence Day
   F. Labor Day

Move the third section with all of its second-level entries to the top of the outline. Delete the entry for Halloween.

CHAPTER OBJECTIVES

After completing this chapter, you should be able to

19.1 Change backup options

19.2 Change display options

19.3 Select initial settings

·19·
Changing the Setup Parameters

Many people use WordPerfect for years without changing the setup parameters that control the package. Not changing these initial settings often leads to having to change the same settings for each new document. By changing WordPerfect's initial settings, you can reset any options you wish to apply to all new documents. In this chapter, you will explore only a few of the many changes that you can make to WordPerfect's initial settings. Since the same process can be used to update other settings, you can explore additional options on your own.

Among the setup parameters is an option for automatically protecting your work. You can have WordPerfect create a backup of the current file at any time interval you select. If your system goes down, you can retrieve the backup file, which will contain any changes you made up to the last time that WordPerfect saved the backup.

WordPerfect's display options allow you to customize the way in which various text styles, sizes, and features are displayed on the screen. You can select from an entire palette of colors for each feature if you have a color monitor.

SKILLS CHECK

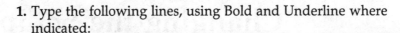

(Do not clear the screen until you have completed the last exercise.)

1. Type the following lines, using Bold and Underline where indicated:

WordPerfect allows you to change several settings. You can set WordPerfect to back up files automatically. You can also change the screen's appearance by selecting the colors WordPerfect uses. <u>These are just a few of the selections available.</u>

2. Save the document as DEFAULT.

3. Rename the DEFAULT file to SETTINGS.

4. Reveal codes to see WordPerfect's code for a soft return.

19.1   CHANGE BACKUP OPTIONS

WordPerfect can create automatic backups of your current document at a fixed time interval. If you request this option, WordPerfect asks you to wait each time it writes your document to disk at the requested interval. If you are working with two documents, it creates files named WP{WP}.BK1 and WP{WP}.BK2, respectively, for them. If your system goes down without warning, you can rename the backup files when you start another WordPerfect session.

To have WordPerfect create automatic timed backups of your work:

a. Press the Setup (SHIFT-F1) key.

b. Type a **b** or a **1** to change the backup settings.

c. Type a **t** or a **1** to change the timed backup settings.

d. Type a **y** to have WordPerfect make timed backups or an **n** to discontinue the feature.

e. If you typed a "y" in step d, type the desired number of minutes between automatic saves, and press ENTER.

f. Press the Exit (F7) key to return to your document.

Examples

1. Timed backups offer protection against power failures or other accidents that remove a document from your computer's memory. To create timed backups, press the Setup (SHIFT-F1) key. Next, type a **b**, a **t**, a **y**, and **30**. Press ENTER and the Exit (F7) key. WordPerfect will back up your documents every half hour.

2. If you lose a document, you can rename the backup copy when you start WordPerfect again. First, press the Setup (SHIFT-F1) key. Next, type a **b**, a **t**, a **y**, and a **1**, and press ENTER and the Exit (F7) key. To have something to back up, type

WordPerfect has an automatic timed backup feature.

To have WordPerfect back up the document, wait a minute. WordPerfect displays this message on the status line when it saves the file:

`* Please wait *`

To show how you can use this timed backup, reboot the machine without exiting from WordPerfect. First, open the door on drive A if you are using a hard disk system, or place the DOS disk in drive A if you are using a floppy disk system. Next, press the CTRL-ALT-DEL key combination. Once the computer has loaded DOS, load WordPerfect. When you load WordPerfect, it displays this message:

Are other copies of WordPerfect currently running? (Y/N)

Type an **n**. When the blank document screen appears, press the Retrieve (SHIFT-F10) key, type **wp{wp}.bk1**, and press ENTER. The document that WordPerfect backed up for you appears on the screen. Save this file under a new name by pressing the Save (F10) key, typing **backup**, and pressing ENTER. Add the word **efficient** in front of "automatic" to alter the entry and cause WordPerfect to back up the document. When WordPerfect first tries to back up this file in the current WordPerfect session, it will display this message:

Old backup file exists, 1 Rename; 2 Delete:

Since you retrieved the data from the backup file and saved it in another file, you can type a **d** for Delete.

Exercises

1. Reset the timed backup to 2 hours (120 minutes).

2. Reset the timed backup to 30-minute intervals.

CHANGE DISPLAY OPTIONS   19.2

WordPerfect allows a significant amount of screen customiza-. tion. If you have a color monitor, you can change the screen colors to make different WordPerfect features appear different on screen. You can use a special character to display hard returns on your screen. You can also choose whether or not to display the filename of the current document on the screen.

To change the screen colors:

a. Press the Setup (SHIFT-F1) key.

b. Type a **d** or a **3** to select Display.

c. Type a **c** or a **2** to select color options.

d. Type an **s** or a **1** to select Screen Colors.

e. Move the cursor to the row of the feature that you want to change.

f. Move the cursor to the Foreground or Background column.

g. Type the letter marking the color you want to use.

h. Press the Exit (F7) key twice to return to the document.

The colors that are available depend upon the equipment you are using. WordPerfect displays a sample of how the feature appears in the right-hand column of the colors setup screen. Some monitors also include a font column, which allows you to use an alternate font for a feature. If you change your mind while selecting colors, press the Cancel (F1) key instead of the Exit (F7) key until you return to the document.

To change the character that represents a hard return:

a. Press the Setup (SHIFT-F1) key.

b. Type a **d** or a **3** to select Display.

c. Type an **h** or a **6** to select Hard Return Display Character.

d. Type the character you want to represent hard returns.

e. Press the Exit (F7) key.

The hard return code [HRt] appears as usual when you press the Reveal Codes (ALT-F3) key.

To change the display of the filename in the status line:

a. Press the Setup (SHIFT-F1) key.

b. Type a **d** or a **3** to select Display.

c. Type an **f** or a **4** to select the filename option.

d. Type a **y** to display the filename on the status line or an **n** to leave the space blank.

e. Press the Exit (F7) key.

Examples

1. You can change the colors WordPerfect uses to block text. First, press the Setup (SHIFT-F1) key. Next, type a **d**, a **c**, and an **s**. If your colors setup screen has a font column, press the RIGHT ARROW key. When the cursor is in the Foreground column, the top of the screen looks like this:

```
Setup: Colors        A B C D E F G H I J K L M N O P
                     A B C D E F G H I J K L M N O P
Attribute            Foreground  Background  Sample
Normal                    H           B      Sample
Blocked                   P           A      Sample
```

Press the DOWN ARROW key, and type an **a** to select black foreground letters. Next, press the RIGHT ARROW key, and type

a c to select a green background. The new appearance is shown in the sample in the right-hand column. Press the Exit (F7) key twice to return to the document. (The available options and the effects they have on your screen depend on your computer equipment.)

2. You can change the character that represents a hard return. WordPerfect's default setting displays a hard return as a blank space. You can change this feature when you are unsure of the location of hard returns and want them to be more obvious. First, type

Hard Return Characters
    Emphasizing the hard return characters allows you to discover where you have pressed ENTER and where WordPerfect has wrapped the text for you.

Next, press ENTER and the Setup (SHIFT-F1) key. Then, type a **d** and an **h**. To display the hard return character as a plus sign, type +, and press the Exit (F7) key. Now the text looks like this:

Hard Return Characters+
    Emphasizing the hard return characters allows you to discover where you have pressed ENTER and where WordPerfect has wrapped the text for you.+

3. You can suppress display of the filename in the status line. First, press the Setup (SHIFT-F1) key. Next, type a **d**, an **f**, and an **n**, and press the Exit (F7) key. The filename will no longer appear in the status line after you retrieve a document or save a new document without exiting from it.

Exercises

1. Change the foreground color of bold text to black.

2. Set the colors of italic text to the ones for normal text.

3. Change the hard return display character to the "less than" symbol (<).

4. Reset the hard return display character to the space.

5. Set WordPerfect to display the filename in the status line.

19.3   SELECT INITIAL SETTINGS

WordPerfect's initial settings provide additional customization capabilities. You can control the computer's beep with these commands. You can also affect the display of the date and other options.

To change the occurrence of the beep sound:

a. Press the Setup (SHIFT-F1) key.

b. Type an **i** or a **5** for Initial Settings.

c. Type a **b** or a **1** for Beep Options.

d. Type an **e** or a **1** to change whether WordPerfect should beep when an error occurs; then type a **y** to have WordPerfect beep or an **n** not to have it beep.

e. Type an **s** or a **3** to change whether WordPerfect should beep when a search fails; then type a **y** to have WordPerfect beep or an **n** to have it not beep when it cannot find a search string.

f. Press the Exit (F7) key to return to the document.

WordPerfect's third beep option, Beep on Hyphenation, determines whether WordPerfect beeps when it prompts you to select a location for a hyphen in a word that won't fit on a line. Appendix A discusses hyphenation in detail.

To change the date display:

a. Press the Setup (SHIFT-F1) key.

b. Type an **i** or a **5** for Initial Settings.

c. Type a **d** or a **2** for Date Format.

d. Type the appropriate numbers and symbols for the date format you want.

e. Press ENTER.

f. Press the Exit (F7) key.

Examples

1. You can direct WordPerfect to beep when you are searching for text. This alerts you when WordPerfect cannot find a search string or when it finishes a replace operation. First, press the Setup (SHIFT-F1) key. Next, type an **i**, a **b**, an **s**, and a **y** to set WordPerfect to beep when a search fails. Finally, press the Exit (F7) key to return to the document. When you search the document for text or codes, WordPerfect will beep when it cannot find the search string.

2. WordPerfect can insert the current date into a document. You can change the date display for WordPerfect's Date feature. First, press the Setup (SHIFT-F1) key. Then, type an **i** and a **d**. The date format screen provides many options to format dates and times. The screen displays the numbers and symbols you can use. Type the appropriate numbers and symbols to specify a date format. To set the date in the format of MM/DD/YY, type **2/1/5**. Finally, press ENTER and the Exit (F7) key. To have WordPerfect insert the date in a document, press the Date/Outline (SHIFT-F5) key, and type a **t** for Date Text. WordPerfect inserts the date at the cursor's location using the format that you specified.

3. You can use the Date feature to insert the current time in your document. First, press the Setup (SHIFT-F1) key. Then, type an **i** and a **d**. To set the time in the format of the hour, a colon, and the minute, type **8:9**. Then, press ENTER and the Exit (F7) key. To have WordPerfect insert the time in a

document, press the Date/Outline (SHIFT-F5) key and type a **t** for Date Text. WordPerfect inserts the time at the cursor's location using the format that you specified.

Exercises

1. Set WordPerfect not to beep when an error occurs.

2. Set WordPerfect to use the date format of day of the week, a comma, a space, the month, another space, and the day of the month.

3. Type the following sentence. Where the sentence has four "X"s, use the Date feature to insert the current date text.

   On XXXX, the Okra Vegetable company begins marketing its new product line, the Seeing Green frozen foods.

EXERCISES

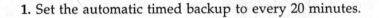

MASTERY
SKILLS CHECK

1. Set the automatic timed backup to every 20 minutes.

2. Set the background for normal text to black.

3. Set the date format to insert the month spelled out, a space, and four digits for the year.

4. Type the following sentence. Where the sentence has four "X"s, use the Date feature to insert the current date text.

   Acme Corporation projects that its personnel will increase 5% during XXXX.

5. Set WordPerfect not to beep when it cannot find the text that you want during a search.

(Do not clear the screen between exercises unless instructed to do so.)

1. Set the automatic timed backup to back up your files every minute. Type **Testing Backups**. Wait until WordPerfect backs up your document. Rename the backup file WP{WP}.BK1 to BCKUPTST. Clear the screen without saving the document.

2. Set the automatic timed backup so that it does not back up your files.

3. Set the date format to the month spelled out, a space, the day of the month, a comma, a space, and the year using four digits.

4. Type the following paragraphs. Use the Date feature to replace the four "X"s with the current date text.

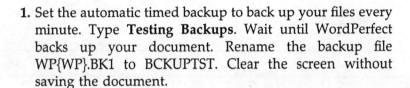

   The company picnic is on XXXX.
   Each person should bring one dish. Please review the schedule, which breaks down the type of dish based upon the person's last name.

5. Make the first sentence boldface. Underline the words "one dish."

6. Set the hard return display character to an asterisk.

7. If you have a color monitor, set the underlined text background to red and the boldfaced text background to light blue.

8. Use the List Files feature to delete the file named WP{WP}.SET. (This restores all of the display settings to their original values.)

9. Save the document as DISH, and exit WordPerfect. Load WordPerfect. Set the automatic timed backup to back up your files every 30 minutes.

Appendixes

·A·

Installing WordPerfect and Selecting a Printer

If you do not have WordPerfect installed on your machine, you will need to install the program before you can use it. The process is not difficult and can be completed in a short time if you follow the instructions provided. Part of the installation process involves selecting one or more printers to use with WordPerfect. If your system is already installed, you will need to repeat the printer installation process if you attach a new printer to your system. The instructions you should use depend upon the computer system you have. This appendix has the installation steps for three different types of computer systems.

Hard disk system using WordPerfect's installation program: Use these instructions if you have a hard disk and all of the WordPerfect disks.

Hard disk system omitting WordPerfect's installation program: Use these instructions if you need to conserve your hard disk space, if you start your computer by putting a disk in drive A, if you want WordPerfect on another hard drive other than C, or if you do not want the WordPerfect subdirectory to be named WP50.

Floppy disk system: Use these instructions if you do not have a hard disk. The instructions assume that you have two floppy disk drives.

The instructions will refer to disk drives by letter names. If your machine has one disk drive, it is drive A. If the computer has two disk drives, the one on the top or the left is drive A, and the one on the bottom or the right is drive B. Drive C is the normal default for a hard disk, although some computers may have hard disks that use other labels.

The instructions are written for 5 1/4-inch disks. If you have a system with 3 1/2-inch disks, these instructions will still work, but you will not need to change disks so frequently. Since the 3 1/2-inch disks have more than double the capacity of 5 1/4-inch disks, one 3 1/2-inch disk will take the place of two 5 1/4-inch disks.

HARD DISK SYSTEM USING WORDPERFECT'S INSTALLATION PROGRAM

WordPerfect contains an installation program to copy the information from the WordPerfect 1, WordPerfect 2, Font/Graphics, Speller, Thesaurus, and PTR Program disks to your hard disk. Your copy of WordPerfect has one of two installation programs. In one version, you can selectively decide which disks you will copy to your hard disk. With this installation program, you must type a **y** or press ENTER and then press any key to copy a disk to your hard drive, or you simply type an **n** to omit copying the disk. In the other installation program, WordPerfect assumes that you will copy the WordPerfect 1, WordPerfect 2, Font/Graphics, Speller, Thesaurus, and PTR Program disks to your hard disk. Word Perfect will tell you when to insert each disk and to press a key when the disk is inserted. These instructions use the first installation program. If you use the second, you will need to press a key only once where the instructions direct you to press ENTER twice. The version of the installation program that you have depends on whether you have the disks distributed with the first release of WordPerfect 5.0 (in May 1988) or a subsequent release.

If WordPerfect is already installed on your machine and you only need to change the printer, you can skip to step 13.

1. Turn on your computer. The computer will load DOS from the hard disk into your computer's memory.

2. Insert the Learning disk in drive A.

3. Type **a:install**, and press ENTER. WordPerfect prompts you to type a **y** or press ENTER if you have a hard disk or type an **n** if you do not.

4. Press ENTER. WordPerfect displays a screen of information. This information tells you that the installation program will create a WP50 subdirectory in drive C if you do not already have one, that it will copy the files on the WordPerfect disks necessary to run the program and the tutorial, and that it will add "FILES=20" to the CONFIG.SYS file if necessary. WordPerfect prompts you to type a **y** or press ENTER to continue or an **n** to abort the installation program.

5. Press ENTER. WordPerfect prompts you to type a **y** or press ENTER to copy the files from the program disks or to type an **n** to skip copying the files to the hard disk.

6. Remove the Learning disk and insert the WordPerfect 1 disk in drive A. Press ENTER twice. WordPerfect reads the files and writes them to the WP50 subdirectory, creating the subdirectory if one does not exist. WordPerfect prompts you to type a **y** or press ENTER to copy the files from the WordPerfect 1 disk or to type an **n** to skip copying the files to the hard disk.

7. If you have 3 1/2-inch disks, both sets of files will be on the same disk, and you can skip this step. Remove the WordPerfect 1 disk, and insert the WordPerfect 2 disk in drive A. Press ENTER twice to copy the files.

8. Remove the WordPerfect 2 disk, and insert the Font/Graphics disk in drive A. Press ENTER twice.

9. Remove the Font/Graphics disk, and insert the Speller disk in drive A. Press ENTER twice.

10. If you have 3 1/2-inch disks, you copied the Thesaurus files with the Speller files and can skip this step. Remove the Speller disk, and insert the Thesaurus disk in drive A. Press ENTER twice.

11. If you have 3 1/2-inch disks, you copied the PTR Program with the Font/Graphics files and can skip this step. Remove the Thesaurus disk, and insert the PTR Program disk in drive A. Press ENTER twice.

12. Remove the PTR Program disk, and insert the Learning disk in drive A. Press ENTER twice. After the installation program finishes copying the Learning disk, it checks the CONFIG.SYS file for a line containing "FILES =" followed by the number 20 or a greater number. If it cannot find the

line or if the number is too low, WordPerfect modifies the CONFIG.SYS file. When the DOS **C>** prompt reappears, WordPerfect is ready to be used, although you will still need to select a printer.

13. Type **wp**, and press ENTER. As Chapter 1 explains, the WordPerfect screen appears.

14. Hold down the SHIFT key, and press the key labeled F7. This is a function key.

15. Type an **s**, an **a**, and an **o**. WordPerfect prompts you for the location of the printer files.

16. Remove the Learning disk, and insert the Printer 1 disk in drive A.

17. Type **a:**, and press ENTER.

18. If you see your printer listed, skip the next step.

19. Remove the disk, and insert the next Printer disk in drive A. Type an **o** and press ENTER. Repeat this step until your printer or a compatible model is listed.

20. Move the highlight to your printer using the DOWN ARROW key, which is below the 2 on the numeric keypad at the right side of the keyboard. If the highlight does not move, press the key labeled NUM LOCK, and try again.

21. Press ENTER twice. WordPerfect displays messages explaining how different WordPerfect features work with your printer.

22. Press the F7 key. If your printer is not connected to the first parallel port, which is usually labelled LPT1:, type a **p**, and select the appropriate number for the port the printer is connected to. If you select a serial port, WordPerfect

displays settings it will use to send information to the printer. Check your printer manual to determine the proper baud rate, parity, stop bits, character length, and XON/XOFF protocol. If any of the information displayed is incorrect, type the letter or number next to the option with the incorrect setting, and type the letter or number for the correct setting. When the settings are correct, press the F7 key.

23. Press the F7 key four times, and type an **n** and a **y**. You are now back in DOS and ready to start learning Word Perfect. Store the original WordPerfect disks in a safe place.

HARD DISK SYSTEM OMITTING WORDPERFECT'S INSTALLATION PROGRAM

If your hard disk is not drive C, replace the letter "C" in the directions with the proper letter for your drive. If WordPerfect is already installed on your machine and you only need to change the printer, you can start with step 18.

1. Turn on your computer. If your computer needs a DOS disk or a startup disk, insert it in drive A.

2. If the computer prompts you for them, provide the current date and time, pressing ENTER after each entry.

3. Type **cd c:**, and press ENTER. If you used a DOS disk or a startup disk when you turned on your computer, make sure that the write-protect tab is uncovered, and type **a:** instead.

4. Type **type config.sys**, and press ENTER. DOS displays the current contents of the configuration file, which contains instructions that your computer uses every time you start it. If the computer displays the message **File Not Found**, skip the next step.

5. Look for a line that contains "FILES=." If the line is present and the number is at least 20, type **c:**, press ENTER, and skip to step 10.

6. Type **copy config.sys + con config.sys**, and press ENTER. The computer displays **CON**.

7. Type **files=20**, and press ENTER.

8. Hold down the key labeled CTRL, and type a **z**. Then press ENTER. The computer appends the line that you typed to the end of the CONFIG.SYS file or creates a CONFIG.SYS file with that line.

9. Hold down the key labeled CTRL and the key labeled ALT, and press the key labeled DEL. The screen clears as the computer reloads the DOS operating system into the computer using the new CONFIG.SYS file. If necessary, reenter the date and the time.

10. Type **cd c:**, and press ENTER.

11. Type **md\wp50** to create a subdirectory called WP50. To use a different name for the subdirectory, replace "WP50" in this and the next step with the desired name.

12. Type **cd\wp50** to switch to the WP50 subdirectory.

13. Insert the WordPerfect 1 disk in drive A.

14. Type **copy a:*.***, and press ENTER. If the computer does not display the message *# **File(s) copied*** with # representing a number greater than 0, retype the line, making sure to put a space only between the "y" and the "a" and that a colon (not a semicolon) follows the "a."

15. If you have 3 1/2-inch disks, the WordPerfect 1 and WordPerfect 2 disks are combined and you can skip this step. Remove the WordPerfect 1 disk, and replace it with the WordPerfect 2 disk. Type **copy a:*.***, and press ENTER.

16. Remove the disk in drive A and insert the next Word-Perfect disk in its place. Type **copy a:*.***, and press ENTER.

17. Repeat step 16 for each of the WordPerfect disks. You do not need to copy all of the disks to use WordPerfect, but you must copy the WordPerfect 1 and WordPerfect 2 disks to use the program. You will probably want to copy the Speller, Thesaurus, and Font/Graphics disks to use those features. You need to copy the Convert disk only if you are planning to transfer text between WordPerfect and other software packages or a mainframe. Do not copy the disks labeled Printer. WordPerfect will transfer the portions of these disks that it needs when you select a printer.

    When the **C>** prompt reappears on the screen, Word-Perfect is ready for you to use.

18. Type **wp**, and press ENTER. As Chapter 1 explains, the WordPerfect screen appears.

19. If your subdirectory containing WordPerfect is not labeled WP50, hold down one of the two keys labeled SHIFT or that has a large arrow pointing up, and press the key labeled F1. This is a function key. Type an **l**, a **p**, and the path for

the printer files (for example, **c:\wordperf** for a subdirectory named WORDPERF). Then, press ENTER, and press the key labeled F7. This is a function key.

20. Hold down the SHIFT key, and press the F7 key.

21. Type an **s**, an **a**, and an **o**. WordPerfect prompts you for the location of the printer files.

22. Replace the disk in drive A with the Printer 1 disk.

23. Type **a:**, and press ENTER.

24. If you see your printer listed, skip the next step.

25. Replace the printer disk in drive A with the next printer disk. Type an **o**, and press ENTER. Repeat this step until your printer or a compatible model is listed.

26. Move the highlight to your printer using the DOWN ARROW key, which is below the 2 on the numeric keypad at the right side of the keyboard. If the highlight does not move, press the key labeled NUM LOCK, and try again.

27. Press ENTER twice. WordPerfect displays messages explaining how different WordPerfect features work with your printer.

28. Press the F7 key. If your printer is not connected to the first parallel port, usually labeled LPT1:, type a **p**, and select the appropriate number for the port the printer is connected to. If you select a serial port, WordPerfect displays settings it will use to send information to the printer. Check your printer manual to determine the proper baud rate, parity, stop bits, character length, and XON/XOFF protocol. If any of the information displayed is incorrect,

type the letter or number next to the option with the incorrect setting, and type the letter or number for the correct setting. When the settings are correct, press the EXIT (F7) key.

29. Press the F7 key four times, and type an **n** and a **y**. You are now back in DOS and ready to start learning Word-Perfect. Store the original disks in a safe place.

FLOPPY DISK SYSTEM

You will need a blank disk for each WordPerfect disk to create a backup copy of the program.

If WordPerfect is already installed on your machine and you only need to change the printer, you can skip to step 12.

1. Turn on your computer. Insert your DOS disk or startup disk in drive A.

2. Type the date and the time when the computer prompts you for them, pressing ENTER after each entry.

3. Remove the DOS or startup disk from drive A, and replace it with the Learning disk.

4. Type **install**, and press ENTER. WordPerfect displays a screen of information telling you that it will check the CONFIG.SYS file and add the line "FILES=20" to it if necessary. WordPerfect prompts you to type a **y** or press ENTER to continue or to type an **n** to abort the installation program.

5. Type a **y**. The installation program prompts you to insert your DOS disk in drive A.

6. Remove the Learning disk from drive A, and insert your DOS disk. Press any key. After the installation program checks and possibly modifies your CONFIG.SYS file, it displays **A>**.

7. Hold down the key labeled CTRL and the key labeled ALT, and press the key labeled DEL. The screen clears as the computer reloads DOS into memory using the new CON-FIG.SYS file.

8. Type **diskcopy a: b:** and press ENTER. The computer will prompt you to place the source (program) disk in drive A and the target (blank) disk in drive B. If the computer does not display the prompt, retype the line, making sure to put spaces only between the "y" and the "a" and between the first colon and the "b." Also make sure that colons (not semicolons) follow both the "a" and the "b."

9. Remove the DOS or startup disk and insert the Word Perfect 1 disk in drive A. When the computer has finished copying the files to the blank disk, the screen displays a prompt asking whether you want to copy another disk.

10. Replace the WordPerfect 1 disk with the WordPerfect 2 disk in drive A. Remove the disk in drive B, and label it "WordPerfect 1." Place a blank disk in drive B, type a **y**, and press any key.

11. Repeat step 10 for each of the WordPerfect disks. After you have copied the last disk, type an **n** instead of a "y." Store the original disks in a safe place, and use only your copies. You are ready to use WordPerfect, although you must select a printer.

12. Type **wp** and press ENTER. When the computer prompts you to do so, replace the WordPerfect 1 disk with the WordPerfect 2 disk in drive A. As Chapter 1 explains, the WordPerfect screen appears.

13. Press the key labeled F7. This is a function key.

14. Type an **s**, an **a**, and an **o**. WordPerfect prompts you for the location of the printer files.

15. Insert the Printer 1 disk in drive B.

16. Type **b:**, and press ENTER.

17. If you see your printer listed, skip the next step.

18. Replace the printer disk in drive A with the next printer disk. Type an **o** and press ENTER. Repeat this step until your printer or a compatible model is listed.

19. Move the highlight to your printer using the DOWN ARROW key, which is below the 2 on the numeric keypad at the right side of the keyboard. If the highlight does not move, press the key labeled NUM LOCK, and try again.

20. Press ENTER twice. WordPerfect displays messages explaining how different WordPerfect features work with your printer.

21. Press the F7 key. If your printer is not connected to the first parallel port, usually labeled LPT1:, type a **p**, and select the appropriate number for the port the printer is connected to. If you select a serial port, WordPerfect displays settings it will use to send information to the printer. Check your printer manual to determine the proper baud rate, parity, stop bits, character length, and XON/XOFF protocol. If any of the information displayed is incorrect, type the letter or number next to the option with the incorrect setting, and type the letter or number for the correct setting. When the settings are correct, press the EXIT (F7) key.

22. Press the F7 key four times, and type an **n** and a **y**. You are now back in DOS and ready to start learning Word-Perfect.

23. Since you will be storing your documents on disks, you may want to format a few blank disks before beginning word processing. With the DOS disk in drive A, type **Format B :** and press ENTER.

24. Place a blank disk in drive B and press ENTER.

    It is important that you have a blank disk in drive B or at least a disk whose information is not important since the format operation erases all the information the disk. When DOS completes the formatting for this disk, it will display a prompt asking if you want to format additional disks. If you want to format another disk, type a **y**, press ENTER and repeat step 24.

25. If you do not wish to format additional disks, type an **n** and press ENTER to return to DOS.

·B·

Hyphenation

Hyphens are used for several purposes when creating word-processed documents. They are used to separate parts of a compound word and can also be used to split long lines. The splitting of words at the end of lines is referred to as *hyphenation*. Hyphenation splits a word at a syllable break. The first part of a hyphenated word appears at the end of a line, followed by a hyphen (-); the remaining letters appear at the beginning of the next line.

With WordPerfect, you can create documents with or without hyphenation. In documents in which the Hyphenation feature is off, lines always end between words. When you enable Hyphenation, you can elect to use WordPerfect's rules for automatic hyphenation or choose to have Word-Perfect ask you for confirmation for the placement of each hyphen.

Hyphenation can help give your documents a professional appearance. You can add hyphens to your documents yourself for a variety of purposes, or you can have Word-Perfect add them for you. When WordPerfect hyphenates for you, it uses a set of rules in an attempt to determine appropriate breaks in a word. It also uses a hyphenation zone setting to determine when it should hyphenate a word.

Hyphenation may differ when you use WordPerfect on different systems, depending on the printer that you have selected for each system and the base font that you have selected for each document. Since WordPerfect attempts to display your document on screen as it will appear when printed, the selected printer and fonts will determine the number of characters that will fit on each line on the screen. The examples in this appendix were produced with a Hewlett-Packard LaserJet Series II printer attached to an IBM PS/2 Model 60. The examples use the default font for the LaserJet Series II.

Although hyphenation capabilities exist regardless of the printer type, you may be unable to duplicate the results of the examples in this appendix without identical equipment, as more or fewer characters may fit on each line of your screen and the word breaks may not occur at the same places. However, you can follow the examples to learn the procedure you will use when hyphenating your own text.

In addition to describing the types of hyphens inserted by WordPerfect during hyphenation, this appendix covers the use of hard hyphens and hyphen characters, which you can insert yourself. It also includes instructions for turning Hyphenation on and off and affecting the size of the zone used to decide whether hyphenation is appropriate for an individual word.

HYPHEN CHARACTERS AND HARD HYPHENS

There will likely be times when you will need to use hyphens in your typing. Since there are several ways to create a hyphen, you will need to know the options. The use of the wrong type of hyphen can cause undesired changes in an edited document.

You can use *hyphen characters* in compound words. To distinguish hyphens used in compound words from other types of hyphens, WordPerfect requires a special method to create the hyphen character. This instructs WordPerfect to treat the two parts of the word as one. Like other characters the hyphen character does not have a hidden code associated with it.

To enter a hyphen character:

a. Press the HOME key.

b. Press the hyphen (-) key.

Compound words use hyphen characters. Using a hyphen character in these words tells WordPerfect that they should be kept together. First, type

The company is changing its write

Then, press the HOME key, and type a hyphen. Finally, type

off method for receivables.

When you press the Reveal Codes (ALT-F3) key, the sentence looks like this:

The company is changing its write-off method for receivables.█

You can also use a hyphen to break a long word that extends past the right margin. This type of hyphen is called a *hard hyphen*. A hard hyphen has a hidden code: [-]. To create a hard hyphen, simply press the hyphen key. First, type the following line of text.

Companies must report gains and losses from prematurely extin

Since you want this word to continue on the next line, type a hyphen. Then, type the remainder of the sentence:

guishing its debt as an extraordinary gain or loss.

The screen looks like this:

```
Companies must report gains and losses from prematurely extin-
guishing its debt as an extraordinary gain or loss.
```

The hyphen you typed is part of the document, much like the characters in the words. When you edit the sentence, the hyphen stays between the "n" and the "g" in "extinguish." First, move the cursor to the word "must" by pressing the UP ARROW key to move to the first line of the sentence, pressing the HOME key and the LEFT ARROW key to move to the beginning of the line, and pressing the CTRL-RIGHT ARROW key combination to move to the "m" in "must." Next, press the CTRL-BACKSPACE key combination to remove the word. After you press the DOWN ARROW key to reformat the paragraph, the screen will look like this:

```
Companies report gains and losses from prematurely extin-guishing
its debt as an extraordinary gain or loss.
```

TURNING HYPHENATION ON AND HYPHENATING A DOCUMENT

WordPerfect's default setting is for no hyphenation. Word-Perfect checks hyphenation as you type each line if you turn Hyphenation on. If the hidden code for Hyphenation is at the top of your document or you change the initial setting for Hyphenation to on, WordPerfect checks the entire document for hyphenation when you scroll through the document. To temporarily disable hyphenation while you move through large sections of the document or use WordPerfect's features to search for a word or check the document's spelling, you can press the Exit (F7) key in response to the first hyphenation prompt during the operation. Hyphenation resumes when the operation is complete.

If you choose to enable the Hyphenation feature, you can use manual hyphenation, which gives you the opportunity to instruct WordPerfect where to place each hyphen. If you prefer, you can use automatic hyphenation, which offers WordPerfect more leeway to make decisions on its own.

In both automatic and manual hyphenation, WordPerfect places a *soft hyphen* in your document. A soft hyphen is unlike a hard hyphen or hyphen character in that it disappears if the length of the line changes and the hyphen is no longer needed.

To use automatic hyphenation:

a. Press the Format (SHIFT-F8) key.

b. Type an **l** or a **1** for line-formatting options.

c. Type a **y** or a **1** to enable Hyphenation.

d. Type an **a** or a **3** for automatic hyphenation.

e. Press the Exit (F7) key to return to the document.

To use manual hyphenation:

a. Press the Format (SHIFT-F8) key.

b. Type an **l** or a **1** for line-formatting options.

c. Type a **y** or a **1** to enable Hyphenation.

d. Type an **m** or a **2** for manual hyphenation.

e. Press the Exit (F7) key to return to the document.

Hyphenation operates only on the text following the Hyphenation code. WordPerfect uses the codes [Hyph On] and [Hyph Off] to indicate when hyphenation is turned on and off. When Hyphenation is set to automatic, WordPerfect uses a set of rules to determine where it should hyphenate words. If WordPerfect thinks a word should be hyphenated but cannot determine from its rules how to split the word, it temporarily switches to manual hyphenation.

You can turn Hyphenation on before you type a document to ensure that the entire document will be hyphenated. First, press the Format (SHIFT-F8) key. Then, type an l, a y, and an a to enable automatic hyphenation. Next, press the Exit (F7) key. To put automatic hyphenation to use, type

The Donner Company recognizes profit on long-term construction contracts using the percentage-of-completion method of accounting. The profit is the percentage of completion multiplied by the difference between the total contract price and the estimated total construction costs. The percentage of completion is the ratio of incurred costs to the estimated total construction cost.

With automatic hyphenation, the paragraph looks like this on the system used for this example:

```
    The Donner Company recognizes profit on long-term construc-
tion contracts using the percentage-of-completion method of
accounting. The profit is the percentage of completion multi-
plied by the difference between the total contract price and the
estimated total construction costs. The percentage of completion
is the ration of incurred costs to the estimated total construc-
tion cost.
```

You can set the Hyphenation feature to manual when you want to confirm all hyphen locations. First, clear the screen and type

When a company extinguishes debt before maturity, it recognizes the difference between the cash paid and the book value of the debt, including unamortized bond issue costs, as an extraordinary gain or loss from early extinguishment.

Next, press HOME, HOME, and the UP ARROW key to move to the beginning of this document. Then, press the Format (SHIFT-F8) key, and type an l, a y and an **m**. To return to the document, press the Exit (F7) key.

When you move the cursor, WordPerfect wants to know how to hyphenate the existing text. First, it displays this prompt:

Position hyphen; Press ESC recog-nizes

Since the hyphen is shown at an appropriate place in the word, press ESC to accept WordPerfect's placement. Next, WordPerfect displays this prompt:

Position hyphen; Press ESC extraor-dinary

To put the hyphen at a more appropriate place, between "extra" and "ordinary," press the LEFT ARROW key twice, and then press ESC. The screen now looks like this:

When a company extinguishes debt before maturity, it recog-nizes the difference between the cash paid and the book value of the debt, including unamortized bond issue costs, as an extra-ordinary gain or loss from early extinguishment

As you add text to a document with Hyphenation set to manual, WordPerfect prompts you for the location of each hyphen. Move the cursor to the end of the paragraph that you just typed, and press the SPACEBAR. When you press the SPACEBAR, WordPerfect prompts you for the hyphen's location. Since its prompt indicates an acceptable location for the hyphen, press ESC. Finally, finish the sentence by typing

of debt when the current interest rates are higher than the bond's rate of issuance.

You can disable hyphenation for a single word. First, clear the screen. Then, press the Format (SHIFT-F8) key, and type an **l**, a **y**, and an **m**. Next, press the Exit (F7) key, and type

Manual and automatic hyphenation are two features that WordPerfect

When you press the SPACEBAR, WordPerfect prompts you for how you want "WordPerfect" hyphenated. Since proper names generally should not be hyphenated, press the Cancel (F1) key. WordPerfect places the entire word on the next line. When you press the Reveal Codes (ALT-F3) key, the lower half of the screen looks like this:

[Hyph On]Manual and automatic hyphenation are two features that[SRt]
[/]WordPerfect

WordPerfect inserted the [/] code to indicate that "WordPerfect" should not be hyphenated.

You can mark a word to prevent hyphenation as you type it. First, clear the screen. The press the Format (SHIFT-F8) key, and type an **l**, a **y**, and an **m**. Next, press the Exit (F7) key, and type

Manual and automatic hyphenation are two features that

Press the HOME key and type a slash (/). You do not see a change, but when you type the next word, WordPerfect will automatically wrap the word to the next line. Type

WordPerfect offers.

When you press the Reveal Codes (ALT-F3) key, you can see the [/] code before "WordPerfect."

When you edit hyphenated text, WordPerfect remembers where it hyphenated words. Since these hyphens are soft hyphens, WordPerfect will remove them if they are no longer required. First, clear the screen. Then, press the Format (SHIFT-F8) key, and type an **l**, a **y**, and an **m**. Next, press the Exit (F7) key. Press the TAB key, and type

Manual and automatic hyphenation are two of the many features

Then, press the SPACEBAR. WordPerfect suggests splitting "features" between the "a" and the "t." Accept WordPerfect's suggestion by pressing ESC. Then, type

WordPerfect can offer.

To edit the text, press the CTRL-LEFT ARROW key combination seven times to move to the word "of." Then, press the CTRL-BACKSPACE key combination three times to delete "of the many." Reformat the paragraph by pressing the DOWN ARROW key. WordPerfect prompts you to hyphenate "WordPerfect." Press the Cancel (F1) key. When you press the Reveal Codes (ALT-F3) key, the screen looks like this:

```
[Hyph On][Tab]Manual and automatic hyphenation are two fea-tures[SRt]
[/]WordPerfect can offer.█
```

The bold hyphen indicates where WordPerfect hyphenated "features." This code allows WordPerfect to hyphenate the word later if necessary without prompting you for the correct hyphen location again.

You can change WordPerfect's placement of hyphens in words. Using the text just entered, press the Reveal Codes (ALT-F3) key, and move the cursor to the slash code before "WordPerfect." Then, press the DEL key to remove the code. To reformat the paragraph, press the UP ARROW key and the DOWN ARROW key. WordPerfect prompts you for a location for the hyphen. Press the LEFT ARROW key three times to move the hyphen between "Word" and "Perfect," and press ESC.

To change the hyphenation of "features," press the UP ARROW key, the END key, the CTRL-LEFT ARROW key combination twice, and the RIGHT ARROW key three times. Then, press the DEL key to delete the boldfaced hyphen. Next, press the HOME key and the LEFT ARROW key, and press the TAB key three times and the SPACEBAR twice. WordPerfect prompts you for hyphenation. Press ESC to accept the suggestion.

You can disable hyphenation after invoking it. First, clear the screen. Then, press the Format (SHIFT-F8) key, and type an **l**, a **y**, and an **a** to enable automatic hyphenation. Next, press the Exit (F7) key, and type

The sum-of-the-years'-digits is one method of accelerated depreciation. This method determines the amount of depreciation expense for a period by multiplying the depreciation by a fraction.

To disable hyphenation, press the Format (SHIFT-F8) key, and type an **l**, a **y**, and an **f**. WordPerfect inserts the hidden code [Hyph Off]. Next, press the Exit (F7) key, press ENTER, and type

The denominator of the fraction is the sum of the numbers representing each year of useful life. The numerator of the fraction is the number of years of useful life remaining at the beginning of the year.

HYPHENATION ZONES

WordPerfect uses a setting called the *hyphenation zone* to determine whether it should hyphenate a word at the end of a line. The hyphenation zone has both left and right zone settings expressed as a percentage of the line length. A small hyphenation zone increases the number of hyphenated words in a document. A large hyphenation zone reduces the number of hyphenated words. WordPerfect's default hyphenation zone setting is 10% and 4%. This means that the last 10% of the line is the left hyphenation zone, and the right hyphenation zone is equivalent to 4% of the line length past the right margin.

If the last word in a line starts before or at the left hyphenation zone and extends to the right hyphenation zone, WordPerfect will hyphenate the word (with automatic hyphenation) or prompt you for hyphenation (with manual hyphenation). A word that starts after the left hyphenation zone and is long enough to stretch beyond the right zone is wordwrapped. Figure B-1 shows the hyphenation zone in perspective with the right margin.

To change the hyphenation zone:

a. Press the Format (SHIFT-F8) key.

b. Type an l or a 1 for line-formatting options.

c. Type a z or a 2 for Hyphenation Zone.

d. Type the percentage of the line to be used for the left hyphenation zone, and press ENTER.

e. Type the percentage of the line to be used for the right hyphenation zone, and press ENTER.

f. Press the Exit (F7) key to return to the document.

The hidden code for the hyphenation zone setting is [HZone:X%,Y%]. The "X" represents the left hyphenation zone, and the "Y" represents the right hyphenation zone.

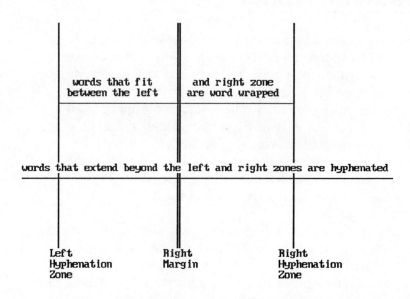

FIGURE B-1.   Hyphenation zone in perspective with the right margin setting

You can decrease the hyphenation zone to increase the number of hyphenated words. First, press the Format (SHIFT-F8) key, and type an l and a z. For the left hyphenation zone, type **5** and press ENTER. For the right hyphenation zone, type **2** and press ENTER. To return to the document, press the Exit (F7) key. To start automatic hyphenation, press the Format (SHIFT-F8) key, type an l, a y, and an a, and press the Exit (F7) key.

To use this new hyphenation zone setting, type

A company often has intangible assets, such as copyrights, patents, and goodwill. These assets do not have a physical shape, like a building, but they have a value. These assets are amortized for a period of not more than 40 years.

As you type the paragraph, you must set the hyphenation for "patents" and "amortized." If you have the same system configuration, the paragraph looks like this:

A company often has intangible assets, such as copyrights, patents, and goodwill. These assets do not have a physical shape
like a building, but they have a value. These assets are amortized for a period of not more than 40 years.

You can increase the hyphenation zone to decrease the number of hyphenated words. Without clearing the screen, press the Format (SHIFT-F8) key. Next, type an l and a z. For the left hyphenation zone, type 15 and press ENTER. For the right hyphenation zone, type 8 and press ENTER. To return to the document, press the Exit (F7) key.

To see how the hyphenation differs, press ENTER and retype the paragraph.

If you wish to use manual hyphenation but are unsure of the correct placement of hyphens, you can refer to almost any dictionary. Words are usually listed with breaks between syllables. Many dictionaries also include a style guide containing information on hyphenation.

·C·

Answers

The following conventions have been used throughout the answers section:

Keystrokes are listed in the order they should be entered. Comments and instructions are enclosed in braces {} to distinguish them from keystrokes.
Special keys, such as the function keys, are enclosed in brackets [].

References to sections covering the material tested in the skills checks, mastery skills checks, and integrated skills checks are provided in brackets at the end of each answer. In the answers for Chapter 1, spaces are indicated by [SPACEBAR]. After Chapter 1, spaces are indicated either by a space in the text or by [SPACEBAR]; the answers use [SPACEBAR] when using a space would cause confusion.

When selections can be made by typing either a letter or a number, the answer gives the letter.

Some exercises have more than one possible solution. Any solution that produces the desired results can be considered correct.

1.1   EXERCISES

1. {for a hard disk system}cd\wp50[ENTER]wp[ENTER]{for a floppy disk system: Place the WordPerfect 1 disk in drive A and a formatted disk for documents in drive B.}b:[ENTER] a:wp[ENTER]{Place the WordPerfect 2 disk in drive A when WordPerfect prompts you, and press any key to continue.}

1.2   EXERCISES

1. {for a hard disk system}cd\wp50[ENTER]wp[ENTER][F7]ny{for a floppy disk system: Place the WordPerfect 1 disk in drive A and a formatted disk for documents in drive B}b:[ENTER] a:wp[ENTER]{Place the WordPerfect 2 disk in drive A when WordPerfect prompts you, and press any key to continue.}[F7]ny

1.3   EXERCISES

1. accounting[F7]nn

2. trees[F7]nn

3. 1989[SPACEBAR]holidays[F7]nn

4. bills,[SPACEBAR]bills,[SPACEBAR]and[SPACEBAR]more[SPACEBAR]bills [F7]nn

EXERCISES

1.4

1. [ENTER][ENTER][ENTER][ENTER][ENTER][ENTER][UP ARROW][UP ARROW][UP ARROW][UP ARROW][UP ARROW][UP ARROW][DOWN ARROW][DOWN ARROW][DOWN ARROW][DOWN ARROW][DOWN ARROW][DOWN ARROW][F7]nn

2. [ESC]10aaaaaaaaaaaa{Press the LEFT ARROW and RIGHT ARROW keys as many times as you like.}[END][ENTER][F7]nn

3. [TAB][TAB][TAB][TAB][LEFT ARROW][LEFT ARROW][LEFT ARROW][LEFT ARROW][F7]nn

4. [CTRL-ENTER][CTRL-ENTER][CTRL-ENTER][CTRL-ENTER]{Press PGUP and PGDN as many times as you like.}[CTRL-HOME]{Type a number from 1 to 5.}[ENTER]{Repeat until you are comfortable with the CTRL-HOME key combination.}[F7]nn

5. the[SPACEBAR]early[SPACEBAR]bird[SPACEBAR]gets[SPACEBAR]the[SPACEBAR]worm.[ENTER][UP ARROW]{Press the CTRL-LEFT ARROW and CTRL-RIGHT ARROW key combinations as many times as you like.} {Press the HOME-LEFT ARROW key combination and the END key as many times as you like.}[F7]nn

6. [ENTER][ENTER][ENTER][ENTER][CTRL-ENTER][ENTER][ENTER][ENTER][ENTER][CTRL-ENTER][ENTER][ENTER][ENTER][ENTER][CTRL-ENTER][ENTER][ENTER][ENTER][ENTER][CTRL-ENTER][ENTER][ENTER][ENTER][ENTER][CTRL-ENTER][ENTER][ENTER][ENTER][ENTER][GREY –][GREY –][GREY +][GREY +][HOME][HOME][UP ARROW][HOME][HOME][DOWN ARROW][F7]nn

7. [NUM LOCK]123456789[NUM LOCK][F7]nn

8. abc[BACKSPACE][LEFT ARROW][LEFT ARROW][DEL]

EXERCISES

1.5

1. [F3]s{for screen}{[ENTER]or[SPACEBAR]to exit Help}

2. he suddenly left.[CTRL-LEFT ARROW][CTRL-LEFT ARROW][LEFT ARROW]
[DEL][DEL][DEL][DEL][DEL][DEL][DEL][DEL][DEL][END][LEFT ARROW][F1]1[F7]nn

3. [F3][F3][ENTER]

4. [F3]d[ENTER]

5. it[SPACEBAR]was[SPACEBAR]a[SPACEBAR]cold,[SPACEBAR]dark,[SPACEBAR]
scary[SPACEBAR]evening[CTRL-LEFT ARROW][CTRL-LEFT ARROW][CTRL-LEFT
ARROW][DEL][DEL][DEL][DEL][DEL][DEL][CTRL-LEFT ARROW][F1]r[F7]}nn

1.6   EXERCISES

1. [SHIFT-j][SHIFT-q][SHIFT-l][SHIFT-y][SHIFT-z][SHIFT-b][SHIFT-e][SHIFT-a][SHIFT-n]
[SHIFT-l][F7]nn

2. [SHIFT-t]he[SPACEBAR][SHIFT-a][SHIFT-b][SHIFT-c][SPACEBAR][SHIFT-c]
orporation[SPACEBAR]makes[SPACEBAR][SHIFT-t]iger[SPACEBAR]sedans.
[F7]nn

3. [SHIFT-t]he[SPACEBAR]lending[SPACEBAR]rate[SPACEBAR]is 15[SHIFT-5].
[ENTER][SHIFT-9]16[SHIFT-8]2[SHIFT-0][SHIFT-=]7 = 39[ENTER][SHIFT-P]
rofit[SPACEBAR][SHIFT-7][SPACEBAR][SHIFT-L]oss[SPACEBAR][SHIFT-S]
tatement[F7]nn

4. [CAPS LOCK]capitalization[SPACEBAR]can[SPACEBAR]emphasize
[SPACEBAR]text[ENTER]wordperfect[CAPS LOCK][SPACEBAR]makes
[SPACEBAR]typing[SPACEBAR][CAPS LOCK]fun.[CAPS LOCK][F7]nn

5. [CAPS LOCK]the[SPACEBAR]local[SPACEBAR]car[SPACEBAR]dealership
[SPACEBAR]is[SPACEBAR]offering[SPACEBAR]16[SHIFT-5][SPACEBAR]apr.
[ENTER]company[SPACEBAR]picnic[SPACEBAR]8/19/89[CAPS LOCK][F7]nn

MASTERY SKILLS CHECK

1. [F7]ny   [1.2]

2. {for a hard disk system}cd\wp50[ENTER]wp[ENTER]{for a   [1.1]
floppy disk system: Place the WordPerfect 1 disk in drive
A and a formatted disk for documents in drive B.}b:
[ENTER]a:wp[ENTER]{Place the WordPerfect 2 disk in drive A
when WordPerfect prompts you, and press any key to
continue.}

3. [SHIFT-a]ugust[SPACEBAR]15th[SPACEBAR]or[SPACEBAR][CAPS LOCK]   [1.4, 1.6]
september[SPACEBAR]3rd[CAPS LOCK][ENTER]3[SHIFT-6]2[SHIFT-=]
[SHIFT-9]8[SHIFT-8]9[SHIFT-0]

4. [F3]e{Press ENTER or SPACEBAR to leave Help.}   [1.5]

5. [F7]nn   [1.3]

6. 10[SHIFT-;]34[SPACEBAR][SHIFT-A][SHIFT-M][ENTER][CAPS LOCK]acme =   [1.4, 1.6]
[SPACEBAR]corporation[CAPS LOCK]

7. [F7]ny   [1.2]

SKILLS CHECK   2

1. [CAPS LOCK]a penny saved is a[CAPS LOCK]penny earned.[F7]n   [1.3, 1.6]
[ENTER]

2. [CAPS LOCK]to[SHIFT-;][SPACEBAR]j[CAPS LOCK]ohn[SPACEBAR][SHIFT-s]mith   [1.4, 1.6]
[ENTER][CAPS LOCK]from[SHIFT-;][SPACEBAR]m[CAPS LOCK]ary[SPACEBAR]
[SHIFT-b]rown[ENTER][CAPS LOCK]subject[SHIFT-;][SPACEBAR][CAPS LOCK]
1989[SPACEBAR][SHIFT-h]oliday[SPACEBAR][SHIFT-s]chedule

3. [ENTER][ESC]65-   [1.4]

[1.4]   **4.** [ENTER][ENTER][ENTER][ENTER][TAB]{Type the text as shown, using the SHIFT key and SPACEBAR where appropriate.}

[1.4, 1.6]   **5.** [CTRL-ENTER][SHIFT-j]anuary[SPACEBAR]1[TAB][TAB][SHIFT-n]ew[SPACEBAR][SHIFT-y]ear's[SPACEBAR][SHIFT-d]ay[ENTER][SHIFT-j]anuary[SPACEBAR]12[TAB]{Note that only one tab was required, since the cursor was already at the first tab stop.}[SHIFT-f]ounders'[SPACEBAR][SHIFT-d]ay[ENTER]{The remaining entries follow the same pattern. The lines for November 28 and December 25 will each require only one tab.}

[1.4]   **6.** [PGUP]

[1.4]   **7.** [HOME][HOME][DOWN ARROW]

[1.4]   **8.** [HOME][HOME][UP ARROW]

[1.3]   **9.** [F7]nn

[1.5]   **10.** [F3]e[ENTER]

[1.2]   **11.** [F7]ny

2.1   EXERCISES

1. {Type the lines as shown, pressing ENTER at the end of the first line and after each sentence.}

2. {Type the paragraph as shown, pressing ENTER only at the end of the paragraph.}

3. {Type the text as shown, pressing ENTER after the words "Descriptions," "light," "black," "translucent," and "diamond."}

4. [TAB]{Type the first paragraph as shown.}[ENTER][TAB]{Type the second paragraph as shown.}[ENTER]

EXERCISES   2.2

1. [SHIFT-a][SPACEBAR]stitch in time saves nine.[F10]stitch[ENTER]

2. [SHIFT-j]im[SPACEBAR][SHIFT-a]llen[ENTER]1123[SPACEBAR][SHIFT-f]ork
[SPACEBAR][SHIFT-r]d.[ENTER][SHIFT-b]altimore,[SPACEBAR][SHIFT-m]
aryland[SPACEBAR]21237[F10]name[ENTER][F7]yname2[ENTER][ENTER]

3. {Type the quote as shown.}[ENTER][ENTER][TAB][TAB][TAB][TAB]Sam
Levenson[F7][ENTER]kids[ENTER][ENTER]

4. {Type the quote as shown.}[ENTER][ENTER][TAB][TAB][TAB][TAB]
Theodore Roosevelt[F10]teddy[ENTER][F7][ENTER]school[ENTER]
[ENTER]

EXERCISES   2.3

1. [SHIFT-F10]stitch[ENTER]

2. [SHIFT-F10]name[ENTER][SHIFT-F10]stitch[ENTER]

3. [SHIFT-F10]teddy[ENTER][SHIFT-F10]teddy[ENTER][F7]n[ENTER]

4. Favorite Quotes[ENTER][SHIFT-F10]kids[ENTER][SHIFT-F10]teddy
[ENTER][F7]nn

EXERCISES   2.4

1. {Type the sentence as shown.}[HOME][HOME][LEFT ARROW]
[CAPS LOCK]abc[SPACEBAR][CAPS LOCK]

2. {Type the sentence as shown.}[CTRL-LEFT ARROW][LEFT ARROW]
,975

3. {Type the sentences as shown.}[CTRL-LEFT ARROW][CTRL-LEFT ARROW][CTRL-LEFT ARROW][CTRL-LEFT ARROW][CTRL-LEFT ARROW][CTRL-LEFT ARROW]{Type the new sentence.}[SPACEBAR][SPACEBAR]

4. She served cake for dessert.[CTRL-LEFT ARROW][CTRL-LEFT ARROW][CTRL-LEFT ARROW]rich, warm, chocolate[SPACEBAR][CTRL-RIGHT ARROW]and creamy, rich, vanilla ice cream[SPACEBAR]

5. {Type the quote as shown.}[ENTER][ENTER][TAB][TAB][TAB][TAB] Philip Guedalla{Move to the "a" in "and."}on the east by obituary,[SPACEBAR]

2.5   EXERCISES

1. {Type the sentences as shown; then use the arrow keys to move to the "C" in "Carol."}[INS][SHIFT-e]llen[INS]

2. {Type the sentence as shown.}[CTRL-LEFT ARROW][CTRL-LEFT ARROW][INS]4[CTRL-LEFT ARROW][CTRL-LEFT ARROW][CTRL-LEFT ARROW][CTRL-LEFT ARROW][CTRL-LEFT ARROW][CTRL-LEFT ARROW]answers the phone [DEL][INS]

3. {Type the sentences as shown; then move to the "c" in "company" in the first sentence.}[INS][CAPS LOCK]j. l. m[INS] [CAPS LOCK][INS]cGregor Corporation

4. The new prices for copies are[ENTER]1 to 100[TAB][TAB].08 each[ENTER]101 to 500[TAB].05 each[ENTER]501 + [TAB][TAB][TAB].02 each[INS]{Move to each price, typing the new figures over the old.}[INS]

5. Your current balance is $789.95.[CTRL-LEFT ARROW][RIGHT ARROW] [INS]3[INS]

EXERCISES

2.6

1. {Type the sentence as shown; then use the arrow keys to move to the "t" in "together"}[DEL][DEL][DEL][DEL][DEL][DEL] [DEL][DEL][DEL]{Move to the period at the end of the sentence.}[BACKSPACE][BACKSPACE][BACKSPACE][BACKSPACE][BACKSPACE] [BACKSPACE][BACKSPACE][BACKSPACE][BACKSPACE][BACKSPACE][BACKSPACE]

2. {Type the sentences as shown; then move to the word "name" in the first sentence.}[CTRL-BACKSPACE][CTRL-BACKSPACE] {Move to "purses."}[CTRL-BACKSPACE]

3. {Type the lines as shown; then move to the beginning of the second slogan.}[CTRL-END][DEL]

4. {Type the text as shown. Move to the beginning of the third line (before the tab).}[CTRL-END][DEL]

5. {Type the text as shown, using the TAB key to place data in columns. Move to the word "SALARY."}[CTRL-BACKSPACE] {Move to the first salary figure.}[CTRL-BACKSPACE]{Repeat this process for the remaining two salary entries.}

MASTERY SKILLS CHECK

1. {Type the paragraph as shown. Do not press ENTER until the end of the paragraph.}   [2.1]

2. {Move to the "X" in "XY."}June 17,[SPACEBAR]   [2.4]

3. {Move to the "I" in "Inc."}[DEL][DEL][DEL][DEL][DEL]   [2.6]

4. {Move to the "n" in "June."}[INS]ly[INS]   [2.5]

5. {Move to the "T" in "This."}[ENTER]   [2.4]

6. [F7][ENTER]seendraw[ENTER]n   [2.2]

[2.3]   **7.** [SHIFT-F10]seendraw[ENTER]

[2.6]   **8.** {Move to "both."}[CTRL-BACKSPACE]

[2.6]   **9.** {Move to the beginning of the second sentence.}[CTRL-END][DEL]

[2.2]   **10.** [F10]draw[ENTER]

INTEGRATED SKILLS CHECK

[1.6]   **1.** {Type the lines as shown, using CAPS LOCK for the first line.}

[1.5]   **2.** [F3]s

[2.2]   **3.** [F10]cookie[ENTER]

[1.3]   **4.** [F7]n[ENTER]

[1.4]   **5.** {Type the line as shown.}[ENTER][ESC]65-[ENTER]

[2.3]   **6.** [SHIFT-F10]cookie[ENTER]

[1.6, 2.4]   **7.** {Use the arrow keys to move to the "C" in "COOKIES."} [CAPS LOCK]and butterscotch chip [CAPS LOCK][SPACEBAR]

8. {Move to the beginning of the last line.}[CTRL-END][DEL]

[2.2]   **9.** [F10]list[ENTER]

[1.2]   **10.** [F7]ny

3   SKILLS CHECK

[1.4, 1.6, 2.1]   **1.** Fourscore and seven years ago our fathers brought forth on this continent, a new nation, conceived in liberty, and dedicated to the propsition that all men are created equal.[ENTER][ENTER][TAB][TAB][TAB][TAB]Gettysburg Address[ENTER]

2. {Move to "Fourscore."[CTRL-BACKSPACE][CTRL-BACKSPACE]   [2.4, 2.6]
[CTRL-BACKSPACE]87[SPACEBAR]

3. [HOME][LEFT ARROW][F1]r[CTRL-BACKSPACE]   [1.4, 1.5]

4. {Move to the "s" in "propsition."}o   [1.4, 2.4]

5. {Move to the "G" in "Gettysburg."}[INS]Abraham   [2.5]
[SPACEBAR]Lincoln[DEL][DEL][DEL][INS]

6. [F10]lincoln[ENTER]   [2.2]

7. [F7]ny   [1.2]

8. {for a hard disk system}cd\wp50[ENTER]wp[ENTER][SHIFT-F10]   [1.1, 2.3]
lincoln[ENTER]{for a floppy disk system: Place the Word-
Perfect 1 disk in drive A and a disk for documents in
drive B.}b:[ENTER]a:wp[ENTER]{When prompted to do so, replace the WordPerfect 1 disk with the WordPerfect 2
disk, and press any key.}[SHIFT-F10]lincoln[ENTER]

9. [F7]nn   [1.3]

EXERCISES ——————————————— 3.1

1. [SHIFT-F10]lincoln[ENTER][SHIFT-F7]f

2. [TAB][TAB][TAB][TAB]12345 Commerce Parkway[ENTER][TAB][TAB]
[TAB][TAB]Beachwood, OH 44123[ENTER][TAB][TAB][TAB][TAB]
December 1, 1988[ENTER][ENTER][ENTER]Samantha Koln[ENTER]
Small Business Administration of Cleveland[ENTER]1235
Public Square[ENTER]Cleveland, OH 44115[ENTER][ENTER]Dear
Ms. Koln,[ENTER][TAB]I am starting a business to manufac-
ture mechanical pencils. Can you provide information on
the services that your organization provides to new com-
panies?[ENTER][ENTER][TAB][TAB][TAB][TAB]Sincerely, [ENTER]
[ENTER][ENTER][ENTER][TAB][TAB][TAB][TAB]Tom Lu[ENTER][TAB][TAB]

[TAB][TAB]President, Various Sundries, Inc.[ENTER][SHIFT-F7]f
[F10]sba[ENTER]

3. {Type the quote as shown.}[ENTER][ENTER][TAB][TAB][TAB][TAB]John
   Ruskin[SHIFT-F7]f

4. [ENTER][ENTER]{Type the quote.}[ENTER][ENTER][TAB][TAB][TAB][TAB]
   Herbert Hoover[SHIFT-F7]f

3.2   EXERCISES

1. [SHIFT-F10]sba[ENTER][SHIFT-F7]f {Move to the end of the paragraph.}[ENTER][TAB]I have enclosed a notice of our upcoming open house for your monthly newsletter.[HOME][HOME]
   [DOWN ARROW][CTRL-ENTER]Attend the Open House Celebration
   at Various Sundries, Inc., on May 15 from 7:30 to 9:30
   P.M.[SHIFT-F7]p

2. Significant Accomplishments 1989 - John Smith[ENTER][CTRL-
   ENTER]Significant Accomplishments 1989 - Mary Brown
   [ENTER][CTRL-ENTER]Significant Accomplishments 1989 - Nancy
   Caster[ENTER][SHIFT-F7]p

3. [PGUP][SHIFT-F7]p[PGUP][SHIFT-F7]p

4. {Type the quotation.}[ENTER][ENTER][TAB][TAB][TAB][TAB]John
   Heywood[ENTER][CTRL-ENTER]{Type the second quotation.}
   [ENTER][ENTER][TAB][TAB][TAB][TAB]Robert Burns[ENTER][PGUP][SHIFT-F7]p

3.3   EXERCISES

1. [SHIFT-F10]lincoln[ENTER][SHIFT-F7]v12

2. To: Sarah Graham, Chief Financial Officer[ENTER]From: Bob
   Kelly, Chief Accounting Officer[ENTER]Re: Financial Statements[ENTER][ESC]65 = [ENTER]Sarah,[ENTER][ENTER][TAB]Enclosed
   are the preliminary financial statements. The attached

text includes all of the footnotes. If you find any corrections or additions, please contact me immediately. [ENTER]
[SHIFT-F7]v312

3. {Type the data as shown.}[SHIFT-F7]v[F7]{Position the cursor after the period at the end of the first sentence.}[CTRL-ENTER]{Position the cursor after the period at the end of the second sentence.}[CTRL-ENTER]{Position the cursor after the period in the third sentence.}[CTRL-ENTER][SHIFT-F7]v{Use PGUP and PGDN to view the document.}

4. {Type the quotes, ending each entry with CTRL-ENTER to start a new page.}[SHIFT-F7]v4{use PGUP and PGDN to move within the document.}[F7][F10]quotes[ENTER]

EXERCISES 3.4

1. [SHIFT-F7]dsba[ENTER][ENTER][F7]

2. [CAPS LOCK]residents opposed to road paving[ENTER]b[CAPS LOCK]lack[ENTER][SHIFT-s]mith[ENTER][SHIFT-c]ampbell[ENTER][SHIFT-g]ilbert[ENTER][SHIFT-l]ong[ENTER][SHIFT-j]ackson[CTRL-ENTER][CAPS LOCK]residents supporting road paving[ENTER]w[CAPS LOCK]ilson[ENTER][SHIFT-b]oswell[ENTER][SHIFT-d]ike[ENTER][F7][ENTER]road[ENTER]n[SHIFT-F7]droad[ENTER][ENTER]droad[ENTER]2 [ENTER][F7]

3. [SHIFT-F7]dquotes[ENTER]2[ENTER][F7]

4. [SHIFT-F7]dquotes[ENTER]2-4[ENTER][F7]

5. [SHIFT-F7]dquotes[ENTER]1,4[ENTER][F7]

MASTERY SKILLS CHECK

1. To: All Managers[ENTER]From: Fred Jones, Director of Human Services[ENTER]Subject: Meetings on the New   [3.3]

Benefit Package[ENTER][ENTER][TAB]The Human Services Department will be conducting a one-hour information meeting on the new benefit package. We have attempted to schedule these meetings at convenient times. Please route the sign-up sheets to your employees and encourage everyone to attend one of these sessions.[ENTER][CTRL-ENTER]Benefit Package meeting - April 5 9:30 A.M.[CTRL-ENTER]Benefit Package meeting - April 5 2:30 P.M.[CTRL-ENTER]Benefit Package meeting - April 6 8:30 A.M.[CTRL-ENTER]Benefit Package meeting - April 6 4:00 P.M.[ENTER] [SHIFT-F7]

[3.1]   **2.** [SHIFT-F7]f

[3.2]   **3.** [HOME][HOME][UP ARROW][SHIFT-F7]p

[3.4]   **4.** [F7][ENTER]benefits[ENTER][ENTER][SHIFT-F7]dbenefits[ENTER]2-5[ENTER] [F7]

INTEGRATED SKILLS CHECK

[1.4, 1.6]   **1.** [TAB]A meeting is scheduled at 5 PM on January 20 to discuss the company's participation in the[CAPS LOCK]cleveland corporate olympics.[CAPS LOCK]The meeting will be held in the fourth-floor conference room.[ENTER][ENTER][TAB]This year, we need a slogan for the banner and a T-shirt design. We also need a list of the employees participating in each activity. Please encourage your staff members to participate.[ENTER][ENTER][TAB]Interested individuals unable to attend the scheduled meeting should contact Steve Spear. His extension is 3963.[ENTER]

[2.6]   **2.** {Move to the "H" in "His".}[CTRL-END]

[1.4, 2.5]   **3.** {Move to the 0 in 20.}[INS]5[INS]

[3.1]   **4.** [SHIFT-F7]f

5. [HOME][HOME][DOWN ARROW]   [1.4]

6. [CTRL-ENTER]   [1.4]

7. Name[TAB][TAB][TAB][TAB][TAB]Activity[ENTER][ESC]8-[TAB][TAB][ESC]10-   [1.4]
[ENTER]Sue Marianetti[TAB][TAB][TAB]Bike Race[ENTER]Sharon
Campbell[TAB][TAB]Tug-of-War[ENTER]John Peterson[TAB][TAB]
[TAB]Tug-of-War[ENTER]Tim Smith[TAB][TAB][TAB][TAB]5K Race
[ENTER]Ted McGregor[TAB][TAB][TAB]Tug-of-War[ENTER]Brandon
Leidy[TAB][TAB][TAB]Swimming[ENTER]Marge Thomas[TAB][TAB]
[TAB]5K Race[ENTER]Anne Kettlewood[TAB][TAB]Bike Race
[ENTER]

8. [SHIFT-F7]v3{Use the PGUP and PGDN keys to view both   [3.3]
pages.}

9. {Position the cursor on page 2.}[SHIFT-F7]p[ENTER]   [3.2]

10. [F7][ENTER]olympics[ENTER][ENTER]   [2.2]

11. [CAPS LOCK]corporate slogan suggestions[ENTER]o[CAPS LOCK]ur   [1.4, 3.4]
Team's the Best[ENTER][SHIFT-F7]dolympics[ENTER]1[ENTER][F7]The
Best at All We Do[ENTER]Scientific Services Employees
Have Brains and Brawn[ENTER]Sticks and Stones Won't
Break Our Bones[ENTER]

SKILLS CHECK   4

1. The next meting of the WordPerfect User's Group will be   [1.4, 1.6]
January 5. Each attendeee will receive a free on the use
of the new graphics features.

2. {Move to the "e" in "meting."}e{Move to the last "e" in   [1.4, 2.4]
"attendeee."}[DEL]{Move to the "o" in "on."}handout
[SPACEBAR]

3. [F3][F3][ENTER]   [1.5]

4. [F10]meeting[ENTER]   [2.2]

[1.3]   **5.** [F7]n[ENTER]

[3.4]   **6.** [SHIFT-F7]dmeeting[ENTER][ENTER][F7]

4.1   EXERCISES

1. Acerson, Karen L.,[F8]WordPerfect: The Complete Reference, Series 5 Edition[F8], Osborne/McGraw-Hill, 1988. [ENTER]Alderman, Eric, and Lawrence J. Magid,[F8]Advanced WordPerfect, Series 5 Edition[F8], Osborne/McGraw-Hill, 1988.[ENTER]Mincberg, Mella,[F8]WordPerfect Made Easy, Series 5 Edition[F8]. Osborne/McGraw-Hill, 1988.

2. We will honor employees with more than[F8]twenty-five years[F8]of service at the annual appreciation dinner. The following employees are honorees at this year's dinner: [ENTER][ENTER][F8][CAPS LOCK]employee[F8][TAB][TAB][F8]years of service[F8][CAPS LOCK][ENTER]J. Smith[TAB][TAB]25[ENTER]R. Taylor [TAB][TAB]35[ENTER]P. Volker[TAB][TAB]31

3. Cost per square foot[SPACEBAR]=[SPACEBAR][F8]Total cost[F8] [ENTER][TAB][TAB][TAB][TAB][SPACEBAR][SPACEBAR][SPACEBAR]Square feet

4. [TAB]{Type the first paragraph as shown.}[ENTER][TAB][F8] Aconteus[F8]looked at[F8]Medusa's[F8]head and turned into stone.[F8]Medusa[F8]was a monster whose hair was made of serpents.[F8]Perseus[F8], the son of[F8]Danae[F8]and[F8] Jupiter[F8], killed[F8]Medusa[F8]. To make himself invisible to[F8]Medusa[F8], he wore[F8]Pluto's[F8]helmet and a pair of winged shoes.

4.2   EXERCISES

1. [CAPS LOCK]account[TAB]balance[CAPS LOCK][ENTER]Rent[TAB][TAB] $5,125[ENTER]Utilities[TAB][F6](1,250)[F6][ENTER]Phone[TAB][F6] ([SPACEBAR][SPACEBAR]950)[F6]

2. Your account balance is[F6]more than 90 days past due[F6].
   Unless you contact us[F6]immediately[F6], we will begin
   legal action to collect the balance of your account.

3. [F6][F8][CAPS LOCK]dept[TAB][TAB]head count[F6][F8][ENTER]acct[TAB]
   [TAB]14[ENTER]fin[TAB][TAB]10[ENTER]mfg[TAB][TAB]84[CAPSLOCK]

4. Foreign words can add variety to your writing. When
   you select foreign phrases, you will want to be certain
   that both you and your readers understand their meaning.[F6]Deo gratias[F6]means thanks to God.[F6]Dei gratia[F6]
   means by the grace of God.[F6]Deo volente[F6]means by
   God's will.[F6]Dieu vous garde[F6]means God protect you.

5. Noble by birth, yet nobler by great deeds.[ENTER][TAB][TAB][F6]
   Henry Wadsworth Longfellow,[F8]Tales of a Wayside Inn
   [F6][F8][ENTER]Who fears t'offend takes the first step to
   please.[ENTER][TAB][TAB][F6]Colley Cibber,[F8]Love in a Riddle
   [F6][F8][ENTER]The art of praising is the beginning of the art
   of pleasing.[ENTER][TAB][TAB][F6]Voltaire,[F8]La Pucelle[F6][F8]

EXERCISES
4.3

1. {Substitute your own name and address for the ones in
   this answer.}[SHIFT-F6]John Smith[ENTER][SHIFT-F6]111 North
   Ave.[ENTER][SHIFT-F6]Cleveland, OH 44040[ENTER]

2. [SHIFT-F6][F6]Tinsel Company[F6][ENTER]

3. [SHIFT-F6]This text is too long for one line. WordPerfect cannot fit the entire entry on one line. When you print the
   text, you will notice that WordPerfect centers only the
   text in the first line.[ENTER]

4. [CAPS LOCK][SHIFT-F6]abc company[ENTER][SHIFT-F6]performance
   report[ENTER][SHIFT-F6]for the quarter ending june 30, 1989
   [ENTER][CAPS LOCK]

4.4 EXERCISES

1. [SHIFT-F6][CAPS LOCK]abc company[ENTER][SHIFT-F6]budget report [ENTER][SHIFT-F6]fiscal 1990[ENTER][CAPS LOCK][ALT-F3]{Look at the codes that cause WordPerfect to center the text.}[ALT-F3]

2. New Sunday store hours are[F6]Noon to 5 P.M.[F6]

3. [ALT-F3][F6][F8]Overdue Accounts[F6][F8]

4. [SHIFT-F6]I think, therefore I am.[ENTER][SHIFT-F6]Rene Descartes[ENTER][ALT-F3][F10]THINK[ENTER]

4.5 EXERCISES

1. [F6]Quality Corporation[F6]is pleased to announce the following Christmas bonus structures:[ENTER][SHIFT-F6]Less than 2 years of service - 2% bonus[ENTER][SHIFT-F6]2 years or more of service - 5% bonus[ENTER]Checks will be available for distribution on[F8]December 23[F8].[ALT-F3]{Use the arrow keys to move around and view the codes. Position the cursor on one of the first pair of Center codes, and press DEL. Repeat for the second centered line.}

2. [ALT-F3][HOME][HOME][HOME][UP ARROW][F2][F6][F2][F7]nn

3. [SHIFT-F10]THINK[ENTER][ALT-F3]{Move to either code for Center ([CNTR]or[C/A/FLRT]) on the first line, and press the DEL key. Repeat for the second line.}

4.6 EXERCISES

1. {Type the text as shown. Move to the "I" in "In."}[ALT-F4].

2. An excuse uncalled for becomes an obvious accusation. [ENTER][TAB][TAB][TAB][TAB]Law Maxim[ENTER]{Move to the first "e" in "excuse."}[ALT-F4][CTRL-RIGHT ARROW][F1][F10]EXCUSE[ENTER]

3. You must submit expense reports by the 15th of the month following travel.{Move to the "1" in "15th."}[ALT-F4] [RIGHT ARROW][RIGHT ARROW][RIGHT ARROW][RIGHT ARROW][F1]

4. {Move to the "m" in "month."}previous[SPACEBAR][ALT-F4] [CTRL-LEFT ARROW][DEL]y

5. [SHIFT-F10]THINK[ENTER][DOWN ARROW][ALT-F4][END][DEL]y

EXERCISES

4.7

1. {Type the text as shown. Move to the "W" in "Word-Perfect" in the first sentence.}[ALT-F4]y[F8]

2. {Move to the "W" in "WordPerfect" in the second sentence.}[ALT-F4]tt[F6]

3. [CAPS LOCK]accounts receivable aging[CAPS LOCK][ALT-F4][CTRL-LEFT ARROW][CTRL-LEFT ARROW][CTRL-LEFT ARROW][F8][ALT-F4][CTRL-RIGHT ARROW] [CTRL-RIGHT ARROW][CTRL-RIGHT ARROW][SHIFT-F6]y

4. [SHIFT-F10]EXCUSE[ENTER][HOME][HOME][DOWN ARROW][ENTER]A bad excuse is better, they say, than none at all.[ENTER][TAB][TAB] [TAB][TAB]Stephen Gosson{Move to the first "e" in the word "excuse" in the first quotation}[ALT-F4][CTRL-RIGHT ARROW][F6] {Move to the first "e" in "excuse" in the second quotation.}[ALT-F4][CTRL-RIGHT ARROW][F6]

5. {Type the quotation as shown.}{Move to the "w" in either occurrence of "wheels."}[ALT-F4]s[F6][ALT-F4][CTRL-LEFT ARROW][F8]{Repeat the process for the other occurrence of "wheels."}

MASTERY SKILLS CHECK

1. [F8]Bylaws of the WordPerfect Users Group[F8][F7]nn   [4.1]

2. [F6]ABC Company[F6]will hold its annual picnic at the[F6]   [4.2] Loch Raven Pavilion[F6]on[F6]July 17th[F6].

[4.4, 4.5]   **3.** [ALT-F3]{Move to the "L" in "Loch."}[BACKSPACE]

[4.1, 4.3]   **4.** [HOME][HOME][HOME][UP ARROW][SHIFT-F6][F8][CAPS LOCK]company picnic announcement[F8][CAPS LOCK]

[4.4, 4.5]   **5.** [ENTER][ENTER][ENTER][ALT-F3][HOME][HOME][HOME][UP ARROW][F2][F8][F2] [SHIFT-F7]f[F7]nn

[4.2, 4.4, 4.5]   **6.** [SHIFT-F6][F6][CAPS LOCK]abc company[ENTER][SHIFT-F6]internal memorandum[ENTER][ENTER]to[SHIFT-;][F6][SPACEBAR]a[CAPS LOCK]ll staff[ENTER][F6][CAPS LOCK]from[SHIFT-;][F6][SPACEBAR]j[CAPS LOCK]ohn [SPACEBAR][SHIFT-s]mith[ENTER][F6][CAPS LOCK]subject[SHIFT-;][F6] [SPACEBAR]c[CAPS LOCK]ompletion of parking lot resurfacing [ENTER][F6][CAPS LOCK]date[SHIFT-;][F6][SPACEBAR]f[CAPS LOCK]ebruary 15, 1989[ENTER][ENTER]The resurfacing of parking lots A and B is complete. Resurfacing of parking lot C is scheduled to begin Monday, February 20. Your[ENTER]continued cooperation is appreciated.[ALT-F3]{Move to the "c" in "continued."}[BACKSPACE][SPACEBAR][F10]PARKING[ENTER]

[4.6, 4.7]   **7.** {Move to the "c" in "complete."}[ALT-F4]ee[F6]{Move to the beginning of the second sentence.}[ALT-F4].[DEL]y[F7]nn

[4.6, 4.7]   **8.** [CAPS LOCK]acct no[TAB]balance[CAPS LOCK][ENTER]1204[TAB][TAB] [SHIFT-4]12,350[ENTER]1567[TAB][TAB][SHIFT-4]17,865[ENTER]2569 [TAB][TAB][SHIFT-4]23,789[ENTER]{Move to the "A" in "ACCT."}[ALT-F4][END][F6][ALT-F4][CTRL-HOME][CTRL-HOME][F8]

INTEGRATED SKILLS CHECK

[1.4, 4.3]   **1.** [SHIFT-F6][CAPS LOCK]abc books[CAPS LOCK][ENTER][SHIFT-F6]1115 Warren Avenue[ENTER][SHIFT-F6]Cleveland, OH 44017[ENTER] [ENTER]{Type the remainder of the text as shown.}

[1.3, 2.2, 3.4]   **2.** [F7][ENTER]myers[ENTER][ENTER][SHIFT-F7]dmyers[ENTER][ENTER][F7]

3. [SHIFT-F10]myers[ENTER]{Move to the "N" in "North."}[INS]   [2.5, 4.6, 4.7]
Sou[INS]{Move to the "S" in "Successful."}[ALT-F4]t[F8]{Move
to the "O" in "October."}[ALT-F4]2[F6]

4. [END][ALT-F4][UP ARROW][HOME][LEFT ARROW][F1]   [4.6, 1.5]

5. [F10][ENTER]y[SHIFT-F7]v[ENTER]f   [2.2, 3.1, 3.3]

SKILLS CHECK _____ 5

1. [SHIFT-F6]Bibliography[ENTER][ENTER]Mincberg, Mella,[F8]   [4.1, 4.3]
WordPerfect 5 Made Easy[F8], Osborne/McGraw-Hill, 492
pages.[ENTER]Campbell, Mary,[F8]1-2-3 Made Easy[F8],
Osborne/McGraw-Hill, 400 pages.[ENTER]

2. {Move to the 4 in 492.}1988[SPACEBAR]{Move to the 4 in   [1.4, 2.4]
400.}1986,[SPACEBAR]

3. [F10]biblio[ENTER]   [2.2]

4. [HOME][HOME][HOME][UP ARROW][F2][F8][F2][BACKSPACE]y[F2][F2][BACKSPACE]y   [4.5]

5. [F7]nn   [1.3]

6. [SHIFT-F7]dbiblio[ENTER][ENTER][F7]   [3.4]

EXERCISES _____ 5.1

1. Some are born great, some achieve greatness, others
have greatness thrust upon 'em.[ENTER][TAB][TAB][TAB][TAB]
William Shakespeare[ENTER][HOME][HOME][UP ARROW][SHIFT-F8]
lm2[ENTER]1.5[ENTER][F7]

2. What makes us discontented with our condition is the absurdly exaggerated idea we have of the happiness of others.[ENTER][TAB][TAB][TAB][TAB]Proverb[ENTER][HOME][HOME][UP ARROW][SHIFT-F8]lm2[ENTER]2[ENTER][F7][ALT-F3]{The code for the margin change is[L/R Mar:2″,2″].}[ALT-F3][SHIFT-F8]lm1.5 [ENTER]1.5[ENTER][F7]{Press the DOWN ARROW key to make Word-Perfect reformat the paragraph with the new margins.}

3. The plural of most compound nouns is formed by add-ing "s" or "es" to the main word in the grouping. For example:[ENTER][TAB]mothers-in-law[ENTER][TAB]runners-up [ENTER][TAB]daughters-in-law[ENTER][HOME][HOME][UP ARROW][SHIFT-F8]lm2.5[ENTER]1.5[ENTER][F7]{Press the DOWN ARROW key to make WordPerfect reformat the paragraph with the new margins.}

4. [CAPS LOCK]abc company - memo[ENTER]d[CAPS LOCK]ate: Friday, Sept 10, 1989[ENTER][ESC]65-[ENTER]When using the copier by the coffee machine, use only the paper stacked next to the machine. Since the machine is old, if you use dif-ferent paper (envelopes, letterheads, etc.), the machine jams.[HOME][HOME][UP ARROW][SHIFT-F8]lm3[ENTER]3[ENTER][F7][SHIFT-F7]v[F7][HOME][HOME][HOME][UP ARROW][DEL]

5.2   EXERCISES

1. [SHIFT-F4][SHIFT-F4][SHIFT-F4][SHIFT-F4]{Type the paragraph as shown.}[ENTER]

2. [F4]{Retype the paragraph from exercise 1.}[ENTER]The meet-ing is scheduled for 9:00 a.m. in the board room.[ENTER]

3. [ALT-F3][HOME][HOME][HOME][UP ARROW][DEL][ALT-F3]

4. [SHIFT-F4]You can use the two indentation keys in the middle of[F4]typing a paragraph. When you press the Indent or the[SHIFT-F4]Indent Left and Right key, WordPerfect indents all new lines that appear until you press ENTER. [ENTER]

EXERCISES _____ 5.3

1. [SHIFT-TAB][SHIFT-TAB]You can use the Margin Release feature to make an indented paragraph begin at the left margin. You can also use it to fit additional characters on a line.

2. Name:[ENTER][SHIFT-TAB][SPACEBAR][SPACEBAR]Address:[ENTER][SHIFT-TAB][SHIFT-TAB][SPACEBAR][SPACEBAR]Phone Number:[ENTER][SHIFT-TAB][SHIFT-TAB][SPACEBAR]Social Sec. #:

EXERCISES _____ 5.4

1. [SHIFT-F8]lt3.3[ENTER][F7][F7]

2. [SHIFT-F8]lt6[ENTER][CTRL-END][F7][F7]

3. [SHIFT-F8]lt4[ENTER]r[F7][F7]

4. [SHIFT-F8]lt2.5[ENTER]d[F7][F7]

5. [SHIFT-F8]lt[HOME][HOME][LEFT ARROW][CTRL-END]2[ENTER]4.5[ENTER][F7][F7][TAB]Jones[TAB]17,850[ENTER][TAB]Culver[TAB]23,489[ENTER][TAB]Walker[TAB]32,500[ENTER][F7]nn

6. [SHIFT-F8]lt[HOME][HOME][LEFT ARROW][CTRL-END]2,.75[ENTER][F7][F7]

7. [SHIFT-F8]lt[HOME][HOME][LEFT ARROW][CTRL-END]0,.5[ENTER][F7][F7]

5.5 EXERCISES

1. [ALT-F6][SHIFT-F5]t[ENTER]

2. [ALT-F6]ABC COMPANY[ENTER]

3. MEMO[ENTER]To: All Employees[ALT-F6]Date:[SHIFT-F5]t
[ENTER]From: Arnold Smith[ALT-F6]Re: Cleaning Computer
Screens[ENTER][ESC]65-[ENTER]Do not use alcohol-based window cleaners to clean your computer screen. Use the
special cleaner that is stored with the blank disks.[ENTER]

5.6 EXERCISES

1. A sense of humor sharp enough to show a man his own
absurdities will keep him from the commission of all sins,
or nearly all, except those that are worth committing.
[ENTER](Samuel Butler from Life and Habit)[ENTER][HOME]
[HOME][UP ARROW][SHIFT-F8]ls2[ENTER][F7][SHIFT-F8]ls3[ENTER][F7][SHIFT-F8]
ls1[ENTER][F7]

2. [TAB]The new Widget maker will expand our current capacity to meet expected demand levels for the next five
to ten years. It has a present net value of $25,687.[ENTER]
[SHIFT-F8]ls2[ENTER][F7][TAB]The manufacturer gives a 10% trade-
in value on its old Widget maker. This is a slightly lower
price than expected in the open market. The capital bud-
geting plan contains the lower trade-in value, but the
company will probably sell the used machine in the
second-hand market.[ENTER][SHIFT-F8]ls3[ENTER][F7][TAB]The new
Widget maker has many new features. One of these, a
free one-year service contract, will save the company
$50,000 in the first year.[ENTER]{Reveal the codes, and de-
lete the line-spacing codes at the beginning of paragraphs 2 and 3. There is no code for paragraph 1, since
the defaults are being used.}[HOME][HOME][HOME][UP ARROW]
[SHIFT-F8]ls2[ENTER][F7]{Move to the beginning of the second
paragraph.}[SHIFT-F8]ls3[ENTER][F7]{Move to the beginning of
the third paragraph.}[SHIFT-F8]ls2[ENTER][F7]

3. When you set the line spacing, WordPerfect uses it for all lines after the code in the document.[SHIFT-F8]ls2[ENTER][F7] If you change the spacing to double spacing in the middle of a paragraph, the lines above the change are single spaced, and the lines after the change are double spaced. [ENTER]

EXERCISES

5.7

1. The Accounts Receivable computer system was installed last January. Due to this new system, the average daily accounts receivable amount dropped by $50. Also, the percentage of bad accounts has dropped from 4% to 2%, mostly due to quicker action on overdue accounts.[ENTER] [SHIFT-F7]v[F7][HOME][HOME][UP ARROW][SHIFT-F8]ljn[F7][SHIFT-F7][F7][SHIFT-F8]ljy[F7]

2. [TAB]When a paragraph is right justified, WordPerfect inserts additional space in lines of the printed copy of the document. This creates even left and right margins. The extra spaces appear only in the printed copy and do not appear on the screen.[ENTER][SHIFT-F8]ljn[F7][TAB]When a paragraph is not right justified, WordPerfect does not insert additional space. The right margin has a jagged appearance.[ENTER][SHIFT-F7]v[F7]

MASTERY SKILLS CHECK

[5.1]

1. {assumes left and right margins are currently 1"}[SHIFT-F8] lm2[ENTER]2[ENTER][F7]Disks store information using magnetized material to hold information. The basic unit of storage is a byte. A byte stores one character of information. [ENTER][F7]ydisk[ENTER]n

[5.2]   **2.** [F4][F4]Disk drives read information from a disk. The disk
               drive spins the disk quickly. A read/write head above the
               disk reads the information as it spins past the head.[ENTER]
               [F7]ydiskread[ENTER]n

[5.4]   **3.** [SHIFT-F8]lt[HOME][HOME][LEFT ARROW][CTRL-END]4[ENTER][F7][F7][TAB]Acme
               Corporation[ENTER][TAB]496 Prospect Road[ENTER][TAB]Cleve-
               land, Ohio 44115[ENTER][TAB]January 3, 1989[ENTER]

[5.6]   **4.** [SHIFT-F10]disk[ENTER][SHIFT-F8]ls2[ENTER][F7][F10][ENTER]y

[5.7]   **5.** [SHIFT-F10]diskread[ENTER][SHIFT-F8]ljn[F7][F10][ENTER]y

[5.5]   **6.** [ALT-F6]ACC-9876[ENTER][ALT-F6]HDG-3218[ENTER][ALT-F6]CRC-
               9873[ENTER]

[5.2, 5.3]   **7.** [F4][SHIFT-TAB]Campbell, Mary,[F8]Teach Yourself Word-
               Perfect[F8], Osborne/McGraw-Hill, 1989.[ENTER]

INTEGRATED SKILLS CHECK

[4.1, 5.1, 5.3]   **1.** [SHIFT-F8]lm1.5[ENTER][ENTER][F7][SHIFT-TAB]Crosby, Samuel,
               "Mergers and Acquisitions,"[F8]Business Yearly[F8], (OMB
               Publishing, 1983), June, p. 46-49.[ENTER][ENTER][SHIFT-TAB]Lee,
               Jane, and Lifeson, Tom, "Effectively Combining Com-
               panies,"[F8]Journal of Business Results[F8], (AMBA, 1987),
               vol 36, Fall, p. 101-9.[ENTER]

[4.3, 4.7, 5.3]   **2.** [SHIFT-TAB][SHIFT-TAB]Acme Corporation[SHIFT-F6]1560 Main
               Street[ALT-F6]Cleveland, Ohio 44103[ENTER][ALT-F4][HOME]
               [HOME][HOME][LEFT ARROW][F8]

[3.1, 4.7, 5.7]   **3.** Joan Smith[ENTER]President, Widgets Inc.[ENTER]7946 Mad-
               ison Avenue[ENTER]New York, New York 10061[ENTER]
               [ENTER]Dear Ms. Smith:[ENTER][ENTER]Enclosed is the pamphlet

you requested, Wrapping Consumer Goods. Our products can shrink-wrap any product. If you send the dimensions of the products that you want to shrink-wrap, one of our representatives will prepare a list of the materials and equipment you will need.[ENTER][ENTER][TAB][TAB][TAB][TAB]Sincerely,[ENTER][ENTER][ENTER][ENTER][TAB][TAB][TAB][TAB]Larry Kennedy[ENTER][TAB][TAB][TAB][TAB]Plastic Covering Co.[ENTER][HOME][HOME][UP ARROW][SHIFT-F8]ljn[F7]{Move to the "W" in "Wrapping."}[ALT-F4][CTRL-RIGHT ARROW][CTRL-RIGHT ARROW][CTRL-RIGHT ARROW][LEFT ARROW][LEFT ARROW][LEFT ARROW][F8][ALT-F3][BACKSPACE][ALT-F3][SHIFT-F7]f

4.

1. j	8. a	[1.4, 2.1, 4.1, 4.2, 4.3, 4.4, 4.7, 5.1, 5.2, 5.3, 5.4, 5.5, 5.6, 5.7]
2. e	9. d	
3. g	10. k	
4. b	11. m	
5. c	12. h	
6. i	13. f	
7. l		

5. [ALT-F6][SHIFT-F5]t[HOME][HOME][HOME][UP ARROW][F2][ALT-F6][F2][BACKSPACE]y   [4.5, 5.5]

SKILLS CHECK   6

1. John Doe[ENTER]23405 Lander Road[ENTER]Cleveland, Ohio 44130[ENTER](216)229-8976[ENTER][ENTER][F6]Education:[F6][SPACEBAR]Cleveland State University, Cleveland, Ohio [ENTER]Business Administration, August 1983[ENTER]Dean's List 7 Quarters, GPA 3.75[ENTER]   [1.4, 4.2]

2. [HOME][UP ARROW][ALT-F4][DOWN ARROW][DOWN ARROW][DOWN ARROW][DOWN ARROW][SHIFT-F6]y   [4.6, 4.7]

[4.6, 4.7]   **3.** [HOME][UP ARROW][ALT-F4][END][F6]

[4.6, 4.7]   **4.** [DOWN ARROW][DOWN ARROW][DOWN ARROW][DOWN ARROW][DOWN ARROW]
[HOME][LEFT ARROW][ALT-F4][CTRL-RIGHT ARROW][LEFT ARROW][LEFT ARROW]
[LEFT ARROW][F8]

[5.4]   **5.** [HOME][HOME][UP ARROW][SHIFT-F8]lt1.5[ENTER][DEL]2[ENTER][DEL]2.2
[ENTER][F7][F7]

[5.2]   **6.** [DOWN ARROW][DOWN ARROW][DOWN ARROW][DOWN ARROW][DOWN ARROW]
[F4][DOWN ARROW][HOME][LEFT ARROW][F4][DOWN ARROW][HOME]
[LEFT ARROW][F4]

[5.3]   **7.** [UP ARROW][UP ARROW][SHIFT-TAB]

[3.1]   **8.** [SHIFT-F7]f

6.1

EXERCISES

1. [SHIFT-F8]pc[F7][SHIFT-F6]Investigation into the Physical Properties of Rust[ENTER][SHIFT-F6]Dissertation[ENTER][SHIFT-F6]Angus
McPhearson[ENTER]

{To view the centered text, press SHIFT-F7 and type a **v**.}

2. {The letter body may be different, and the name at the
bottom should be your own.}[SHIFT-F8]pc[F7]Jules McBride
[ENTER]234 Main Street[ENTER]Lawrence, PA 28634[ENTER]
[ENTER]Dear Jules,[ENTER][ENTER]Thank you for promptly sending the information I requested.[ENTER][ENTER]Sincerely,[ENTER]
[ENTER][ENTER][ENTER]John Doe[ENTER]{To view the centered
text, press SHIFT-F7 and type a **v**.}

3. [SHIFT-F8]pc[F7][SHIFT-F6]1989 Financial Statements[ENTER]
[SHIFT-F6]Acme Corporation[ENTER][SHIFT-F7]v[F7]

4. [SHIFT-F8]pc[F7]MEMO:[ENTER]To: All Employees[ENTER]Re: Paychecks[ENTER][ENTER][TAB]To receive a paycheck September 10th, submit your time card to payroll by September 3rd.[ENTER][SHIFT-F7]v[F7]

EXERCISES   6.2

1. [SHIFT-F8]pm3[ENTER]3[ENTER][F7]{You can press ENTER approximately 29 times before WordPerfect inserts a page break. The exact number depends upon your printer.}

2. [SHIFT-F8]pm0[ENTER]0[ENTER][F7]{You can press ENTER approximately 65 times before WordPerfect inserts a page break. The exact number depends upon your printer.}

3. [SHIFT-F8]pm9.5[ENTER][ENTER][F7]{Type the paragraphs as shown. WordPerfect inserts page breaks.}[SHIFT-F7]v{Press PGUP and PGDN to switch among the pages.}[F7]

EXERCISES   6.3

1. [SHIFT-F8]pp6[F7]Travel Expenses[CTRL-ENTER]Benefits[CTRL-ENTER] Salary Expense[ENTER][SHIFT-F7]v{Press PGUP and PGDN to switch among the three pages.}[F7]

2. [SHIFT-F8]pp6[F7]1[CTRL-ENTER]2[CTRL-ENTER]3[CTRL-ENTER]4[CTRL-ENTER] 5[SHIFT-F7]v{Press PGUP and PGDN to switch among the pages.}[F7]{Press PGDN until the **Pg** indicator displays 5.} [SHIFT-F8]pn1[ENTER][F7][PGUP][SHIFT-F8]pn2[ENTER][F7][PGUP][SHIFT-F8] pn3[ENTER][F7][PGUP][SHIFT-F8]pn4[ENTER][F7][PGUP][SHIFT-F8]pn5 [ENTER][F7]

6.4

EXERCISES

1. [SHIFT-F8]psls[F7]Legal-Size Paper[CTRL-ENTER][SHIFT-F8]psss[F7] Standard-Size Paper[SHIFT-F7]v{Press PGDN and PGUP to see how WordPerfect will print the two pages.}[F7]

2. [SHIFT-F8]pshs[F7]Jim Adler[ENTER]514 Washington Avenue [ENTER]Columbus, OH 43213[ENTER][SHIFT-F7]v[F7]

MASTERY SKILLS CHECK

[4.3, 6.1]   1. [SHIFT-F8]pc[F7][SHIFT-F6]Wilbur Horse Supplies[ENTER][SHIFT-F6] Financial Statements[ENTER][SHIFT-F6]For the Year Ending December 31, 1989[ENTER][SHIFT-F7]v[F7]

[6.2]   2. [HOME][HOME][HOME][UP ARROW][SHIFT-F8]pm3[ENTER][ENTER][F7] [SHIFT-F7]v[F7]

[6.3]   3. [HOME][HOME][UP ARROW][SHIFT-F8]pp2[F7]

[6.3]   4. [HOME][HOME][DOWN ARROW][CTRL-ENTER][SHIFT-F8]pn10[ENTER][F7]

[6.4]   5. [SHIFT-F8]pshs[F7]

INTEGRATED SKILLS CHECK

[4.3]   1. [SHIFT-F6]Archie's California Grapes[ENTER][SHIFT-F6]Production Records[ENTER][SHIFT-F6]For the season ending September 30, 1989[ENTER]

[6.1]   2. [HOME][HOME][HOME][UP ARROW][SHIFT-F8]pc[F7]

[4.7]   3. [ALT-F4][END][F6][CTRL-RIGHT ARROW][ALT-F4][END][F8]

4. [HOME][HOME][DOWN ARROW][CTRL-ENTER][SHIFT-F8]pp3n1[ENTER][F7]   [6.3]

5. [SHIFT-F8]ls2[ENTER][F7][TAB]This year's crop is the largest in the   [5.6]
last 20 years. It is primarily due to improved fertilization
methods and increased rainfall. The plants damaged by
last year's drought were replaced.[ENTER]

6. {Move to the beginning of the paragraph.}[SHIFT-F8]ljn[F7]   [5.7]

7. [SHIFT-F7]f   [3.1]

SKILLS CHECK   7

1. Product Announcement[ENTER][ENTER][TAB]The XY Graphics   [1.4]
Company has announced the release of its new product,
See 'N' Draw. This package creates custom pictures by
combining existing drawings and advanced graphics features. Since each new feature added to an image is considered a unique layer, you can edit one layer without
affecting the others. The print options offer features unavailable in any competing product.[ENTER]

2. [HOME][HOME][UP ARROW][ALT-F4][END][F6]   [1.4, 4.7]

3. [ALT-F4][HOME][LEFT ARROW][SHIFT-F6]y   [4.7]

4. [ALT-F3][UP ARROW][BACKSPACE]   [4.5]

5. [DOWN ARROW][SHIFT-F4]{Press the DOWN ARROW key to make   [5.2]
WordPerfect reformat the paragraph.}

6. [HOME][HOME][UP ARROW][SHIFT-F8]ls2[ENTER][F7]   [5.6]

7. [SHIFT-F8]pc[F7]   [6.1]

8. [SHIFT-F7]p   [3.1]

7.1   EXERCISES

1. On Saturday, May 16, XY Graphics is holding a press conference for their new product, See 'N' Draw. At this conference, the public relations director, Jill Smith, will reveal the company's marketing strategy for the product. [ENTER][HOME][HOME][UP ARROW][F2]Jill Smith[F2]

2. Memory Requirements: 512K[ENTER]Storage Space Required: 200K[ENTER]Number of Disks: 5[ENTER]Tutorial: Yes[ENTER]Demo: Yes[ENTER][HOME][HOME][UP ARROW][F2]5[ENTER] [F2] {or[F2]Disks: 5[F2]}

3. {Type the text as shown.}[HOME][HOME][UP ARROW][F2]forgive [F2][F2][F2][F2][F2][F2][F2]{If you search again, WordPerfect will beep and display the message "∗ Not found ∗" in the status line.}

4. {Type the text as shown.}[HOME][HOME][UP ARROW][F2]sea[F2] {Press F2 twice. Repeat until WordPerfect beeps and displays the "∗ Not found ∗" message. WordPerfect will find "Searching," "seashells," "seashore," "sea," and "season."}[HOME][HOME][UP ARROW][F2][SPACEBAR]sea[SPACEBAR][F2] {WordPerfect will only find "sea" in the last sentence. If you press F2 twice more, WordPerfect will beep and display the "∗ Not found ∗" message.}

7.2   EXERCISES

1. The entire project was moved to Tobler Hall under the direction of John Tomita.[SHIFT-F2]to[F2]{The cursor moves to the "m" in "Tomita."}[SHIFT-F2][F2]{The cursor moves to the "b" in "Tobler."}[SHIFT-F2][F2]{The cursor moves to the space between "to" and "Tobler."}[SHIFT-F2][F2]{WordPerfect beeps and displays the "∗ Not Found ∗" message, and the cursor remains in place.}

2. The meeting is Friday, August 11th.[F8]All must attend.[F8] Discuss previous commitments with Carol Stevens. [SHIFT-F2][F8][F8][LEFT ARROW][BACKSPACE][F2]{The cursor moves to the space after the period at the end of the second sentence.}

3. {Type the text as shown.}[SHIFT-F2]for[F2]{Press SHIFT-F2 and F2 again, and repeat until WordPerfect beeps and displays the "* Not found *" message. WordPerfect will find "forty," "foreigners," "for," and "forum."}[HOME][HOME] [DOWN ARROW][SHIFT-F2][SPACEBAR]for[SPACEBAR][F2]{WordPerfect will find "for" in the first sentence. If you press SHIFT-F2 and F2 again, WordPerfect will beep and display the "* Not found *" message.}

EXERCISES

7.3

1. Sam Cook is the production manager. He has five years' experience in this position. Prior to this position, Sam Cook was a sergeant in the army. Sam Cook succeeded Thomas MacNamara in his current position.[ENTER][ALT-F2]n [UP ARROW]{This sets the search and replace to operate from the end. Press DEL to remove any previous search string.}Sam Cook[F2]Daniel Jones[F2]{The paragraph now reads: Daniel Jones is the production manager. He has five years' experience in this position. Prior to this position, Daniel Jones was a sergeant in the army. Daniel Jones succeeded Thomas MacNamara in his current position.}

2. WordPerfect's Replace feature allows you to selectively replace one string of characters with another character string. You can have WordPerfect prompt you before completing each replacement, or you can have it make the changes automatically.[ENTER][ALT-F2]n[ENTER][UP ARROW] WordPerfect[F2]WordPerfect 5.0[F2]

3. The Public Relations Director for your area is XX. XX has been with the company for many years and can answer

your questions.[ENTER][ALT-F2]n[UP ARROW]XX[F2]Nancy Clark
[F2][ALT-F2]nNancy Clark[F2]Martin Smith[F2]

4. You can use WP's Replace feature to shorten typing in a
ms or doc. In a ms or doc, you type the abbreviations in
place of the words and have WP replace the abbreviations with the words they represent.[ENTER][ALT-F2]n
[UP ARROW]ms [F2]manuscript[F2][ALT-F2]ndoc[F2]document
[F2][HOME][HOME][UP ARROW][ALT-F2]nWP[F2]WordPerfect[F2]

MASTERY SKILLS CHECK

[7.1]

1. WordPerfect lets you search for text. You can search
either backward or forward. This means that you do not
have to move the cursor to a specific location before you
can use this feature.[ENTER][HOME][HOME][UP ARROW][F2]search
[F2][F2][F2]

[7.1]

2. [HOME][HOME][UP ARROW][F2]you[F2][F2][F2][F2][F2][F2][F2][F2][F2]
{WordPerfect beeps and displays the "* Not found *"
message after finding "you" four times.}

[7.2]

3. [HOME][HOME][DOWN ARROW][SHIFT-F2]for[F2]{The cursor moves to
the second "e" in "before" in the second sentence.}
[SHIFT-F2][F2]{The cursor moves to the "w" in "forward."}
[SHIFT-F2][F2]{The cursor moves to the space between "for"
and "text" in the first sentence.}[SHIFT-F2][F2]{WordPerfect
beeps and displays the "* Not found *" message.}

[7.3]

4. Aeneades was a Trojan prince. He was the son of
Diomedes and Achilles. Aeneades married Lavinia.
[ALT-F2]n[UP ARROW]Aeneades[CTRL-END][F2]Aeneas[F2]

INTEGRATED SKILLS CHECK

[4.1, 4.3, 4.4,
7.1]

1. [SHIFT-F6][F8]Proposal[F8][ENTER][ENTER]The Quick Time division
of New Men's Look, Inc., would like to expand their

product line to include pocket watches. Adding pocket watches would fit into the division's current production capacity. The plant is operating 30% below capacity. The technology required is already available. This product would also complement the suits produced by another subsidiary, the Taylor division.[ENTER][HOME][HOME][UP ARROW] [F2][F8][F2][ALT-F3]

2. [ALT-F2]nQuick Time[F2]QUICK TIME[F2]   [7.3]

3. [ALT-F2]nTaylor[F2]Tailor[F2]   [7.3]

4. [HOME][HOME][UP ARROW][SHIFT-F8]pc[F7]   [6.1]

5. [SHIFT-F7]v[F7]   [3.3]

SKILLS CHECK   8

1. [SHIFT-F8]lm2[ENTER]2[ENTER][F7][SHIFT-F8]pm2[ENTER]2[ENTER][F7]   [5.1, 6.2]

2. [SHIFT-F8]pp1[F7]   [6.3]

3. [SHIFT-F8]lt[HOME][HOME][LEFT ARROW][CTRL-END]1,1[ENTER][F7][F7]   [5.4]

4. Dale Thompson[ENTER]Birds of a Feather[ENTER]2398   [4.7]
Manzanita Park[ENTER]Stanford, CA 94321[ENTER][ENTER]
Dear Dale,[ENTER][ENTER]According to your advertisement in
Feathered Friends, you are interested in purchasing two
white cockatoos. I own several and would like to sell
them. Please contact me at (813)212-2634.[ENTER][ENTER]
[TAB][TAB][TAB][TAB]Sincerely,[ENTER][ENTER][ENTER][ENTER][TAB][TAB]
[TAB][TAB]Byron Wilson[ENTER]{Move to the "F" in
"Feathered."}[ALT-F4][CTRL-RIGHT ARROW][CTRL-RIGHT ARROW]
[LEFT ARROW][LEFT ARROW][F8]

[7.3]   **5.** [HOME][HOME][UP ARROW][ALT-F2]nwhitecockatoos[F2]parakeets [F2]

[3.1, 6.1]   **6.** [SHIFT-F7]f[HOME][HOME][UP ARROW][SHIFT-F8]pc[F7][SHIFT-F7]f

[4.5]   **7.** [HOME][HOME][UP ARROW][ALT-F3][BACKSPACE][BACKSPACE][BACKSPACE]
[BACKSPACE][ALT-F3]

8.1   EXERCISES

1. A complex sentence consists of an independent clause, which can stand alone, and one or more dependent clauses. A compound sentence is two or more simple sentences joined by a conjunction, such as "and," "or," "but," or "for." A simple sentence expresses a single action or thought.[SPACEBAR][SPACEBAR][ENTER]{Move the cursor to a character in the first sentence.}[CTRL-F4]sm{Move the cursor past the end of the last sentence.}[ENTER]{Move the cursor to a character in what is now the middle sentence.}sm{Move the cursor to the top of the document.}[ENTER]

2. [TAB]The sun's temperature is 11,000 degrees Fahrenheit at the surface and 35,000,000 degrees in the center. It releases 1.94 calories per square centimeter per minute. [ENTER][TAB]The diameter of the sun is 865,000 miles. It is small by comparison to other stars. The sun's proximity to the earth makes it appear larger than other stars.[ENTER] [UP ARROW][CTRL-F4]pm[HOME][HOME][UP ARROW][ENTER]

3. A nebula is a mass of gas in space.[CTRL-ENTER]A meteoroid is a small object in space.[CTRL-ENTER]A constellation is a group of stars.[CTRL-ENTER][HOME][HOME][UP ARROW][CTRL-F4]am [HOME][HOME][DOWN ARROW][ENTER]

4. [TAB]Keyboards usually come in two types. A standard keyboard has ten function keys at the side. An enhanced

keyboard has 12 function keys across the top.[ENTER]
[TAB]With WordPerfect, if you have an enhanced
keyboard, you can use F11 in place of ALT-F3. You can
also use F12 in place of ALT-F4.[ENTER]{Move the cursor to
the second sentence.}[CTRL-F4]sm[DOWN ARROW][SPACEBAR]
[SPACEBAR][ENTER][CTRL-F4]pm[DOWN ARROW][DOWN ARROW][ENTER][ENTER]

EXERCISES

8.2

1. See 'N' Draw, XY Graphics' new product, should capture
   a large part of the graphics market for first-time users.
   [ENTER][UP ARROW][UP ARROW][ALT-F4][CTRL-RIGHT ARROW][CTRL-RIGHT
   ARROW][CTRL-RIGHT ARROW][CTRL-F4]bm[CTRL-RIGHT ARROW][CTRL-RIGHT
   ARROW][CTRL-RIGHT ARROW][CTRL-RIGHT ARROW][ENTER]

2. The new machinery funnels the cake mix into preprinted
   boxes, weighs a predetermined amount of the cake mix,
   and seals the bag.[ENTER]{Move to the "w" in "weigh."}
   [ALT-F4]{Move to the "a" in "and."}[CTRL-F4]bm[HOME][HOME]
   [UP ARROW][CTRL-RIGHT ARROW][CTRL-RIGHT ARROW][CTRL-RIGHT ARROW]
   [ENTER]

3. Review meeting agenda.[ENTER]Nominate potential candi-
   dates for new director position.[ENTER]Review financial
   statements.[ENTER]Review minutes from the last meeting.
   [ENTER]Introduce new corporate treasurer to board.[ENTER]
   [UP ARROW][UP ARROW][ALT-F4][DOWN ARROW][DOWN ARROW][CTRL-F4]bm
   [UP ARROW][UP ARROW][ENTER]

4. When you move a block, you should check to include
   any hidden codes in your text. WordPerfect moves all of
   the codes within the block. If the text that you move is
   part of a larger block of text that has special print
   attributes (for example, bold or underline), the special
   print characteristics appear in both the moved text and
   the original. To view the codes, press the Reveal Codes
   (ALT-F3) key.[ENTER]{Move to the "W" in "WordPerfect."}
   [ALT-F4]..[RIGHT ARROW][RIGHT ARROW][CTRL-F4]bm[PGUP][ENTER]

8.3   EXERCISES

1. The Office of Human Resources reports that hiring has increased by 14%. This increase is a result of last year's expansion of the Largo division. The increased hiring, which created 1000 new jobs, should not affect next year's personnel needs.[ENTER]{Move the cursor to the period at the end of the first sentence.}[ALT-F4][CTRL-RIGHT ARROW][CTRL-RIGHT ARROW][CTRL-RIGHT ARROW][CTRL-RIGHT ARROW] [LEFT ARROW][CTRL-F4]bd,

2. As of May 15, the corporation must increase sales by 15,000 units per month, renovate the corporate offices, and divest itself of its Romper division to meet its 1989 objectives.[ENTER]{Move the cursor to the "r" in "renovate."}[ALT-F4]{Move the cursor to the "a" in "and."}[DEL]y

3. Today's Projects[ENTER]Prepare capital budget request for two computers.[ENTER]Review receivables older than 90 days.[ENTER]Prepare next year's forecast.[ENTER][ALT-F4] [UP ARROW][UP ARROW][CTRL-F4]bd

4. Last February, the widget assembler became jammed. While the cause was poor maintenance, the machine's condition requires above-normal maintenance to prevent the problem from recurring. To prevent this problem from recurring, the company should purchase a new machine.[ENTER]{Move the cursor to the second sentence.} [CTRL-F4]sd

8.4   EXERCISES

1. Name: Patrick Rabbit[ENTER]Address: 777 Carrot Lane[ENTER] [ALT-F4][UP ARROW][UP ARROW][CTRL-F4]bc[DOWN ARROW][DOWN ARROW] [ENTER]{Move to the "P" in "Patrick" in the copy.}[INS] Nancy[DEL][DEL]{Move to the first 7 in 777 in the

copy.}515[INS][DOWN ARROW][CTRL-F4]rb

2. First, put the correct pens in the plotter. This is an important step. Next, put the paper or transparency in the plotter.[ENTER]{Move the cursor to the second sentence.} [CTRL-F4]sc{Move the cursor to the end of the third sentence.}[SPACEBAR][SPACEBAR][ENTER]

3. Current Month:[ESC]7.[ENTER]Sales:[ESC]7.[ENTER]Cost of Goods Sold:[ESC]7.[ENTER][UP ARROW][UP ARROW][UP ARROW][ALT-F4][DOWN ARROW][DOWN ARROW][DOWN ARROW][CTRL-F4]bc[ENTER][CTRL-F4]rb [CTRL-F4]rb[CTRL-F4]rb

4. Directions to the Cloverleaf Hall: Take the interstate to the Bay Street exit. At the exit, turn right, and take the next left after the light. Stay on this road until you pass the shopping mall on the right. After passing the shopping mall,[SPACEBAR]{Move to the "t" in "take."}[ALT-F4]. [CTRL-F4]bc[HOME][DOWN ARROW][END][ENTER]

MASTERY SKILLS CHECK

1. The cost of goods sold is $2,363,782. The beginning inventory is $689,578. The ending inventory is $234,245. [ENTER][HOME][UP ARROW][CTRL-F4]sm[CTRL-RIGHT ARROW][CTRL-RIGHT ARROW][CTRL-RIGHT ARROW][CTRL-RIGHT ARROW][CTRL-RIGHT ARROW][ENTER]   [8.1]

2. The new and improved widget maker has several features. One of these features is the internal painter. This feature evenly coats each widget and limits the fumes, which reduces the number of employees needed to operate the machine.[ENTER]{Move the cursor to the comma in the third sentence.}[ALT-F4].[LEFT ARROW][CTRL-F4]bm{Move the cursor to the period ending the second sentence.}[ENTER]   [8.2]

[8.1, 8.3]   3. Tuesday, the heads of the accounting, production, and MIS departments will review the steps that they can take to reduce the time between the receipt of an order and its completion.[ENTER]{Move the cursor to the beginning of the word "that."}[ALT-F4][CTRL-RIGHT ARROW][CTRL-RIGHT ARROW][CTRL-RIGHT ARROW][CTRL-RIGHT ARROW][DEL]y[CTRL-F4]pd

[8.4]   4. Today's weather will be lovely. The temperature will rise to 82 and will cool to an evening low of 70. The low humidity will contribute to the day's pleasant weather. [ENTER][UP ARROW][CTRL-F4]pc[ENTER][CTRL-F4]rb[CTRL-F4]rb

INTEGRATED SKILLS CHECK

[1.4, 8.1]   1. {Type the text as shown.}[CTRL-ENTER][UP ARROW][CTRL-F4] pm[DOWN ARROW][ENTER]

[5.2]   2. [F4][HOME][HOME][DOWN ARROW][F7]nn

[1.4, 6.1]   3. Marketing Strategy[ENTER][CAPS LOCK]ABC WIDGETS [CAPS LOCK][ENTER]Prepared on July 7, 1988[ENTER][UP ARROW] [CTRL-BACKSPACE][CTRL-BACKSPACE][HOME][HOME][UP ARROW][SHIFT-F8]pc[F7] [SHIFT-F7]v[F7][F7]nn

[1.4, 8.4]   4. Date:[ENTER]Name:[ENTER]Amount:[ENTER]Explanation:[ENTER] Signature:[ENTER][CTRL-ENTER][HOME][HOME][UP ARROW][ALT-F4] [PGDN][CTRL-F4]bc[ENTER]

[8.4]   5. [CTRL-F4]rb[CTRL-F4]rb[CTRL-F4]rb

[3.1, 6.3]   6. [HOME][HOME][UP ARROW][SHIFT-F8]pp2[F7][SHIFT-F7]f

[7.3]   7. [ALT-F2]nExplanation[F2]For[F2]

9   SKILLS CHECK

[5.1]   1. [SHIFT-F8]lm2[ENTER]2[ENTER][F7]

2. [SHIFT-F8]pp1[F7]   [6.3]

3. {Type the text as shown}[ENTER][SHIFT-F2]spell[F2][SHIFT-F2][F2]   [7.2]

4. [HOME][HOME][UP ARROW][ALT-F2]yit[F2]WordPerfect[F2]ynyn[F7]   [7.3]

5. [HOME][HOME][DOWN ARROW][LEFT ARROW]{Enter the text shown}   [8.3, 8.4]
[UP ARROW][UP ARROW]{to move to the second sentence}
[CTRL-F4]sc[HOME][HOME][DOWN ARROW][LEFT ARROW][SPACEBAR]
[SPACEBAR][ENTER]{Move to "when" in the last sentence.}
[ALT-F4].[LEFT ARROW][DEL]y{Type the new text as shown.}

EXERCISES ———————————— 9.1

1. {Type the words exactly as shown.}[HOME][HOME][UP ARROW]
[CTRL-F2]wawwwaw[F7]

2. {Type the text exactly as shown.}[HOME][HOME][UP ARROW]
[CTRL-F2]wawwawwwwwdwwcwwwhw[F7]

3. {Type the text exactly as shown.}[HOME][HOME][UP ARROW]
[CTRL-F2]w2w2wwdwwb[F7]

4. {Type the text exactly as shown.}[HOME][LEFT ARROW][CTRL-F2]
w4[RIGHT ARROW][RIGHT ARROW][SPACEBAR][F7]ww4p[F7]w4[RIGHT
ARROW][RIGHT ARROW][SPACEBAR][F7]ww4p[DEL][F7]w4[RIGHT ARROW]
[RIGHT ARROW][RIGHT ARROW][SPACEBAR][F7]ww4[RIGHT ARROW]
[RIGHT ARROW][RIGHT ARROW][SPACEBAR][F7]w[SPACEBAR]

EXERCISES ———————————— 9.2

1. {Type the paragraph as shown.}[CTRL-F2]db2aa[ENTER]

2. {Type the paragraph as shown.}[CTRL-F2]dagaa[ENTER]

3. {Type the paragraph as shown.}[CTRL-F2]d2aia[F7]

4. {Type the paragraph as shown.}[CTRL-F2]daadd[F7]

9.3 EXERCISES

1. {Type the paragraph as shown.}[CTRL-F2]d333[SPACEBAR]

2. {Type the paragraph as shown.}[CTRL-F2]d333aa3333[SPACEBAR]

3. {Type the paragraph as shown.}[CTRL-F2]d333333[SPACEBAR]

4. WordPerfect does[ENTER]does not[ENTER]not check to see if the[ENTER]the last word of one paragraph is the same word as the[ENTER]first word word of the next paragraph. [ENTER][CTRL-F2]d3{The speller finds only the double word in the last two lines.}

9.4 EXERCISES

1. {Type the names and addresses as shown.}[CTRL-F2]d33333[ENTER]

2. {Type your name.}[CTRL-F2]d{Type **3** to add any part of your name to the dictionary if WordPerfect does not recognize it.}[ENTER]

3. Abbreviations[ENTER]ATMOS - Atmosphere[ENTER]IDP - Integrated Data Processing[ENTER]OCS - Officer Candidate School[ENTER]SWAZ - Swaziland[ENTER][CTRL-F2]d3333[SPACEBAR]

4. {Type the paragraph as it appears.}[CTRL-F2]d333[SPACEBAR]

9.5 EXERCISES

1. [SHIFT-F10]wp{wp}en.sup[ENTER]{Position the cursor on the first character in a word you wish to remove.}[CTRL-BACKSPACE][DEL]{For each word you wish to remove, move

the cursor to the word, and repeat the keystrokes.[F10]
[ENTER]y

2. [F7]nn[SHIFT-F10]wp{wp}en.sup[ENTER]{Press the DOWN ARROW key
to move the cursor to "ATMOS" if it is not already
there.}[CTRL-BACKSPACE][DEL]{Press the DOWN ARROW key to move
the cursor to "IDP."}[CTRL-BACKSPACE][DEL]{Press the DOWN
ARROW key to move the cursor to "OCS."}[CTRL-BACKSPACE]
[DEL]{Press the DOWN ARROW key to move the cursor to
"SWAZ."}[CTRL-BACKSPACE][DEL][F10][ENTER]y

3. [F7]nn[SHIFT-F10]wp{wp}en.sup[ENTER]{Press the DOWN ARROW key
to move the cursor to "Aphrodite" if it is not already
there.}[CTRL-BACKSPACE][DEL]{Press the DOWN ARROW key to move
the cursor to "Audrey."}[CTRL-BACKSPACE][DEL]{Press the DOWN
ARROW key to move the cursor to "Galatea."}[CTRL-BACKSPACE]
[DEL]{Press the DOWN ARROW key to move the cursor to
"Pygmalion."}[CTRL-BACKSPACE][DEL][F10][ENTER]y

EXERCISES ————————————————— 9.6

1. The fair four the bridge to get to the fare is for dollars.
[ENTER][ALT-F2]y[UP ARROW]fair[CTRL-END][F2]fare[F2]y[HOME][LEFT
ARROW][ALT-F2]yfare[F2]fair[F2]ny[HOME][LEFT ARROW][ALT-F2]
yfor[F2]four[F2]y[HOME][LEFT ARROW][ALT-F2]yfour[F2]for[F2]yn

2. Their demonstrating there new product over they're.
[ALT-F2]ythere[UP ARROW][F2]their[F2]y[HOME][LEFT ARROW][ALT-F2]
ythey're[F2]there[F2]y[HOME][LEFT ARROW][ALT-F2]ytheir[F2]
they're[F2]yn

EXERCISES ————————————————— 9.7

1. [ALT-F1]table[ENTER][F7]

2. [ALT-F1]adjoining[ENTER][F7]

3. rich[ALT-F1]c[F7]

4. [ALT-F1]limit[ENTER][RIGHT ARROW]d[RIGHT ARROW]ehdd[LEFT ARROW] [LEFT ARROW]44[F7]

9.8   EXERCISES

1. {Type the sentence as shown.}[CTRL-LEFT ARROW][ALT-F1]1j

2. {Type the sentence as shown. Then, move the cursor to "division."}[ALT-F1]1m

3. {Type the sentence as shown. Then, move the cursor to "Business."}[ALT-F1][RIGHT ARROW]1a

4. {Type the paragraph.}[ENTER][UP ARROW][UP ARROW][CTRL-RIGHT ARROW][ALT-F1]1k[CTRL-RIGHT ARROW][CTRL-RIGHT ARROW][CTRL-RIGHT ARROW][ALT-F1]1n[CTRL-RIGHT ARROW][CTRL-RIGHT ARROW][CTRL-RIGHT ARROW][CTRL-RIGHT ARROW][ALT-F1]1l[CTRL-RIGHT ARROW][CTRL-RIGHT ARROW][CTRL-RIGHT ARROW][CTRL-RIGHT ARROW][CTRL-RIGHT ARROW] [CTRL-RIGHT ARROW][ALT-F1]1m

MASTERY SKILLS CHECK

[9.1]

1. {Type each word as shown, pressing ENTER at the end of each one.}[HOME][HOME][UP ARROW][CTRL-F2]wawawaw[F7]

[9.2]

2. {Type the paragraph as shown.}[ENTER][CTRL-F2]dzc3b3 [SPACEBAR]

[9.4]

3. {Type the letter as shown.}[CTRL-F2]d{Type a **3** for each proper name suggested as a misspelling to add it to the dictionary.}

4. [SHIFT-F10]wp{wp}en.sup[ENTER]{Move the cursor to the first   [9.5]
   name; press CTRL-BACKSPACE and the DEL key. Repeat this
   process for each name that you added.}[F10][ENTER]y

5. {Type the paragraph as shown.}[HOME][HOME][UP ARROW]   [9.6]
   [ALT-F2]yfor[F2]four[F2]y{Repeat the replace process for the
   homonyms "it's" and "its," "moor" and "more," "too"
   and "to," and "two" and "to."}

6. [ALT-F1]bar[ENTER]e3light[ENTER][F7]   [9.7]

7. {Type the sentence as shown.}[HOME][HOME][UP ARROW][CTRL-   [9.8]
   RIGHT ARROW][CTRL-RIGHT ARROW][ALT-F1]1e

INTEGRATED SKILLS CHECK

1. [SHIFT-F8]lm3[ENTER]3[ENTER][ENTER]pm3[ENTER]3[ENTER][F7]   [5.1, 6.2]

2. {Type the paragraph as shown.}[ENTER][CTRL-F2]   [9.2]
   daaaaa[SPACEBAR]

3. {Type the paragraph as shown.}[CTRL-F2]d33a[SPACEBAR]   [9.2, 9.4]

4. [CTRL-F4]pm[HOME][HOME][UP ARROW][ENTER]   [8.1]

5. {Move to the beginning of the second paragraph.}[ALT-F4]   [8.4]
   [ENTER][CTRL-F4]bc[ENTER][CTRL-F4]rb[CTRL-F4]rb

6. {Type the sentence; then move the cursor to the word   [9.8]
   "light."}[ALT-F1]1m

7. [SHIFT-F7]f   [3.1]

8. [F10]words[ENTER]   [2.2]

9. [SHIFT-F10]wp{wp}en.sup[ENTER]{Move the cursor to   [9.5]
   "Howard."}[CTRL-BACKSPACE][DEL]{Repeat this procedure for
   "Moore."}[F10][ENTER]y

10

SKILLS CHECK

[9.2]   **1.** {Type the paragraph as shown.}[CTRL-F2]daa

[9.8]   **2.** {Move the cursor to "decides."}[ALT-F1]1gs{The "s" changes the verb tense to fit the context of the sentence.}

[8.1]   **3.** [HOME][HOME][UP ARROW][CTRL-F4]sm[HOME][HOME][DOWN ARROW][LEFT ARROW][SPACEBAR][SPACEBAR][ENTER]

[7.1]   **4.** [HOME][HOME][UP ARROW][F2]date[F2]{Repeat the F2 sequence until the "* Not found *" message appears.}

[8.3]   **5.** {Move the cursor to the last sentence.}[CTRL-F4]sd

10.1

EXERCISES

1. [SHIFT-F8]pm5[ENTER]5[ENTER][F7]{Type the paragraphs as shown.}[HOME][HOME][UP ARROW][SHIFT-F8]lwy[F7]{Move the cursor down the screen.}

2. [SHIFT-F8]pm5[ENTER]5[ENTER][F7]{Type the paragraph as shown.}[HOME][HOME][UP ARROW][SHIFT-F8]lwy[F7]{Move the cursor to the bottom of the document to reformat the paragraph.}[F10]lifo[ENTER]

3. [SHIFT-F10]lifo[ENTER][ALT-F3][DEL][ALT-F3][SHIFT-F8]pm[ENTER]9[ENTER] [F7]{Press the DOWN ARROW key until you reach the bottom of the document.}[F7][ENTER][ENTER]y[ENTER]

4. [SHIFT-F10]lifo[ENTER][SHIFT-F8]lm3[ENTER]3[ENTER][F7]{Press the DOWN ARROW key until you reach the bottom of the document.} [F7][ENTER][ENTER]y[ENTER]

10.2

EXERCISES

1. [SHIFT-F8]phapAcme Inc. Income Statement[F7][F7][SHIFT-F7]v1 [F7]

2. [SHIFT-F8]pfap[F6]{Type your name}[F6][F7][F7][SHIFT-F7]v{Press the DOWN ARROW key repeatedly until the footer appears on the screen.}[F7]

3. [SHIFT-F8]phap[SHIFT-F6]- [CTRL-B] -[F7][F7][SHIFT-F7]v[F7]

4. [SHIFT-F8]phao[CTRL-B][F7]hbv{Type your name.}[F7][F7][CTRL-ENTER][SHIFT-F7]v[PGDN][F7]

EXERCISES   10.3

1. {Type the sentence as shown.}[CTRL-F7]fc{Type the footnote text.}[F7][F7]nn

2. Once upon a time, . . . [CTRL-F7]fcGrimm Brothers Fairy Tales[F7][ENTER]Mary had a little lamb[CTRL-F7]fcMother Goose[F7][ENTER]The Goose That Laid a Golden Egg [CTRL-F7]fcAesop's Fables[F7][ENTER]

3. [HOME][HOME][UP ARROW][CTRL-F4]pm[HOME][HOME][DOWN ARROW] [ENTER]{You may need to press the DOWN ARROW key to make WordPerfect renumber the footnote.}

4. [CTRL-F7]fe3{Make the changes specified.}[F7]

MASTERY SKILLS CHECK

1. [SHIFT-F8]pm[ENTER]9[ENTER][F7]{Type the text as shown.}[ENTER] [HOME][HOME][UP ARROW][SHIFT-F8]lwy[F7]{You may need to press the DOWN ARROW key to make WordPerfect reformat the paragraph.}   [10.1]

2. {Place the cursor before the tab at the beginning of the paragraph.}[CTRL-ENTER][HOME][HOME][DOWN ARROW][LEFT ARROW] [CTRL-F7]fc{Type the footnote text.}[F7]   [10.3]

3. {Move the cursor to the end of the second sentence.} [CTRL-F7]fc{Type the footnote text.}[F7]   [10.3]

[10.3] **4.** [CTRL-F7]fe1{Make the changes shown.}[F7]

[10.2] **5.** [HOME][HOME][UP ARROW][SHIFT-F8]phapPreparing a Trial Balance
[F7][F7][CTRL-END][DEL][DEL]

[10.2] **6.** [SHIFT-F8]pfao{Type your name.}[F7][F7][SHIFT-F7]v{Page through the document with the PGUP and PGDN keys.}

INTEGRATED SKILLS CHECK

[1.4] **1.** {Type the address labels as shown. Move to the end of the first ZIP code}[CTRL-ENTER]{Repeat for the other addresses.}

[9.7] **2.** {Move to the bottom of the first page, press ENTER twice, and type the letter text as shown.}{Move the cursor to "continue."}[ALT-F1][F7]{Move the cursor to "receive."}
[ALT-F1][F7]

[9.2] **3.** [CTRL-F2]d{The only words the Spell feature should highlight are "Elsie," "Johann," and "Sebastian;" you can skip them or add them to the dictionary.}

[10.3] **4.** {Move the cursor to the space after the comma following "publication."}[CTRL-F7]fc{Type the footnote text.}[F7]

[10.3] **5.** [CTRL-F7]fe1{Make the change shown.}[F7]

[8.4] **6.** {Move the cursor to the beginning of the letter.}[ALT-F4]
{Move the cursor to the bottom of the letter.}[CTRL-F4]
bc{Move the cursor to the end of the ZIP code in Karl Davis's address.}[ENTER][ENTER][ENTER]{Move the cursor to the end of the ZIP code in Angus Fuller's address.}[ENTER]
[ENTER] [CTRL-F4]rb

[10.2] **7.** [HOME][HOME][UP ARROW][SHIFT-F8]phap[ALT-F6]{Type your name}
[F7][F7]

SKILLS CHECK

11

1. {Type the paragraphs, pressing ENTER after each one.}
[UP ARROW][CTRL-F4]pm[UP ARROW][UP ARROW][UP ARROW][ENTER]

[8.1]

2. [CTRL-F2]d{Fix any spelling errors as WordPerfect finds
them; the original had none.}

[9.2]

3. {Move to "redeem."}[ALT-F1]11

[9.8]

4. [HOME][HOME][UP ARROW][SHIFT-F8]pm5[ENTER]5[ENTER][F7]

[6.2]

5. [SHIFT-F8]lwy[F7]

[10.1]

6. {Move to the end of the convertible bonds paragraph.}
[CTRL-F7]fcUsually in exchange for common stock[F7]

[10.3]

7. [F7][ENTER]stocks[ENTER][ENTER]

[2.2]

EXERCISES

11.1

1. The pension plan is expected to earn 6% per year. New
employees become vested in the plan after five years
with the company.[ENTER][F10]plan[ENTER][F7]nn[F5][ENTER]{Move
the highlight to the PLAN filename.}cearn[ENTER][F7]

2. {Place a disk in drive A.}[F5][ENTER]{Move the highlight to
the PLAN filename.}ca:plan[ENTER][F7]

3. [SHIFT-F10]plan[ENTER][F10]vested[ENTER]

4. [F5][ENTER]{Move the highlight to the EARN filename.}
cpenplan[ENTER][F7]

5. [SHIFT-F10]vested[ENTER]{Place a disk in drive A.}[F10]a:vested
[ENTER]

11.2   EXERCISES

1. [F5] = \finance[ENTER]y

2. [F5] = letters[ENTER]y

3. [F5] = \finance\finc1989[ENTER]y

4. [F5] = \finance\finc1990[ENTER]y

11.3   EXERCISES

1. [F5] = \finance[ENTER][F1]

2. [F5] = \wp50\letters[ENTER][F1]

3. [F5] = \finance\finc1989[ENTER][F1]

4. [F5] = \finance\finc1990[ENTER][F1]

5. [F5] = \wp50[ENTER][F1]

11.4   EXERCISES

1. {Put the disk containing the PLAN file in drive A.}
   [F5]a:[ENTER]{Move the highlight to the PLAN file.}dy[F7]

2. [F5][ENTER]{Move the highlight to the LETTERS
   subdirectory.}dy[F7]

3. [F5]\finance[ENTER]{Move the highlight to the FINC1989
   subdirectory.}dy[F7]

4. [F5]\finance[ENTER]{Move the highlight to the FINC1990
   subdirectory.}dy[F7]

EXERCISES
11.5

1. [F5][ENTER]{Move the highlight to the PLAN file.} mpension3
[ENTER][F7]

2. [F5][ENTER]{Move the highlight to the EARN file.}m[END]ed
[ENTER][F7]

3. [SHIFT-F10]EARNED[F10]ERN _ INC[ENTER][F7]n[ENTER][F5][ENTER]
{Move the highlight to the ERN _ INC filename.}m{Move
the cursor to the "R" in "ERN,"}a[ENTER][F7]

EXERCISES
11.6

1. [SHIFT-F8]dsdBlank Quit Claim Sales Contract[ENTER]sUnde-
veloped Real Estate[ENTER]aJonas Smith[ENTER]tKaren Polk
[ENTER]cThis blank contract covers most undeveloped land
sales in the state of Florida. This contract has four Xs
where you must fill in information. Paragraphs contained
in braces are optional. Remove them if they are unnecessary for a particular contract.[F7][F7][F7][ENTER]contract[ENTER]n

2. The August 17th meeting discussed the following issues:
[ENTER]Installation of new parking lot lights[ENTER]Hiring of
security personnel to patrol the parking lots after dark
[ENTER]Completion of new research and development
building[ENTER]Improved insurance benefits[ENTER][SHIFT-F8]
dsdAugust 17th meeting notes[ENTER][F7][F10]issues[ENTER]

3. WordPerfect's Graphics features are among the most
advanced in the industry. Investing some time in mastering these features could offer a significant payoff for our
company. Outside service costs for creating newsletters
and brochures can be reduced significantly.[ENTER]
[SHIFT-F8]dsdCut costs with WordPerfect's Graphics[ENTER]
cReduce newsletter and brochure development costs
with Graphics features. We can recover the cost of the
upgrade to 5.0 with the first job.[F7][F7][F7][ENTER]saving
[ENTER][ENTER]

4. [SHIFT-F10]issues[ENTER][SHIFT-F8]dst[CTRL-END]Martha King[ENTER][F7]

11.7 EXERCISES

1. [F5][ENTER]wdAugust[ENTER]{The ISSUES file will have an asterisk next to it; additional files may be marked.}[F7]

2. [F5][ENTER]wfAcme Corporation[ENTER]{The PENSCONT file will have an asterisk next to it; additional files may be marked.}[F7]

3. [F5][ENTER]weplan[ENTER]{The EARNED, EARN_INC, PENSION, PENSCONT, PENSION3, and VESTED files will have asterisks next to them; additional files may be marked.}[F7]

4. [F5][ENTER]we{Type your first name.}[ENTER]{Various files may have asterisks next to them.}we{Type your last name.}[ENTER]{Various files may have asterisks next to them.}we{Type your first name, a semicolon, and your last name.}[ENTER]{Various files may have asterisks next to them.}we{Type your first name, a comma, and your last name.}[ENTER]{Various files may have asterisks next to them.}[F7]

5. [F5][ENTER]wdcompany;product[ENTER][F7]

6. [F5][ENTER]wepension,contract[ENTER][F7]

11.8 EXERCISES

1. [F5][ENTER]{Move the highlight to the EARNED filename.}[ENTER]{Look through the file.}[F7][F7]

2. [F5][ENTER]{Move the highlight to the CONTRACT file.}[ENTER]{Look through the file.}[F7][F7]

3. [F5][ENTER]{Move the highlight to the ISSUES filename.}
[ENTER]{Look through the file.}[F7][F7]

4. [F5][ENTER]{Move the highlight to the PENPLAN filename.}
[ENTER]{Look through the file.}[F7][F7]

5. [F5][ENTER]{Move the highlight to the STOCKS filename.}
[ENTER]{Look through the file.}[F7][F7]

MASTERY SKILLS CHECK

1. [F5][ENTER]obudget90[ENTER]y[F7]   [11.2]

2. Acme Corporation - 1990 Budget[ENTER][ENTER]Estimated   [11.1]
Sales[TAB][TAB]$1,000,000[ENTER]Fixed Costs[TAB][TAB][TAB]
$[SPACEBAR][SPACEBAR]400,000[ENTER]Variable Costs[TAB][TAB]
$[SPACEBAR][SPACEBAR]400,000[ENTER]Gross Profit[TAB][TAB][TAB]
$[SPACEBAR][SPACEBAR]200,000[ENTER][F10]BUDGET[ENTER][F7]nn
[F5][ENTER]{Move the highlight to the BUDGET filename.}
cbudget90[ENTER][F7]

3. [F5]=budget90[ENTER][F1]   [11.3]

4. [F5][ENTER]{Move the highlight to the BUDGET filename.}   [11.1]
cbdgt1990[ENTER][F7]

5. [F5][ENTER]{Move the highlight to the BUDGET filename.}   [11.4]
dy[F7]

6. [F5][ENTER]{Move the highlight to the BDGT1990   [11.5]
filename.}m[END][LEFT ARROW][LEFT ARROW][BACKSPACE]
[BACKSPACE][ENTER][F7]

7. [SHIFT-F10]bdgt90[ENTER][SHIFT-F8]dsdBudget 1990[ENTER]sAcme   [11.6]
Corporation[ENTER]aJane Smith[ENTER]tJohn Dow[ENTER]
cMichael McCormick must have this report by
September 30, 1989.[F7][F7]

[11.6]   **8.** [F10][ENTER]y

[11.7]   **9.** [F5][ENTER]wdBudget[ENTER][F7]

[11.8]   **10.** [F7]nn[F5][ENTER]{Move the highlight to the BDGT90 filename.}[ENTER]{Use the cursor movement keys to look at the file.}[F7][F7]

[11.3]   **11.** [F5]=\wp50[ENTER][F1]

INTEGRATED SKILLS CHECK

[9.2]   **1.** {Type the paragraphs, pressing ENTER at the end of each one.}[CTRL-F2]d{Fix any spelling errors as WordPerfect finds them; the original has none.}

[2.2]   **2.** [F10]prefer[ENTER]

[11.1]   **3.** [F5][ENTER]{Move the highlight to the PREFER filename.} cpreferrd[ENTER][F7]

[11.3]   **4.** [F5][ENTER]ostock[ENTER]y[F7]

[1.3]   **5.** [F7]nn

[11.1]   **6.** [F5][ENTER]{Move the highlight to the PREFERRD filename.}cstock[ENTER][F7]

[11.3]   **7.** [F5]=stock[ENTER][F1][SHIFT-F10]preferrd[ENTER]

[8.1]   **8.** {This answer moves "participation" to the bottom and "conversion" between "callable" and "cumulative;" there are other methods to accomplish this.}
[DOWN ARROW][DOWN ARROW][CTRL-F4]pm[PGDN][ENTER][UP ARROW]
[CTRL-F4]pm[UP ARROW][UP ARROW][UP ARROW][ENTER]

[6.2]   **9.** [HOME][HOME][UP ARROW][SHIFT-F8]pm5[ENTER]5[ENTER][F7]

10. [SHIFT-F8]lwy[F7]   [10.1]

11. [F10][ENTER]y   [2.2]

12. [F5]c:\wp50[ENTER]{Move the cursor to the PREFER   [11.4]
    filename.}dy[F7]

13. [F2]dividend[F2]{"Dividend" first occurs in the explanation   [7.1]
    of "Cumulative."}

14. {Move the cursor to "fluctuates."}[ALT-F1]{Look at the   [9.7]
    synonyms.}[F7]{Move the cursor to "extent."}[ALT-F1]{Look
    at the synonyms.}[F7]

SKILLS CHECK   **12**

1. {Type the paragraph as shown.}[CTRL-F2]da3aa{Press any   [9.2]
   key.}

2. {Move the cursor to the word "customize."}[ALT-F1]1f   [9.8]

3. [HOME][HOME][UP ARROW][SHIFT-F8]phapWordPerfect Print   [10.2]
   Features[F7]fap[SHIFT-F6]Page[SPACEBAR][CTRL-B][F7][F7][SHIFT-F7]v3[F7]

4. [SHIFT-F8]dsdDescribing WordPerfect's Print features[ENTER]   [11.6]
   sTeach Yourself WordPerfect[ENTER]a{Type your name.}
   [ENTER]t{Type your name.}[ENTER][F7]

5. [F10]advprint[ENTER][F5][ENTER]{Move the highlight to the   [11.1, 11.4, 11.5]
   ADVPRINT file.}cprintadv[ENTER]mprntfeat[ENTER][F7]{Since
   WordPerfect does not refresh the screen when you copy
   files, you must leave List Files and reenter it.}[F5]
   [ENTER]{Move the highlight to the PRINTADV file.}dy[F7]

EXERCISES   **12.1**

1. {Type the paragraph as shown.}[ENTER][SHIFT-F7]n3[ENTER]f
   [F7][ENTER]filedel[ENTER]n

2. {Type the paragraph as shown.}[ENTER][SHIFT-F7]n2[ENTER]f
[F7][ENTER]rename[ENTER]n

3. [SHIFT-F7]n3[ENTER]dprintopt[ENTER][ENTER][F7]

4. [SHIFT-F7]n2[ENTER]dwpset[ENTER][ENTER][F7]

5. [SHIFT-F7]dfiledel[ENTER][ENTER]n1[ENTER]dwpset[ENTER][ENTER][F7]

12.2   EXERCISES

1. [SHIFT-F7]n3drename[ENTER][ENTER]c[F7]

2. [SHIFT-F7]drename[ENTER][ENTER]n2[ENTER]dfiledel[ENTER][ENTER]n1
[ENTER]dwpset[ENTER][ENTER]c{Wait until WordPerfect finishes
all three jobs.}[F7]

12.3   EXERCISES

1. [SHIFT-F7]n5[ENTER]drename[ENTER][ENTER]cc{Type the number of
the RENAME print job}[ENTER][F7]

2. [SHIFT-F7]n3drename[ENTER][ENTER]dfiledel[ENTER][ENTER]dwpset
[ENTER][ENTER]cc*y[F7]

3. {Turn the printer off.}[SHIFT-F7]n1[ENTER]dfiledel[ENTER][ENTER]cc
{Type the number of the FILEDEL print job.}[ENTER][F7]

4. [SHIFT-F7]dwpset[ENTER][ENTER]dfiledel[ENTER][ENTER]drename
[ENTER][ENTER]cc{Type the number of the WPSET print
job.}[ENTER]c{Type the number of the RENAME print
job.}[ENTER][F7]{Turn the printer on.}

12.4   EXERCISES

1. [SHIFT-F7]drename[ENTER][ENTER]dfiledel[ENTER][ENTER]dprintopt
[ENTER][ENTER]cr{Type the number of the PRINTOPT print
job.}[ENTER]y[F7]

2. [SHIFT-F7]dwpset[ENTER][ENTER]dfiledel[ENTER][ENTER]drename [ENTER][ENTER]cr{Type the number of the RENAME print job.}[ENTER]{Since the first one has not started printing, the third print request will print before the first one, and WordPerfect will not prompt you for interrupting the current print job.}{Turn the printer on.}g[F7]

EXERCISES _____ 12.5

1. [SHIFT-F10]wpset[ENTER][SHIFT-F7]tmf

2. [SHIFT-F7]thf

3. [SHIFT-F7]tdf

EXERCISES _____ 12.6

1. When you change the font, all characters after the font change are affected.[CTRL-F8]f{Move the highlight to a font that has a smaller CPI, smaller pitch, or larger point size than the one originally highlighted.}[ENTER]Characters before the font change use the initial setting of your printer.[SHIFT-F7]v1[F7]

2. Fonts can also be proportionally spaced.[CTRL-F8]f{If your printer has a proportionally spaced font, move the highlight to a font that has a "PS" after it, preferably with the same CPI, pitch, or point size than the one originally highlighted; if your printer does not have a proportionally spaced font, move the highlight to a font that has a smaller point size, smaller pitch, or higher CPI.}In proportionally spaced fonts, each character uses a different amount of space. For example, an I takes less space than an m.[SHIFT-F7]v[F7]

12.7

EXERCISES

1. {Type the paragraph as shown.}[HOME][HOME][UP ARROW][ALT-F4].[CTRL-F8]sf[SHIFT-F7]v[F7]

2. H[CTRL-F8]sb2[RIGHT ARROW]O[ENTER][ENTER]E = mc[CTRL-F8]sp2[RIGHT ARROW][ENTER][ENTER]Subscripted text appears[CTRL-F8]sbbelow the normal text.[RIGHT ARROW][ENTER][ENTER]Superscripted text appears[CTRL-F8]spabove the normal text.[RIGHT ARROW][ENTER][ENTER][SHIFT-F7]v[F7]

3. [CTRL-F8]seYour printer prints Extra Large text like this.[RIGHT ARROW][ENTER][CTRL-F8]svYour printer prints Very Large text like this.[RIGHT ARROW][ENTER][CTRL-F8]slYour printer prints Large text like this.[RIGHT ARROW][ENTER][CTRL-F8]ssYour printer prints Small text like this.[RIGHT ARROW][ENTER][CTRL-F8]sfYour printer prints Fine text like this.[RIGHT ARROW][SHIFT-F7]v[F7]

MASTERY SKILLS CHECK

[12.6]

1. {Type the paragraph as shown.}[HOME][HOME][UP ARROW][CTRL-F8]f{Move the highlight to another font that has the same PT or pitch as the first one highlighted and has "italics" following it; if italic is not available, select another font.}

[12.7]

2. {Move the cursor to the "C" in "CPI."}[ALT-F4][RIGHT ARROW][RIGHT ARROW][RIGHT ARROW][CTRL-F8]sl{Move the cursor to the "P" in "PT."}[ALT-F4][RIGHT ARROW][RIGHT ARROW][CTRL-F8]sl{Move the cursor to the "P" in "Pitch."}[ALT-F4][CTRL-RIGHT ARROW][LEFT ARROW][CTRL-F8]sl

[12.1, 12.5]

3. [SHIFT-F7]n4[ENTER]tdf

[12.3]

4. [SHIFT-F7]cc{Type the number that appears next to "(Screen)."}[ENTER][F7]

5. [SHIFT-F7]n2[ENTER]thf[SHIFT-F7]n4[ENTER]tdf[SHIFT-F7]cr{Type the number that appears next to the print job that displays the "Text = Draft" message under Print Options.}[ENTER][F7]

[12.1, 12.4, 12.5]

INTEGRATED SKILLS CHECK

1. {Type the paragraph as shown.}[CTRL-F2]d{The original paragraph has no spelling mistakes; correct any typing mistakes that WordPerfect finds. Press any key to return to the document.}

[9.2]

2. [F10]wordwrap[ENTER][F10]fontadj[ENTER][F5][ENTER]{Move the highlight to the WORDWRAP file.}dy[F7]

[11.1, 11.4]

3. {Move to the "f" in "fine."}[ALT-F4][CTRL-RIGHT ARROW][LEFT ARROW][CTRL-F8]sf[RIGHT ARROW][ALT-F4][CTRL-RIGHT ARROW][LEFT ARROW][CTRL-F8]se[CTRL-RIGHT ARROW][CTRL-RIGHT ARROW][ALT-F4][CTRL-RIGHT ARROW][LEFT ARROW][CTRL-F8]ss[SHIFT-F7]v[F7]

[12.7]

4. [HOME][HOME][UP ARROW][CTRL-F8]f{Move the highlight to a font that has a smaller CPI, smaller pitch, or larger point size than the one originally highlighted.}[ENTER]{Move to the beginning of the last sentence.}[CTRL-F8]f{Move the highlight to a font that has a larger CPI, larger pitch, or smaller point size than the one originally highlighted.} [ENTER][SHIFT-F7]v[F7]

[12.6]

5. {Move to the end of the first sentence.}[CTRL-F7]fcChanging the font does not change WordPerfect's other default settings, such as margins and page size.[F7]

[10.3]

6. [SHIFT-F7]thn4f[SHIFT-F7]n3f[SHIFT-F7]tdn2f[SHIFT-F7]cr{Type the job number of the draft print request.}[ENTER]y[F7]

[12.1, 12.4, 12.5]

7. [F5][ENTER]{Move the highlight to the FONTADJ file.}[ENTER][F7][F7]

[11.8]

13 SKILLS CHECK

[10.3]

1. {Type the text as shown.}[ENTER]{Move the cursor to the first space after the period at the end of the first sentence.}[CTRL-F7]fcThese bonds were originally issued to upgrade production facilities.[F7]

[10.2]

2. [HOME][HOME][UP ARROW][SHIFT-F8]pfap{Type your name.}[F7][F7]

[10.2]

3. [SHIFT-F8]phapPage[SPACEBAR][CTRL-B][F7][F7]

[12.5]

4. [SHIFT-F7]td[F7]

[12.6, 12.7]

5. {If your printer has an italic base font:}[CTRL-F8]f{Move the highlight to a font that is followed by the word "Italic."}[ENTER][F7]yxtragain[ENTER]n {If your printer does not have an italic base font:}[ALT-F4][HOME][HOME][DOWN ARROW][CTRL-F8]ai[F7]yxtragain[ENTER]n

[11.2]

6. [F5][ENTER]onotes[ENTER]y[F7]

[11.1]

7. [F5][ENTER]{Move the highlight to XTRAGAIN.}cnotes[ENTER][F7]

[3.4]

8. [SHIFT-F7]dnotes\xtragain[ENTER][ENTER][F7]

[11.4]

9. [F5]notes[ENTER]{Move the highlight to XTRAGAIN.}dy[F7]

[11.4]

10. [F5][ENTER]{Move the highlight to the NOTES subdirectory.}dy[F7]

13.1 EXERCISES

1. Production used 1200 ball bearings to replace the machinery's worn ones.[ENTER][SHIFT-F3][SHIFT-F10]final[ENTER]{Move

the cursor to the end of the letter.}[CTRL-ENTER][F7][ENTER][ENTER]yy[F7][ENTER]skates[ENTER]n.

2. {Type the text as shown.}[ENTER][F10]stmt1[ENTER][SHIFT-F3][SHIFT-F10]stmt1[ENTER]{Move to the end of the paragraph, and type the text as shown.}[F10]stmt2[ENTER][F7]ny[F7]nn

3. [SHIFT-F10]stmt2[ENTER][SHIFT-F3][SHIFT-F10]stmt1[ENTER][F7]ny[F7]nn

EXERCISES   13.2

1. [CTRL-F3]w10[ENTER][CTRL-F3]w24[ENTER]

2. [CTRL-F3]w8[ENTER][CTRL-F3]w18[ENTER]

3. [SHIFT-F3][CTRL-F3]w14[ENTER]

4. [CTRL-F3]w8[ENTER]

EXERCISES   13.3

1. The discrepancy between the amount due and what the client believes is the proper amount is the sales tax of [SHIFT-F3][SHIFT-F10]final[ENTER][SHIFT-F3]$31.50.{Type the remaining text.}

2. The president, Amanda Williams, started with the company as chief production officer fifteen years ago.[SHIFT-F3] Ms. Williams' experience includes chief production officer, divisional vice president, production vice president, and president.[SHIFT-F3][SPACEBAR][SPACEBAR]After four years as production officer, she was promoted to divisional vice president of the appliance division.[F7]ypresidnt[ENTER]y [F7]ypresresu.me[ENTER]n

EXERCISES   13.4

1. [TAB]Peter Sullivan is production vice president. He has held this position for the past three years.[ENTER][TAB]

Paula Atchinson is the financial vice president. She has held this position for the past five years.[ENTER][UP ARROW][UP ARROW][UP ARROW][UP ARROW][CTRL-F4]pm[SHIFT-F3][ENTER]

2. Terry Kesley[ENTER]Kesley Associates[ENTER]496 Berry Avenue[ENTER]Newport, Rhode Island 03563[ENTER][ALT-F4][HOME][HOME][UP ARROW][CTRL-F4]bc[SHIFT-F3][ENTER]

MASTERY SKILLS CHECK

[13.1]   **1.** {Type the text as shown.}[SHIFT-F3]

[13.2]   **2.** [CTRL-F3]w12[ENTER]

[13.2]   **3.** [SHIFT-F3][CTRL-F3]w8[ENTER]

[13.4]   **4.** [HOME][UP ARROW][DOWN ARROW][CTRL-F4]pc[SHIFT-F3][ENTER]

[13.4]   **5.** [SHIFT-F3][CTRL-F4]pm[SHIFT-F3][ENTER]

INTEGRATED SKILLS CHECK

[11.1]   **1.** [TAB]The company leases most of its office space and mainframe computer equipment. It owns all of its production facilities.[ENTER][TAB]Total rental expense is $1,709,000 for the current year, $998,000 for 1988, and $923,000 for 1987.[ENTER][F10]leases[ENTER][F10]leases.bak [ENTER]

[13.1]   **2.** [SHIFT-F3][SHIFT-F10]leases.bak[ENTER]

              3. [HOME][DOWN ARROW]{Type the text as shown.}[ENTER][UP ARROW][CTRL-F4]pc[SHIFT-F3][ENTER]

[13.1]   **4.** [F7][ENTER]leases.new[ENTER]y

5. [SHIFT-F8]dsdNotes for financial statements[ENTER]sFor 1989   [11.6]
financial statements[ENTER]a{Type your name.}[ENTER]t{Type
your name.}[ENTER][F7]

6. [F5][ENTER]{Move the highlight to the LEASES.BAK   [11.4]
file.}dy[F7]

7. [HOME][HOME][UP ARROW][SHIFT-F8]phapFinancial Statement   [10.2]
Notes[F7][F7]

8. [SHIFT-F8]pfap{Type your name.}[F7][F7]   [10.2]

9. {Turn the printer off.}[SHIFT-F7]n2[ENTER]f[SHIFT-F7]{Type the job   [12.1,12.3]
number shown under "Current Job."}[F7]{Turn the printer
on.}

SKILLS CHECK   14

1. [SHIFT-F8]lt[CTRL-END]1.5[ENTER]4[ENTER][F7][F7]{Type the text as   [9.2]
shown, pressing the TAB key twice for the address and
closing lines.}[CTRL-F2]d{Spelling as shown is correct. Press
any key to end the spelling check when WordPerfect
displays the word count.}

2. {Move to the "M" in "Mark."}[ALT-F4]{Move to the line be-   [8.2]
low the address.}

3. [CTRL-F4]bc[SHIFT-F3][ENTER]   [13.4]

4. [SHIFT-F3][CTRL-F3]w12[ENTER]   [13.1, 13.2]

5. [F10]request[ENTER]   [2.2]

6. [SHIFT-F7]n2[ENTER]f   [12.1]

7. [SHIFT-F7]f[SHIFT-F7]f[SHIFT-F7]cc*y[F7]   [12.1, 12.3]

[1.4, 9.2]   **8.** {Move the cursor to the blank line between the letter
body and the closing.}[TAB]I have enclosed a list of the
sales representatives who will be attending the forum.
[ENTER][HOME][HOME][DOWN ARROW][CTRL-ENTER]Jim Styverson[ENTER]
Karen Acermann[ENTER]Julie Greenlowe[ENTER]Paul Hatterfield[ENTER][CTRL-F2]p33333{Press any key.}

[10.2]   **9.** {Move the cursor to the top of the page.}[SHIFT-F8]
phapForum Attendees[F7][F7]

[11.1]   **10.** [F5][ENTER]{Move to the REQUEST filename.}cletter.bk
[ENTER][F7]

[10.2, 13.4]   **11.** [SHIFT-F3][SHIFT-F8]phapBooth Assignments[F7][F7][SHIFT-F3][ALT-
F4][HOME][HOME][DOWN ARROW][CTRL-F4]bc[SHIFT-F3][HOME][HOME][DOWN
ARROW][ENTER]

[5.4]   **12.** [SHIFT-F8]lt[HOME][LEFT ARROW][CTRL-END]4[ENTER][F7][F7][END][TAB]8:00 -
10:00[DOWN ARROW][TAB]10:00 - 1:00[DOWN ARROW][TAB]1:00 -
3:00[DOWN ARROW][TAB]3:00 - 5:30

[12.1, 12.4]   **13.** [SHIFT-F7]n1drequest[ENTER][ENTER]drequest[ENTER][ENTER]p[SHIFT-F7]
cr{Type the number of the "(Screen)" print job.}[ENTER]
[F7]

[2.2, 11.5]   **14.** [F10]times[ENTER][F5][ENTER]{Move the highlight to the TIMES
filename.}mbooth[ENTER][F7]

[11.7]   **15.** [F5][ENTER]weKaren[ENTER]{LETTER.BK and BOOTH will be
marked with asterisks; others may also be.}[F7]

[11.8]   **16.** [F7]ny[F7]nn[F5][ENTER]{Move the highlight to the BOOTH
filename.}[ENTER]{View the file.}[F7][F7]

[11.6]   **17.** [SHIFT-F10]booth[ENTER][SHIFT-F8]dsd{Type a descriptive filename.}[ENTER]a{Type an author name.}[ENTER]t{Type a
typist name.}[ENTER][F7]

18. {if you have a hard disk}[F5]=\[ENTER][ENTER][F7]{if you are using floppy disks}[F5]a:[ENTER][F7] [11.3]

19. {if you have a hard disk}[F5][ENTER]otrdeshow[ENTER]y[F7] [11.2, 11.4]
[F5][ENTER]{Move the highlight to the TRDESHOW subdirectory.}dy[F7][F5]=wp50[ENTER][F1]{if you are using floppy disks}[F5][ENTER]o\trdeshow[ENTER]y[F7][F5][ENTER]{Move the highlight to the TRDESHOW subdirectory.}dy[F7]

20. [SHIFT-F8]pfap{Type today's date.}[ALT-F6]Page[SPACEBAR][CTRL- [10.2, 13.2]
B][F7][F7][F7][ENTER][ENTER]yn[CTRL-F3]w24[ENTER]

21. [SHIFT-F10]wp{wp}en.sup[ENTER]{Move the cursor to [9.5]
"Acermann."}[CTRL-END][DEL]{Move the cursor to
"Greenlowe."}[CTRL-END][DEL]{Move the cursor to
"Hatterfield."}[CTRL-END][DEL]{Move the cursor to
"Julie."}[CTRL-END][DEL]{Move the cursor to "Styverson."}
[CTRL-END][DEL][F7][ENTER][ENTER]yn

EXERCISES   14.1

1. B. J. Smith[F9]231-46-4232[F9][SHIFT-F9]eCarroll Lawrence
[F9]564-90-5327[F9][SHIFT-F9]e{Follow the same pattern to en-
ter the last two records.}

2. [SHIFT-F10]names[ENTER][HOME][HOME][DOWN ARROW]{Type the text
as shown, pressing F9 to end the first, second, third,
fifth, sixth, and seventh lines.}[SHIFT-F9]e

3. {Type your name.}[F9]{Type your title.}[F9]{Type your
company's name.}[F9]{Type your street address.}[ENTER]
{Type your city, state, and ZIP code.}[F9]{Type your so-
cial security number.}[F9]{Type your first name.}[F9][SHIFT-
F9]e[F10][ENTER]y

14.2   EXERCISES

1. The Association of Computer Graphic Artists wishes to thank[SHIFT-F9]f1[ENTER]from[SHIFT-F9]f3[ENTER]for his or her assistance with the Taking Computer Graphics One Step Further forum.[ENTER][F7][ENTER]thanks[ENTER]n

2. [SHIFT-F9]f1[ENTER][ENTER][SHIFT-F9]f2[ENTER][ENTER][SHIFT-F9]f3[ENTER] [ENTER][SHIFT-F9]f4[ENTER][ENTER][ENTER]Dear[SPACEBAR][SHIFT-F9]f6 [ENTER],[ENTER][ENTER]{Type the paragraph as shown.}[SHIFT-F9]f3[ENTER][ENTER][SHIFT-F9]f4[ENTER][ENTER][SHIFT-F9]f5[ENTER][ENTER] Contact:[TAB][SHIFT-F9]f1[ENTER][ENTER][TAB][TAB][SHIFT-F9]f2[ENTER] [ENTER]{Type the last paragraph and the closing.}[F7] [ENTER]cards[ENTER]n

14.3   EXERCISES

1. [CTRL-F9]mthanks[ENTER]names[ENTER][F10]thanks.out[ENTER]

2. [CTRL-F9]mcards[ENTER]names[ENTER][F10]cards.out[ENTER]

14.4   EXERCISES

1. [SHIFT-F7]dthanks.out[ENTER][ENTER]

2. [SHIFT-F7]dcards.out[ENTER][ENTER]

MASTERY SKILLS CHECK

[14.1]

1. Karen Simon[F9]34220 Euclid Avenue[F9]Cleveland, OH 44134[F9][SHIFT-F9]eJim Darcy[F9]12353 Carnegie Avenue [F9]Lakewood, OH 44116[F9][SHIFT-F9]e[F10]names2[ENTER]

2. [SHIFT-F9]f1[ENTER][ENTER][SHIFT-F9]f2[ENTER][ENTER][SHIFT-F9]f3[ENTER]   [14.2, 14.3, 14.4]
[F7][ENTER]lbls[ENTER]n[CTRL-F9]mlbls[ENTER]names2[ENTER][SHIFT-F7]f

3. [SHIFT-F10]names2[ENTER][DOWN ARROW][DOWN ARROW][DOWN ARROW]   [14.1]
Karen[F9][DOWN ARROW][DOWN ARROW][DOWN ARROW][DOWN ARROW]
Jim[F9][F7][ENTER][ENTER]y[ENTER]

4. [SHIFT-F9]f1[ENTER][ENTER][SHIFT-F9]f2[ENTER][ENTER][SHIFT-F9]f3[ENTER]   [14.2, 14.3, 14.4]
[ENTER][ENTER]Dear[SHIFT-F9]f4[ENTER],[ENTER][ENTER]{Type the text
as shown.}[F7][ENTER]photos[ENTER]n[CTRL-F9]mphotos[ENTER]
names2[ENTER][SHIFT-F7]f

5. [SHIFT-F10]photos[ENTER]{Move to the "w" in "we."}[SHIFT-F9]   [14.2, 14.3, 14.4]
f4[ENTER],[SPACEBAR][F7][ENTER][ENTER]y[ENTER][CTRL-F9]mphotos
[ENTER]names2[ENTER][SHIFT-F7]f

INTEGRATED SKILLS CHECK

1. Thomas Douglas[F9]Dept. Manager, Accounting[F9]X3963   [14.1]
[F9][SHIFT-F9]eTanya Smith[F9]Dept. Manager, Data Processing[F9]X3959[F9][SHIFT-F9]e[F7][ENTER]names.two[ENTER][ENTER]

2. Memo[ENTER]To:[TAB][TAB][SHIFT-F9]f1[ENTER][ENTER][TAB][SHIFT-F9]f2   [14.2]
[ENTER][ENTER][TAB][SHIFT-F9]f3[ENTER][ENTER]{Type the remainder of
the memo as shown, including the date and your name
where indicated.}

3. [PGUP][SHIFT-F6]   [4.6, 4.7]

4. [END][ENTER][ESC]65-   [1.4]

5. [F10]smokers[ENTER][F7]nn   [1.3, 2.2]

6. [CTRL-F9]msmokers[ENTER]names.two[ENTER]   [14.3]

7. [SHIFT-F7]n2[ENTER]f   [12.1, 14.4]

[1.3, 2.3, 13.1, 13.2]

8. [F7]n[ENTER][SHIFT-F10]names.two[ENTER][SHIFT-F3][SHIFT-F10]smokers [ENTER][CTRL-F3]w12[ENTER]

15 SKILLS CHECK

[5.4]

1. [SHIFT-F8]lt[HOME][LEFT ARROW][CTRL-END]1.5[ENTER]2[ENTER]4[ENTER][F7][F7] [SHIFT-F8]lt[CTRL-END]0,.5[F7][F7]

[4.1, 4.2]

2. We have written several times to inquire about the status of[F6]order number 98754[F6]. Please check the status of the backorder items. If you are unable to fill the remainder of the order within[F8]10 days[F8], please notify us so that we can contact other suppliers.[ENTER]

[1.4]

3. 150[ENTER][SPACEBAR]50[ENTER]100[ENTER][ESC]3-[ENTER]300[ENTER]

[4.2, 12.1]

4. You can use an[F6]'s[F6] to create the plural of letters,numbers, symbols, and words. For example, you could write that there are four[F6]s's[F6]and four[F6]i's[F6]in[F6]Mississippi[F6].[SHIFT-F7]n2[ENTER]f

[8.4]

5. Errors, like straws, upon the surface flow;[ENTER]He who would search for pearls, must dive below.[ENTER][ENTER][TAB] [TAB][TAB][TAB]John Dryden[ENTER][ALT-F4][PGUP][CTRL-F4]bc[ENTER] [CTRL-F4]rb

[12.1]

6. [SHIFT-F7]n1[ENTER][F7]

15.1 EXERCISES

1. [SHIFT-F8]lt[CTRL-END]3[ENTER]d[F7][F7][ALT-F7]mSalaries[TAB]50,000 [ENTER]Benefits[TAB]8,500 [ENTER] Travel[TAB]18,000[ENTER] Rent[TAB]120,000[ENTER][TAB] + [ALT-F7]a[ALT-F7]m

2. {Move the cursor to the 5 in the "Benefits" amount.} [INS]9[INS][ALT-F7]a

EXERCISES ———————————— 15.2

1. [SHIFT-F8]lt[CTRL-END]1.5[ENTER]3.7[ENTER]d4.7[ENTER]d[F7][F7][ALT F7]
   e123[DOWN ARROW][DOWN ARROW][LEFT ARROW][LEFT ARROW]00[F7]
   mMachine repairs[ENTER][ENTER]Model 5210[ENTER][TAB]Factory
   1[TAB]10[ENTER][TAB]Factory 2[TAB]5[ENTER]Total Repairs 5210
   [TAB] + [ENTER][ENTER]Model 6511[ENTER][TAB]Factory 1[TAB]48[ENTER]
   [TAB]Factory 2[TAB]9[ENTER]Total Repairs 6511 [TAB] + [ENTER]
   [ENTER]TOTAL ALL MODELS[TAB][TAB] = [ALT- F7]a{The subtotals should be 15 and 57; the total should be 72.}[ALT-
   F7]m

2. EMPLOYEE BENEFIT PARTICIPATION[ENTER][SHIFT-F8]lt
   [CTRL-END]1.3[ENTER]1.5[ENTER]4.5[ENTER]d5.5[ENTER]d6.5[ENTER]d
   [F7][F7][ALT-F7]e11233[DOWN ARROW][DOWN ARROW] [LEFT ARROW][LEFT
   ARROW][LEFT ARROW]000[F7]m[TAB]Employees in Savings Plan
   [ENTER][TAB][TAB]Thrift[TAB]500[ENTER][TAB][TAB]S&L[TAB]250[ENTER]
   [TAB][TAB]Bonds[TAB]250[ENTER][TAB]Total in Savings[TAB] + [ENTER]
   [TAB]Employees in Stock Option Plan[ENTER][TAB][TAB]Plan
   A[TAB]100[ENTER][TAB][TAB]Plan B[TAB]100[ENTER][TAB]Total in
   Stocks[TAB] + [ENTER][TAB]Total Employees in Investment
   Plans[TAB] = [ENTER][ENTER][TAB]Employees in Medical Plan
   [ENTER][TAB][TAB]White Cross[TAB]500[ENTER][TAB][TAB]Cheap Docs
   [TAB]500[ENTER][TAB]Total Medical[TAB] + [ENTER][TAB]Employees in
   Life Insurance Plan[ENTER][TAB][TAB]Quick Save[TAB]100[ENTER]
   [TAB][TAB]High Risk[TAB]100[ENTER][TAB]Total Life[TAB] + [ENTER]
   [TAB]Total Employees in Insurance Plans[TAB] = [ENTER][ENTER]
   TOTAL NUMBERS IN BENEFIT PLANS[TAB][TAB][TAB]
   *[ALT-F7]a[ALT-F7]m

MASTERY SKILLS CHECK ————————————

1. [SHIFT-F8]lt[CTRL-END]2.8[ENTER]d[F7][F7][ALT + F7]e[DOWN ARROW][DOWN   [15.1]
   ARROW]0[F7]mHEADCOUNT BY LOCATION[ENTER][ENTER]
   Chicago[TAB]120[ENTER]Dallas[TAB]38[ENTER]Denver[TAB]105

[ENTER]New York[TAB]302[ENTER][ENTER]TOTAL[TAB] + [ALT-F7]a[ALT-F7]m

[15.1]

2. {Move the cursor to the "T" in "TOTAL."}U.S.[SPACEBAR] [ALT-F3]{Move the cursor to the [Math Off] code.}[ALT-F3] [ENTER][ENTER]Paris[TAB]82[ENTER]London[TAB]106[ENTER]Lisbon [TAB]34[ENTER]Frankfort[TAB]192[ENTER][ENTER]FOREIGN TOTAL [TAB] + [ALT-F7]a

[15.2]

3. [SHIFT-F8]lt[CTRL-END]1.5[ENTER]3.5[ENTER]d4.5[ENTER]d[F7][F7][ALT-F7] e123[DOWN ARROW][DOWN ARROW][LEFT ARROW][LEFT ARROW]00[F7] mProduct 1 Sales[ENTER][TAB]Jim[TAB]12,500[ENTER][TAB]Fred [TAB]38,900[ENTER][TAB]Harry[TAB]23,500[ENTER]Total Product 1[TAB] + [ENTER][ENTER]Product 2 Sales[ENTER][TAB]Jim[TAB]23,450 [ENTER][TAB]Fred[TAB]56,750[ENTER][TAB] Harry [TAB]78,900[ENTER] Total Product 2[TAB] + [ENTER][ENTER]Total Products 1 & 2[TAB] [TAB] = [ALT-F7]a[ALT-F7]m

[15.2]

4. [SHIFT-F8]lt[CTRL-END]3.7[ENTER]d4.7[ENTER]d5.7[ENTER]d[F7][F7][ALT-F7] e233[F7]mOffice Supplies[ENTER][TAB]10.00[ENTER][TAB]15.50 [ENTER][TAB]25.60[ENTER]Total Supplies[TAB] + [ENTER]Office Furniture[ENTER][TAB]345.00[ENTER][TAB]545.00[ENTER]Total Furniture[TAB] + [ENTER]Total Office Products[TAB][TAB] = [ENTER][ENTER]Coffee Supplies[ENTER][TAB]25.00[ENTER][TAB]15.80 [ENTER]Total Coffee[TAB] + [ENTER]Paper Products[ENTER][TAB] 115.00[ENTER]Total Paper[TAB] + [ENTER]Total Miscellaneous [TAB][TAB] = [ENTER][ENTER]TOTAL PURCHASES[TAB][TAB][TAB] *[ALT-F7]a[ALT-F7]m

INTEGRATED SKILLS CHECK

[4.3, 5.5, 10.2]

1. {Type the text as shown.}[ENTER][HOME][HOME][UP ARROW][SHIFT-F8]phapABC COMPANY[ALT-F6][SHIFT-F5]t[F7]fap[SHIFT-F6]Page [SPACEBAR][CTRL + B][F7][F7]

2. [PGDN][ENTER][SHIFT-F8]lt[CTRL-END]3[ENTER]3.5[ENTER]d4.5[ENTER] 5[ENTER]d[F7][F7][ALT-F7]e121[DOWN ARROW][DOWN ARROW][LEFT

ARROW][LEFT ARROW]0[RIGHT ARROW]0[F7]m[TAB][F8]Last[TAB][TAB]This   [4.1, 5.4, 15.1]
[ENTER][TAB]Year[TAB][TAB]Year[F8][ENTER][ENTER]Travel[TAB][TAB]
52,900[TAB][TAB]86,900[ENTER]Consultants[TAB][TAB]104,585
[TAB][TAB]190,800[ENTER]Entertainment[TAB][TAB]3,900[TAB][TAB]
9,800[ENTER]Supplies[TAB][TAB]1,200[TAB][TAB]15,900[ENTER]Phone
[TAB][TAB]25,000[TAB][TAB]49,000[ENTER][ENTER]TOTALS[TAB][TAB] +
[TAB][TAB] + [ALT-F7]a

3. [ALT-F7]m[ENTER][SHIFT-F8]lt[CTRL-END]1,.5[ENTER][F7][F7][TAB]{Type the   [5.4, 15.1]
text as shown.}[ENTER]

4. [SHIFT-F7]n2[ENTER]f   [12.1]

SKILLS CHECK   16

1. [F5]\[ENTER]oaccount[ENTER]y[F7]   [11.2]

2. [F5][ENTER]oletters[ENTER]y[F7]   [11.2]

3. [ESC]55*   [1.4]

4. [ENTER][SHIFT-F6][F6][F8]{Type the text as shown.}[F8][F6][ENTER]   [4.1, 4.2, 4.3]

5. [SHIFT-F7]v   [3.3]

6. {Move the cursor to the first asterisk.}[CTRL-F4]pm{Move the   [8.2]
cursor to the line below the text.}[ENTER]

EXERCISES   16.1

1. {Type the first paragraph.}[ENTER][CTRL-F3]12[ESC]40[RIGHT ARROW]
[F7][RIGHT ARROW][ENTER]{Type the second paragraph.}

2. [CTRL-F3]ll[DOWN ARROW][DOWN ARROW][DOWN ARROW]2[RIGHT ARROW]
[RIGHT ARROW][RIGHT ARROW][RIGHT ARROW][RIGHT ARROW][RIGHT ARROW]
[DOWN ARROW][DOWN ARROW][DOWN ARROW][DOWN ARROW][DOWN ARROW]
[F7][SHIFT-F7]v12[F7]

16.2   EXERCISES

1. First Name:[SPACEBAR][CTRL-F3]ll[DOWN ARROW][DOWN ARROW][DOWN
ARROW][ESC]15[RIGHT ARROW][UP ARROW][UP ARROW][UP ARROW][ESC]15
[LEFT ARROW][F7][END][DOWN ARROW][DOWN ARROW][DOWN ARROW][ENTER]
Last Name:[SPACEBAR][CTRL-F3]l[DOWN ARROW][DOWN ARROW][DOWN
ARROW][ESC]15[RIGHT ARROW][UP ARROW][UP ARROW][UP ARROW][ESC]15[LEFT
ARROW][F7]{This makes boxes 3 rows by 15 columns. Your
boxes may be a different size.}

2. [CTRL-F3]l[ESC]14[RIGHT ARROW][ESC]5[DOWN ARROW][ESC]14[LEFT ARROW]
[ESC]5[UP ARROW][F7][ALT-F4][PGDN][CTRL-F4]rc[PGUP][END][TAB][TAB][ENTER]
[PGDN][ENTER][ENTER][ENTER][TAB][TAB][TAB][TAB][TAB][CTRL-F4]rr[ESC]7[RIGHT
ARROW][CTRL-F3]l[ESC]4[UP ARROW][ESC]7[LEFT ARROW][UP ARROW][UP ARROW]
[UP ARROW][ESC]11[LEFT ARROW][F7]

16.3   EXERCISES

1. [CTRL-F3]l2[ESC]6[RIGHT ARROW]5[ESC]6[LEFT ARROW][F7]

2. [CTRL-F3]ll[ESC]4[DOWN ARROW][ESC]5[RIGHT ARROW][ESC]4[UP ARROW]
[ESC]5[LEFT ARROW][RIGHT ARROW][RIGHT ARROW]5[RIGHT ARROW][DOWN
ARROW][DOWN ARROW][DOWN ARROW][DOWN ARROW][LEFT ARROW][F7]

16.4   EXERCISES

1. [CTRL-F3]l2[ESC]4[DOWN ARROW][ESC]15[RIGHT ARROW][ESC]4[UP ARROW][ESC]
15[LEFT ARROW]6[ESC]20[RIGHT ARROW]2[DOWN ARROW][DOWN ARROW]
[ESC]12[RIGHT ARROW][UP ARROW][UP ARROW][ESC]12[LEFT ARROW][F7]

2. [CTRL-F3]11[ESC]10[RIGHT ARROW]6[ESC]5[LEFT ARROW]1[ESC]10[DOWN ARROW]6[ESC]5[LEFT ARROW]1[ESC]10[RIGHT ARROW]6[ESC]10[RIGHT ARROW] 1[ESC]10[RIGHT ARROW]6[ESC]5[LEFT ARROW]1[ESC]10[UP ARROW]6[ESC]5 [LEFT ARROW]1[ESC]10[RIGHT ARROW]6[ESC]10[RIGHT ARROW]1[ESC]10[RIGHT ARROW]6[ESC]5[LEFT ARROW]1[ESC]10[DOWN ARROW]6[ESC]5[LEFT ARROW]1 [ESC]10[RIGHT ARROW][F7]

EXERCISES   16.5

1. [CTRL-F3]149[SHIFT-F3][ESC]10[DOWN ARROW][ESC]20[RIGHT ARROW][ESC]10[UP ARROW][ESC]20[LEFT ARROW][F7]

2. [CTRL-F3]144[ESC]30[RIGHT ARROW][F7]

EXERCISES   16.6

1. {Answer assumes that you draw the boxes and then type the text. This answer creates boxes that are 3 rows by 20 columns. If you use different numbers, replace the 3 and the 20 in the answers with the numbers that you use.} [TAB][TAB][TAB][TAB][TAB][CTRL-F3]12[ESC]3[DOWN ARROW][ESC]20[RIGHT ARROW][ESC]3[UP ARROW][ESC]20[LEFT ARROW][F7][DOWN ARROW][DOWN ARROW][DOWN ARROW][END][ENTER][ENTER][ENTER][HOME][UP ARROW][CTRL-RIGHT ARROW][ALT-F4][DOWN ARROW][DOWN ARROW][DOWN ARROW][END] [CTRL-F4]rc[DOWN ARROW][DOWN ARROW][DOWN ARROW][ENTER][ALT-F4] [DOWN ARROW][DOWN ARROW][DOWN ARROW][END][CTRL-F4]rc[UP ARROW][UP ARROW][UP ARROW][END][SPACEBAR][ENTER][ALT-F4][DOWN ARROW][DOWN ARROW][DOWN ARROW][END][CTRL-F4]rc[UP ARROW][UP ARROW][UP ARROW] [END][SPACEBAR][ENTER][ESC]10[RIGHT ARROW][CTRL-F3]11[UP ARROW][ESC] 43[LEFT ARROW][DOWN ARROW][UP ARROW][ESC]21[RIGHT ARROW][DOWN ARROW][UP ARROW][UP ARROW][UP ARROW][F7][INS][UP ARROW][UP ARROW] [CTRL-LEFT ARROW][RIGHT ARROW][RIGHT ARROW]Root Directory[DOWN ARROW][DOWN ARROW][DOWN ARROW][DOWN ARROW][DOWN ARROW][DOWN ARROW][CTRL-LEFT ARROW][CTRL-LEFT ARROW][CTRL-LEFT ARROW][RIGHT ARROW][RIGHT ARROW]BUDGET[CTRL-RIGHTARROW][CTRL-RIGHT ARROW]

[RIGHT ARROW][RIGHT ARROW]PRODUCT[CTRL-RIGHT ARROW][CTRL-RIGHT ARROW][RIGHT ARROW][RIGHT ARROW]REPORTS[INS]

2. [CTRL-F3]l1[ESC]4[DOWN ARROW][ESC]50[RIGHT ARROW][ESC]4[UP ARROW][ESC]50[LEFT ARROW][F7][INS][DOWN ARROW][RIGHT ARROW][RIGHT ARROW]All of the paintings displayed in this[DOWN ARROW] [CTRL-LEFT ARROW][RIGHT ARROW][RIGHT ARROW] restaurant are for sale on a consignment[DOWN ARROW][CTRL-LEFT ARROW] [RIGHT ARROW][RIGHT ARROW]basis. For more details, see the manager. [INS]

MASTERY SKILLS CHECK

[16.1, 16.3, 16.4]   1. [CTRL-F3]l1[ESC]40[RIGHT ARROW]6[ESC]20[LEFT ARROW]5[ESC]3[RIGHT ARROW][F7][F7]nn

[16.1, 16.2, 16.6]   2. [SPACEBAR][SPACEBAR][SPACEBAR][CTRL-F3]l1[ESC]3[DOWN ARROW][ESC] 10[RIGHT ARROW][ESC]3[UP ARROW][ESC]10[LEFT ARROW][ESC]3[DOWN ARROW][ESC]5[RIGHT ARROW][DOWN ARROW][ESC]5[LEFT ARROW][ESC]5[DOWN ARROW][ESC]10[RIGHT ARROW][ESC]5[UP ARROW][ESC]5[LEFT ARROW] 6[ESC]5[DOWN ARROW]1[DOWN ARROW][ESC]5[RIGHT ARROW][ESC]3[DOWN ARROW][ESC]10[LEFT ARROW][ESC]3[UP ARROW][ESC]5[RIGHT ARROW][F7] [INS][ESC]9[UP ARROW][LEFT ARROW][LEFT ARROW][LEFT ARROW]Receive[ESC] 7[LEFT ARROW][DOWN ARROW]Invoice[DOWN ARROW][DOWN ARROW][DOWN ARROW][ESC]7[LEFT ARROW]Compare[DOWN ARROW][ESC]7[LEFT ARROW] to[DOWN ARROW][LEFT ARROW][LEFT ARROW]Purchase[ESC]8[LEFT ARROW][DOWN ARROW]Order[ESC]5[LEFT ARROW][DOWN ARROW][DOWN ARROW][DOWN ARROW]Prepare[ESC]7[LEFT ARROW][DOWN ARROW] Voucher[INS]

[16.5]   3. [CTRL-F3]l49:[F7]

[16.1, 16.4]   4. [ENTER][SPACEBAR][SPACEBAR]Construction Schedule[TAB][TAB] Dates[ENTER][ENTER][SPACEBAR][SPACEBAR]Start renovation[ENTER] [ENTER][SPACEBAR][SPACEBAR]Start interior remodeling[ENTER] [ENTER][SPACEBAR][SPACEBAR]Start repaving parking lot[ENTER] [ENTER][SPACEBAR][SPACEBAR]End repaving parking lot[ENTER]

[ENTER][SPACEBAR][SPACEBAR]End interior remodeling[ENTER][ENTER]
[SPACEBAR][SPACEBAR]End renovation[ENTER][ESC]5[UP ARROW][END]
[CTRL-F3]11[ESC]20[RIGHT ARROW][UP ARROW][UP ARROW][ESC]18[LEFT
ARROW]6[UP ARROW][UP ARROW][LEFT ARROW]1[ESC]21[RIGHT ARROW][ESC]
6[DOWN ARROW][ESC]23[LEFT ARROW]6[DOWN ARROW][DOWN ARROW][ESC]
9[LEFT ARROW]1[ESC]34[RIGHT ARROW][ESC]10[UP ARROW][ESC]32[LEFT
ARROW][F7]

5. [CTRL-F3]16[ESC]17[RIGHT ARROW]5[ESC]5[RIGHT ARROW][DOWN ARROW]   [16.3, 16.4]
[DOWN ARROW][ESC]5[LEFT ARROW][DOWN ARROW][DOWN ARROW][ESC]5
[RIGHT ARROW][DOWN ARROW][DOWN ARROW][ESC]5[LEFT ARROW][DOWN
ARROW][DOWN ARROW][ESC]5[RIGHT ARROW][DOWN ARROW][DOWN ARROW]
[ESC]5[LEFT ARROW][F7][ESC]10[UP ARROW][INS][RIGHT ARROW]5/1[DOWN
ARROW][DOWN ARROW][ESC]3[LEFT ARROW]6/15[DOWN ARROW][DOWN
ARROW][ESC]4[LEFT ARROW]7/1[DOWN ARROW][DOWN ARROW][ESC]3[LEFT
ARROW]7/31[DOWN ARROW][DOWN ARROW][ESC]4[LEFT ARROW]8/30
[DOWN ARROW][DOWN ARROW][ESC]4[LEFT ARROW]9/30[INS]

6. [PGUP]{If you do not have a blank line above the construc-   [16.5]
tion schedule, press ENTER and the UP ARROW key.}[CTRL-F3]13
[ESC]14[DOWN ARROW][ESC]52[RIGHT ARROW][ESC]14[UP ARROW][ESC]51
[LEFT ARROW][F7]

INTEGRATED SKILLS CHECK

1. Last name:[SPACEBAR][CTRL-F3]11[DOWN ARROW][DOWN ARROW][ESC]   [16.2]
20[RIGHT ARROW][UP ARROW][UP ARROW][ESC]20[LEFT ARROW][F7][DOWN
ARROW][DOWN ARROW][END][ENTER]First name:[SPACEBAR][CTRL-F3]
1[DOWN ARROW][DOWN ARROW][ESC]20[RIGHT ARROW][UP ARROW][UP
ARROW][ESC]20[LEFT ARROW][F7][DOWN ARROW][DOWN ARROW][END][ENTER]
Department:[SPACEBAR][CTRL-F3]1[DOWN ARROW][DOWN ARROW][ESC]
20[RIGHT ARROW][UP ARROW][UP ARROW][ESC]20[LEFT ARROW][F7][DOWN
ARROW][DOWN ARROW][END][ENTER]Years with the company:
[SPACEBAR][CTRL-F3]1[DOWN ARROW][DOWN ARROW][ESC]20[RIGHT ARROW]
[UP ARROW][UP ARROW][ESC]20[LEFT ARROW][F7][DOWN ARROW][DOWN
ARROW][END][ENTER]

[4.1, 16.1]   **2.** [F8]Acme's Main Product Line[F8][ENTER]Solder[ENTER]Silver necklaces[ENTER]Silver flatware[ENTER][UP ARROW][END][CTRL-F3] 11[ESC]10[RIGHT ARROW][ESC]3[UP ARROW][UP ARROW][ESC]19[LEFT ARROW]6[DOWN ARROW][ESC]10[RIGHT ARROW]1[ESC]9[RIGHT ARROW]

[11.4]   **3.** [F5]\[ENTER]{Move the highlight to the ACCOUNT subdirectory.}dy[F7]

[11.4]   **4.** [F5][ENTER]{Move the highlight to the LETTERS subdirectory.}dy[F7]

[4.2, 4.3, 16.2, 16.5, 16.6]   **5.** [CTRL-F3]149∗[ESC]10[DOWN ARROW][ESC]50[RIGHT ARROW][ESC]10[UP ARROW][ESC]50[LEFT ARROW][F7][INS][DOWN ARROW][DOWN ARROW][RIGHT ARROW][RIGHT ARROW][TAB][TAB][F6]Clark Corporation is Moving [DOWN ARROW][DOWN ARROW][CTRL-LEFT ARROW][RIGHT ARROW][RIGHT ARROW]On Friday the 23rd, Clark Corporation is[DOWN ARROW][CTRL-LEFT ARROW][RIGHT ARROW][RIGHT ARROW]closing its Lakewood offices. Its new[DOWN ARROW][CTRL-LEFT ARROW][RIGHT ARROW] [RIGHT ARROW] headquarters are in Barlow, Florida. It is [DOWN ARROW][CTRL-LEFT ARROW] [RIGHT ARROW][RIGHT ARROW] moving there to move closer to its prospering[DOWN ARROW][CTRL-LEFT ARROW] [RIGHT ARROW][RIGHT ARROW]land-development subsidiary.[INS]

[4.7]   **6.** [PGUP][ALT-F4][PGDN][SHIFT-F6]y

17   SKILLS CHECK

[4.7]   **1.** {Type the text as shown.}[ENTER][HOME][HOME][UP ARROW][CTRL-RIGHT ARROW][ALT-F4][CTRL-RIGHT ARROW][CTRL-RIGHT ARROW][CTRL-RIGHT ARROW][CTRL-RIGHT ARROW][LEFT ARROW][F8][F10]graphbox[ENTER]

[13.3]   **2.** [SHIFT-F3][SHIFT-F10]graphbox[ENTER][HOME][HOME][DOWN ARROW][ENTER] {Type the text as shown.}

3. [HOME][HOME][UP ARROW][SHIFT-F8]phapWordPerfect's Graphics   [10.2]
Features[F7][F7]

4. {Move to the beginning of the word "captions."}[ALT-F4]   [4.7]
[CTRL-RIGHT ARROW][LEFT ARROW][F6]{Repeat the procedure for
each of the other two words.}

5. [SHIFT-F7]v[F7][SHIFT-F3][SHIFT-F7]v[F7]   [3.3, 13.3]

EXERCISES _____ 17.1

1. [ALT-F9]uc[F7]{Press ENTER 21 times.}

2. [ALT-F9]fc[F7]{Type the paragraph as shown.}

3. [ALT-F9]tc[F7][SHIFT-F7]v[F7]

4. [ALT-F9]bc[F7][ENTER][ENTER][ENTER][ENTER][ENTER][ALT-F9]fc[F7][SHIFT-F7]
v[F7]

5. [ALT-F9]tc[F7][ALT-F9]fc[F7]{Press ENTER 22 times.}[SHIFT-F7]v[F7]

EXERCISES _____ 17.2

1. [ALT-F9]tce[F8]Project[F8][TAB][TAB][TAB][F8]Date[F8][ENTER]Systems
analysis[TAB]5/1[ENTER]Order equipment[TAB][TAB]6/15[ENTER]
Design software[TAB][TAB]7/1[ENTER]Test software[TAB][TAB]
7/31[ENTER]Implement software[TAB]8/30[ENTER]Evaluation
[TAB][TAB][TAB]9/30[ENTER][F7][F7][SHIFT-F7]v[F7]

2. {Type the paragraph as shown.}[F7][ENTER]picture[ENTER]n[ALT-
F9]bcfpicture[ENTER][F7][SHIFT-F7]v[F7]

3. [ALT-F9]tce{Type the text as shown, pressing ENTER after the
heading and after each step.}[F7][F7][SHIFT-F7]v[F7]

17.3   EXERCISES

{If your graphics images are not in the WordPerfect subdirectory, type a backslash, the subdirectory name, a backslash, and the filename where the answers provide only the filename.}

1. [ALT-F9]tcfmapsymbl.wpg[ENTER][F7][SHIFT-F7]v[F7]

2. [ALT-F9]bcfarrow1.wpg[ENTER][F7][SHIFT-F7]v[F7]

3. [ALT-F9]fcfborder.wpg[ENTER][F7][SHIFT-F7]v[F7]

4. [ALT-F9]ucfgavel.wpg[ENTER][F7][SHIFT-F7]v[F7]

17.4   EXERCISES

1. [ALT-F9]bcc[SPACEBAR]To be filled in later[F7][F7][SHIFT-F7]v[F7]

2. [ALT-F9]tceinsert Ms. Mitchell's picture here[F7]c[SPACEBAR] Susan Mitchell, President[F7][F7][SHIFT-F7]v[F7]

3. [ALT-F9]fcfphone.wpg[ENTER]c[SPACEBAR]When It Rings, We Answer[F7][F7][SHIFT-F7]v[F7]

4. [ALT-F9]fcfno1.wpg[ENTER]c[SPACEBAR]First in the Business[F7][F7] [SHIFT-F7]v[F7]

17.5   EXERCISES

1. [ALT-F9]bcv.4[ENTER][F7]{type the paragraph as shown.}[SHIFT-F7] v[F7]

2. [ALT-F9]fch1[F7][SHIFT-F7]v[F7]

3. [ALT-F9]ucfcheck.wpg[ENTER]sh5[ENTER][F7][SHIFT-F7]v[F7]

4. [ALT-F9]tce{Type the paragraph as shown.}[F7][F7][SHIFT-F7]v[F7] [ALT-F9]te1[ENTER]sw2.5[ENTER][F7][SHIFT-F7]v[F7][ALT-F9]te1[ENTER] sb3[ENTER]2[ENTER][F7][SHIFT-F7]v[F7]

5. [ALT-F9]fcfapplause.wpg[ENTER]sh4[ENTER]hc[F7][SHIFT-F7]v[F7]

EXERCISES   17.6

1. [ALT-F9]tcfarrow1.wpg[ENTER][F7][SHIFT-F7]v[F7][ALT-F9]te1[ENTER] fcheck.wpg[ENTER]y[F7][SHIFT-F7]v[F7]

2. [ALT-F9]bcfconfiden.wpg[ENTER][F7][SHIFT-F7]v[F7][ALT-F9]be1[ENTER] f[CTRL-END][ENTER]y[F7][SHIFT-F7]v[F7]

3. [ALT-F9]tc[F7][ALT-F3][LEFT ARROW][DEL][ALT-F3]

4. [ALT-F9]fcfnewspapr.wpg[ENTER][F7]{Press ENTER 19 times.}[ALT-F9]fcfpresent.wpg[ENTER][F7]{Press ENTER 25 times.}[HOME][HOME] [UP ARROW][ALT-F3][BACKSPACE][HOME][HOME][DOWN ARROW][F1]r[HOME] [HOME][UP ARROW]{Press DEL 19 times.}[SHIFT-F7]v[F7]

EXERCISES   17.7

1. {assumes that your printer can print graphics and text simultaneously}[ALT-F9]tcfand.wpg[ENTER][F7][SHIFT-F7]gdf

2. {assumes that your printer can print graphics and text simultaneously}[ALT-F9]bcfkey.wpg[ENTER][F7]{Type the paragraph as shown, allowing WordPerfect to wrap the text around the text box.}[SHIFT-F7]gmthf

3. {assumes that your printer can print graphics and text simultaneously}[ALT-F9]ucfquill.wpg[ENTER][F7]{Type the paragraph as shown, allowing WordPerfect to wrap the text around the user-defined box.}[SHIFT-F7]ghf

4. {assumes that your printer can print graphics and text simultaneously}[ALT-F9]fcfpencil.wpg[ENTER][F7][ALT-F9] fcfbook.wpg[ENTER][F7]{Type the paragraph as shown, allowing WordPerfect to wrap the text around the two figures.}[SHIFT-F7]gmf

MASTERY SKILLS CHECK

[17.1]	**1.** [ALT-F9]fc[F7][SHIFT-F7]v[F7]
[17.1, 17.5]	**2.** [ALT-F9]fchl[F7][SHIFT-F7]v[F7]
[17.3, 17.6]	**3.** [ALT-F9]fe1[ENTER]fquill.wpg[ENTER][F7][SHIFT-F7]v[F7]
[17.2, 17.6]	**4.** [ALT-F9]fe2[ENTER]e{Type the text as shown, pressing ENTER after the colon and after each author.}[F7][F7][SHIFT-F7]v[F7]
[17.6]	**5.** [ALT-F9]fe1[ENTER]fthinker.wpg[ENTER]y[F7][SHIFT-F7]v[F7]
[17.4]	**6.** [ALT-F9]fe1[ENTER]c[SPACEBAR]Rodin's[F8]The Thinker[F8][F7][F7][SHIFT-F7]v[F7]
[17.5]	**7.** [ALT-F9]fe1[ENTER]sh2[ENTER][F7][SHIFT-F7]v[F7]
[17.5]	**8.** [ALT-F9]fe2[ENTER]sw4[ENTER][F7][SHIFT-F7]v[F7]
[17.2, 17.6]	**9.** [ALT-F9]fe2[ENTER]e[DOWN ARROW][ENTER][DOWN ARROW][DOWN ARROW] [ENTER][DOWN ARROW][DOWN ARROW][ENTER][F7][F7][SHIFT-F7]v[F7] ·
[17.7]	**10.** [SHIFT-F7]tmghf[F7]nn
[17.3, 17.4, 17.5]	**11.** [ALT-F9]h1tcfarrow1.wpg[ENTER]c[SPACEBAR]Read This! It Is Important![F7][F7][SHIFT-F7]v[F7]

INTEGRATED SKILLS CHECK

[17.2]	**1.** {Type the paragraph as shown.}[F7]yimages[ENTER]n[ALT-F9] bcfimages[ENTER][F7]{Press ENTER 17 times.}[SHIFT-F7]v[F7]

2. [ALT-F9]tcfclock.wpg[ENTER]c[SPACEBAR]A stitch in time saves nine[F7][F7][SHIFT-F7]v[F7]   [17.3, 17.4]

3. [ALT-F9]te1[ENTER]sb4[ENTER]4[ENTER][F7][SHIFT-F7]v[F7]   [17.5]

4. [SHIFT-F3][SHIFT-F10]images[ENTER][DOWN ARROW][DOWN ARROW][DOWN ARROW][CTRL-F4]sd[F10][ENTER]y[SHIFT-F7]v[F7]   [13.3]

5. [SHIFT-F3][ALT-F9]be1[ENTER]f[ENTER]y[F7][SHIFT-F7]v[F7]   [13.3, 17.6]

6. [ALT-F9]be1[ENTER]e{Move to the "W" in "WordPerfect Made Easy."}[ALT-F4]y[F8][F7][F7][SHIFT-F7]v[F7]   [4.7, 17.6]

7. [SHIFT-F7]gdtdf[SHIFT-F7]v[F7]   [17.7]

8. [ALT-F3][HOME][HOME][DOWN ARROW][BACKSPACE][ALT-F3][SHIFT-F7]v[F7]   [17.6]

9. [ALT-F9]fcfannounce.wpg[ENTER][F7]{Press ENTER 19 times.} [SHIFT-F7]v[F7]   [17.3]

10. [ALT-F3][HOME][HOME][UP ARROW][BACKSPACE][HOME][HOME][DOWN ARROW] [F1]r[HOME][HOME][UP ARROW]{Press the DEL key until the [Figure:1;ANNOUNCE.WPG;] code is at the beginning of the document.}[ALT-F3][SHIFT-F7]v[F7]   [17.6]

11. [SHIFT-F8]phap[ALT-F9]ucfairplane.wpg[ENTER]hb[F7][F7][F7][SHIFT-F7]v[F7]   [10.2, 17.3, 17.5]

12. [SHIFT-F7]ghf[SHIFT-F7]v[F7]   [17.7]

SKILLS CHECK   18

1. [F4]{Type the paragraph as shown.}   [5.2]

2. [SHIFT-F4]{Type the paragraph.}   [5.2]

[5.4]

3. [SHIFT-F8]lt[CTRL-END]4[ENTER][F7][F7]Joe Jones[TAB]Accounting
[ENTER]Paul Balber[TAB]Finance[ENTER]Norlin Rugers[TAB]
Management[ENTER]Mary Rogers[TAB]Accounting[ENTER]

[5.1, 12.1]

4. [SHIFT-F8]lm2[ENTER]2[ENTER][F7]{Type the text as shown.}
[SHIFT-F7]n2[ENTER]f

18.1   EXERCISES

1. [CAPS LOCK]high school sports[ENTER][SHIFT-F5]o[ENTER][SPACEBAR]
[TAB]baseball[ENTER][SPACEBAR][TAB]football[ENTER][SPACEBAR]swim-
ming[ENTER][SPACEBAR][TAB]hockey[SHIFT-F5]o[CAPS LOCK][F7][ENTER]
sports[ENTER][ENTER]

2. [CAPS LOCK]breeds of dogs[CAPS LOCK][ENTER][SHIFT-F5]o[ENTER][F4]
Hounds[ENTER][TAB][F4]Greyhound[ENTER][TAB][F4]Whippet
[ENTER][F4]Sporting Dogs[ENTER][TAB][F4]Labrador Retriever
[ENTER][TAB][F4]Irish Setter[ENTER][F4]Terriers[ENTER][TAB][F4]
Airedale[ENTER][TAB][F4]Welsh Terrier[ENTER][F4]Working Dogs
[ENTER][TAB][F4]Collie[ENTER][TAB][F4]Siberian Husky[SHIFT-F5]
o[F7][ENTER]dogs[ENTER][ENTER]

18.2   EXERCISES

1. [SHIFT-F10]sports[ENTER][SHIFT-F5]o[HOME][HOME][DOWN ARROW][ENTER]
[SPACEBAR][TAB]BASKETBALL[ENTER][SPACEBAR][TAB]TRACK
{Move the cursor after the final "L" in "BASEBALL."}
[ENTER][TAB][SPACEBAR][TAB]John Doe[ENTER][TAB][SPACEBAR][TAB]Bill
Black[DOWN ARROW]{Repeat the process, entering the names
of the captains for the other sports.}

2. [SHIFT-F10]dogs[ENTER]{Move the cursor to the first "I" in
"II."}[ALT-F4][DOWN ARROW][DOWN ARROW][DOWN ARROW][CTRL-F4]bm
[PGDN][ENTER][ENTER]{You may need to press the DEL key if
WordPerfect inserts an extra number before "Sporting
Dogs."}[RIGHT ARROW]

EXERCISES

18.3

1. [SHIFT-F5]dl[F7]o[ENTER][F4] Estate Planning[ENTER][TAB][F4]Trust [ENTER][TAB][F4]Will[SHIFT-F5]o

2. [SHIFT-F5]db[F7]oThe following employees are being honored for 25 years of service:[ENTER][TAB][TAB][TAB][F4]Jane Parker[ENTER][TAB][TAB][TAB][F4]Bill Black[SHIFT-F5]o

MASTERY SKILLS CHECK

1. [SHIFT-F5]do[F7]o[CAPS LOCK]portfolio holdings[CAPS LOCK][ENTER] [F4]Zero coupon bonds[ENTER][F4]Treasury bills[ENTER][F4]Blue chip stocks[ENTER][F4]Mutual fund shares   [18.1]

2. {Move the cursor to the second outline entry.}[CTRL-F4]pm {Move the cursor to the end of the last outline entry.} [ENTER][ENTER]{You may need to press the DEL key if Word-Perfect inserts an extra number before "Treasury bills."} [RIGHT ARROW]   [18.2]

3. [END][ENTER][F4]Stock options[SHIFT-F5]o[F7][ENTER]invest[ENTER] y[E-NTER]   [18.1]

4. [SHIFT-F5]o[ENTER][F4]New Construction[ENTER][TAB][F4]Mayfield Village[ENTER][TAB][F4]Highland Heights[ENTER][TAB][TAB][F4]1114 Miner Road[ENTER][TAB][TAB][F4]4811 Highland Ave.[ENTER][F4] Remodeling Projects[ENTER][TAB][F4]Gates Mills[ENTER][TAB][TAB] [F4]112 Sherman Road[ENTER][TAB][TAB][F4]230 Saddleback Lane[ENTER][TAB][F4]Chagrin Falls   [18.1]

5. [ENTER][TAB][F4]Solon{Move the cursor to after the period in "Highland Ave."}[ENTER][TAB][TAB][F4]5311 Wilson Mills Road [SHIFT-F5]o[F7][ENTER]jobs[ENTER][ENTER]   [18.2]

INTEGRATED SKILLS CHECK

[1.4, 3.1, 18.3]

1. {Type the top of the memo and the first paragraph as shown.}[SHIFT-F5]db[F7]o[ENTER][TAB][TAB][TAB][F4]Jim Miller[ENTER][TAB][TAB][TAB][F4]Mary Parker[ENTER][TAB][TAB][TAB][F4]Paul Drake[SHIFT-F5]o{Move the cursor to after the period in the last sentence.}[CTRL-ENTER][SHIFT-F7]f

[18.1, 18.3]

2. [SHIFT-F5]dl[F7]o[ENTER][F4]WordPerfect's Math Features[ENTER][TAB][F4]Add numbers[ENTER][TAB][TAB][F4]Produce a subtotal for a column of numbers[ENTER][TAB][TAB][F4]Add subtotals to produce totals[ENTER][TAB][TAB][F4]Add totals to produce a grand total[ENTER][TAB][F4]Perform formula calculations across columns[SHIFT-F5]o[F7][ENTER]math[ENTER][ENTER]

[4.1, 12.1, 18.1, 18.2]

3. [SHIFT-F5]do[F7]o[ENTER][F4]WordPerfect Books[ENTER][TAB][F4][F8]WordPerfect Made Easy[F8][ENTER][TAB][F4][F8]WordPerfect: The Complete Reference[F8][ENTER][F4]1-2-3 Books[ENTER][TAB][F4][F8]1-2-3 Made Easy[F8][ENTER][TAB][F4][F8]1-2-3: The Complete Reference[F8]{Move to the end of the last entry in the first section.}[ENTER][TAB][F4][F8]Teach Yourself WordPerfect[F8][SHIFT-F5]o[SHIFT-F7]n2[ENTER]f

[8.2, 18.1, 18.2]

4. [SHIFT-F5]o[ENTER][F4]Vacation days[ENTER][F4]Sick leave[ENTER][F4]Holidays[ENTER][TAB][F4]Christmas[ENTER][TAB][F4]Thanksgiving[ENTER][TAB][F4]Memorial Day[ENTER][TAB][F4]Halloween[ENTER][TAB][F4]Independence Day[ENTER][TAB][F4]Labor Day{Move the cursor to the first "I" in "III."}[ALT-F4][HOME][HOME][DOWN ARROW][CTRL-F4]bm[HOME][HOME][UP ARROW][ENTER]{Move to the beginning of the line for "Halloween."}[CTRL-END][DEL][HOME][HOME][DOWN ARROW]

19

SKILLS CHECK

[4.1, 4.2]

1. [F6]WordPerfect allows you to change several settings.[F6] You can set WordPerfect to back up files automatically.

You can also change the screen's appearance by selecting the colors WordPerfect uses.[F8]These are just a few of the selections available.[F8]

2. [F10]default[ENTER]   [2.2]

3. [F5][ENTER]{Move the cursor to the DEFAULT file.}msettings[ENTER][F7]   [11.5]

4. [ALT-F3]{Soft returns appear as **[SRt]**.}   [4.4]

EXERCISES ——————————————————— 19.1

1. [SHIFT-F1]bty120[ENTER][F7]

2. [SHIFT-F1]bty30[ENTER][F7]

EXERCISES ——————————————————— 19.2

1. [SHIFT-F1]dcs[DOWN ARROW][DOWN ARROW][DOWN ARROW][DOWN ARROW]{Press the RIGHT ARROW key if you have a Font column.}a[F7][F7]

2. [SHIFT-F1]dcs[DOWN ARROW][DOWN ARROW][DOWN ARROW][DOWN ARROW][DOWN ARROW][DOWN ARROW][DOWN ARROW][DOWN ARROW]{Press the RIGHT ARROW key if you have a Font column.}{Type the letter for the normal font in the Foreground column.}[RIGHT ARROW]{Type the letter for the normal font in the Background column.}[F7][F7]

3. [SHIFT-F1]dh<[F7]

4. [SHIFT-F1]dh[SPACEBAR][F7]

5. [SHIFT-F1]dfy[F7]

19.3

EXERCISES

1. [SHIFT-F1]iben[F7]

2. [SHIFT-F1]id6,[SPACEBAR]3[SPACEBAR]1[ENTER][F7]

3. On[SHIFT-F5]t, the Okra Vegetable company begins marketing its new product line, the Seeing Green frozen foods.

MASTERY SKILLS CHECK

[19.1]   1. [SHIFT-F1]bty20[ENTER][F7]

[19.2]   2. [SHIFT-F1]dcs{Press the RIGHT ARROW key if you have a Font column.}[RIGHT ARROW]a[F7][F7]

[19.3]   3. [SHIFT-F1]id3[SPACEBAR]4[ENTER][F7]

[19.3]   4. Acme Corporation projects that its personnel will increase 5% during[SHIFT-F5]t.

[19.3]   5. [SHIFT-F1]ibsn[F7]

INTEGRATED SKILLS CHECK

[1.3, 11.5, 19.1]   1. [SHIFT-F1]bty1[ENTER][F7]Testing Backups{Wait until WordPerfect backs up the document.}[F5][ENTER]{move the highlight to the WP{WP}.BK1 file.}mbckuptst[ENTER][F7][F7]nn

[19.1]   2. [SHIFT-F1]btn[ENTER][F7]

[19.3]   3. [SHIFT-F1]id3[SPACEBAR]1,[SPACEBAR]4[ENTER][F7]

[19.3]   4. [TAB]The company picnic is on[SHIFT-F5]t.[ENTER][TAB]Each person should bring one dish. Please review the schedule, which breaks down the type of dish based upon the person's last name.[ENTER]

5. [HOME][HOME][UP ARROW][ALT-F4][END][F6]{Move to the "o" in   [4.7]
"one."}[CTRL-LEFT ARROW][ALT-F4]h[F8]

6. [SHIFT-F1]dh*[F7]   [19.2]

7. [SHIFT-F1]dcs{Press the RIGHT ARROW key if you have a Font   [19.2]
column.}[DOWN ARROW][DOWN ARROW][RIGHT ARROW]e{assuming e is
the selection for red}[DOWN ARROW][DOWN ARROW]d{assuming d
is the selection for light blue}[F7]

8. {for a hard disk system}[F5][ENTER]{Move the highlight to   [11.4]
the WP{WP}.SET file.}dy{for a floppy disk system}[F5]a:
[ENTER]{Move the highlight to the WP{WP}.SET file.}dy

9. [F7][ENTER]dish[ENTER]y{for a hard disk system}wp[ENTER]{for a   [1.1, 1.2, 19.1]
floppy disk system: Place the WordPerfect 1 disk in drive
A.}a:wp[ENTER]{Place the WordPerfect 2 disk in drive A
when WordPerfect prompts you, and press any key to
continue.}[SHIFT-F1]bty30[ENTER][F7]

Trademarks

Index

The manuscript for this book was prepared and submitted to Osborne/McGraw-Hill in electronic form. The acquisitions editor for this project was Cynthia Hudson, and the technical reviewer was Robert Wanetick.

Text design by Judy Wohlfrom, using Palatino for text body and display.

Cover art by Bay Graphics Design Associates. Color separation by Colour Image. Cover supplier, Phoenix Color Corporation. Screens produced with InSet, from InSet Systems, Inc. Book printed and bound by R.R. Donnelley & Sons Company, Crawfordsville, Indiana.